PRISON LETTERS

... to them ... physical + psychological ... it is already so much the disability ...

... the man who says: I will be ...

... facts me most is your half-way strength ...

... the courage & determination ... to memory. Of the ...

... the average & not it in the end bring you ...

... keep this constantly in mind ...

... role of Chris Butelezi. Tour ...

... to the Royal family because ...

PRISON LETTERS

NELSON MANDELA

EDITED BY **SAHM VENTER**
FOREWORD BY **ZAMASWAZI DLAMINI-MANDELA**

LIVERIGHT PUBLISHING CORPORATION
A Division of W. W. Norton & Company
Independent Publishers Since 1923
New York · London

Owing to the limitations of space, all acknowledgments for permission to reprint
previously published and unpublished material can be found on page 357.

For information about permission to reproduce selections from this book,
write to Permissions, Liveright Publishing Corporation, a division of
W. W. Norton & Company, Inc., 500 Fifth Avenue, New York, NY 10110

For information about special discounts for bulk purchases, please contact
W. W. Norton Special Sales at specialsales@wwnorton.com or 800-233-4830

Manufacturing by LSC Communications, Harrisonburg

Produced and originated by Blackwell and Ruth Limited
405 IronBank, 150 Karangahape Road, Auckland 1010, New Zealand
www.blackwellandruth.com

The Library of Congress has cataloged the hardcover edition as follows:

Names: Mandela, Nelson, 1918–2013, author. | Venter, Sahm, editor. |
Dlamini-Mandela, Zamaswazi, 1979– writer of foreword.
Title: The prison letters of Nelson Mandela / edited by Sahm Venter ; foreword
by Zamaswazi Dlamini-Mandela.
Description: First edition. | New York : Liveright Publishing Corporation, A Division of
W. W. Norton & Company, 2018. | Includes bibliographical references and index.
Identifiers: LCCN 2018009933 | ISBN 9781631491177 (hardcover)
Subjects: LCSH: Mandela, Nelson, 1912–8013—Correspondence. | Political
prisoners—South Africa—Correspondence. | Mandela, Nelson, 1918–2013—
Imprisonment. | Anti-apartheid movements—South Africa. | Government, Resistance
to—South Africa. | South Africa—Politics and government—20th century.
Classification: LCC DT1974 .M343 2018 | DDC 968.06092—dc23
LC record available at https://lccn.loc.gov/2018009933

ISBN 978-1-63149-596-0 (pbk.)

Liveright Publishing Corporation
500 Fifth Avenue, New York, N.Y. 10110
www.wwnorton.com

W. W. Norton & Company Ltd.
15 Carlisle Street, London W1D 3BS

NELSON MANDELA
FOUNDATION
Living the legacy
www.nelsonmandelafoundation.org

1 2 3 4 5 6 7 8 9 0

CONTENTS

FOREWORD

By the time I was born, my grandfather had already been in prison for seventeen years. In a letter to my grandmother, Winnie Madikizela-Mandela, shortly after his sixty-second birthday, he lists the people that he has received telegrams and cards from, including my Aunt Zindzi, my sister, Zaziwe, and me, and the people he's expecting and hoping to hear from. 'So far I have received not a single one of the multitude that friends have sent from all over the world,' he jokes. 'Nevertheless, it is very comforting to know that so many friends still think of us after so many yrs.' It's one of many examples in this book that shows how communication from the outside world bolstered him through his twenty-seven years in prison, and just how much he yearned for those letters.

During his incarceration, my grandfather wrote many hundreds of letters. The selection that appears in this book intimately acquaints readers not only with Nelson Mandela the political activist and prisoner, but with Nelson Mandela the lawyer, father, husband, uncle and friend, and illustrates how his lengthy incarceration, far away from everyday life, impeded him in carrying out these roles. It revisits a very dark time in South Africa's history where those caught opposing the apartheid government's system to oppress an entire race of people, endured terrible punishments. Through his letters he documents the ongoing persecution of my grandmother and provides insight into what it must have been like for his children, Thembi, Makgatho, Makaziwe, Zenani, and Zindzi, to have an absent father that they could barely communicate with or – this I found unbearable – even visit until they turned sixteen. As much as he tried to parent his children from prison, he couldn't.

What has particularly affected me, especially as a mother, is witnessing through my grandfather's letters what my mother and my Aunt Zindzi went through as children. Often they were left parentless while my grandmother was imprisoned as well, sometimes because of her involvement in anti-apartheid activities but often for being the wife of one of South Africa's most well-known political prisoners.

Most heartrending, is the wistful optimism in many of the letters to my grandmother and his children where my grandfather suggests, 'Perhaps one day we will . . .' and 'One day we shall . . . '. That happily-ever-after day never came for my grandparents, my mom, and my aunts and uncles. The children suffered the most, and ultimately the consequences of forfeiting a stable family life for his ideals was a sacrifice that my grandfather just had to make peace with.

My grandfather always reminded us that we should never forget our past or where we come from. The democratic society that both my grandparents and their comrades fought for was achieved after a lot of suffering and loss of life. This book is a reminder that we could easily go back to that place of hatred, but it also shows that personal resilience can overcome unendurable situations. From day one in prison, my grandfather resolved that he would not break or waver; instead he would insist that he and his fellow prisoners be treated with dignity. In a letter to my grandmother in 1969, he recommends she boosts her spirits by reading psychologist Norman Vincent Peale's 1952 bestseller *The Power of Positive Thinking*. He writes: 'I attach no importance to the metaphysical aspects of his arguments, but I consider his views on physical & psychological issues valuable.

'He makes the basic point that it is not so much the disability one suffers from that matters but one's attitude to it. The man who says: I will conquer this illness & live a happy life, is already halfway through to victory.'

This inspirational outlook sustained my grandfather's unwavering pursuit of justice and an equal society for all South Africans, and is one that I think can be applied to many of life's challenges.

This collection has answered many of the questions that used to baffle me: How did my grandfather survive twenty-seven years in jail? What kept him going? Through his words we can find the answers.

Zamaswazi Dlamini-Mandela

INTRODUCTION

A raft of draconian regulations governing the writing of letters by South African political prisoners and their random implementation by mean-spirited guards was designed to control the most precious aspects of a prisoner's soul – their contact with loved ones and news of the outside world.[1]

After political prisoners were sentenced in court, they were assigned to the prison where they were supposed to serve their punishment. In Nelson Mandela's case, his life as a condemned prisoner began in Pretoria Local Prison after he received a five-year sentence on 7 November 1962 for leaving the country without a passport and inciting workers to strike. Already a prisoner, he was brought back to court on sabotage charges in 1963, and on 12 June 1964 he received a lifelong sentence. His wife, Winnie Mandela, visited him in Pretoria that day, and hours later, without warning, he and six of the seven comrades sentenced with him were taken from Pretoria for the long flight in a military aircraft to the notorious prison on Robben Island. They arrived on a bitterly cold winter morning on 13 June 1964. Unlike inmates who had committed 'common law' crimes like rape, robbery, and assault, who were classified as C Grade and sometimes B Grade on arrival, political prisoners were assigned to D Grade, the lowest possible classification with the least privileges. They were allowed only one visitor every six months and were entitled to write and receive only one letter of five hundred words every six months. So unpredictable was the process of sending and receiving letters that six years after he was imprisoned, Mandela met with his lawyers on Robben Island and listed examples of 'unreasonable and vexatious behaviour and conduct of the authorities'. He said that the disruptions to his correspondence, 'indicate a deliberate intention and policy on the part of the authorities to cut me off and isolate me from all external contacts, to frustrate and demoralise me, to make me despair and lose all hope and eventually break me.'[2]

Later on, when the censors tired of counting words, they began accepting letters of a page and a half.[3] Letters to their lawyers and prison authorities did not come from their quota. Saturdays and Sundays were earmarked for visits, and letters were delivered on a Saturday. Prisoners could give up a visit in exchange for the receipt of two letters. Initially, both visits and correspondence had to be with 'first degree relatives'. Prisoners were forbidden from mentioning other prisoners in their letters or from writing about prison conditions or anything the authorities may have construed as being 'political'.[4] Every letter went through the Censor's Office on Robben Island, where incoming and outgoing mail was checked.[5] Decades later, Mandela recalled:

> They didn't want you to discuss things other than family matters and especially when they were considered by them to be of a political nature. And that was the reason, that you must confine yourself purely to family matters. And then there was ignorance of language. If you used the word 'war', it doesn't matter what context, they would say, 'Take it out' because they didn't understand the language very well. And war is war; it can't have any other meaning. If you said the 'war of ideas', then you had said something you were not supposed to say.[6]

In his book about the fifteen years he spent as a prisoner on Robben Island, in the same section as Mandela, Eddie Daniels paints a picture of the 'frustration' of arbitrary, incompetent, and 'vindictive' censoring and holding back of letters.[7]

Conditions began to improve slightly from 1967, arguably due to the intervention of Helen Suzman – an opposition member of Parliament to whom Mandela reported 'a reign of terror' on the Island. The International Committee of the Red Cross and the prisoners' own efforts also contributed to these changes. They were then allowed to write and receive one letter every three months and be visited every three months.[8]

A prisoner was supposed to remain in a category of privileges for two years, meaning that after six years D Grade prisoners would be in A Grade, with the most privileges. Mandela, however, remained in D Grade for ten years. We can see from his letters, where he sometimes wrote his grade (the prisoners also referred to this as a 'group'), that he was in B Grade in 1972 and finally received A Grade designation in 1973, allowing the writing and receiving of six letters each month.[9]

Before being upgraded, a prisoner had to have their behaviour assessed by the prison board, which conducted discussions with prisoners that Mandela said were for the purposes of 'victimising' political prisoners.[10]

Despite the relentless censoring by bureaucrats, Nelson Mandela the prisoner became a prolific correspondent. He copied down his letters in notebooks to aid him with rewriting them when the censors refused to send them unless he removed certain paragraphs or when letters went missing in transit. He also liked to keep a record of what he'd said to whom. Jailed from 5 August 1962 until 11 February 1990, he wrote hundreds of letters. Not all of them, however, reached their destination in one piece. Some were censored to the extent that they became unintelligible, others were delayed for no reason, and some were not sent at all. Some he managed to smuggle out in the belongings of prisoners being released.

Prisoners were rarely informed if a letter remained unsent and usually discovered this if a recipient complained of not having received a letter. It is not known, for instance, whether all the letters he wrote to Adelaide Tambo under the guise of various nicknames reached her in London where she was living in exile with her husband, Oliver Tambo, president of the African National Congress (ANC) and Mandela's former law partner. The letters were likely intended for both of them. We do know from fellow prisoner Michael Dingake that Mandela had 'demanded the right to correspond with O. R. Tambo and exchange views on the liberation struggle.'[11]

A father of five young children when he was first taken into prison, Mandela was not allowed to see his children until they were sixteen years old. Letters became a vital tool of his parenting.

In an official letter of complaint to officials twelve years into his imprisonment, Mandela wrote, 'I sometimes wish science could invent miracles and make my daughter get her missing birthday cards and have the pleasure of knowing that her Pa loves her, thinks of her and makes efforts to reach her whenever necessary. It is significant that repeated attempts on her part to reach me and the photos she has sent have disappeared without trace whatsoever.'

The most painful of Mandela's letters is the series of 'Special Letters' in addition to his quota, written after the deaths of his beloved mother, Nosekeni, in 1968, and of his firstborn, his son Thembi, a year later. Forbidden from attending their funerals, he was reduced to consoling his children and other family members in letters through this harrowing time, and writing to thank senior family members for stepping up and ensuring that his mother and son got the send-offs they deserved.

A lawyer by profession, Mandela habitually used the written word to press officials to uphold prisoners' human rights, and on at least two occasions he wrote to officials demanding that they release him and his comrades.

Dingake described Mandela's role in prison from the early 1960s as that of a 'battering ram'.[12] In the face of 'atrocious' conditions, he could not be ignored, 'not only because of his status, but because he would "not let them do it" '.[13] His relentless campaigning for prisoners' rights eventually broke down the resolve of the authorities to have each prisoner raise their complaints individually.[14] Mandela 'defiantly continued to describe general conditions' in his letters to the commissioner of prisons, and the rest of the prisoners began laying personal complaints 'at every opportunity'. It was 'impossible', Dingake writes, for guards to record the 'complaints from every single one of more than a thousand inmates'.[15] The rule was 'repealed by practice' and individuals or groups from each section in the prison were allowed to speak on behalf of all the prisoners.[16]

During his discussions and in letters to government officials in the late 1980s, Mandela urged for the release of his comrades. See for instance his letter to the commissioner of prisons dated 11 September 1989 (page 315). Finally Mandela's efforts bore fruit when the remaining five men sentenced with him to life were freed on 15 October 1989. (Denis Goldberg had been freed in 1985 and Govan Mbeki in 1987.) He walked out of prison less than four months later.

Nelson Mandela has left us a rich archive of letters documenting his twenty-seven years in prison, which echo his anger, his self-control, and his love for family and country.

A NOTE ON THE LETTERS

Nelson Mandela's prison letters are not housed under one roof, and compiling this book has taken almost ten years. These letters have been drawn from various collections: Mandela's prison files held by the National Archives and Records Service of South Africa, the Himan Bernadt Collection, and the collections of Meyer de Waal, Morabo Morojele, Fatima Meer, Michael Dingake, Amina Cachalia, Peter Wellman, Ray Carter, Adelaide and Paul Joseph, Sylvia Neame, Mzobanzi Mboya and Helen Joseph. Letters are also taken from the Donald Card Collection, named for the former security policemen who in 2004 returned to Mandela the hardcover notebooks in which he copied his letters before he handed them in for posting. Both the Himan Bernadt Collection and the Donald Card Collection are held by the Nelson Mandela Foundation. The books were taken from his cell in 1971, and he complains about this in a letter to authorities on 4 April 1971. For a list of where the individual letters are housed, see page 352.

The National Archives and Records Service of South Africa houses by far the majority of Mandela's prison letters. Encased alongside other official paperwork in string-tied bundles assembled in cardboard folders, they fill some fifty-nine boxes. The letters represent the Prisons Department's record of letters he wrote and received. In some cases the originals remain as evidence that they were never sent.

Since most of these letters are copies of the originals, their legibility depends on the way in which they were photocopied, the paper used, and how the ink has faded over time. Some letters are missing words that have been left off the sides during photocopying by prison officials or sliced out of the paper during censoring. In the case of some of the letters, we will never know exactly what Mandela wrote.

Heartbreakingly, a long and loving letter to his youngest daughter, Zindziswa, still neatly folded in its plain white envelope, was found in his prison archives nineteen years after his release from prison. It was accompanied by a note from a prison official who wrote that Mandela was not allowed to send a letter with a Christmas card. Written on 9 December 1979, it is a beautiful reaching out from a father longing for his daughter. She was supposed to have received it in time for her nineteenth birthday from the father she lost when she was a baby of twenty months. Such was the arbitrary and cruel control over correspondence.

The letters in this selection have been reproduced in their entirety apart from in several cases where we have omitted information in the interests of privacy. To avoid repetition, we have also omitted Mandela's address from nearly all of the letters. The book is divided into sections according to the four different prisons and two different hospitals he was housed in.

We have reproduced the text exactly as Mandela wrote it apart from correcting the odd misspelt word or name (of which there are, typically, very few), very occasionally adding or removing punctuation for ease of reading, or removing superscript in numbers that appear in dates. We have retained his various styles of writing dates and his abbreviations. One cannot know precisely why he frequently wrote 'yr' for 'year' and 'chdn' for 'children', but it may have been to keep the letters to the set limit of one and a half pages after prison censors stopped counting the number of words. When discussing books, Mandela usually formatted their titles in quotation marks. In instances where he hasn't, we have formatted these in italics as per standard editorial conventions. Mandela often used square brackets instead of parentheses. However, to avoid confusing his original text with editorial interpolations, we have replaced his square brackets with parentheses unless otherwise noted.

We have retained the underlining that appears under certain words and passages in particular letters. Usually these were made by prison censors suspicious of individuals or events being discussed. Sometimes Mandela underlined passages. We've noted where underlining appears to be the censors' work, where it appears to be Mandela's own, and where it is too hard to tell. Mandela often wrote letters in Afrikaans and isiXhosa, the language he grew up speaking, and we have noted which of these letters have been translated into English for inclusion in this publication. Some letters were also typed by prison officials and we have also noted these instances.

Mandela signed off his letters in various ways depending on who the recipient was. In official correspondence he includes his signature, 'NR Mandela', the 'R' representing his given name, Rolihlahla. In letters to his wife, Winnie Mandela, and certain family members he often signs off as Dalibunga, the name given to him after he underwent the traditional initiation into manhood at the age of sixteen. To others he is Nelson or Nel, the name given to him at his first school by his teacher, Miss Mdingane, according to the custom at the time where African children were given an English name. To his children he is Tata, 'father' in isiXhosa, and to his grandchildren, he is Khulu, 'granddad' in isiXhosa.

It has not been possible to identify every individual mentioned but, where available, enlightening detail about individuals, locations, and events referred to in the letters has been included in the footnotes. An extensive glossary at the end of the book includes additional information about many of the individuals and events frequently referred to by Mandela.

To avoid readers having to keep track of the host of individuals Mandela refers to, many of whom are often known by more than one name, such as Winnie Mandela, or who are mentioned in letters many years apart, we have treated each letter as its own entity. Therefore, the first time an individual is mentioned in a letter, we have included a footnote explaining who they are despite the same reference appearing in earlier or subsequent letters. We have also applied this approach to the referencing of events and places. Although in some cases this may seem repetitive, we decided it was the most reader-friendly approach, particularly for the reader who chooses to dip in and out of this book which we hope you do, many times.

NELSON MANDELA'S PRISON NUMBERS

Rather than being identified by name, prisoners were issued with prison numbers by which they were, at first, always referred to and which they had to use in any correspondence. The first part of the number was based on how many prisoners had been admitted to a particular prison that year; the second part of the number listed the year. Nelson Mandela's best-known prison number is 466/64. Years after his release, at a concert in Cape Town launching an HIV awareness campaign using his prison numbers, he said: 'I was supposed to have been reduced to that number.'[17]

Mandela was on Robben Island twice, which meant that he was allocated two different prison numbers for that prison. During his twenty-seven years of incarceration, Mandela was held in four prisons after he was sentenced and was issued with six different prison numbers.

19476/62	Pretoria Local Prison: 7 November 1962–25 May 1963
191/63	Robben Island: 27 May 1963–12 June 1963
11657/63	Pretoria Local Prison: 12 June 1963–12 June 1964
466/64	Robben Island: 13 June 1964–31 March 1982
220/82	Pollsmoor Prison: 31 March 1982–12 August 1988 Tygerberg Hospital: 12 August 1988–31 August 1988 Constantiaberg MediClinic: 31 August 1988–7 December 1988
1335/88	Victor Verster Prison: 7 December 1988–11 February 1990

PRETORIA LOCAL PRISON

||||||||||||

NOVEMBER 1962–MAY 1963

For just six months in 1962, while on his clandestine tour out of South Africa to African countries and London, UK, Mandela lived the life of a free man when he was not subjected to apartheid rules and could move around as he chose. On Thursday, 11 January 1962 he secretly left South Africa by road for a tour of the newly independent African states. Mandela was asked by the underground structures of his organisation, the African National Congress, or ANC, to speak at a conference of African nations in Ethiopia and also to travel the continent raising funds and support for the fight ahead. Two years earlier, in 1960, the ANC had been outlawed and a year later it had accepted the inevitability of an armed struggle to campaign for equal rights and democracy in South Africa. In the middle of 1961 the organisation had decided to form an armed wing, and Umkhonto weSizwe (Spear of the Nation) was born. Also known as MK for short, it was launched with a series of explosions of strategic targets with the intent to avoid loss of life.

If this known opponent of the apartheid regime had applied for a passport, it would have been refused. Besides, he was wanted by the police for continuing underground the activities of the illegal ANC.

He travelled under the name David Motsamayi, a name he had borrowed from a client at his law firm, and used at least one fake passport. Ethiopia had provided one and, it is said, so did Senegal.

The journey took him to sixteen independent African countries and in two of them, Morocco and Ethiopia, he underwent military training. In between he visited London for ten days where he caught up with old friends and comrades, including Oliver Tambo and his wife Adelaide. Tambo, who later became president of the ANC in 1967 after the death of Chief Albert Luthuli, had joined Mandela on some of his travels in Africa.

Mandela's freedom came to an end one Sunday afternoon on a country road near Howick, a small town in the east of South Africa. It was 5 August 1962. He and fellow anti-apartheid activist and theatre director Cecil Williams were en route by car to Johannesburg. Mandela had been in the area to brief ANC president Chief Albert Luthuli[i] and others about his trip. A meal with friends the day before was to be his last celebration for nearly three decades.

As part of his repertoire of disguises, Mandela would often masquerade as the chauffeur of a white man. On that day, however, Williams was behind the wheel of his Austin when the driver of a Ford V8 suddenly overtook them and ordered Williams to stop. It was the police. Dressed in a coat and cap and wearing dark glasses, Mandela denied that he was in fact Nelson Mandela and insisted he was David Motsamayi, but they were sure they had their man and so was he. He considered making a run for it but knew that the game, so to speak, was up. Speaking about it just more than thirty years later, Mandela said: 'I was very fit those days, and I could virtually climb any wall. And then I looked at the back, just at the rearview mirror. I saw there were two cars behind, then I felt that no it would be ridiculous for me to try and escape, they'll shoot me. And we stopped.'[18]

The men summarily were arrested and the police drove them back some 9 miles to Pietermaritzburg where Mandela was held overnight, appearing briefly before a local magistrate the next morning. He was driven on to Johannesburg and locked up at the Old Fort Prison, preserved today as a museum within the precint of the Constitutional Court of South Africa. Over the next ten days Mandela appeared twice in the Johannesburg Magistrates' Court and his case was remanded for trial on 15 October. On Saturday, 13 October he was informed that he would be moved to the city of Pretoria, where, on Monday, 15 October, he appeared in the Old Synagogue, temporarily named a 'special regional court', for his trial. His appearance stunned the public gallery and officials alike. Around his broad shoulders he wore a kaross made of multiple jackal skins sewn together on a large piece of fabric. The rest of his ensemble included a T-shirt, khaki trousers, sandals, and a yellow and green beaded necklace. He wanted to be seen as African in an unequal society.[19]

The lawyer Mandela who, having passed the requisite attorneys'

---

i   Chief Albert Luthuli (1898–1967), president-general of the ANC, 1952–67 – see the glossary.

admission examination in 1952, had practised in his own firm for years, defended himself, taking advice from Advocate Bob Hepple,[i] who, ironically, would join him and nine others on trial for sabotage the next year. Mandela employed the tactic of speaking from the dock, which freed him from testifying under cross-examination. In his first speech to the court, on 22 October 1962, he called for the recusal of the magistrate, Mr. W. A. van Helsdingen, saying that as a black man he would not get a fair trial.[20] After hearing his plea, Van Helsdingen refused to step down.

Mandela recalled how on the last day of the trial, 7 November 1962, the prosecutor, Mr. D. J. Bosch, whom he knew from his days as a lawyer, went to the holding cell and apologised to him about having to ask for his conviction. 'He then just embraced me and kissed me on the cheeks, and he says, "Today I didn't want to come to court. For me to come to court to ask for conviction against you is something that upset me." So I thanked him.'[21]

Hepple reluctantly left the room while they spoke, and later wrote: 'When Bosch came out of the cell about five minutes later, I saw tears streaming down his face. I asked Mandela: "What the hell's going on?" He replied: "You won't believe this but he asked me to forgive him." I exclaimed, "Nel, I hope you told him to get stuffed." To my surprise, Mandela responded: "No, I did not. I told him I knew he was just doing his job, and thanked him for his good wishes."'[22]

In his judgment, Van Helsdingen said it was clear that Mandela had been 'the mastermind' behind a strike in May 1961 against South Africa's plans to abandon its membership of the Commonwealth and become a republic.[23]

Mandela made another lengthy speech from the dock after being convicted on both charges, and said: 'Whatever sentence you pass on me, you can rest assured that, when it is completed, I will still be moved by my dislike of race discrimination and will take up again the fight against injustices until they are removed once and for all.'[24]

Van Helsdingen called the case 'distressing and difficult' and declared that Mandela's actions should be 'put down with a strong hand'. It was clear, he maintained, that what Mandela was really doing was trying to 'overthrow the Government'.[25]

At the end of the short trial in which he had mounted no defence

---

i   Bob Hepple (1934–2015), lawyer, academic, and anti-apartheid activist – see the glossary.

apart from his two speeches, Mandela was sentenced to three years' imprisonment on the charge of inciting a strike and to an additional two years' imprisonment for leaving the country without a South African passport. He was forty-four years old.

Immediately after he was sentenced, Mandela had his status changed from that of a prisoner awaiting trial to that of a convict in the same prison. He was held with Robert Mangaliso Sobukwe, a university lecturer and a former ANC colleague who had led a split from the party to found the Pan Africanist Congress (PAC),[i] and several other members of that organisation. Sobukwe and his comrades had been sentenced two years earlier for their involvement in an anti-pass protest in which sixty-nine unarmed demonstrators were shot dead by police. It became known as the Sharpeville Massacre.

The first letter in this collection is one Mandela wrote the day before his conviction and sentencing, to Mr. Louis Blom-Cooper, a British advocate sent by the organisation then known as Amnesty to observe the trial. During the case, Mandela applied a second time for the recusal of the magistrate after Blom-Cooper informed him that he had seen Van Helsdingen driving from the court in the company of the investigating officer. Van Helsdingen again rejected the application, saying only that he 'did not communicate with the two detectives'.[26]

After his release Mandela described Blom-Cooper as 'tremendous', and said of the incident: 'He behaved just like an Englishman, you know, their desire to challenge anything that looks wrong. Whilst I was cross-examining the state witnesses, the magistrate was seen to leave the courthouse with an investigating officer, and Blom-Cooper immediately prepared an affidavit and went to the registrar to sign it before the registrar of the Supreme Court. And he came to me with this affidavit and he says, "Here is an affidavit."'[27]

---

i   For the Pan Africanist Congress (PAC), see the glossary.

To the secretary, Amnesty

6.11.62

The Secretary
Amnesty
LONDON

Dear Sir,

We are most grateful to your organisation for sending Mr L Blom Cooper to attend the trial.

His mere presence, as well as the assistance he gave, were a source of tremendous inspiration and encouragement to us.

The fact that he sat next to us furnished yet another proof that honest and upright men, and democratic organisations, throughout the civilised world are on our side in the struggle for a democratic South Africa.

Finally, I must ask you to accept this note as a very firm, warm and hearty handshake from me.

Yours very sincerely,
Nelson

6/11/62   FOR 19

Nelson Mandela   The Secretary
19476/62   Amnesty.
                             LONDON

Dear Sir,

We are most grateful to your

organisation for sending Mr

L Blom-Cooper to attend the

trial.

His mere presence, as well as

the assistance he gave, were

source of tremendous inspiration

and encouragement to us.

The fact that he sat next to

us furnished yet another proof

Page from a letter to the Secretary of Amnesty, written the day before his conviction and sentencing in
November 1962, see opposite.

ROBBEN ISLAND MAXIMUM SECURITY PRISON

||||||||||||

MAY 1963–JUNE 1963

n late May 1963, Mandela was unexpectedly taken from Pretoria to Robben Island with three PAC prisoners.

Crammed in the back of a police van, Mandela and the three others were driven for a day and a half until they reached Cape Town where they boarded a ferry. They arrived on the notorious island on 27 May 1963. It was bleak, brutal, and bitterly cold.

The four men were steered into one cell and made to undress. Each item of clothing was searched by guards and then thrown onto a wet floor. Mandela got into an argument, and one guard moved threateningly towards him. The story Mandela told of the incident became the hallmark of his relationship with the prison authorities going forward. He would not be cowed: 'So I say, "You dare touch me, I will take you to the highest court in this land, and by the time I'm finished with you, you will be as poor as a church mouse." And he stopped. I was not, I was frightened; it was not because I was courageous, but one had to put up a front and so he stopped.'[28]

Less than three weeks later, Mandela was told to pack and was transferred back to Pretoria. He was never given any explanation and later dismissed a notion that it was in relation to the Rivonia Trial because his colleagues were arrested after he'd been transferred – two of them were detained on 24 June 1963 in Soweto and the rest on 11 July 1963.

Mandela found himself back in the Pretoria jail cells in June 1963, and within some weeks discovered that fellow MK operatives Andrew Mlangeni and Elias Motsoaledi had been arrested on their return from a trip to China for military training. One morning Mandela was running up the stairs for his morning meal (at Pretoria he was given the same food as white prisoners and said he looked forward to it) and he saw a group of fellow prisoners he recognised as some of the workers at Liliesleaf Farm, which he and his comrades had used as a hideout. 'That spoiled my whole appetite,' he said.[29]

He describes encountering Thomas Mashifane, who had been the foreman at Liliesleaf Farm, in *Long Walk to Freedom*: 'I greeted him warmly, though I realised that the authorities had undoubtedly led him to my corridor to see if I recognised or acknowledged him. I could not but do otherwise. His presence there could mean only one thing: the authorities had discovered Rivonia.'[30]

Worse was still to come. Once they had completed nearly three months in solitary confinement, Mandela met up with a group of close comrades. 'I was summoned to the prison office where I found Walter [Sisulu]; Govan Mbeki; Ahmed Kathrada; Andrew Mlangeni; Bob Hepple; Raymond Mhlaba, a member of the MK High Command who had recently returned from training in China; Elias Motsoaledi, also a member of MK; Denis Goldberg, an engineer and a member of the Congress of Democrats; Rusty Bernstein, an architect and also a member of the COD; and Jimmy Kantor,[i] an attorney. . . . We were all charged with sabotage, and scheduled to appear in court the next day.'[31]

During this new period while he was awaiting trial, Mandela kept up a steady stream of correspondence to the prison authorities – a habit that was to become a hallmark of his imprisonment.

Mandela and ten of his colleagues, including Bob Hepple, appeared in the Palace of Justice, a court in Pretoria, on 9 October 1963. The others were Walter Sisulu, Govan Mbeki, Ahmed Kathrada, Denis Goldberg, Raymond Mhlaba, Elias Motsoaledi, Andrew Mlangeni, Rusty Bernstein, and James Kantor. The case was remanded until 20

---

i   For details on all these individuals, see their entries in the glossary.

October, and on that day the defence applied to quash the indictment of more than 235 acts of sabotage which it alleged were part of a grand plan of 'violent revolution'.[32] The defence had decided to challenge it because they found it to be 'a shoddy and imprecise document' which 'made it impossible to discern' what the charges were and who committed them.[33] Lawyer Joel Joffe wrote that the defence team had resolved 'to make it clear from the outset to the court and the prosecution that we would not be swayed by the hysteria in the country' and 'we would not abandon any of the normal legal rights'.[34]

On 30 October their application was successful and all the accused, excluding Bob Hepple who had his charges withdrawn and was freed, were immediately rearrested in court and charged with sabotage. Hepple had persuaded the prosecution that he would testify for the State as a state witness, but he did not want to testify against people he 'admired and respected',[35] so he and his wife Shirley fled the country.

Back in court, a new indictment was introduced on 12 November. On 25 November the 199 acts of sabotage were reduced to 193, and the defence again applied to have the indictment quashed. Their application was dismissed on 26 November, and the next time the accused appeared in court was 3 December, when all ten pleaded not guilty.

On judgment day, 11 June 1964, Mandela and seven others were convicted. Bernstein was acquitted. Kantor had been acquitted on 4 March.[i]

◇◇◇◇◇◇◇◇◇◇◇◇

---

i   James Kantor's attorney John Croaker applied for Kantor's discharge 'on the basis that there was no case
     for him to answer' (Joel Joffe, *The State vs. Nelson Mandela: The Trial that Changed South Africa*, p. 144).
     Justice de Wet said he did not intend giving his reasons for discharge. On judgment day when Bernstein
     was acquitted and Mandela and seven others convicted, Justice de Wet said, 'I have very good reasons for
     the conclusions to which I have come. I don't propose to read these reasons.' (Ibid, p. 244.)

To the commanding officer, Pretoria Local Prison

25th October, 1963

The Commanding Officer
The Prison
PRETORIA

I refer you to my letter of the 8th instant in which I applied for my eyes to be tested by a specialist.

In the letter aforesaid, I indicated that the application was being made on the recommendation of the Prison Medical Officer. I must add that the condition of my eyes is deteriorating very rapidly and I must ask you to give the matter your urgent attention.

I must further add that I am seriously handicapped in the preparations for the forthcoming trial against me on the 29th instant. The said preparations entail the reading of numerous documents as well as a lot of writing. I find all this trying and dangerous to my health.

Finally, I must ask you to allow me to use my own clothing outfit for the purpose of appearing in court on the 29th instant.

[Signed N R Mandela]
Prisoner no. 11657/63

◇◇◇◇◇◇◇◇◇◇◇◇

Sylvia Neame was a member of the banned South African Communist Party[i] and the partner, at the time, of Ahmed Kathrada, a co-accused with Nelson Mandela in the Rivonia Trial. She was, herself, held in detention for one and a half months in October–November 1963 and again in July–August 1964. She was charged, with others, for membership of the SACP and remained in custody while awaiting trial. When Kathrada was in solitary confinement for interrogation purposes, they corresponded on tissue paper, hidden in the girdle of his pyjamas, sent out for washing. When Mandela, Kathrada and their comrades were standing trial in Pretoria they corresponded via letters handled by Advocate Bram Fischer, who led the defence team.

---

i   Sylvia Neame (1937–) anti-apartheid activist, and a member of the Communist Party. She originally belonged to the Communist Party of South Africa, which was established in 1921. It disbanded in 1950 when the apartheid regime passed the Suppression of Communism Act. It reformed in 1953 as the South African Communist Party and operated underground. It was legalised in 1990.

In this undated letter, received before the end of the Rivonia trial on 12 June 1964, Mandela critiques her draft university Honours thesis. She assumes that he asked to see it when Kathrada mentioned it to him.[i] In April 1965 she was convicted and sentenced to two terms of two years to run concurrently for belonging to the Communist Party, but was soon taken from Johannesburg to the Eastern Cape, where, like hundreds of others, she faced charges concocted by the apartheid regime to destroy opposition to it. She successfully appealed against both the conviction and sentence, and following her release from prison left South Africa for England and then Germany, where she lived in exile until her return to South Africa in 2014.

To Sylvia Neame, a friend

[date unknown][ii]

Dear S,[iii]

I have thoroughly enjoyed reading your manuscript. I wish you to know that I regard it as an impressive effort which will, I hope, in its final form, serve as an important source of information for students of the S.A. political scene. I trust that it will one day be published in book form so that it can reach a wider public and be available to all those interested in studying the history of evolution of African political thought in our country.

You attempt to answer the question: "Why were the Communists expelled"[iv] from the I.C.U.?[v] I make certain suggestions below in the hope that you may consider them relevant and helpful.

---

i   'I have a feeling that it was not so long before sentencing in the Rivonia Trial that Madiba had asked for it. I know I have always borne in mind that they were facing the death sentence at the time and yet Madiba had an interest in a thesis on our history. The only person who would have transported it to Madiba and back to me was Bram [Fisher].' (Sylvia Neame in an email to Sahm Venter, 26 September 2018.)

ii   It is likely that the letter was received in 1964 as Sylvia was in detention until the end of November 1963. Sylvia recalls she received it during the Rivonia Trial, and that it was probably smuggled out via Ahmed Kathrada (for Ahmed Kathrada, see the glossary). (Sylvia Neame in an email to Sahm Venter, 26 September 2019.)

iii   The fact that Mandela wrote 'Dear S' and signed it 'Friend' is a sign that it was smuggled out as such a letter would not have been allowed.

iv   Communists were expelled from the ICU in December 1926.

v   Industrial and Commercial Workers' Union, founded in 1919.

1. Reading through the document, I gain the impression that in investigating the facts relating to the expulsion there is a tendency to be one-sided, leaning heavily, and almost exclusively, on the version put forward by the Party.[i] The point of view of the leaders of the I.C.U. on the matter, is not sufficiently canvassed. Numerous articles from the "S.A. Worker" are quoted and hardly any from the "Workers Herald", the organ of the I.C.U. or from the spokesmen of the organisation. I believe a work of this nature is expected to be thoroughly objective to enable the reader to decide for himself whether the conclusions made are in fact borne out by the facts given. At no stage must you appear to be partisan in your approach or gloss over problems. It might be useful to bring out the reasons advanced by the I.C.U. for expelling the Communists.

2. You pose the question: "Were the Communists calling for militant action which Kadalie[ii] for one reason or another did not want to carry out?" Your conclusions on this particular point are very convincing precisely because they are based mainly on statements made by responsible leaders of the I.C.U. In all these statements the officials interviewed make it clear that they are not in favour of strike action. I do, however, wish to recommend that, without in any way changing your theme, you should, in addition, bring out the other aspect of the matter as well.

It is easy for us when we look back and attempt to assess the policies of the pioneers of African liberation, with all the advantages which a later generation must possess, to be severe in our judgment. You will probably concede that, speaking generally, the striking feature of most liberatory movements in the early stages of their history is their adherence to constitutional forms of struggle and their aversion of militant action. For example, this is exactly what happened with the Congress in India [Refer to the "History of the Indian Congress", Vol. I, either the Introduction or Chapter I. I have unfortunately forgotten the <u>author's name</u>.*[iii] These 2 volumes should be available at the University Library and Yusuf C.[iv] may help you in regard to the author's

---

i   Communist Party of South Africa.

ii   Clements Kadalie (c.1896–1951), founder of the ICU.

iii   The underlining of the words 'author's name' with an asterisk is linked to a sentence in the margin thought to be in Ahmed Kathrada's hand, which reads '*I think the author is Dr Sitaraymaya' (for Ahmed Kathrada, see the glossary).

iv   Yusuf Cachalia (1915–95), Amina Cachalia's husband, political activist and secretary of the South African Indian Congress – see the glossary.

name.] In its struggle for national independence, the Indian Congress started off with the hope and confidence that by passing resolutions, putting forward moderate demands and sending deputations, the British Government would eventually grant full independence to India. Subsequent experience, after many years of fruitless constitutional endeavours, completely shattered this illusion, and resulted in a change to more militant forms of action.

Although the African National Congress in this country was formed in 1912 and although now and again spirited skirmishes occurred, involving strikes and demonstrations, these were few and far between, and more of an exception than the rule. It was not until Dec. 1949, after 37 yrs of its history, that the A.N.C. adopted the famous Programme of Action and consciously embarked on militant forms of action such as the boycott weapon, civil disobedience, strikes and other mass demonstrations. In this connection, you may consider it relevant to examine the question whether the Party was justified in its criticism of the I.C.U. leaders in 1927/8 for their failure to resort to direct action, a form of struggle which the Party itself had apparently not employed to any appreciable extent at the time.

3. You also pose the question: "Were the Liberals influencing Kadalie?" This topic is dealt with in Chapter III and answered in the affirmative. Again I find the arguments advanced in support of your conclusions equally convincing. But your arguments would carry even more conviction if you made some sort of acknowledgement of the efforts made by the Independent Labour Party to assist the I.C.U. by providing it with an organiser to straighten out the affairs of the organisation, providing funds and a library. Having made this concession, you could then point out, just as you do, that instead of confining themselves to this good work; they attempted to build up the I.C.U. "as a bulwark against Communism" and tried to turn it away from the path of militant struggle.

Whilst dealing with this point you might also wish to examine the question whether the Party, in the early stages of its history, did not in fact go to the other extreme, to create problems in the I.C.U. which were regarded by some people as having had the same effects as those perpetrated by the Liberals. The domination of the Party by whites, its dogmatic approach to political problems and sectarianism, and its attempt to transform the I.C.U. into a carbon copy of the Party may have created the impression to leaders of political thought amongst

Africans that Communism was a foreign ideology, hostile to the spirit of African nationalism and a concept to be resisted by genuine African patriots. To what extent was the expulsion influenced by this fact?

4. On page 71 appears the following statement: "It was not racialism that led to the expulsion of the Communists although Kadalie used the racial appeal". Would it not be correct to say that to use the racial appeal to secure the expulsion of Communists is racialism? To me this appears to amount to the same. I am, however, in full agreement with the statement appearing on page 72, that Gomas[i] put the matter strongly when he said that Communists were anti-Black or anti-African. It is absurd to suggest that the Communists would be against the only force that would guarantee their victory. But it is not enough merely to dismiss Gomas' views as an exaggeration. The matter is important enough to merit fuller consideration. The Party – dissolved in 1950 – did not drop from the heavens but was born out of the squalid society of our country with all its evils. Its members were ordinary human beings who were drawn from the country's peoples and who brought into the Party all the prejudices of S.A. society. If the whites were dominant, it would not be surprising to find within the ranks of the Party some of these evils. As a matter of fact the attitude of Bill Andrews[ii] was to a very large extent influenced by the ingrained prejudice and contempt for the masses of the Africans commonly found amongst whites in this country.

5. On several occasions in history, it has happened that the working cooperation between a non-Marxist political organisation and the C.P. ceases because policy differences emerged, as they have for example in India between the Congress and the C.P.; & in several Middle Eastern countries. To what extent was the expulsion the result of genuine policy differences between the I.C.U. and the C.P. To what extent were these policy differences accentuated by attacks of the type made by Greene in the "S.A. Worker" of the 26th Aug. 1926, an action which you correctly criticise on page 82?

6. Although you are dealing with why the Communists were expelled from the I.C.U., and not with the history of this organisation, the topic is introduced somewhat abruptly in Chapter II. Perhaps you may like to supplement the Introduction with one or two passages

i   John Gomas (1901–79), provincial secretary of the ICU until his expulsion in 1926 because he was a
       communist.
ii   William H. Andrews (1870–1950), first general secretary of the Communist Party of South Africa.

explaining the aims and objects of this body. This may perhaps be difficult since you are not in possession of a Constitution earlier than the 1925 Revised one.

7. It may be helpful to annex to the document the Constitution of the I.C.U. or at least to summarise it sufficiently to make clear the powers and functions of the bodies you mention especially in Chapter I of the "manuscript". This will make it easy to appreciate the points you are making. Just as an illustration on page 2 reference is made to "Section 19, para. (a) (k)". Further references are made to "the National and Provincial Secretary assisted by the office clerk . . . functioning in place of the Executive". The "Board of Arbitration", the "National Council" and "Congress" make it necessary for one who reads the document to refer to the constitution.

Further on p. 1. you say that "Jimmy La Guma[i] had been General Secretary of the I.C.U. before the expulsion of Dec. 1926.". On pages 9 & 10, on the other hand, Kadalie refers to himself as General Secretary. On page 10 La Guma is described as the Assistant Secretary. Perhaps you would like to sort out these inconsistencies.

Finally, I must assure you once more that this work fascinates me immensely and I make these comments in the hope that they may help to tie up the loose ends of what I regard as an excellent dissertation. Fondest regards.

Sincerely,
Friend

◇◇◇◇◇◇◇◇◇◇◇◇

Just as he did the day before he was sentenced in 1962, Mandela wrote another letter of thanks on the day of his conviction for sabotage. It was again to a foreigner who had served as an observer during his trial.

He expressed his gratitude to Mr. Coen Stork, the Dutch ambassador to South Africa, who had attended the Rivonia Trial.

The death sentence was a very real possibility and he and his comrades decided that if it was imposed, they would not appeal.[36]

If he was afraid, he was not showing it. In fact, Mandela observed that as Judge de Wet began to read his judgment, it was he who appeared nervous.[37]

---

i   James La Guma (1894–1961), a communist who was expelled by Kadalie.

After an eight-month trial the eight men were sentenced to life imprison-ment. Mandela had already been in prison for 678 days.

In South Africa then, for political prisoners, 'life' meant exactly that – life. At the age of forty-five he was about to spend the rest of his life in prison.

He only knew the name of the prison that would hold him when he arrived early the next morning.

––––––––

To Coen Stork, the Dutch ambassador to South Africa

11th June, 1964

Dear Mr Stork,

I am writing to you before the final outcome of this case because, thereafter, it will not be possible for me to do so.

My colleagues and I deeply appreciate the invaluable assistance you have given us. The personal interest you have shown in the case, and the strong support we are receiving from all sections of the Dutch population, give us enormous reserves of strength and courage.

We would like you to know that we regard you as one of our great-est friends, and are sure you will continue to be of assistance to our people in their struggle against racial discrimination.

UNGADINWA NANGOMSO.[i]

Yours very sincerely
[Signed NRMandela]

––––––––

i   'Nangamso' is an isiXhosa word that expresses deep gratitude to a person who has gone beyond the call of duty. Mandela sometimes spelled it nangomso.

Pretoria Prison
Republic of South Africa
11th June, 1964.

Dear Mr. Stork,

I am writing to you before the final outcome of this case because, thereafter, it will not be possible for me to do so.

My colleagues and I deeply appreciate the invaluable assistance you have given us. The personal interest you have shown in the case, and the strong support we are receiving from all sections of the Dutch population, give us enormous reserves of strength and courage.

We would like you to know that we regard you as one of our greatest friends, and are sure you will continue to be of assistance to our people in their struggle against racial discrimination.

UNGADINIMA NANGOMSO.

Yours very sincerely
NRMandela

Letter to Coen Stork, Dutch ambassador to South Africa, 11 June 1964, see page 19.

ROBBEN ISLAND MAXIMUM SECURITY PRISON

||||||||||||

JUNE 1964–MARCH 1982

Within hours of being sentenced to life imprisonment, Nelson Mandela and six of his comrades were taken from their cells in Pretoria Local Prison, handcuffed, and driven to a nearby military air base. They arrived on Robben Island early the next morning, Saturday, 13 June 1964. Denis Goldberg, the only white accused convicted with them, remained in Pretoria to serve his sentence – apartheid laws decreed that he was forbidden from being incarcerated with black prisoners.

This was Mandela's second time in Robben Island maximum security prison; his few weeks as a prisoner there in mid-1963 had prepared him for the harsh conditions, and he counselled his comrades on the importance of keeping their dignity intact.

Soon after he and three others had arrived his previous time on Robben Island in May 1963, prison guards barked orders for them to walk briskly in twos, herding them like cattle. When they continued walking at the same pace, the guards threatened them. 'Look here, we will kill you here – and your parents, your people, will never know what has happened to you,' Mandela recalled them saying. He and Steve Tefu, a prisoner who belonged to the PAC, then took the lead, maintaining their own pace. 'I was determined that we should put our stamp clearly, right from the first day we must fight because that would determine how we were going to be treated. But if we gave in on the first day, then they would treat us in a very contemptuous manner. So we went to the front and we walked even more steadily. They couldn't do anything, they didn't do anything.'[38]

Conditions on Robben Island were brutal. The prisoners were only allowed to stop doing hard labour fourteen years later in 1978, and until then their existence on the island was stark and cruel, lightened only by their own attitude, as well as visits and letters from family.

In the beginning, the food was barely edible[i] and divvied up according to racist policies. Breakfast for African prisoners was 12 ounces of maize meal porridge and a cup of black coffee, so-called coloured and Indian prisoners got 14 ounces of maize meal porridge with bread and coffee.[39] There were no white prisoners on the island.

'We were like cattle kept on spare rations so as to be lean for the market,' former prisoner Indres Naidoo writes. 'Bodies to be kept alive, not human beings with tastes and a pleasure in eating.'[40]

The weather conditions on the island were extreme – 'blistering hot in summer' and in winter 'bitterly cold, raining or drizzling most of the time', recalled former prisoner Mac Maharaj.[41] In the beginning, African prisoners had to wear short pants and sandals year-round, whereas Indian and coloured prisoners were issued with long pants and socks.[ii] Prisoners were given a thin jersey on 25 April, which was taken away again on 25 September.[42] There were no beds for the first ten years – prisoners slept on the concrete floor on a sisal mat with three 'flimsy' blankets.[43] It was so cold in winter, they slept fully clothed. For the first ten years, Mandela and his colleagues bathed with cold water.

Throughout the week, prisoners were put to work in the yard, breaking stones with hammers. On the weekends, they were locked in their cells for twenty-three hours a day, unless they had a visitor. At the beginning of 1965, they were set to work digging in the lime quarry.[iii] It was gruelling work, and the glare of the sun on the white limestone seared their eyes. For three years, repeated requests to the prison authorities for dark glasses were rejected. By the time permission was given, the eyesight of many of the prisoners, including Mandela's, had been irreparably damaged.

In 1968, Mandela's mother, Nosekeni, died, and he was refused permission to bury her. The following year, his eldest son, Thembi, was killed in a car accident, and this time his plea to be at the graveside

---

i   In a memorandum to the commissioner of prisons written on Robben Island in January 1970, Mandela writes: 'On numerous occasions since 1964, we have repeatedly stressed that our diet is not adequately nutritional, insufficiently varied and unpalatable.'

ii   In a memorandum to the commissioner of prisons written on Robben Island in January 1970, Mandela writes: 'In May 1967, we were issued with a new outfit which went a long way towards fulfilling the requirements stipulated in the above regulations. But we cannot make maximum use of the improvements because of the standing orders which require us to give up long trousers and jersies in summer and the mechanical manner in which these orders are enforced irrespective of the actual state of the weather conditions.'

iii   In the same memorandum Mandela writes: 'We have been forced to do heavy and uncreative work which sapped our energy and in some cases even adversely affected our health.'

was ignored. He was forced to stand on the sidelines while friends and relatives played his role in the burials. His letters during this period spell out his raw anguish over these tremendous losses.

Around the same time, his beloved wife Winnie was detained by police and spent fourteen months in custody. His letters to her and others about her imprisonment demonstrate his frustration and anguish at not being able to help her or his children during this nightmare.

He kept up a regular correspondence with prison authorities to assert his rights as a prisoner, and even went as far as to demand the release of himself and his comrades or to be treated as political prisoners.

In 1975, on the initiative of his comrades, he began to secretly write his memoirs with the assistance of Walter Sisulu, Ahmed Kathrada, and two other comrades and prisoners, Mac Maharaj and Laloo Chiba. The plan was for the autobiography to be published abroad in time for his sixtieth birthday on 18 July 1978. On his release in late 1976, Maharaj smuggled off the island, hidden within the covers of notebooks, a transcribed version of the manuscript. When part of the original manuscript was discovered buried in a tin near the prison block in 1977, Mandela and his comrades had their study privileges withdrawn from the start of 1978. The manuscript, however, made it to London, but it was not published until 1994 as *Long Walk to Freedom*.

Bram Fischer[i] was a white Afrikaner advocate who defended Mandela and his colleagues in the Treason Trial of 1956 to 1961[ii] and in the Rivonia Trial. But more than that, he was a comrade and a good friend. He first visited the Rivonia trialists on Robben Island in 1964 to confirm their earlier decision not to appeal their conviction and sentences.

Mandela and some of his colleagues had known Fischer and his wife, Molly, well and had spent many joyful hours at their home in Johannesburg. But on that prison visit when Mandela asked after Molly, Fischer turned and walked away. After he had left the island, a senior prison official told Mandela that she had drowned when their car left the road and plunged into a river. The major gave permission for Mandela to write Fischer a condolence letter. It was never delivered.

The letter to Fischer is formal, befitting correspondence from a prisoner to his lawyer – and in this case from a prisoner who was also a lawyer. As prisoners held a special dispensation to write to their legal advisors, it would have been preferable not to create the impression that it was a personal letter, which he may not have had permission to write.

In 1965, Fischer was arrested and tried the next year for furthering the aims of the Communist Party[iii] and conspiring to overthrow the government. He was sentenced to life imprisonment. While in Pretoria Local Prison he was diagnosed with cancer and fell badly in 1974. The authorities finally bowed to public pressure and released him to his brother's house from which he was forbidden from moving. He died in 1975 and the Prisons Department had him cremated. His ashes have never been located.

To Bram Fischer,[iv] his comrade and advocate in the Rivonia Trial

2nd August 1964

---

i   Bram Fischer, lawyer and political and anti-apartheid activist – see the glossary.
ii   The Treason Trial (1956–61) was a result of the apartheid government's attempt to quell the power of the Congress Alliance, a coalition of anti-apartheid organisations. In early-morning raids on 5 December 1956, 156 individuals were arrested and charged with high treason. By the end of the trial in March 1961 all the accused either had the charges withdrawn or, in the case of the last twenty-eight accused (including Mandela), were acquitted.
iii For the South African Communist Party (SACP), see the glossary.
iv   Bram Fischer (1908–75), lawyer and political and anti-apartheid activist – see the glossary.

Dear Mr Fischer,

You will recall that when you visited the Island last time, you discussed with Major Visser whether it would be permissible for you to arrange for me to receive the *South African Law Journal*.

I have to date not received the journal and I thought it advisable to remind you about the matter, should pressure of work have made it difficult for you to make the arrangements with Juta's & Co.

I have also not received the lecture from Wolsey Hall, London, and the law books and I would be pleased if you would kindly check up with Mr Joffe.[i]

Yours faithfully
[Signed NRMandela]
Prisoner no. 466/64

Advocate A Fischer, S.A,.
c/o Innes Chambers,
Corner Von Brandis & Pritchard Sts.
Johannesburg

◇◇◇◇◇◇◇◇◇◇◇◇

Mandela studied the Afrikaans language in prison in search of a better knowledge of the history and culture of the ruling National Party and its followers. He believed this would help him to communicate more effectively with his enemy.

It worked. It assisted in breaking down barriers with prison guards and later with government officials and even the country's president, P. W. Botha.[ii]

Here, while making the point that legitimate requests are often ignored, he is reiterating his plea to be able to prepare for his exams by studying past papers of an organisation which promoted Afrikaans, an official South African language from 1925, as well as asking for back copies of an Afrikaans-language women's magazine, Huisgenoot.

---

i   Mandela's attorney, Joel Joffe.
ii   P. W. Botha, president of South Africa 1978–84 and state president 1984–89 – see the glossary.

To Major Visser, prison official

[Stamp dated 25.8.1965]

Major Visser,

During the inspection on the 14th August 1965, I tried to speak to you but you did not give me the opportunity of doing so. While the inspection was in progress Chief Warder Van Tonder, who accompanied you, promised to tell you that I had some requests to make, but you left without seeing me. I am now writing to you because the matter has become urgent.

1. I am preparing to write an examination on the 29th October 1965. In March this year and early in May, I had made written applications to the Commanding Officer for leave to order old examination papers from the Saamwerk-Unie of Natal as part of my preparation for this examination. You have repeatedly assured me that you have written to the SWU and ordered the required papers and that you awaited their reply. Although the examination is now 2 months away I still have not received the papers.

2. I owe the University of South Africa the sum of R40.0 being the balance of fees for an Honours Degree course which I had planned to write in February 1966. In terms of the contract this amount must be paid before the 1st September 1965. On the last occasion I discussed the matter with you, you informed me that you had written to the university. A few days ago, I received the account for this amount and I am anxious to have the matter finalised before it is too late. In this connection I might add that I ordered my study books from Messrs Juta & Co. I asked them to order them if they did not have them in stock and to advise me when they would have them available to enable me to plan my work. I have not heard from them and I would be glad if you would kindly advise me whether the matter has been attended to.

3. You also told me that you had ordered the old *Huisgenoot*[i] num-

---

i   *Huisgenoot* is an Afrikaans-language magazine.

bers I required for purposes of study and I wish to remind you that I have not yet received them.

4. Several times last year and early this year I applied for a loan of books from the State Library and for enrolment forms. I have not heard from them.

I am seriously considering whether in view of the difficulties I have mentioned above, I should write the forthcoming examinations, and I should be pleased if you would give me the opportunity to discuss the whole matter with you.

[Signed NRMandela]

◇◇◇◇◇◇◇◇◇◇◇◇

It is clear from correspondence in Mandela's prison files held by the National Archives and Records Service of South Africa, that he wrote on several occasions to Adelaide Tambo, the wife of his former law partner and the president of the ANC, Oliver Tambo, who was living in exile with his family in London, and running the organisation from abroad. It is unlikely that Adelaide Tambo received the letters before the latter part of his prison sentence. In 1968 Mandela wrote to her care of his wife and used her African name, Matlala, and the surname Mandela. A note in Afrikaans at the end of one of the letters shows that the prison authorities had worked out the identity of the real recipient because someone has written 'A Tambo' on the letter. Just this information would have been enough for them to hold it back. It is highly probable that all the underlined text in this letter is the work of the prison censors, drawing attention to individuals that are known to them or whom they want to identify.

══════════

To Adelaide Tambo,[i] friend, anti-apartheid activist, and the wife of Oliver Tambo, ANC president and Mandela's former law partner[ii]

5.3.68

[Note in another hand says 'My sister'.]

---

i   Adelaide Tambo (1929–2007) – see the glossary.
ii   The underlining of words appears to have been done by the censor to question the names of the people he mentions.

Kgaitsedi yaka,[i]

I send you my warmest love. You, Reginald,[ii] Thembi,[iii] and Dalindlela[iv] and the baby have been in my thoughts during the past five years, and it gives me great pleasure to be able to tell you this.

I hope you have all been keeping well. Zami[v] gives me scraps of information about you in her letters and whenever she comes down, but the last occasion I heard from you directly was when I received Reggie's[vi] inciting telegram during my first case. I was tremendously inspired. It arrived almost simultaneously with that from the late Chief, and both messages gave a new dimension to the issues.

News of the widespread efforts made by our household[vii] during the first half of '64 played a similar role. Such efforts fortified our spirits and relieved the grimness of that period.

But I must return to you Matlala.[viii] Just exactly where do I start? Certainly not from the day in the early fifties when Reggie and I drove to the Helping Hand[ix] where you presented him with a smart jersey that you had especially knitted for the occasion. That would take us far back. Suffice to say that I thought you played your cards very well. Nor do I wish to remind you [of] the pertinent observations you used to make during the numerous consultations we attended together with the late Rita, Effie[x] and others on matters that vitally affected the interests of your profession,[xi] the savoury meals I enjoyed when I visited you in the East shortly after your wedding as well as in June '62 over there.[xii] The correspondence we had in '61 was stimulating and was widely discussed among us at the time. These and numerous other incidents have flashed across my mind on many occasions and I love to recall them.

I was sorry to learn that you had abandoned your studies.[xiii] In July

---

i   'My sister' in both Sesotho and Setswana.
ii   Oliver Reginald Tambo (1917–93) – Mandela's friend, former law partner, and the president of the ANC – see the glossary. His middle name was Reginald.
iii   The Tambos' eldest daughter.
iv   The Tambo's son, Dali.
v   Zami is one of Winnie Mandela's names.
vi   Oliver Reginald Tambo (his middle name Reginald was shortened to Reggie).
vii   'Our household' is code for the ANC.
viii 'Matlala', a nickname for Adelaide Tambo.
ix   Adelaide Tambo and Winnie Mandela both stayed at the Helping Hand Hostel in Hans Street, Jeppestown, when they moved to Johannesburg.
x   Possibly Effie Schultz, a medical doctor and activist.
xi   He might be referring to Adelaide Tambo's vocation as a nurse. Also see footnote xiii on this page.
xii   He is referring to his visit to London where he saw the Tambos in June 1962 while on his clandestine trip out of South Africa.
xiii Adelaide Tambo was a nurse and matron at the hospital where she worked. She had a master's degree in gerontology from the University of Oxford and after being encouraged by the doctors at the hospital,

'62 I had mentioned the matter to <u>Xamela</u>[i] and others, and the news of which they approved fully, had much excited them. In fact we were calculating only the other day that you had either completed or [were] at least doing the final year. Anyway I am sure you and Reggie must have weighed the matter very carefully and, there must have been a good reason for terminating the studies.

<u>Thembi, Dali and the baby</u>[ii] must have grown and I would love to hear about them. Please give them my love. I hope Thembi still remembers the Saturday morning when you and herself visited Chancellor House.[iii] In the general office and with all the clients around I complimented her on her new dress, whereupon she promptly [displayed] the dress, boasting that "i ne stiffening" to the amusement of everybody there.

I also think of <u>Malume</u> and the <u>heavyweight from the western areas</u>[iv] and hope that they still <u>find time to dye</u> their hair. Incidentally, during our sojourn with Reggie, I remarked that he was beginning to turn grey and drew from him the grave comment: "Please don't tell me that, don't tell me that". I am sure my good friend <u>Gcwanini</u>,[v] always polite and peaceful for the [first] five days of the week and who always allowed himself relaxation from these virtues and a bit of rioting on weekends still will remember the night we spent at home together with <u>Peter</u>. Then there is the nocturnal Ngwali, who never got tired of waking us up at midnight to burden us with numerous problems, and the ubiquitous <u>Bakwe</u>.[vi] I believe problems of weight have slowed down the activities of both. <u>Madiba</u> of Orlando East, the two <u>Gambus</u>, <u>Alfred</u>, <u>Mzwayi</u>, <u>Tom</u>, <u>Dinou</u>, <u>Maindy</u>,[vii] and Gabula, I remember them all. I hope you still see <u>Tough Guy</u> and <u>Hazel</u>. Has he produced

---

    enrolled to study medicine. She discontinued her studies when it became apparent that she would need to give up her job, the income from which her family relied on. (Dali Tambo in an email to Sahm Venter, 28 November 2017.)

i   Walter Sisulu (1912– 2003), ANC and MK activist and fellow Rivonia trialist who was imprisoned with Mandela – see the glossary. Mandela is referring to him by his clan name Xamela (sometimes spelt by Mandela as Xhamela) as he is not permitted to write about other prisoners.

ii   The Tambos' children.

iii Chancellor House was the building in which Mandela and Oliver Tambo started their law practice, Mandela and Tambo, in 1952.

iv Mandela is possibly speaking about people in code here.

v   Advocate Duma Nokwe (1927–78), political activist and advocate – see the glossary. Gcwanini is his clan name.

vi Bakwe (Joe) Matthews (1929–2010), political activist and son of Frieda and Z. K. Matthews – see the glossary for these three individuals.

vii Maindy Msimang (1928–2018), also known as Mendi Msimang, was an administrative officer of the ANC in London.

anything new after "The Road to . . . ?" Any new literature from Todd and Esme,[i] or musical composition? Do you hear of <u>Cousin, Mlahleni, and Mpumi</u>?[ii] I would like to be remembered to all of them.

Our family has always attached a great deal of importance to education and progress, and the widespread illiteracy facing us has always been a matter of grave concern. Efforts to overcome this problem have always been frustrated by lack of <u>funds</u> and of adequate <u>facilities</u> for <u>academic</u> and <u>vocational training</u>. Now <u>these problems are being gradually tackled and solved</u> and increasing numbers of school-going youths are finding their way into boarding schools and technical colleges. It <u>flatters one's pride to know</u> that those who have <u>completed</u> their <u>courses</u> and <u>who have been given posts and assignments are doing so exceptionally well</u>. Heartiest congratulations and fondest regards to all.

The pronoun "I" has been prominent in this correspondence. I would have preferred "we". But I am constrained to use <u>terminology acceptable</u> to the practice of this <u>establishment</u>, however much it may be incompatible with my own individual [taste]. I am sure you will pardon me for the egotism.

Once again, I wish you to know that you, Reggie, the kids and all my friends are constantly in my thoughts. I know you must be worried about my incarceration. But let me assure you that I am well, fit and on top of the world, and nothing would please me more than to hear from you.

In the meantime my warmest to you and fondest regards to all.

Sincerely,
Nel

[Written in another hand in Afrikaans] (Contents from inside the envelope).

[Envelope]

---

i   Todd Matshikiza (1920–68), writer and musician who composed the musical score for the internationally successful South African musical *King Kong* (1959) and his wife Esme Matshikiza, a social worker.

ii   Mlahleni is Professor Nyisani and his wife Mpumi.

Miss Matlala Mandela,[i]
8155, Orlando West,
Johannesburg.

━━━━━━━

To Knowledge Guzana,[ii] attorney and leader of the Transkei homeland's Democratic Party[iii]

[Stamp dated 14.10.1968]

WHEN ACKNOWLEDGING RECEIPT HEREOF PLEASE WRITE THE FOLLOWING WORDS AT THE TOP OF YOUR LETTER: "REPLY TO SPECIAL LETTER."

Dear Dambisa,[iv]

Two days ago my brother-in-law, Timothy Mbuzo,[v] informed me that you attended my mother's funeral and I should like to thank you for this considerate gesture.

Only a keen sense of public duty would enable a man in your position, and on whom there must be heavy and pressing demands for his services, to find time to devote himself to the public good, and I should like you to know that I am greatly indebted to you.

It was never easy for one anywhere to lose a beloved mother. Behind bars such misfortune can be a shattering disaster. This could easily have been the case with me when I was confronted with these tragic news on September 26, which ironically enough was my wife's birthday. Fortunately for me, however, my friends here, who are endowed with virtues far in excess of anything I can hope to command, are remarkable for their ability to think and feel for others. I have always

---

i   Using Adelaide Tambo's nickname and the surname Mandela indicates further that he wishes to disguise her identity.
ii   Knowledge Guzana (1916–unknown) – see the glossary.
iii   The Democatic Party, which was formed in 1963, rejected 'independence' of black homelands or Bantustans and was the official opposition party in the Transkei. Guzana led the party from 1966 until 1976.
iv   Knowledge Guzana's clan name.
v   Sibali Timothy Mbuzo, a close relative of Mandela's brother-in-law Daniel Timakwe and a long-standing leading member of the ANC in the Transkei homeland.

leaned heavily on their comradeship and solidarity. Their offers of goodwill and encouragement enabled me to face this tragic loss with resignation.

Sibali[i] Mkhuze told me that my relatives and friends responded admirably and rallied to the graveside. This was a magnificent demonstration of solidarity which gave me a shot in the arm, and it is a source of tremendous inspiration for me to count you amongst those who gave me this encouragement.

I have also written to your friend and head of the Tembu[ii] Royal House,[iii] Jonguhlanga, to thank him for undertaking the strenuous task of planning the funeral, and this in spite of his declining health and heavy commitments. His touching devotion to his relatives, friends and people generally has created a profound impression far and wide. I only hope that his health might improve.

This is a special letter allowed me only for the purpose of thanking you for attending the funeral and it is not possible to refer to wider issues. It is sufficient for me to say that I am happy to note that the interest you showed in public affairs as a student at S.A.N.C[iv] 30 years ago has not flagged. I hope that in this note I have succeeded in placing on record not only my deep gratitude to you for honouring the occasion with your presence but also in indicating to you the regard I have for you and family.

Bulisa elusasheni na ku[v] [name is difficult to read]. Na ngomso![vi]

Yours very sincerely,
Nelson

K Guzana, Esq.,
Ncambedlana,
P.O. Umtata.[vii] Transkei

---

i   *Sibali* means 'brother-in-law' in isiXhosa.
ii   More commonly this is spelt 'Thembu'.
iii   Mandela was a member of the Thembu royal house – see the glossary. In a letter to Fatima Meer, dated 14 June 1989, Mandela said the correct spelling was Thembu.
iv   South African Native College, another name for University College of Fort Hare.
v   'Give my regards to the family' in isiXhosa.
vi   'Nangamso' is an isiXhosa word that expresses deep gratitude to a person who has gone beyond the call of duty. It is usually spelled nangamso, sometimes Mandela spelled it nangomso and in this case, na ngomso.
vii   Umtata (now called Mthatha) was the capital of the Transkei homeland.

To Mangosuthu Buthelezi,[i] family friend and Zulu prince

[In another hand] 466/64 Nelson Mandela

                    [Stamp dated and signed] Censor Office 4–11–1968
My dear Chief,

I should be pleased if you would kindly convey to the Royal Family
my deepest sympathy on the death of King Cyprian Bhekuzulu.[ii] His
passing away took me completely by surprise for I did not have even
the slightest hint of the King's fatal illness. Although a few years back I
had heard that his health was somewhat indifferent, a friend had later
informed me that he had much improved, a fact which seemed to be
confirmed by photographs that I subsequently saw in various publications and which on the face of it appeared to indicate that he was in good
health. The unexpected news consequently shocked me immensely, and
I have since been thinking of the Royal Family in their bereavement.

You and the late King were closely related and bound to each other
by a long and fruitful friendship, and his death must have been a severe
blow to you. I met him twice only; in my Johannesburg home and in my
office, and on both occasions he was accompanied by you. It afforded
me great pleasure to note how deeply he valued your friendship and
how highly he appreciated your advice. In him we caught glimpses
of the astuteness and courage that was the source of so much of the
glittering achievements of his famous ancestors. In serving him as you
did, you were carrying on the tradition established by my chiefs, Ngq-
engelele and Mnyamana, your ancestors, whose magnificent role in
the task of national service is widely acknowledged.

The vast crowds that must have attended the funeral, the words of
comfort delivered at the graveside and the messages of sympathy from
organisations and individuals all over the country would by now have
fully demonstrated that the Royal Family is not alone in mourning his
unfortunate loss to the country.

The death of a human being, whatever may be his station in life,

---

i   Mangosuthu Buthelezi (1928–) – see the glossary.
ii   King Cyprian Bhekuzulu kaSolomon, king of the Zulu nation – see the glossary.

is always a sad and painful affair; that of a noted public figure brings not only grief and mourning to his family and friends, but very often entails implications of a wider nature. It may mean tampering with established attitudes and the introduction of new ones, with all the uncertainty that normally accompanies the change of personalities at the head of affairs. In due course Amazulu will no doubt be summoned to the Royal capital to deliberate over the whole situation and to make the necessary decisions. I am confident that the statesmen and elders whose vast wealth of wisdom, ability and experience have guided the fortunes of this celebrated House in the past, will, on this occasion, offer solutions which will be inspired by the conviction that the interests and welfare of all our countrymen is the first and paramount consideration. In this regard, your immense knowledge and able advice will be as crucial now as it has been in the past.

Incidentally, in December 1965 I wrote a special letter to Nkosikazi Nokhukhanya[i] and requested her, amongst other things, to mention me to your late cousin and to you. I indicated then that on my release I would visit Zululand to pay my respects to my traditional leader. I hope the message was received. This resolution remains unchanged, and although it will no longer be my privilege to pay homage to the late King personally, it will be an honour for me to visit Nongoma[ii] and thereafter Mahlabatini.[iii]

Finally, I should like you to know that I think of you and Umndlunkulu[iv] with warm and pleasant memories, and sincerely wish you great happiness and good health. My fond regards to Umntwana,[v] your mother, and to your mother-in-law.

Yours very sincerely,
[Signed NR Mandela]
NELSON R[vi] MANDELA

Chief Mangosuthu Buthelezi
P.O. Box 1, Mahlabatini
Zululand

---

i   Nokhukhanya Luthuli, widow of Chief Albert Luthuli – see the glossary.
ii   Residence of the Zulu King and the seat of the royal family.
iii   Buthelezi's birthplace and residence.
iv   A royal reference to Mangosuthu Buthelezi's wife, Irene Buthelezi.
v   'The child' in isiZulu.
vi   The initial R stands for his given name, Rolihlahla.

◇◇◇◇◇◇◇◇◇◇◇◇◇

*Apart from the letters they were allowed to write to officials and their law-
yers, prisoners could only initially write to direct family members. In the
beginning it was one letter of 500 words every six months. They were also
only allowed one family visit every six months. Children over two years old
could only visit their fathers when they turned sixteen. By the time of Mandela's first imprisonment in 1962, his five children – two boys and three
girls – were aged between twenty-three months and seventeen years old.*

To Zenani and Zindzi Mandela,[i] his middle and youngest daugh-
ters

4.2.69

My Darlings,

The nice letter by Zindzi reached me safely, and I was indeed very glad
to know that she is now in Standard 2. When Mummy came to see me
last December, she told me that both of you had passed your examinations and that Zeni was now in Standard 3. I now know that Kgatho[ii]
and Maki[iii] have also passed. It pleases me very much to see that all my
children are doing well.

I hope that you will do even better at the end of the year.

I was happy to learn that Zeni can cook chips, rice, meat, and many
other things. I am looking forward to the day when I will be able to
enjoy all that she cooks.

Zindzi says her heart is sore because I am not at home and wants
to know when I will come back. I do not know, my darlings, when I
will return. You will remember that in the letter I wrote in 1966, I told
you that the white judge said I should stay in jail for the rest of my life.

It may be long before I come back; it may be soon. Nobody knows
when it will be, not even the judge who said I should be kept here. But
I am certain that one day I will be back at home to live in happiness
with you until the end of my days.

i   Zenani Mandela (1959–) and Zindziswa Mandela (1960–) – see the glossary.
ii   Makgatho (Kgatho) Mandela (1950–2005), Mandela's second-born son – see the glossary.
iii   Makaziwe (Maki) Mandela (1954–), Mandela's eldest daughter – see the glossary.

Do not worry about me now. I am happy, well and full of strength and hope. The only thing I long for is you, but whenever I feel lonely I look at your photo which is always in front of me. It has a white frame with a black margin. It is a lovely photo. For the last 2 years I have been asking Mummy to send me a group photo with Zindzi, Zeni, Maki, Kgatho, Nomfundo[i] and Kazeka. But up to now I have not received it. The photo will make me even more happy than I am at the present moment.

Many thanks for the wonderful Christmas cards you sent me. Apart from yours, I received one from Kgatho and another from Mummy. I hope you received more.

Mummy visits me two or three times a year. She also arranges for Kgatho and others to see me. Father Long of the Roman Catholic Church, St Patrick, Mowbray, Cape Town, still visits me once a month. In addition, I am allowed to receive and write one letter every month. All these things keep me happy and hopeful.

Please pass my fondest regards to Father Borelli and tell the Mother Superior[ii] that I am greatly indebted to her and all the sisters there for the help and guidance they are giving you. Perhaps someday I may be able in some small way to return this kindness.

In December 1965 I received a letter from Zeni in which she also asked me to come back home, just as Zindzi says in hers. The English was good and the handwriting clear. But I was completely surprised to get one from Zindzi. Her English was also good and the writing was just as clear. You are doing well, my darlings. Keep it up.

With lots and lots of love and a million kisses.

Affectionately,
Tata[iii]

MISSES ZENI & ZINDZI MANDELA
HOUSE NO. 8115 ORLANDO WEST
JOHANNESBURG

---

i   Olive Nomfundo Mandela, daughter of Mandela's sister Notancu.
ii   Zindzi and Zenani were at a Catholic school in neighbouring Swaziland.
iii   'Father' in isiXhosa.

To Makaziwe Mandela,[i] his eldest daughter

16.2.69

My Darling,

I was indeed very happy to learn that you, Kgatho, Zeni & Zindzi[ii] had passed your respective examinations. Please accept my warmest congratulations. Your success in all the examinations that you have written up to now show that all of you have the ability to study and I do hope this will inspire you to work even harder this year. You are now doing the final year of the Junior Certificate and I feel that when the time comes to sit for the examinations at the end of the year, you will again pass, provided you work hard and continuously right from the beginning. I expect you to tell me in your reply your subjects this year, and the titles of the English and Xhosa/Zulu set works. I should like to read them. But for the time being I say: "Well done!"

I believe you, Tembi[iii] & Kgatho were expected to go down to Umtata[iv] to visit Makhulu's[v] grave and to pay your last respects to her. Did you succeed? I was very sorry to receive the news of her death for I had hoped to be able to look after her in her last days on earth and to bury her when she died. But Mummy and others tell me that relatives and friends, led by Paramount Chief Sabata,[vi] attended in large numbers and gave a burial that aroused deep feelings. I know that Zeni & Zindzi attended and would be equally happy to be told that you were also able to do so.

I hope you received the Xmas card I sent you and Kgatho and that you enjoyed your Xmas and New Year. It was a real pleasure for me to get your undated letter in November 1967. The language and

---

i   Makaziwe Mandela (1954–) – see the glossary.
ii   Mandela's son Makgatho (1950–2005) and his daughters Zenani (1959–) and Zindziswa (1960–).
iii Mandela's eldest son, Madiba Thembekile (1945–69). Mandela variously shortened it to 'Thembi' or 'Tembi'.
iv   Umtata (now called Mthatha) was the capital of the Transkei homeland.
v   'Grandmother' in isiXhosa. Here Mandela is referring to his mother, Nosekeni Mandela, who died in 1968.
vi   King Sabata Jonguhlanga Dalindyebo (1928–86), paramount chief of the Transkei homeland and leader of the Democratic Progressive Party, the opposition party in Transkei which opposed apartheid rule – see the glossary. The term 'paramount chief' was developed by the British colonisers as the highest title in a region with a chief-based system. Paramount Chief Sabata was actually a king. The British maintained that only the British monarch could hold that title.

style were good and the writing clear. It pleased me very much to hear that you were enjoying yourself in school and that you liked English the best. I was also happy to know that your ambition is to become a doctor or scientist. Both are strenuous professions and you must work hard and steadily during school terms and have a good rest during school holidays. I see that you are afraid of being kidnapped one day when you have discovered a dangerous drug. Do not worry much, darling, about kidnappers. Their world is getting smaller and smaller and their friends fewer. One day there will be a new world when all of us will live in happiness and peace. That world will be created by you and me; by Kgatho, Zeni & Zindzi; by our friends and country-men. When you become a doctor or scientist and use your knowledge, training and skill to help your people who are poor and miserable and who have no opportunity to develop, you will be fighting for that new world.

In your letter you told me that Kgatho was doing first year matric and that he was doing well at school. The reports I have received both before and after your letter confirm your statement. I am pleased to learn that Kgatho is keen on his studies and that he is making good progress. You also told me that Thembi was working, and that he had a 2 year baby who was plumpy and lovely. You ended your letter on this point, by pointing out that Thembi was helping in every way, that he was buying clothes and all that you needed. It pleased me much to be informed that he is of assistance to you. Anything that eases your difficulties and that adds to your happiness fills my heart with joy, and I am really grateful to Thembi for all that he does for you.

I am however sorry to learn that he elected to leave school before he had obtained even the Junior Certificate. I wrote to him in 1967 and advised him to return to school together with his wife, or to continue the studies by correspondence. I received no reply from him nor have I any information on just what work he is doing.

I thank you for letting me know that But' Sitsheketshe[i] is married and that he stays in Pimville.[ii]

I have been trying for the last 2 years to get a group photo of you, Kgatho, Zeni, Zindzi, Nomfundo[iii] and Chief Mdingi's daughter.[iv] I

[i]   Mandela's cousin.
[ii]   A suburb of Soweto.
[iii] Olive Nomfundo Mandela, daughter of Mandela's sister Notancu.
[iv]   Chief Mdingi is a relative of Mandela's and the Thembu chief who named Mandela's two younger
       daughters. The eldest he named 'Zenani' meaning 'What have you brought?', and the Madikizelas

should be grateful if you would help in arranging for the photo to be taken and sent down as soon as possible.

Please ask Mme Ngakane[i] to give me, through you, the respective qualifications, profession or trade of Mookamedi[ii] Makgatho, Letanka, Msane and Mabaso. You will give me this information in your reply.

The sentiments you expressed in the last paragraph of your letter were very sweet and they gave me a lot of inspiration and strength, darling. You are now 14 and the day is not far off when you will be able to visit me. I am told that you have grown tall and charming and I am anxious to see you. In the meantime I should like you to know that I think of you, Kgatho, Zeni, and Zindzi every day and your school progress makes me happy and proud of you. With lots and lots of love.

Affectionately,
Tata

29.7.69

I had written the above letter & handed it in for posting to you on February 16 this year but for some reason or other it was not sent away. I have already written to your mother and Kgatho and Zeni and Zindzi giving you all my deepest sympathy, darling. My application for permission to attend the funeral was not granted, and I hope it was possible for you and Kgatho to do so.

In March I received the group photo I asked for, and you need no longer worry about it. I had previously been promised a photo of Thembi and his family, and will write to Molokozana[iii] about it as soon as Kgatho gives me the particulars I had asked for.

With much love,
Tata

(Winnie Mandela's family) named her Nomadabi Nosizwe – 'battlefield of the nation'. Mdingi named the youngest daughter Mantu Nobutho Zindziswa.

i   Neighbours of the Mandelas.
ii   'President' in Sesotho. Although we haven't been able to identify to whom Mandela is referring, it is probably not an actual president.
iii   'Daughter-in-law' in isiXhosa. He is referring to Thoko Mandela, his son Thembi's widow.

◇◇◇◇◇◇◇◇◇◇◇◇

It appears that by the end of the 1960s, Mandela was allowed to write to those outside his family circle. But such correspondence was not exempt from the obstacles that had become a hallmark of the prisoner and his life-line to the world. In this series of letters, Mandela has rewritten his original letter with its original date, and then explained this to the recipient in a postscript.

To Lilian Ngoyi,[i] his friend & comrade

3.3.69

Kgaitsedi yaka, yaratehang[ii]

I wrote to you before I was sentenced in Nov 1962. You also heard from me sometime thereafter when I asked you, as the eldest daughter in the family, always to play the role of peacekeeper. Since then I have been anxious to write to you but the main difficulty has always been the fact that you would not have been able to reply.[iii] Now, however, you are free to communicate with me & I should like you to know that I always think of you, the Old Lady,[iv] Hlatse,[v] Memo[vi] & Oupa[vii] with warm & affectionate memories. I hope you are all keeping well & am looking forward to hear something on each one of you.

I was very sorry to hear of the death of Percy[viii] & was even more so that I was unable to attend the funeral. He was not only your brother but a friend whose kindness and charm made him dear to me & I regretted very much when I heard that he was no more. Even though years have passed since the happening of this event, I should be pleased if you would kindly give the Old Lady my deepest sympathy.

---

i   Lilian Ngoyi (1911–80), politician, and anti-apartheid and women's rights activist – see the glossary.
ii   'My dear sister' in Sesotho or Setswana.
iii   She wouldn't have been able to reply due to the fact that she was not family and also that she was a known political activist.
iv   Annie, Lilian Ngoyi's grandmother.
v   Lilian Ngoyi's daughter.
vi   Peletsi 'Memory' Mphahlele, Lilian Ngoyi's adopted daughter.
vii Edith's son Tebogo and Lilian Ngoyi's nephew.
viii Lilian Ngoyi's brother.

It was very sweet of you to send Hlatse to the Rivonia Trial. We deeply appreciated the trouble she took in travelling the 32 miles to Pretoria & accepted her presence in court as an act of solidarity from you and family that gave us much courage & inspiration. In all the important issues that we took up you were always in the forefront, sharing common hardships with your friends & giving them encouragement & hope. Your humble contribution was made in the Defiance Campaign,[i] COP,[ii] Women's Protest March to Pretoria[iii] & the Treason Trial,[iv] to mention but a few.

We knew that although you could not be present in person you were, nevertheless fully, with us in spirit as we went through that memorable case, & were indeed very glad to see Hlatse there. Is Sonny[v] keeping well?

You may not be in a position to give my fondest regards to Helen.[vi] I should like her to know that I think of her as well. I have always respected her for her noble ideas & immense courage. We travelled together almost daily to & from Pretoria during the Treason Trial & we became very close to each other. Together we worked in Pretoria Prison preparing her evidence during the State of Emergency[vii] & I watched her as she was mercilessly being hammered by the prosecution for several days.[viii] She did very well indeed & my confidence

---

i   Initiated by the ANC in December 1951, and launched with the South African Indian Congress on 26 June 1952 against six apartheid laws, the Defiance Campaign Against Unjust Laws (known as the Defiance Campaign for short) involved individuals breaking racist laws such as entering premises reserved for 'whites only', breaking curfews, and courting arrest. Mandela was appointed national volunteer-in-chief and Maulvi Cachalia as his deputy. Over 8,500 volunteers were imprisoned for their participation in the Defiance Campaign.

ii   The Congress of the People, held on 25–26 June 1955 in Kliptown, Johannesburg, was attended by 3,000 delegates and was the culmination of a year-long campaign where members of the Congress Alliance visited homes across the length and breadth of South Africa recording people's demands for a free South Africa. These were included in the Freedom Charter, which was adopted on the second day of the Congress of the People, and which espoused equal rights for all South Africans regardless of race, along with land reform, improved working and living conditions, the fair distribution of wealth, compulsory education, and fairer laws.

iii   On 9 August 1956, 20,000 women marched to the government's Union Buildings in Pretoria to protest against the extension of passes to African women.

iv   The Treason Trial (1956–61) was a result of the apartheid government's attempt to quell the power of the Congress Alliance, a coalition of anti-apartheid organisations. In early-morning raids on 5 December 1956, 156 individuals were arrested and charged with high treason. By the end of the trial in March 1961 all the accused either had the charges withdrawn or, in the case of the last twenty-eight accused (including Mandela), were acquitted.

v   Edith Ngoyi's husband.

vi   Helen Joseph (1905–92), teacher, social worker, and anti-apartheid and women's rights activist – see the glossary.

vii   Declared on 30 March 1960 as a response to the Sharpeville Massacre, the 1960 State of Emergency was characterised by mass arrests and the imprisonment of most African leaders. On 8 April 1960 the ANC and Pan Africanist Congress were banned under the Unlawful Organisations Act.

viii   When the South African government declared a State of Emergency in 1960, the accused in the Treason in her grew deeper. Her training as a social worker, & probably her experience as an army officer, made her very sensitive to the welfare of her needy colleagues & she was always ready to offer some kind of material help. Now & again I get some snatches of information about her & I am happy to know that my confidence in her was not misplaced. My only regret was that I was unable to see her book on the Treason Trial after it was published.[i]

I was privileged to read the manuscript & found it very stimulating. I would have liked to see the finished article. Perhaps now that she is living in semi-retirement she may be devoting her good talents to more writing.

My fondest regards also go to Ntsiki,[ii] Greta,[iii] Doreen, Muriel, Joana, Caroline, Catherine, Mrs Taunyane, Lily Seroke, Virginia,[iv] Onica & Dorcas, my cousin Nobelungu & Hilda.[v] All of them are courageous girls & I regard it as a privilege to have been associated with them in the past.[vi]

I am presently reading on the great African Chiefs, Sekukuni & Mampuru, sons of Sekwati,[vii] & on the struggle between them for the Bapedi Throne. Even by modern standards these were intelligent & capable men who loved their country & people. The role of Sekukuni in the history of the country is known far & wide, but I have often wondered what the course of that history would have been if these & other chiefs in the country had sunk their differences & tried to solve their mutual problems through common efforts. Ngoana waKgosi Godfrey[viii] has every reason to be proud of the achievements of his famous grandfather. I hope he and his family are keeping well. It is

---

Trial who had been on bail were taken into custody. The defence team withdrew in protest and those accused who were lawyers assisted their colleagues in preparing for the trial. Mandela provided legal assistance to his fellow trialist Helen Joseph.

i   Helen Joseph, *If This Be Treason* (Cape Town: Kwagga Publishers, 1963).

ii   Albertina Sisulu (1918–2011), anti-apartheid and women's rights activist, and wife of Mandela's comrade Walter Sisulu – see the glossary. Ntsiki is short for Nontsikelelo, her African name.

iii   Greta Ncapayi, an ANC Women's League activist and friend of Albertina Sisulu.

iv   Virginia Mngoma, political activist.

v   Hilda Bernstein (1915–2006), author, artist, and anti-apartheid and women's rights activist. She was a founding member of the South African Peace Council and of the Federation of South African Women. After her husband, Lionel (Rusty), was acquitted in the Rivonia Trial, they crossed into neighbouring Botswana on foot.

vi   All these women are likely to have been friends and associates of Mandela's who were anti-apartheid activists.

vii Sekukuni or Matsebe Sekhukhune (1814–82) and Mampuru were sons of Bapedi king Sekwati and became rivals for the throne following his death in 1861. Sekhukhune was killed by Mampuru in 1882, and Mampuru was executed the following year. His remains have never been found.

viii Godfrey Mogaramedi Sekhukhune became a freedom fighter with the ANC's military wing Umkhonto weSizwe, and at some point was imprisoned on Robben Island.

quite some time since I last heard of Motsoala John. May he also be in good health & as lively as we knew him to be.

In January 1966 I received a sweet & inspiring letter from Ma Nokukanya,[i] in which she informed us that we were always in her thoughts. Her words of encouragement did us a world of good. When the chief died I was allowed to write a special letter of condolence, but it never reached. I hear that her son-in-law is in hospital & I should be glad to hear about his condition. Once again I should like you to know that I think of you & family with warm & affectionate memories & nothing would please me more than to hear from you.

With love,
Yours very sincerely,
Nel

Mrs Lilian Ngoyi
c/o Miss Nonyaniso Madikizela,[ii]
House No. 8115, Orlando West,
Johannesburg.

29.7.69

This letter had been written & handed in for posting to you on March 3 this year. I now know that you never received it. Here it is again & though much has occurred since I wrote it, I have nevertheless preferred to reproduce it exactly as it was when I first wrote it. I can only hope that this time it will reach you.

Thank you very much for your moving message of condolence which has given me much strength & inspiration. I received the tragic news on July 16 & my reaction was the same as yours. I could hardly believe that Thembi was really gone. My application to attend the funeral was not approved, just as happened on the occasion of my mother's death 10 months ago. In both cases I was denied the opportunity to pay my last respects to those who are dearest to me. But my colleagues did all they could to soften the blow & make me happy. Your message has meant much to me & the sentiments it expresses

---

i   Nokhukhanya Luthuli, widow of Chief Albert Luthuli.
ii   Winnie Mandela's sister.

have given me mighty courage. Once more I feel on top of the world and ready to face whatever the fates may have in store for me. Nel

---

To Gibson Kente,[i] his nephew and a renowned playwright and composer[ii]

For the month of February 1969 B.I.P. V.B[iii]

3.3.69

My dear Nephew,

Zami[iv] has told me of my niece, Evelyn,[v] your wife. Unfortunately, the time allowed for visits is never long enough to enable us to cover fully such family matters as we should like to discuss & she was consequently unable to give me all the information I need know about her. I have not had the privilege of meeting her before but I am sure she must be a talented & charming girl to win your affection & I should be glad to receive her family background. I am looking forward to seeing both of you one day. In the meantime I wish you a fruitful marriage & happy future.

I should like to know whether the Union of S. A. Artists[vi] is still growing strong. Who are the present officials & what is the name of their publication (if any) & subscription fee? I am collecting albums of African songs[vii] – Sotho, Zulu & Xhosa – but I am experiencing difficulties. I am aware of Mohapeloa's[viii] collection but I was unable to

---

i   Gibson Kente (1932–2004) – see the glossary.

ii   Because Gibson Kente came from the Madiba clan, as Mandela did, he called him a nephew.

iii   These initials are in Mandela's handwriting. It is not clear what the initials stand for.

iv   Zami is one of Winnie Mandela's names.

v   Nomathemba Evelyn Kasi, a top model, was married to Gibson Kente, her second husband, from 1969 to 1974. She later moved to the USA and married attorney Alan Jackman, becoming known as Thembi Jackman. She went missing in South Africa in 2008 and was presumed dead by court order in 2012.

vi   The Union of South African Artists was formed in 1952 and by 1958 was one of the most successful entertainment promotional bodies in South Africa.

vii   When asked if the Robben Island prisoners had access to music, fellow Robben Island prisoner and former comrade of Mandela's, Mac Maharaj (see the glossary), recalls that 'There was a brief (very short) period in the late sixties (I think) when the authorities installed a speaker system in our section which they used to play music from the control room in the main office. If I recall correctly we then asked to be allowed to select and buy records that could be played by the officers for us over the broadcast system. The records were kept by the prison authorities, we made requests as to which piece of music and song should be played. The authorities discontinued within a few months. But up to the time of my departure (1976), we were not allowed to buy and keep and music albums in our cells, (Mac Maharaj in an email to Sahm Venter).

viii   Joshua Pulumo Mohapeloa (1908–82), a lyricist and Sesotho composer who worked with Gibson Kente obtain them from the Cape Town firm which specialises in this field. I managed to get a look at choral folk songs for mixed voices by Williams & Maselwa,[i] but I am more interested in albums of modern African music. Perhaps you may advise me how to go about it.

I learn from various sources that you have been doing rather well these days in drama & that *Sikalo*[ii] and *Lifa*[iii] have drawn fairly big audiences. This is quite an achievement for which I give you my warmest congratulations & good luck in future efforts. I should have much liked to see both plays; perhaps one day it may be possible for me to at least read the scripts. It was not clear from the reports whether you wrote both the scripts & produced the plays, & whether the audiences were drawn mainly from Africans or whites. I am interested to know the impact of drama on Africans generally. I believe *Nongqawuse*[iv] was quite a draw; who wrote the script? Are these available as publications?

I believe Miriam[v] continues to do well overseas & that she is either engaged or married to Carmichael.[vi] She has shown great talent & her views on social questions seem to be more advanced than I ever knew. I am told that Dolly[vii] is also in the States. I hope that she will be as lucky & make as great an impact as Miriam has done. In London I met Dambuza, Joe & Rufus.[viii] At the time, they were planning to tour Africa & I hope they succeeded. I was sorry to miss Gwigwi,[ix] who made quite an impression to our fellows abroad & I should like to be

on his musical productions (Sahm Venter, telephonic conversations with Gibson Kente's niece, Vicky Kente, 23 July 2017).

i　　H. C. N. Williams and J. N. Maselwa (New York: G. Schirmer, 1960), *Choral Folksongs of the Bantu, for Mixed Voices*.

ii　　Commercially successful musical *Sikalo* (Lament) was produced by Gibson Kente in 1965. The story centres upon a young man who tries to avoid becoming part of a gang but ends up going to jail.

iii　　*Lifa* was also a successful show produced by Gibson Kente in 1967.

iv　　Legendary figure Nongqawuse has been written about frequently. She was a young Xhosa prophetess who delivered an instruction in 1856 to kill all the cattle and burn all the grain in order for the dead to come back to life so that they could assist the Xhosa in living free of European rule. However, as a result of carrying out her instructions the Xhosa people suffered a severe famine and the British enforced colonial rule. The first play about the Xhosa, *UNongqause*, written by Mary Waters, was produced in 1925. It is likely that Mandela was referring to a contemporary version of the Nongqawuse story here.

v　　Zenzile Miriam Makeba (1932–2008), South African singer, actor, United Nations goodwill ambassador, and activist.

vi　　Stokely Carmichael (1941–98), Trinidadian-American involved in the US Civil Rights and Pan-African movement, who became the 'Honorary Prime Minister' of the Black Panther Party and later of the All-African Peoples Revolutionary Party.

vii　　Dolly Rathebe (1928–2004), South African jazz singer and actress.

viii　　Nathan 'Dambuza' Mdledle (1923–95), Joe (Kolie) Mogotsi (1924–2011), and Rufus Khoza – three of four members of the Manhattan Brothers, a popular South African jazz band of the 1940s and 1950s that incorporated Zulu harmonies and African choral music into its music. They were the first band to have a Billboard Top 100 hit in the United States with their song 'Lovely Lies' in 1956.

ix　　Gwigwi Mrwebi (1936–73), founder of the Union of South African Artists. A saxophonist, he was a member of The Jazz Maniacs, Harlem Swingsters, and Jazz Dazzlers.

remembered to him if he is back. We hardly hear anything about Peggy Phango[i] & Hugh Masekela[ii] & hope they are doing well. All these are talented artists for whom we have the greatest regard, & nothing would please us more than to know that they are making full use of the opportunities now available to them.

Who are the new stars at home & how good are they? Who are the respective secretaries of the B.M.S.C.,[iii] the D.O.C.C.,[iv] & Moroka Centres? I served for several years on the Board of Trustees & Board of Management of the D.O.C.C. & was able to gain some insight into the value of such institutions provided the secretary is a man with a go.

Now & again Zami gives me details of how helpful you are to her & children, & I should like you to know that I deeply appreciate the interest that you continue to show. Nangomso![v] I think of you with warm & pleasant memories. Lots of love to Evelyn, Zami & kids.

Yours very sincerely,
Uncle Nel

29.7.69 P.S. Temba (Union Wide) remembers you.

Mr Gibson Kente
c/o Mrs Nobandla Mandela, House no. 8115, Orlando West,
Johannesburg

---

i   Peggy Phango (1928–98), South African jazz singer and actor who played the female lead in the musical *King Kong* on London's West End in 1961.

ii   Hugh Ramopolo Masekela (1939–2018), South African trumpeter, singer, and composer who has written anti-apartheid songs including 'Bring Him Back Home', recorded in 1986, which demands the release of Nelson Mandela. He went into exile following the Sharpeville Massacre of 1960, in which 69 protesters were shot dead, and studied music in London, then New York.

iii The Bantu Men's Social Centre (BMSC), founded in Johannesburg, in 1924, was an important cultural, social, and political meeting place for black South Africans. Its facilities included a gym and a library, and it hosted boxing matches, political meetings, and dances. Mandela and others founded the ANC Youth League there in 1944.

iv The Donaldson Orlando Community Centre was a community space in Soweto that hosted dances, concerts, and boxing matches. It was built by the Donaldson Trust, established in 1936 by Lieutenant Colonel James Donaldson D.S.O. to 'advance the status, improve the conditions and remove the disabilities suffered by the black African population of South Africa; and generally to seek their benefit and betterment'. Nelson Mandela used to box there in the 1940s and 1950s and spent many of his evenings training at the gym with his eldest son, Thembi.

v   'Nangamso' is an isiXhosa word that expresses deep gratitude to a person who has gone beyond the call of duty. Mandela sometimes spelled it nangomso.

29.7.69 P.S. This letter had been written & handed in for posting to you on March 3 this year. I know that you never received it. Here it is again & though much has occurred since I wrote it, I have, nevertheless, preferred to reproduce it exactly as it was when I first wrote it. I can only hope that this time it will reach you.

Uncle Nel

==========

To Winnie Mandela,[i] his wife

2.4.69

Darling,

I was taken completely by surprise to learn that you had been very unwell as I did not have even the slightest hint that you suffered from blackouts. I have known of your heart condition & pleurisy attacks.

I am however happy to hear that the specialists have diagnosed the particular condition you suffer from & that the blackouts have now disappeared. I should like to be given details of the doctors' diagnosis.

I am pleased to know that our family doctor has been wonderful as usual & I wish you speedy & complete recovery Ngutyana[ii] & all that is best in life.

"The Power of Positive Thinking"[iii] & "The Results of Positive Thinking",[iv] both written by the American psychologist Dr Norman Vincent Peale, may be rewarding to read. The municipal library should stock them. I attach no importance to the metaphysical aspects of his arguments, but I consider his views on physical & psychological issues valuable.

He makes the basic point that it is not so much the disability one suffers from that matters but one's attitude to it. The man who says: I will conquer this illness & live a happy life, is already halfway through to victory.

---

i   Nomzamo Winifred Madikizela-Mandela (1936–2018) – see the glossary.
ii   One of Winnie Mandela's names. She comes from the amaNgutyana clan.
iii   Norman Vincent Peale, *The Power of Positive Thinking* (New York: Prentice-Hall, Inc., 1952).
iv   Norman Vincent Peale, *The Amazing Results of Positive Thinking* (New York: Fawcett Crest, 1959).

2. 4. 69.

Darling,

I was taken completely by surprise to learn that you had been very unwell as I did not have even the slightest hint that you suffered from blackout. I have known of you but somtimes flewissy attacks. I am however happy to hear that the specialists have diagnosed the particular condition you suffer from, that the blackouts have now disappeared. I should like to be given details of the doctors' diagnosis. I am pleased to know that our family doctor has been wonderful as usual. I wish you speedy ~~recovery~~ & complete recovery Ngutyana & all that is best in life. "The power of positive thinking" & "The Results of Positive Thinking" both written by the American psychologist Dr Norman Vincent Peale, may be rewarding to read. The municipal library should stock them. I attach no importance to the metaphysical aspects of his arguments but I consider his ~~theories~~ views on physical & psychological issues valuable. He makes the basic point that it is not so much the disability one suffers from, that matters but one's attitude to it. The man who says: I will conquer this illness, live a happy life, is already half way through to victory. Of the talents you possess, the one that attracts me most is your courage & determination. This makes you stand head & shoulders above the average & will in the end, bring you the triumph of high achievement. Do conscientiously keep this constantly in mind.

Last nov. I wrote to Chief Buteleza, cousin of the late King Cyprian & asked him to convey our sympathies to the Royal family. I received an interesting reply plus a letter of condolence for ma's death. The Dec. letters went to Nali & Kgatho, Jan. to Wonga, & in feb. I wrote to Maki, & zeni & zindzi Lily & Gibson should by now have received the march letters. Advise me whether they were all received. On 17/3 I wrote a special letter to mother & I am glad to note that the family rift has been settled. Sabata has not replied 2 letters I wrote him. The relative to whom funds could be sent, was mentioned in kgatho's letter. On 8/3 I was due for a visit that did not come off. who was it? why did he not come? Funds have run out ~~for me~~. Have received the American journal. Have you had from Marry kind about Swet & Maxwell. I hear that my brother Reqe is experiencing difficulties with the kids & that Malome is ill. Can you elaborate? Fondest regards to our friends & Masesa maud.

Page from a letter to Winnie Mandela, 2 April 1969, see opposite.

Of the talents you possess, the one that attracts me most is your courage & determination. This makes you stand head & shoulders above the average & will in the end bring you the triumph of high achievement. Do consciously keep this constantly in mind.

Last Nov. I wrote to Chief Butelezi [*sic*], cousin of the late King Cyprian, & asked him to convey our sympathies to the Royal Family. I received an interesting reply plus a letter of condolence for ma's death.

The Dec. letters went to Nali & Kgatho; Jan. to Wonga,[i] & in Feb. I wrote to Maki, & Zeni & Zindzi. Lily[ii] & Gibson[iii] should by now have received the March letters. Advise me whether they were all received....

Sabata[iv] has not replied [to] 2 letters I wrote him.

The relative to whom funds could be sent were mentioned in Kgatho's letter.

On 8/3 I was due for a visit that did not come off. Who was it? Why did he not come? My funds have run out. Have received the *American Journal*.

Have you heard from Mary[v] & Paul[vi] about Sweet & Maxwell?[vii] I hear that my brother Regie[viii] [*sic*] is experiencing difficulties with the kids & that Malome[ix] is ill. Can you elaborate?

Fondest regards to our friends Moosa & Maud.[x]...

A family photo at last 'what a masterpiece'. Kgatho & sisters are terrific & it gave me such joy to see ma's photo. Your small picture almost created an upheaval. "Ayingo Nobandla lo!"[xi] "Is this not her younger sister!" "Madiba has been too long in jail, he does not know

---

i   K. D. Matanzima (1915– 2003), Mandela's nephew, a Thembu chief, and chief minister for the Transkei
      – see the glossary. His middle name was Daliwonga, which was abbreviated to Wonga.
ii   Lilian Ngoyi (1911–80), politician, and anti-apartheid and women's rights activist – see the glossary.
iii   Gibson Kente (1932–2004), playwright, composer, and director. Like Mandela, he was from the
      Madiba clan, so Mandela referred to him as a nephew – see the glossary.
iv   King Sabata Jonguhlanga Dalindyebo (1928–86), paramount chief of the Transkei homeland and leader
      of the Democratic Progressive Party, the opposition party in Transkei which opposed apartheid rule –
      see the glossary.
v   Mary Benson (1919–2000), friend, author, journalist, and anti-apartheid activist – see the glossary.
vi   Paul Joseph (1930–) and Adelaide Joseph (1932–) were South African political activists who went into
      exile in London in 1965. When Mandela was arrested in 1962, Adelaide brought him food in prison.
vii   Bookshop in London from which Mandela ordered legal books for his studies.
viii Oliver Reginald Tambo (1917–1993) – Mandela's friend, former law partner, and the president of the
      ANC – see the glossary. His middle name was Reginald and Mandela referred to him as Reggie.
ix   'Uncle' in isiXhosa.
x   Moosa Dinath and his wife Maud Katzenellenbogen. Mandela first met Moosa Dinath when he was
      a member of the Transvaal Indian Congress and businessman in Johannesburg. They renewed their
      acquaintance in prison in 1962 while Mandela was awaiting trial and Dinath was serving a sentence for
      fraud. He and Maud Katzenellenbogen, who befriended Winnie, hatched a plan to free Mandela from
      prison, but it was shelved after Winnie became suspicious of it.
xi   'This is not Nobandla' in isiXhosa.

his sister-in-law," all these & other remarks were flung at me from all directions.

To me the portrait aroused mixed feelings. You look somewhat sad, absent-minded & unwell but lovely all the same. The big one is a magnificent study that depicts all I know in you, the devastating beauty & charm which 10 stormy years of married life have not chilled. I suspect that you intended the picture to convey a special message that no words could ever express. Rest assured I have caught it. All that I wish to say now is that the picture has aroused all the tender feelings in me & softened the grimness that is all around. It has sharpened my longing for you & our sweet & peaceful home.

These days my thoughts have wandered far & wide; to Hans St[i] where a friend would jump into a blue van & unburden herself of all the solemn vows that are due from fiancée to her betrothed & immediately thereafter dash across to an Olds on the opposite end of the block with vows equally sweet & reassuring; the skill with which she manipulated her evening 'studies' in Chancellor House[ii] & made it possible to receive & entertain old friends as soon as new ones proceeded to a boxing gym. All these have come back over & over again as I examine the portrait.[iii]

Finally Mhlope,[iv] I should like you to know that if in the past my letters have not been passionate, it is because I need not seek to improve the debt I owe to a woman who, in spite of formidable difficulties & lack of experience, has nonetheless succeeded in keeping the home fires burning & in attending to the smallest wants & wishes of her incarcerated life companion. These things make me humble to be the object of your love & affection. Remember that hope is a powerful weapon even when all else is lost. You & I, however, have gained much over the years & are making advances in important respects. You are in my thoughts every moment of my life. Nothing will happen to you darling. You will certainly recover and rise.

---

i   Winnie Mandela stayed at the Helping Hand Hostel in Hans Street, Jeppestown, when she moved to Johannesburg. Mandela is reminding her of when he would pick her up from there.

ii   Winnie would do her studies at Mandela's law firm in Chancellor House when he worked after hours.

iii Nelson and Winnie Mandela met in 1957 and went on their first date on 10 March that year. They married on 14 June 1958 in Winnie's home town of Bizana. In a letter to Fatima Meer dated 14 June 1989, he wrote: 'The wedding party left Johannesburg at midnight on 12 June and reached Bizana the next day in the afternoon. As we were expected to reach the bride's place, Mbongweni, at dusk we spent some time at Dr Gordon Mabuya's place where he and his wife, Nontobeko, entertained us.'

iv One of Winnie Mandela's names.

A million kisses & tons & tons of love.
Dalibunga

NKOSIKAZI NOBANDLA MANDELA.
HOUSE NO. 8115, ORLANDO WEST.
JOHANNESBURG.

[PS] Good luck to Kgatho in his exams & tell Mtshana Nomfundo,[i] that I am glad to note that she is not discouraged. Let her remember that perseverance is key to success. I hope you managed to forward the letter to Cecil.[ii]

◇◇◇◇◇◇◇◇◇◇◇

Mandela ran his relationship with the prison authorities on the basis of respect seasoned with the wry observation that an ordinary guard made the difference between an extra blanket in winter or not. The basis of all these interactions, however, was the recognition of the humanity of the other, all the while being sure to maintain his own dignity and to protect his rights.

His many letters to the prison authorities for requests to see an eye specialist or a dentist, or pushing for more study rights, were not obligatory. Prisoners were presented every week with the opportunity of making complaints or requests to an officer. But, according to his comrade and fellow prisoner Mac Maharaj, while prisoners had an opportunity to make verbal requests, they were not given the opportunity to elaborate on them or provide any background information. Mandela probably wanted to keep a written record and at the same time was shrewdly managing each request for possible improvements from which the other prisoners may benefit.[49]

He also boldly wrote to senior officials and, in some cases, the minister of justice himself. Just less than five years into his prison sentence he wrote to the minister of justice demanding that he and his colleagues be released or treated as political prisoners according to rules of the Geneva Convention. His knowledge of the battles between the Afrikaners and the British colonial powers was brought to bear to support his arguments.

---

i   *Mtshana* means 'niece' or 'nephew' in isiXhosa. He is referring to Olive Nomfundo Mandela, his niece.
ii   Cecil Eprile (1914–93), friend, journalist, and newspaper editor. Wrote and edited for *Arthur Barlow's Weekly*, the *Sunday Times*, and *Sunday Express*. Editor-in-chief of *Golden City Post* (*Drum* magazine's sister paper), 1955–67, where he trained many prominent black South African journalists.

Comparing his plight and that of his fellow prisoners with the way in which the Afrikaner freedom fighters had been treated in jail, Mandela made a solid case for their freedom. But his captors were not the British; and the apartheid regime, which ran the country on force and oppression, was fearful that letting Mandela go would weaken it in the eyes of its supporters.

To the minister of justice, c/o the commissioner of prisons

[Typed]

<u>The Commissioner of Prisons,</u>
PRETORIA.

I should be pleased if you would kindly approve of the following letter to the Minister of Justice.

                                                                22.4.69

The Minister of Justice,
Parliament Buildings,
CAPE TOWN.

Dear Sir,

My colleagues have requested me to write and ask you to release us from prison and, pending your decision on the matter, to accord us the treatment due to political prisoners. At the outset we wish to point out that in making this application we are not pleading for mercy but are exercising the inherent right of all people incarcerated for their political beliefs.

The persons whose names appear in schedule A attached to this letter live in the Single Cell Section of Robben Island Prison and are completely isolated from the rest of the prisoners on the Island. For this reason we are unable to furnish you with a full list of all the persons on this Island and in other prisons on behalf of whom this application is made.

Prior to our conviction and imprisonment we are[i] members of well-known political organisations which fought against political and racial persecution, and which demanded full political rights for the African, Coloured and Indian people of this Country. We completely rejected as we still do, all forms of white domination, and more particularly the policy of separate development, and demanded a democratic South Africa free from the evils of Colour oppression, and where all South Africans, regardless of race or belief, would live together in peace and harmony on a basis of equality.

All of us, without exception, were convicted and sentenced for political activities which we embarked upon as part and parcel of our struggle to win for our people the right of self-determination, acknowledged throughout the civilized world as the inalienable birthright of all human beings. These activities were inspired by the desire to resist racial policies and unjust laws which violate the principle of human rights and fundamental freedoms that form the foundation of democratic government.

In the past the governments of South Africa have treated persons found guilty of offences of this nature as political offenders who were released from prison, in some cases, long before their sentences expired. In this connection we refer you to the cases of Generals Christiaan De Wet, JCG Kemp and others who were charged with high treason arising out of the 1914 Rebellion.[ii] Their case was in every respect more serious than ours. 12,000 rebels took to arms and there were no less than 322 casualties. Towns were occupied and considerable damage caused to government installations, while claims for damage to private property amounted to R500,000. These acts of violence were committed by white men who enjoyed full political rights, who belonged to political parties that were legal, who had newspapers that could publicise their views. They were free to move up and down the country espousing their cause and rallying support for their ideas. They had no justification whatsoever for resorting to violence. The

---

i   The letter was typed by a prison official and the word 'are' rather than 'were' must have been typed by
        mistake.
ii   During World War I the British government called on its dominions to assist it. South Africa was
        specifically asked to fight against Germany in the neighbouring South West Africa. While Prime Minister
        Louis Botha supported Britain, a number of his generals did not and rebelled against the South African
        government.

leader of the Orange Free State rebels, De Wet, was sentenced to 6 years' imprisonment plus a fine of R4,000. Kemp received a sentence of 7 years and a fine of R2,000. The rest were given comparatively lighter sentences.

In spite of the gravity of their offences, De Wet was released within 6 months of his conviction and sentence, and the rest within a year. This event occurred a little more than half a century ago, yet the Government of the day showed much less intransigence in its treatment of this category of prisoner than the present Government seems prepared to do 54 years later with black politicians who have even more justification to resort to violence than the 1914 rebels. This Government has persistently spurned our aspirations, suppressed our political organisations and imposed severe restrictions on known activists and field workers.

It has caused hardship and disruption of family life by throwing into prison hundreds of otherwise innocent people. Finally it has instituted a reign of terror unprecedented in the history of the Country and closed all channels of constitutional struggle. In such a situation, resort to violence was the inevitable alternative of freedom fighters who had the courage of their convictions. No men of principle and integrity could have done otherwise.[i] To have folded arms would have been an act of surrender to a Government of minority rule and a betrayal of our cause. World history in general, and that of South Africa in particular, teaches that resort to violence may in certain cases be perfectly legitimate.

In releasing the rebels soon after their convictions the Botha Smuts Government acknowledged this vital fact. We firmly believe that our case is no less different, and we accordingly ask you to make this privilege available to us. As indicated above, there were 322 casualties in the Rebellion.

By way of contrast, we draw attention to the fact that in committing

---

i   At the time of Mandela's arrest, Umhkonto weSizwe (MK), which was launched on 16 December 1961, had set off explosive devices after hours, to avoid loss of life, at locations including municipal and post offices, pass offices, a resettlement office, and an electricity substation. At that stage there was no loss of life.

acts of sabotage we took special precautions to avoid loss of life, a fact which was expressly acknowledged by both the trial Judge[i] [and] the prosecution in the Rivonia case.[ii]

An examination of the attached schedule shows that if we use De Wet's case as the standard, then every one of us ought to have been released by now. Of the 23 persons whose names are listed therein, 8 are doing life imprisonment, 10 are serving sentences ranging from 10 to 20 years, and 5 between 2 and 10 years.

Of those doing imprisonment for life, 7 have completed 4 years 10 months and 1 has done 4 years and 4 months. The man with the longest sentence amongst those serving terms between 10 and 20 years is Billy Nair[iii] who has already completed ¼ of his sentence. Joe Gqabi,[iv] Samson Fadana and Andrew Masondo,[v] the first to be convicted in this group have each completed 6 years of their respective sentences of 12, 8 and 13 years. The last men to be sentenced in the same group were Jackson Fuzile[vi] and Johannes Dangala who received 12 and 7 years respectively. Fuzile has completed a ¼ of the sentence whereas Dangala will have done exactly half of his on 19th May 1969. Every one of those serving terms between 2 and 10 years has at least completed ¼ of his sentence.

Our claim for release becomes even stronger when examined in

---

i   'Counsel for the defence successfully convinced the judge that MK – and therefore the defendants – was not responsible for all the acts of sabotage', wrote Kenneth S. Braun in *Saving Nelson Mandela: The Rivonia Trial and the Fate of South Africa* (Oxford University Press: Oxford, 2012), p. 147. 'This fact was also acknowledged by the court during closing argument and lent support to another – perhaps even more important – point in the judge's failure to sentence them to death. No act of sabotage actually attributed to them or their organizations had resulted in death or injury to any person.' (Ibid.)

ii   Attorney Joel Joffe wrote that his colleague Arthur Chaskalson showed that 'of the 193 acts of sabotage which the State had proved to have happened, only about a dozen had been proved legally' and 'not one involved any danger whatsoever to human life'. Joel Joffe, *The State vs. Nelson Mandela: The Trial that Changed South Africa* (London: One World Publications, 2007), pp. 238 and 239.

iii Billy Nair (1929–2008), comrade and MK member who was charged with sabotage in 1963. He was held in B Section with Mandela on Robben Island and was released in 1984 – see the glossary.

iv   Joe Gqabi (1929–81) was convicted of sabotage for MK activities and was imprisoned on Robben Island for ten years. He was assassinated in 1981 whilst living in exile in Zimbabwe.

v   Andrew Masondo (1936–2008) was convicted of sabotage for MK activities and was imprisoned on Robben Island for thirteen years.

vi   Mxolisi Jackson Fuzile (1940–2011) was convicted of sabotage for his activities on behalf of the ANC and sentenced to imprisonment for twelve years.

relations to the cases of Robey Leibrandt,[i] Holm,[ii] Pienaar, Strauss[iii] and others. Leibrandt, a national of the Union of South Africa,[iv] arrived in the Union from Germany at a time when that country was at war with the Union. He then proceeded to set up a para-military underground organisation with the purpose of overthrowing the Government and establishing in its place one modelled on that of Nazi Germany. He was found guilty of high treason and sentenced to death, later commuted to imprisonment for life. Holm, Pienaar and Strauss were also imprisoned for high treason, it being alleged that they collaborated with the enemy in prosecuting the war against the Union and its allies. On coming to power, however, the present Government released these and other prisoners sentenced for treason and sabotage, notwithstanding the fact that they had been arrested in circumstances which made them appear to many South Africans as traitors to their own country. Again, by way of contrast, we draw attention to the fact that our activities were at all times actuated by the noblest ideals that men can cherish, namely, the desire to serve our people in their just struggle to free themselves from a Government founded on injustice and inequality.

We further wish to remind you that in 1966 your predecessor released Spike de Keller,[v] Stephanie Kemp,[vi] Allan Brooks[vii] and Tony Trew,[viii] all of whom originally appeared jointly with Edward Joseph Daniels[ix] (whose names appear in the schedule) on a charge of Sab-

---

i   Sidney Robey Leibbrandt (1913–66), a South African Olympic boxer of German and Irish descent, was a Nazi supporter who, after training with the Germany army, became a central part of Operation Weissdorn, a plan approved by Hitler, to assassinate General Jan Smuts, the head of South Africa's government, and bring about a coup d'etat in South Africa. He was initially sentenced to death for treason, but Smuts later commuted this to life imprisonment. When the National Party came to power in 1948, he was pardoned and released.

ii   Eric Holm was engaged by Zeesen Radio which broadcast Nazi propaganda to South Africa.

iii   Possibly Mandela is referring to Strauss von Moltke, a former leader of the Greyshirts, a South African fascist organisation which sympathised with German Nazis, who handed over documents stolen from the Jewish Board of Deputies to anti-Semitic elements in South Africa's National Party.

iv   The Union of South Africa was formed in 1910 from the four self-governing British colonies of the Cape, Natal, the Transvaal, and the Orange River Colony.

v   David 'Spike' de Keller, member of the African Resistance Movement and the Liberal Party, who spent a year in prison.

vi   Stephanie Kemp (1941–), member of the African Resistance Movement and the Communist Party, who spent a year in prison.

vii   Allan Brooks (1940–2008), member of the African Resistance Movement and the Communist Party, who spent a year in prison.

viii   Tony Trew (1941–), member of the African Resistance Movement who spent a year in prison.

ix   Eddie Daniels (1928–2017), member of the African Resistance Movement who spent fifteen years on Robben Island – see the glossary.

otage. Kemp, Brooks and Trew pleaded guilty to an alternative charge and a separation of trial was ordered. The case against Daniels and De Keller proceeded on the main charge and on 17th November 1964 they were found guilty and sentenced to 15 and 10 years respectively. Kemp, Brooks and Trew were found guilty on the alternative and sentenced to 5, 4 and 4 years respectively, each of which was partly suspended. We are informed that De Keller was released after he had served approximately 2 years, or less, of his sentence of 10 years, whilst Kemp, Brooks and Trew were also released before they had completed their sentences.

We do not in any way begrudge those who were fortunate enough to be released and who escaped the hardship of prison life and are happy to know that they now lead a normal life. But we refer to their case for the limited purpose of showing that our request is reasonable, and also to stress that a Government is expected to be consistent in its policy and to accord the same treatment to its citizens.

There is one important difference between our case and that of De Wet and Leibrandt. They were released only after the rebellion had been crushed and after Germany had been conquered and they were thus no threat to the safety of the State when they were freed. In our case, however, it may be argued that our revolution is planned for the future and that security considerations require that we be treated differently. Add to this fact that our convictions have not changed and our dreams are still the same as they were before we were jailed. All of which would seem to confirm the opinion that our case is distinguishable from all previous ones. We feel sure, however, that you will not be tempted to think along these lines, as such an argument would carry sinister implications. It would mean that if security considerations today require that we should be kept in prison, we would not be released when we complete our respective sentences, if the present situation remains unaltered, or if the position worsens. The plain truth is that the racial strife and conflict that seriously threatens the country today is due solely to the short-sighted policies and crimes committed by this Government.

The only way to avert disaster is not to keep innocent men in jail but to abandon your provocative actions and to pursue sane and enlightened policies. Whether or not evil, strife and bloodshed are to occur in this country rests entirely on the Government. The continued suppression of our aspirations and reliance on rule through coercion drives our people more and more to violence. Neither you nor I can predict [what] the country will have to pay at the end of that strife. The obvious solution is to release us and to hold a round table conference to consider an amicable solution.

Our main request is that you release us and, pending your decision, to treat us as political prisoners. This means that we should be provided with good diet, proper clothing outfits, bed and mattresses, newspapers, radios, bioscope,[i] [and] better and closer contact with our families and friends here and abroad. Treatment as political prisoners implies the freedom to obtain all reading material that is not banned and to write books for publication, we would expect to be given the option to work as one desires and to decide the trades one would like to learn. In this connection we wish to point out that some of these privileges were enjoyed both by the 1914 rebels as well as by Leibrandt and colleagues, all of whom were treated as political prisoners.

The prison authorities attempt to answer our demand for treatment as political prisoners by pointing out that we were convicted by the courts for contravening the laws of the county, that we are like any other criminals and, therefore, cannot be treated as political offenders.

This is a spurious argument which flies in the face of the facts. On this view De Wet, Kemp, Maritz, Leibrandt and others were ordinary criminals. Treason, sabotage, membership of an illegal organisation were criminal offences then as now. Why then were they treated differently? It seems to us that the only difference between the two cases is one of colour.

Serious differences of opinion on a specific issue had emerged amongst the whites, and those who lost in the contest that flowed from those differences eventually found themselves behind bars. On all other issues, especially on the major question of colour, both victor and vanquished were in agreement. The conflict having been solved it was possible for the Government to adopt a conciliatory attitude and to extend to the prisoners all sorts of indulgences. But today the position is altogether different. This time the challenge comes, not from white men, but mainly from black politicians who disagree with the

---

i   A cinema or film.

Government on almost everything under the sun. The victory of our cause means the end of white rule.

In this situation the Government regards the prison not as an institution of rehabilitation but as an instrument of retribution, not to prepare us to lead a respectable and industrious life when released, and to play our role as worthy members of society, but to punish and cripple us, so that we should never again have the strength and courage to pursue our ideals. This [is] our punishment for raising our voices against the tyranny of colour. This is the true explanation for the bad treatment we receive in prison – pick and shovel work continuously for the last 5 years, a wretched diet, denial of essential cultural material and isolation from the world outside jail. This is the reason why privileges normally available to other prisoners, including those convicted of murder, rape and crimes involving dishonesty are withheld from political offenders.

We get no remission of sentence. Whilst the ordinary prisoner is classified in C group on admission, political offenders are put in D which carries the least privileges. Those of us who managed to reach A group are denied privileges normally enjoyed by criminals in the same group. They are compelled to do pick and shovel work, are not allowed newspapers, radios, bioscope, contact visits and even groceries are given grudgingly.

As already indicated in the second paragraph above, I make this application on behalf of all my colleagues on the Island and in other jails and I trust that any concessions that may be granted will be made available to all without exception.

The Prisons Act 1959 gives to you the necessary powers to grant the relief we seek. Under its provisions you are entitled to release us on parole or probation. De Wet and others were released under the former method.

In conclusion we place on record that the years we have spent on this Island have been difficult years.[i] Almost every one of us has had [our] full share in one way or another of the hardships that face non-white prisoners. These hardships have at times been the result of official indifference to our problems, other times they were due to plain

---

i   By 1969, Mandela and the other accused Rivonia trialists incarcerated on Robben Island had been there for almost five years.

persecution. But things have somewhat eased and we hope even better days will come. All that we wish to add is that we trust that when you consider this application you will bear in mind that the ideas that inspire us, and the convictions that give form and direction to our activities constitute the only solution to the problems of our country and are in accordance with the enlightened conceptions of the human family.

Yours faithfully,
[Signed N. Mandela]

◇◇◇◇◇◇◇◇◇◇◇◇

In May 1969, Mandela's wife Winnie was hauled from her Soweto home in darkness in front of their two terrified small daughters and spent the following fourteen months in solitary detention which she called 'tortuous mental agony'.[50] In prison she suffered anaemia, bronchitis, and heart problems.

During this time the couple did not know who was taking care of the children and in what condition they were forced to live. Mandela could not be sure that his letters ever reached her. And we can only be sure that any letters were received once there was a reply referring to previous correspondence. While his wife was no stranger to police harassment, one can only imagine the anxiety of two imprisoned parents trying to take care of their children.

He wrote to his wife, their children and various family members in desperate attempts to find out what was happening in their parentless lives outside prison.

———————

To Frank, Bernadt & Joffe, his attorneys

[In another hand] N. Mandela   S.B[i]

[Stamped] Reception Office Robben Island, 20 May 1969

Messrs Frank, Bernadt & Joffe
PO Box 252.
Cape Town.

---

i   S.B. indicates that this is a special letter. B stands for 'Brief' in Afrikaans. Special letters were not taken off a prisoner's quota.

Dear Sirs,

Attention: Mr Brown[i]

I understand that my wife has been arrested with several other persons in Johannesburg and that she is presently under detention.

In this connection, I should be pleased if you would kindly instruct your Johannesburg correspondent to furnish me with the following information:

1. The date of the arrest and the nature of the charge.
2. Whether or not she has been released on bail and the amount thereof?
3. The full names and addresses of her co-detainees.
4. Whether she received my letter of 4th April?
5. The name of the person, if any, who is now in charge of our Johannesburg home.

Your prompt attention will be highly appreciated.

   Yours faithfully,
[Signed NRMandela]
NELSON MANDELA

◇◇◇◇◇◇◇◇◇◇◇

Mandela called his Soweto home at 8115, on the corner of Vilakazi and Ngakane streets, Orlando West, Johannesburg, 'the centrepoint' of his world.[1a] *He and his first wife, Evelyn, and their baby, Thembekile, moved there in 1946. They raised their children there and Mandela's mother stayed there from time to time. The three-room house cost 17s. 6d. per month in rent (black people weren't allowed to own property). It was at 8115 that Mandela and his second wife, Winnie, were welcomed back after their wedding in June 1958 and where their children were also raised. It was to 8115 that he returned when he was released from prison, and from which Winnie Mandela was arrested on several occasions while her husband was in prison.*

---

i   Henry Brown worked at Frank, Bernadt & Joffe in Cape Town as an articled clerk from 1957 to 1962, and then as a partner from 1962 to 1971. Brown represented Mandela during his imprisonment on Robben Island from 1966 until 1971, when he emigrated to the UK.

Messrs Frank, Bernadt & Joffe,
P. O. Box 252.
Cape Town.
Dear Sirs,   <u>Attention: Mr Brown</u>

I understand that my wife has been arrested with several other persons in Johannesburg and that she is presently under detention.
In this connection, I should be pleased if you would kindly instruct your Johannesburg Correspondent to furnish me with the following information:

1. The date of the arrest and the nature of the charge.
2. Whether or not she has been released on bail and the amount thereof?
3. The full names and addresses of her Co detainees.
4. Whether she received my letter of 4th April?
5. The name of the person, if any, who is now in charge of our Johannesburg home.

Your prompt attention will be highly appreciated.

Yours faithfully,
NRMandela.
NELSON MANDELA.

Letter to attorneys Messrs Frank, Bernadt & Joffe, 20 May 1969, see pages 61–2.

Zenani and Zindzi Mandela,[i] his middle and youngest daughters

23.6.69

My darlings,

Once again our beloved Mummy has been arrested and now she and Daddy are away in jail. My heart bleeds as I think of her sitting in some police cell far away from home, perhaps alone and without anybody to talk to, and with nothing to read. Twenty-four hours of the day longing for her little ones. It may be many months or even years before you see her again. For long you may live like orphans without your own home and parents, without the natural love, affection and protection Mummy used to give you. Now you will get no birthday or Christmas parties, no presents or new dresses, no shoes or toys. Gone are the days when, after having a warm bath in the evening, you would sit at table with Mummy and enjoy her good and simple food. Gone are the comfortable beds, the warm blankets and clean linen she used to provide. She will not be there to arrange for friends to take you to bioscopes,[ii] concerts and plays, or to tell you nice stories in the evening, help you read difficult books and to answer the many questions you would like to ask. She will be unable to give you the help and guidance you need as you grow older and as new problems arise. Perhaps never again will Mummy and Daddy join you in House no. 8115 Orlando West,[iii] the one place in the whole world that is so dear to our hearts.

This is not the first time Mummy goes to jail. In October 1958, only four months after our wedding, she was arrested with 2000 other women when they protested against passes in Johannesburg[iv] and spent two weeks in jail. Last year she served four days, but now she has gone back again and I cannot tell you how long she will be away this time. All that I wish you always to bear in mind is that we have a brave and determined Mummy who loves her people with all

---

i   Zenani Mandela (1959–) and Zindziswa Mandela (1960–) – see the glossary.
ii A cinema or film.
iii The family home in Soweto.
iv In the mid-1950s the National Party government began issuing black women with pass books which they were required to carry at all times. This led to a series of organised protests and campaigns which led to thousands of arrests. In a speech given in 1976 after the Soweto Uprising, Winnie Mandela was reported as saying: 'We have to carry passes which we abhor because we cannot have houses without them, we cannot work without them, we are endorsed out of towns without them, we cannot register births without them, we are not even expected to die without them.'

23. 6. 69

My darlings,

Once again our beloved Mummy has been arrested and now she and Daddy are away in jail. My heart bleeds as I think of her sitting in some cell far away from home, perhaps alone and without anybody to talk to, and with nothing to read. Twenty-four hours of the day longing for her little ones. It may be many months or even years before you see her again. For long you may live like orphans, without your own home and parents, without the natural love, affection and protection Mummy used to give you. Now you will get no birthday or Christmas parties, no presents or new dresses, no shoes or toys. Gone are the days when, after having a warm bath in the evening, you would sit at table with Mummy and enjoy her good and simple food. Gone are the comfortable beds, the warm blankets and clean linen she used to provide. She will not be there to arrange for friends to take you to bioscopes, concerts and plays, or to tell you nice stories in the evening, help you read difficult books and to answer the many questions you would like to ask. She will be unable to give you the help and guidance you need as you grow older and as new problems arise. Perhaps never again will Mummy and Daddy join you in House no. 8115 Orlando West, the one place in the whole world that is so dear to our hearts.

This is not the first time Mummy goes to jail. In October 1958 only four months after our wedding she was arrested with 2000 other women when they protested against passes in Johannesburg and spent two weeks in jail. Last year she served few days, but now she has gone back again and I cannot tell you how long she will be away this time. All that I with you to always bear in mind is that we have a brave and determined Mummy who loves her people with all her heart. She gave up pleasure and comfort in return for a life, full of hardship and misery, because of the deep love she has for her people and country. When you become adults and think carefully of the unpleasant experiences Mummy has gone through, and the stubbornness with which she has held to her beliefs, you will begin to realise the importance of her contribution in the battle for truth and justice and the extent to which she has sacrificed her own personal interests and happiness.

Mummy comes from a rich and respected family. She is a qualified Social

Page from a letter from Mandela to daughters Zindzi and Zenani dated 23 June 1969, after learning that Winnie had been arrested (see pages 64–7).

her heart. She gave up pleasure and comfort for a life full of hardship and misery because of the deep love she has for her people and country. When you become adults and think carefully of the unpleasant experiences Mummy has gone through, and the stubbornness with which she has held to her beliefs, you will begin to realise the importance of her contribution in the battle for truth and justice and to the extent to which she has sacrificed her own personal interests and happiness.

Mummy comes from a rich and respected family. She is a qualified Social Worker and at the time of our marriage in June 1958[i] she had a good and comfortable job at the Baragwanath Hospital. She was working there when she was arrested for the first time and at the end of 1958 she lost that job. Later she worked for the Child Welfare Society in town, a post she liked very much. It was whilst working there that the Government ordered her not to leave Johannesburg, to remain at home from 6pm to 6am, and not to attend meetings, nor enter any hospital, school, university, courtroom, compound or hostel, or any African township save Orlando where she lived. This order made it difficult for her to continue with her work at the Child Welfare Society and she lost this particular job as well.

Since then Mummy has lived a painful life and had to try to run a home without a fixed income. Yet she somehow managed to buy you food and clothing, pay your school fees, rent for the house and to send me money regularly.

I left home in April 1961 when Zeni was two years and Zindzi three months. Early in January 1962 I toured Africa and visited London for ten days, and returned to South Africa towards the end of July the same year. I was terribly shaken when I met Mummy. I had left her in good health with a lot of flesh and colour. But she had suddenly lost weight and was now a shadow of her former self. I realised at once the strain my absence had caused her. I looked forward to some time when I would be able to tell her about my journey, the countries I visited and the people I met. But my arrest on August 5 put an end to that dream.

When Mummy was arrested in 1958 I visited her daily and brought her food and fruits. I felt proud of her, especially because the decision to join the other women in demonstrating against the passes was taken by her freely without any suggestion from me. But her attitude to my own arrest made me know Mummy better and more fully. Immediately

---

i   They married on 14 June 1958 in Winnie Mandela's home village of Bizana in the Transkei.

I was arrested our friends here and abroad offered her scholarships and suggested that she leave the country to study overseas. I welcomed these suggestions as I felt that studies would keep her mind away from her troubles. I discussed the matter with her when she visited me in Pretoria Jail in October 1962. She told me that although she would most probably be arrested and sent to jail, as every politician fighting for freedom must expect, she would nevertheless remain in the country and suffer with her people. Do you see now what a brave Mummy we have?

Do not worry, my darlings, we have a lot of friends; they will look after you, and one day Mummy and Daddy will return and you will no longer be orphans without a home. Then we will also live peacefully and happily as all normal families do. In the meantime you must study hard and pass your examinations, and behave like good girls. Mummy and I will write to you many letters. I hope you got the Christmas card I sent you in December and the letter I wrote both of you on February 4 this year.

With lots & lots of love and a million kisses.

Yours affectionately,
Daddy

MISSES ZENI & ZINDZI MANDELA
C/O MRS IRIS NIKI XABA.[i]
P.O. BOX 23,
DUBE VILLAGE
SOWETO, JOHANNESBURG.

To Niki Xaba,[ii] his wife's sister

15.7.69

My dear Niki,

I had originally planned to write this letter to Uncle Marsh.[iii] But I consider you mother to Zami[iv] & not just her eldest sister, & when I

---

i   Winnie Mandela's eldest sister – see the glossary.
ii   Niki Xaba (1932–1985), Winnie Mandela's eldest sister – see the glossary.
iii   Niki Xaba's husband, Marshall Xaba.
iv   Zami is one of Winnie Mandela's names.

received the news of the detention of Nyanya,[i] in addition to that of Zami, I realised just how much the whole affair must have disturbed you. In the circumstances I decided to send the letter to you instead.

In the letter I wrote to Ma[ii] at Bizana on May 4, I told her I spent a lot of time thinking of Zami, the painful experiences she was having & the numerous problems that face her as a result of my absence. I pointed out that my confidence & regard for her had risen considerably, & that my only hope was that one day I might be able to give her the peace, comfort & happiness that would compensate for her dreadful hardships. Little did I know at the time that only 8 days thereafter Zami would be back in jail. Her arrest is a real disaster to the family & I must confess that I am very concerned. She is unwell[iii] & prison might worsen her condition. When I was arrested I had the fortune that she was outside & free. Before I was convicted she saw me on every visiting day without exception, brought me delicious provisions & clean clothes, & wrote me sweet & charming letters, & never missed a single day of my 2 trials to which she brought many friends & relatives, including my mother. I will never forget the day of sentence in the Rivonia Case for, besides the immense crowds of supporters & well-wishers that turned up, there sat behind us Zami, Ma, Nali[iv] & Nyanya. It was a rare moment which comes seldom in a man's career & it deepened my love & respect for Zami & drew me closer to my relatives – to Ma, Nali, Nyanya & to all of you. During my 5 years on this island Zami has visited me no less than 9 times & organised 10 other visits which brought me into contact with relations & friends I much value & respect. Even when difficulties on her side were growing, when she was without a job and her health was giving trouble, she thought first & foremost of me & my happiness & never failed to send me funds, wonderful letters, birthday & wedding anniversary cards. All these things have meant much to me. One has to be a prisoner to appreciate fully the true value of many things we take much for granted in life outside prison. During the nearly 7 years of my imprisonment Zami has been truly at my side. Now it is her turn & she needs all my love & affection, all my sympathy & help, & yet I can do absolutely nothing for her. She can look forward to no visit from me that would bring some welcome change from the depressing

---

i   Winnie Mandela's youngest sister, Nonyaniso Madikizela, who was also known as Nyanya.
ii   Nophikela Hilda Madikizela, Winnie Mandela and Niki Xaba's stepmother – see the glossary.
iii   Winnie Mandela had a heart condition.
iv   Nali Nancy Vutela, Winnie Mandela's sister.

routine to which she is now subjected, no tasty provisions that would suit her indifferent health, no warm & affectionate letters that would bring back happy memories. If she should ultimately be charged, it will not be possible for me to show solidarity through physical presence, & none of the countless things she did for me as prisoner shall I be able to do for her.

The tender faces of small children, distorted by fear & drowsiness, seeing their dear mother escorted away in the dead of night, & unable to understand the issues involved is a memory that could haunt the most fearless mother. Add to this picture the fact that for years her children may live like orphans & that she may be completely deprived of the opportunity of giving her children the help & guidance which they would need in the most critical years of their lives. I know how Zami is devoted to the children & if there is one thing that would do further harm to her health it is the uncertainty & insecurity that now threatens them. These are the reasons why I regard her arrest as a family disaster, Niki. I am not in a position to make any predictions as to how she will face up to the situation & I shall certainly not risk any prophecy. But her record up to now has shown her as a woman of great courage who has stuck to her principles in spite of severe trials. My only hope is that she will find it possible to survive even this one in spite of her indifferent health. I am equally proud of Nyanya & have grown to love her much more than I ever did in the past. I sometimes think that if I were at home these last 8 years she would have made good progress both in her studies & ideas in life. In my last letter to Bawo I expressed my concern over the fact that she was idling at home & suggested that she should at least be given some vocational training. I hope she will also benefit from this experience.

At the time of writing to Ma I was actually expecting a visit from Zami as I had last seen her in December & I had had no visit since then. Our friend Radebe (Mgulwa)[i] was due to visit me in February but for reasons unknown to me he did not come. I had looked forward to that visit because it offered me the only opportunity of hearing something about Zami & the kids as apparently none of the letters I have written monthly since December last has reached its destination. On June 28

---

i   Alfred Mgulwa (Radebe is his clan name), Winnie Mandela's uncle.

another good friend, Moosa Dinath,[i] who was coming down from Johannesburg for the express purpose of discussing family problems caused by Zami's detention, also failed to turn up & again the prison authorities were unable to give me an explanation for this mysterious behaviour on the part of my visitors. I now know that before May 12 Zami had applied for a visiting permit for Kgatho for May 24. The authorities never even told me of this particular visit. The result is that I have been completely cut off from my family & friends at a time when such contact has been absolutely essential. On June 23 I wrote Zeni & Zindzi a long letter which I sent to Brig. Aucamp[ii] of the Headquarters, Pretoria, & asked him to forward it to you. I hope at least this one has reached you. In December I wrote to Nali, February to Zeni & Zindzi, March, to my nephew Gibson Kente[iii] and to Lilian.[iv] All these letters were addressed to 8115, Orlando West. The fact that I received no acknowledgement compels me to infer that the letters were not received & perhaps Uncle Marsh[v] will make the investigations & let you know. I have also written to Tellie[vi] requesting her to find out about the letters to Kgatho[vii] & Maki[viii] in January & February. I was sorry to hear that you were involved in a car accident in which you fractured a leg. I hope you are recovering & am anxious to get some details in your next letter. How are the children getting on & what are their names? How old are they? How many children has Bantu?[ix] Love and fondest regards to Marsh, Bantu & hubby, Tellie, Mfundo, etc.

Sincerely,
Nel

MRS NIKI IRIS XABA, 8115, ORLANDO WEST, JOHANNES-
BURG

---

i   Mandela first met Moosa Dinath when he was a member of the Transvaal Indian Congress and businessman in Johannesburg. They renewed their acquaintance in prison in 1962 while Mandela was awaiting trial and Dinath was serving a sentence for fraud.
ii   Brigadier Aucamp, commanding officer of Robben Island – see the glossary.
iii Gibson Kente (1932–2004), playwright, composer, and director. Like Mandela, he was from the Madiba clan, so Mandela referred to him as a nephew – see the glossary.
iv   Lilian Ngoyi (1911–80), politician, and anti-apartheid and women's rights activist – see the glossary.
v   Marshall Xaba, husband of Niki Xaba, Winnie Mandela's eldest sister (for Niki Xaba, see the glossary).
vi   Telia (Telli or Tellie) Mtirara, a relative of Mandela's.
vii Makgatho (Kgatho) Mandela (1950–2005), Mandela's second-born son – see the glossary.
viii Makaziwe (Maki) Mandela (1954–), Mandela's eldest daughter – see the glossary.
ix   Nobantu Mniki, one of Winnie Mandela's sisters.

◇◇◇◇◇◇◇◇◇◇◇◇◇

As if 1969 could not have got any worse, a telegram came, carrying devastating news. Mandela's firstborn child, Madiba Thembekile 'Thembi', had been killed in a car accident outside Cape Town. His wife, Thoko, had survived the collision but his passing left his two little daughters fatherless. Mandela had not yet met his daughter-in-law or his two granddaughters, Nandi and Ndileka. He would have to wait until they had reached sixteen, the required visiting age, for that privilege.

Winnie Mandela was still in prison, and he poured out his sorrow to her and Thembi's mother – his first wife, Evelyn – and many other members of the family. Letters remained the only tool for his remote control parenting and they were not enough, notwithstanding their unpredicatable journey into the outside world. Unable to physically console anyone or to stand at the grave as his son was buried, Mandela had to rely on his comrades for comfort and his own inner strength.

Once they were free, Mandela's colleagues were able to relate their own anguish at seeing him wrapped tightly in a brown prison-issue blanket, sitting in his cell alongside his friend Walter Sisulu.[i]

To Winnie Mandela,[ii] **his wife**

Special letter to Zami[iii]

16.7.69

My Darling,

This afternoon the Commanding Officer received the following telegram from attorney Mendel Levin:[iv]

---

i   Walter Sisulu (1912– 2003), ANC and MK activist and fellow Rivonia trialist who was imprisoned with Mandela – see the glossary.
ii   Nomzamo Winifred Madikizela-Mandela (1936–2018) – see the glossary.
iii Special letters were not taken off a prisoner's quota. Zami is one of Winnie Mandela's names.
iv   Mendel Levin was a lawyer Winnie Mandela's friend Maud Katzenellenbogen proposed to defend Winnie Mandela. After consultation with Mandela she did not use him and eventually chose Joel

"Please advise Nelson Mandela his Thembekile[i] passed away 13th instant result motor accident in Cape Town."

I find it difficult to believe that I will never see Thembi again. On February 23 this year he turned 24. I had seen him towards the end of July 1962, a few days after I had returned from the trip abroad. Then he was a lusty lad of 17 that I could never associate with death. He wore one of my trousers which was a shade too big & long for him. The incident was significant & set me thinking. As you know he had a lot of clothing, was particular about his dress & had no reason whatsoever for using my clothes. I was deeply touched for the emotional factors underlying his action were too obvious. For days thereafter my mind & feelings were agitated to realise the psychological strains & stresses my absence from home had imposed on the children. I recalled an incident in December 1956 when I was an awaiting trial prisoner at the Johannesburg Fort. At that time Kgatho[ii] was 6 and lived in Orlando East. Although he well knew that I was in jail he went over to Orlando West & told Ma[iii] that he longed for me. That night he slept in my bed.

But let me return to my meeting with Thembi. He had come to bid me farewell on his way to a boarding school. On his arrival he greeted me very warmly, holding my hand firmly & for some time. Thereafter we sat down & conversed. Somehow the conversation drifted to his studies, & he gave me what I considered, in the light of his age at the time, to be an interesting appreciation of Shakespeare's *Julius Caesar* which I very much enjoyed. We had been corresponding regularly ever since he went to school at Matatiele & when he later changed to Wodehouse.[iv] In December 1960 I travelled some distance by car to meet him. Throughout this period I regarded him as a child & I approached him mainly from this angle. But our conversation in July 1962 reminded me I was no longer speaking to a child but to one who was beginning to have a settled attitude in life. He had suddenly raised himself from a son to a friend. I was indeed a bit sad when we ultimately parted. I could neither accompany him to a bus stop nor see him off at the station, for an outlaw, such as I was at the time, must be ready to give up even important parental duties. So it was that my son, no! my friend, stepped out alone to fend for himself in a world where I could only meet him

Carlson instead.

i   Madiba Thembekile (Thembi) Mandela (1945–69), Mandela's eldest son – see the glossary.
ii   Makgatho Mandela (1950–2005), Mandela's second-born son – see the glossary.
iii   He is most likely referring to his mother, Nosekeni Fanny Mandela, who stayed with them for a while.
iv   Wodehouse Junior Secondary School in Cofimvaba, Transkei.

secretly & once in a while. I knew you had bought him clothing & given him some cash, but nevertheless I emptied my pockets and transferred to him all the copper and silver that a wretched fugitive could afford. During the Rivonia Case he sat behind me one day. I kept looking back, nodding to him & giving him a broad smile. At the time it was generally believed that we would certainly be given the extreme penalty & this was clearly written across his face. Though he nodded back as many times as I did to him, not once did he return the smile. I never dreamt that I would never see him again. That was 5 years ago.

During the intervening period, you gave me many interesting reports on him in your letters & during your visits. I was particularly pleased to note his attachment to the family & the personal interest he took in matters affecting his relations. This attachment & interest is demonstrated by the warm letter he wrote you in June 1967, meeting you at the airport when you visited me the same month, looking after Ma[i] in Cape Town & bringing her to the Docks to board the Island boat, visiting you when he recently came up to Johannesburg with his family & taking Zeni & Zindzi[ii] out. I do not know whether he managed to go down to see Ma's grave. He has sent messages through Kgatho & gave me the parental honour of asking me to name his baby. Maki[iii] also told me that he bought Kgatho & herself clothing & all the other things they need. I know what a shattering blow his death is to you darling & I write to give you my deepest sympathy. I have sent Ntoko[iv] our condolences. Though taken away so early in his life, he will rest in peace for he has done his duty to his parents, brother & sisters & to his relations. We will all miss him. It is a pity that neither you nor I could pay him the last respects that are due from parents to a beloved son who has departed. To lose a mother & a first-born, & to have your life partner incarcerated for an indefinite period, and all within a period of ten months, is a burden too heavy for one man to carry even in the best of time. But I do not at all complain my darling. All I wish you to know is that you are my pride & that of our wide family.

Never before have I longed for you than at the present moment. It is good to remember this in this day of bitter misfortunes & bitter

---

i   Nelson Mandela's mother and Thembi's grandmother who passed away in September 1968.
ii   Zenani (1959–) and Zindzi (1960–) Mandela, his youngest daughters – see the glossary.
iii   Makaziwe Mandela (1954–), Mandela's eldest daughter – see the glossary.
iv   Evelyn Ntoko Mandela (1922–2004), Mandela's first wife (1944–1958) and the mother of Thembi – see the glossary.

reverses. The writer, P. J. Schoeman, told the story of an African Commander-in-Chief who took his army of magnificent black warriors for
a hunt. During the chase the son of the Commander was killed by a
lioness & the Commander himself was badly mauled by the beast.
The wound was then sterilised with a red-hot spear & the wounded
dignitary writhed with pain as the wound was being treated. Later
Schoeman asked how he felt & he replied that the invisible wound was
more painful than the visible one. I now know what the commander
meant. I think of you every moment of the day. Tons & tons of love &
a million kisses, Mhlope.[i]

Devotedly,
Dalibunga

NKOSIKAZI NOBANDLA MANDELA. 8115 ORLANDO WEST
JOHANNESBURG

To Evelyn Mandela,[ii] his former wife and mother of Thembi[iii]

16.7.69

Special letter[iv]
Dear Evelyn,

This afternoon the Commanding Officer informed me of a telegram
received from attorney Mendel Levin of Johannesburg in which he
reported the death of Thembi in a motor accident in Cape Town on
July 13.

I write to give you, Kgatho & Maki[v] my deepest sympathy. I know
more than anybody else living today just how devastating this cruel blow
must have been for you for Thembi was your first-born & the second

---

i   One of Winnie Mandela's names.
ii   Evelyn Ntoko Mandela (1922–2004), Mandela's first wife (1944–1958) and the mother of Thembi – see
      the glossary.
iii   Madiba Thembekile (Thembi) Mandela (1945–69), Mandela's eldest son – see the glossary.
iv   Special letters were not taken from a prisoner's quota.
v   His remaining living children with Evelyn Mandela – Makgatho (Kgatho) Mandela (1950–2005),
      Mandela's second-born son (see the glossary) and Makaziwe (Maki) Mandela (1954–), Mandela's eldest
      daughter (see the glossary).

16 7 69

Special letter

Dear Evelyn,

This afternoon the Commanding Officer informed me of a telegram received from attorney Mendel Levin of Johannesburg in which he reported the death of Thembi in a motor accident in Cape Town on July 13.

I write to give you, Kgatho & Maki my deepest sympathy. I know more than anybody else living today just how devastating this cruel blow must have been to you for Thembi was your first born & the second child that you have lost. I also am fully conscious of the passionate love that you had for him & the efforts you made to train & prepare him to play his part in a complex modern industrial society. I am also aware of how Kgatho & Maki adored & respected him, the holidays & good time they spent with him in Cape Town. In his letter written in October 1967 Maki told me that Thembi helped you in buying them all they needed. My late ma gave me details of the warm hospitality she received she received from him when she visited me on the Island. Throughout the last five years up to March this year, Nobandla gave me interesting accounts of his attachment & devotion to the family & the personal interest he took in all his relatives. I last saw him five years ago during the Rivonia Trial & I always looked forward to these accounts for they were the main channel through which I was able to hear something of him.

The blow has been equally grievous to me. In addition to the fact that I had not seen him for at least sixty months, I was neither privileged to give him a wedding ceremony nor to lay him to rest when the fatal hour had struck. In 1967 I wrote him a long letter drawing his attention to some matters which I thought it was in his interest to attend to without delay. I looked forward to further correspondence to & to meeting him and his family when I returned. All these expectations have now been completely shattered for he has been taken away at the early age of 24 and we will never again see him. We should all be consoled & comforted by the fact that he had

Page from a special letter to Evelyn Mandela, 16 July 1969, see pages 74–6.

child that you have lost.[i] I am also fully conscious of the passionate love that you had for him & the efforts you made to train & prepare him to play his part in a complex modern industrial society. I am also aware of how Kgatho & Maki adored & respected him, the holidays & good time they spent with him in Cape Town. In her letter written in October 1967 Maki told me that Thembi helped you in buying them all they needed. My late Ma gave me details of the warm hospitality she received from him when she visited me on the Island. Throughout the last five years up to March this year, Nobandla[ii] gave me interesting accounts of his attachment & devotion to the family & the personal interest he took in all his relatives. I last saw him five years ago during the Rivonia Trial & I always looked forward to these accounts for they were the main channel through which I was able to hear something of him.

The blow has been equally grievous to me. In addition to the fact that I had not seen him for at least sixty months, I was neither privileged to give him a wedding ceremony nor to lay him to rest when the fatal hour had struck. In 1967 I wrote him a long letter drawing his attention to some matters which I thought was in his interest to attend to without delay. I looked forward to further correspondence & to meeting him and his family when I returned. All these expectations have now been completely shattered for he has been taken away at the early age of 24 and we will never again see him. We should all be consoled & comforted by the fact that he had many good friends who join with us in mourning his passing away. He fulfilled his duties to us as parents and has left us with an inheritance for which every parent is proud – a charming Molokazana[iii] & two lovely babies. Once more I extend to you, Kgatho & Maki my sincere condolences & trust that you will muster enough strength & courage to survive this painful tragedy.

Fondest regards to Sam & Tshezi,[iv] to Nomanage, Lulu, Phindi, Nosisi, Mxolisi, Mongezi & Waza.[v] Nobandla joins me in this message of sympathy.

Yours very sincerely,
Nelson.

---

i   His first daughter with Evelyn died of an illness at the age of nine months. She was named Makaziwe. They subsequently gave the same name to their second daughter.
ii   One of Winnie Mandela's names.
iii isiXhosa for 'daughter-in-law'. He is referring to his late son Thembi's wife, Thoko Mandela – see the glossary.
iv   Evelyn Mandela's brother and sister-in-law.
v   Members of Evelyn Mandela's family.

To Makgatho Mandela,[i] his second-born son

28.7.69

My dear Kgatho,

I have been shown your telegram of July 17 in which you advised me of Thembi's[ii] death in a car accident. The previous day the Commanding Officer had received a similar telegram from Attorney Mendel Levin of Johannesburg. I hope your mother[iii] has by now received the letter I wrote on July 16 expressing my condolences to her and to you and Maki.[iv]

It is a wise rule never to brood over past calamities, however disastrous they may appear to be, and we should try to reconcile ourselves to the grim fact that Thembi, your beloved brother, is no more and that never again shall we see him. None the less, his passing away is a serious loss to the family and it has left a deep and painful wound that may take many years to heal.

I think of your mother who must have been severely shocked to lose a son so early in his life and who had already begun to take over some of the heavy duties of a parent that will now press on her from all sides. I think more particularly of you and Maki because I realise fully just how hard a blow Thembi's death must have been to both of you. He sincerely loved you, and you, in turn, were very fond of him. He was not just a brother but the person to whom you naturally turned for advice and assistance. He was the shield that protected you against danger, and that helped you to build up the self-confidence and courage you need to deal with the numerous problems that you meet as you grow. You could take him into confidence in regard to many matters a child would hesitate to disclose to his parents, and now that he is gone you must be feeling lost, lonely and sad. In Cape Town he provided a home for you where you could happily spend exciting holidays, meet new friends and learn more about your country and people. His death means that no more will you be able to enjoy these advantages and that from now on you will have to fight and win your own battles and to depend on your own resources.

---

i   Makgatho Mandela (1950–2005) – see the glossary.
ii   Madiba Thembekile (Thembi) (1945–69), Mandela's eldest son – see the glossary.
iii   Evelyn Ntoko Mandela (1922–2004), Mandela's first wife (1944–1958) – see the glossary.
iv   Makaziwe (Maki) Mandela (1954–), Mandela's eldest daughter – see the glossary.

I think it fit and proper to highlight but one striking virtue of his which created a deep impression on me. His love and devotion to you, Maki, Zeni,[i] Zindzi[ii] and to relatives generally, created the image of a man who respected family ties and who was destined to play an important role in the upbringing, education and development of the children. He had already developed himself to a position where he had become the object of his sisters' love, admiration and respect and a source of pride to the family.

From 8115[iii] I was kept constantly informed of his unflagging interest in all of us and details of his hospitality during his recent visit with his family to Johannesburg were outlined. The late Granny[iv] never missed the chance of saying something complimentary about him whenever she visited me here and I sincerely regret that death has denied him the opportunity to bring this magnificent gift of his in full play in the service of the family.

I hate giving lectures, Kgatho, even to my own children and I prefer discussing matters with everyone on a basis of perfect equality, where my views are offered as advice which the person affected is free to accept or reject as it pleases him. But I would be failing in my duty if I did not point out that the death of Thembi brings a heavy responsibility on your shoulders. Now you are the eldest child and it will be your duty to keep the family together and to set a good example for your sisters, to be a pride to your parents and to all your relatives. This means that you will have to work harder on your studies, never allow yourself to be discouraged by difficulties or setbacks, and never give up the battle even in the darkest hour. Remember that we live in a new age of scientific achievement, the most staggering of which is the recent landing of man on the moon. That is a sensational event that will enrich man's knowledge of the universe and that may even result in a change or modification of many fundamental assumptions in many fields of knowledge. The younger generation must train and prepare themselves so that they can easily grasp the far-reaching repercussions of developments in the realm of space. This is an era of intense and vicious competition in which the richest rewards are reserved for those who have undergone the most thorough training and who have attained the highest academic qualifications in their respective fields. The issues

---

i   Zenani (Zeni) Mandela (1959–), Mandela's middle daughter.
ii   Zindziswa (Zindzi) Mandela (1960–), Mandela's youngest daughter.
iii   Mandela's house in Vilakazi street, Orlando West, Soweto.
iv   Nelson Mandela's mother, Nosekeni Fanny Mandela, who died in 1968 – see the glossary.

that agitate humanity today call for trained minds and the man who is deficient in this respect is crippled because he is not in possession of the tools and equipment necessary to ensure success and victory in service of country and people. To lead an orderly and disciplined life, and to give up the glittering pleasures that attract the average boy, to work hard and systematically in your studies throughout the year, will in the end bring you coveted prizes and much personal happiness. It will inspire your sisters to follow the example of their beloved brother, and they will benefit greatly through your scientific knowledge, vast experience, diligence and achievements. Besides, human beings like to be associated with a hardworking, disciplined and successful person, and by carefully cultivating these qualities you will win yourself many friends. This is what I should like to stress. Perhaps you would like to discuss the matter with Sisi Tellie[i] in 8115 who will arrange a permit[ii] for you to come down so that we can discuss future plans relating to your education.

Last January I wrote you a lengthy letter discussing precisely this matter and other personal questions. I wrote Maki a similar one on February 16. Your failure to reply made me suspect that both of you had not received the letters. I made enquiries and found that there was no evidence that the letters had been posted to you. I was indeed shocked to hear that my letters do not reach you and other members of the family & friends as they are the only means I have to communicate with you. I hope at least this one will reach you. Please let me know about your supplementary results.

Finally I must thank you most earnestly for advising me of the death of Thembi and I will think of you in this family tragedy. Do let me have the full name of Molokazana,[iii] her present address as well as the names of Abazukulu.[iv] Fond regards to all.

Affectionately
Tata.[v]

MR MAKGATHO LEWANIKA MANDELA, HOUSE NO. 8115 ORLANDO WEST, JOHANNESBURG.

---

i   Telia (Telli or Tellie) Mtirara, a relative of Mandela's. *Sisi* means 'sister' in isiXhosa and is often used to refer to a woman in the samge age group.

ii   Permits were required by all visitors.

iii   'Daughter-in-law' in isiXhosa. He is referring to Thembi's wife, Thoko Mandela – see the glossary.

iv   'Grandchildren' in isiXhosa and isiXulu. Mandela is referring to Thembi and Thoko Mandela's children Ndileka (1965–) and Nandi (1968–) Mandela – see the glossary.

v   'Father' in isiXhosa.

To Sefton Vutela, the husband of Nancy (Nali) Vutela, Winnie Mandela's sister

28.7.69

My dear Sef,

I have been shocked to discover that almost every letter I have written since December last to members of my family, relations & friends has not reached its destination, including one I wrote you 7 months ago. I hope this one will reach safely & that the invisible forces that have been responsible for the mysterious but systematic disappearance of my correspondence, & that have completely cut me off from my family and relations will be prompted by considerations of fairplay & sportsmanship to give me a break & let this one through.

I owe you a debt which I may find difficult to repay. The day my colleagues and I were sentenced in the Rivonia Trial,[i] Nali, Zami,[ii] my late mother and Nyanya[iii] sat amongst the audience. The offence for which we had been convicted the previous day carried a capital sentence, & there were many who feared that we would in due course be condemned to the countless legions of the dead. As a matter of fact, on the very first day of consultations, counsel felt obliged to inform us that the prosecution had indicated that they would demand the extreme penalty, at least against some of the accused. The gravity of the situation was sufficiently stressed & we were duly warned to prepare ourselves for this grim and grievous end to all our dreams. I am neither brave nor bold, & since the days of my youth, I have been stalked by the chronic weakness of being anxious to live & be an eye-witness to the introduction of the radical developments for which my countrymen have fought so bravely in the course of the last three centuries. As disciplined and dedicated comrades fighting for a worthy cause, we should be ready to undertake any tasks which history might assign to us however high the price to be paid may be. This was the guiding principle throughout our political careers, & even as we went through

---

i   See the glossary.
ii   Another name for Winnie Mandela.
iii   Nonyaniso (Nyanya) Madikizela, Winnie Mandela's youngest sister.

the various stages of the trial. I must, however, confess that for my own part the threat of death evoked no desire in me to play the role of martyr. I was ready to do so if I had to. But the anxiety to live always lingered. But familiarity does breed contempt even for the hideous hand of death. The critical phase lasted a few hours only, & I was a worried & exhausted man as I went to bed the day I heard of the Rivonia swoop.[i] But when I got up in the morning the worst was over & I had somehow mustered enough strength & courage even to rationalise that if there was nothing else I could do to further the cause we all so passionately cherished, even the dreadful outcome that threatened us might serve a useful purpose on wider issues. This belief served to feed & replenish my slender resources of fortitude until the last day of the proceedings. It was reinforced by the conviction that our cause was just & by the wide support we received from influential bodies & individuals on both sides of the Colour line. But all the flourish of trumpets & the hosannas sung by us & our well-wishers in the course of the trial would have been valueless if courage had deserted us when the decisive moment struck.[ii] The immense crowds that turned up when sentence was pronounced on June 12 gave us real inspiration. As we entered the courtroom that morning my eyes immediately fell on Nyanya, Nali, Ma & Zami. Ma & Zami have always been a tower of strength to me & have very often succeeded in spurring me to accomplish much more than my limited talents warranted. I was delighted to see them on this occasion. But for me Nali's attendance was a shot in the arm; it had a significance that went somewhat beyond the mere physical presence of a sister-in-law. I regarded it as an act of solidarity on your part because of the major principle that was at stake. I shall always remember that day.

In 1967 Nali travelled the 1,000 miles between Johannesburg & Cape Town reaching the Island on February 4. She brought me a visit which really excited me. She looked well & terrific & I was indeed very happy to see her once more.

Some time before that you had personally packed & sent me the literature I needed for my studies & your pencil signature in the books meant much to me. Above all is the invaluable help you have given Zami, the details of which she repeatedly placed before me through

---

i   The police raid on Liliesleaf Farm on 11 July 1963 in which most of Mandela's fellow Rivonia Trialists were arrested.

ii   Mandela and his comrades received much support from within and outside South Africa during the Rivonia Trial. The courage he is referring to here is related to the expectation that they would be sentenced to death.

correspondence & during her visits. It may not be out of place to make the point here that often in normal life, when happy & free, we build for ourselves ivory towers into which we retreat & within which we swell with pride & conceit & treat with indifference & even contempt the generosity & affection of friends. Behind iron bars such artificial towers easily crumble & acts of hospitality become priceless jewels. I do want to assure you in all sincerity that I deeply appreciated all that you and Nali did for me & Zami. The northern areas are miles away from your native village in the Transkei, from the plains & hills where your childhood was spent, & from your kith & kin. Often I have sat down & thought long & deeply over you & Nali, & the ideas that have crossed my mind have been legion, all that I need say at the present moment is that I wish both of you & the children (about whom I should like to hear when you reply) good health, strength & much luck & fortune in the days that lie ahead.

Zami also told me of the help given by Cameron,[i] my suave brother-in-law, & I should be pleased if you would kindly tell him that his assistance made a profound impression on me. I have not had the privilege of meeting his wife & I do look forward to seeing her one day. I think of Kha & Tami as well. I do not know if I would find it easy to recognise her as I saw her once or twice, but I still remember that she is a beautiful girl, as all the Madikizela females are, otherwise how do you think they succeeded in dragging you, Tami & me to the altar?

Fondest regards to Tshutsha, NKOMO & VUYIZANA Dabane, Mthuthu & his Joyce.[ii] Warmest love to Nali.

Yours very sincerely,
Nel

MISS NANCY MADIKIZELA,
C/O MRS NIKI IRIS XABA.[iii]
HOUSE NO. 8115 ORLANDO WEST, JOHANNESBURG

---

i   One of Winnie Mandela's brothers.
ii   Nothuthuzelo and Joyce Mgudlwa, Winnie's relatives.
iii   Niki Xaba (1932–1985), Winnie Mandela's eldest sister – see the glossary.

To Zenani and Zindzi Mandela,[i] his middle and youngest daughters

August 3, 1969

My Darlings,

On July 17 I received a telegram from Kgatho[ii] in which he told me that Buti[iii] Thembi, your beloved brother, had died in a car accident. The accident occurred in Touws River, near Cape Town, on July 13. I am told that apart from him two Europeans, who recently came to this country from Italy, also died. Your brother will be buried in Johannesburg today. In his telegram Kgatho informed me that he was sending the full details of how Thembi died. But my letters take a very long time to reach me and, at the time of writing Kgatho's letter, had not arrived, and I am thus not in a position to give you more particulars on the matter.

I write on behalf of Mummy and myself to give you our deepest sympathy. All of us were very fond and proud of Thembi, and he, in turn, was devoted to us, and it is indeed very sad to think that we will never see him again. I know just how he loved you. Mummy wrote to me on March 1 and advised me that he spent his holidays with his family in Johannesburg, and that during that period he took you out several times and gave you much pleasure and joy.

Mummy has also informed me that he had invited you to spend the forthcoming December holidays with him in Cape Town and that you were looking forward to a lot of fun. There you would have seen the sea; places like Muizenberg and the Strand where you could swim. You would also have seen the Castle, a large stone fort which was completed about the year 1679. Here the Governors of the early Cape lived. It was also here that the famous African king, Cetywayo, was kept for a while after the Battle of Isandhlwana in January 1879 where the Zulu army defeated the English. In Cape Town you would also have seen Table Mountain which is about 3,549 feet high. From the top of the mountain you would see Robben Island across the waves. Thembi's death means that you will not be able to spend your December holidays down there, and you will also miss the pleasures and

---

i   Zenani Mandela (1959–) and Zindzi Mandela (1960–) – see the glossary.
ii   Makgatho (Kgatho) Mandela (1950–2005), Mandela's second-born son – see the glossary.
iii   'Brother' in isiXhosa and isiZulu.

beautiful places I have mentioned above, and we are all very sorry that our Thembi is really gone. He meant much to us and we will miss him.

It was not possible for Mummy and myself to attend his funeral. Both of us are in jail and our request for permission to go to the funeral was not granted. You also did not attend, but when you return from school Kgatho will arrange for you to be taken to see the grave and bid your departed brother farewell. Perhaps one day Mummy and I will be able also to visit the grave. But now that he is gone, we must forget about the painful fact of his death. Now he sleeps in peace, my darlings, free from troubles, worries, sickness or need; he can feel neither pain nor hunger. You must continue with your schoolwork, play games and sing songs.

This time I have written you a sad letter. On June 23 I had written you another letter which was just as sad, because it dealt with the arrest of Mummy. This year has been a bad one indeed for us, but happy days will come when we will be full of joy and laughter. What is even more important is that one day Mummy and I will come back and live happily together with you in one house, sit at table together, help you with the many problems you will experience as you grow. But until then Mummy and I will write to you regularly. Tons and tons of love, my darlings.

Affectionately,
Tata.[i]

MISSES ZENI AND ZINDZI MANDELA
C/O MRS NIKI IRIS XABA,[ii]
HOUSE NO. 8115 ORLANDO WEST, JOHANNESBURG.

===

To Irene Buthelezi,[iii] a friend and the wife of Chief Mangosuthu Buthelezi[iv]

---

i   'Father' in isiXhosa.
ii   Niki Xaba (1932–1985), Winnie Mandela's eldest sister – see the glossary.
iii   See the glossary.
iv   Chief Mangosuthu Buthelezi (1928–), Zulu prince and politician – see the glossary.

3-8-69

Our dear Mndhlunkulu,[i]

I was moved by the message of condolence contained in the telegram sent by my chief, Mangosuthu, on behalf of the family & which I received on July 18 (my birthday), & I should like him to know that I deeply appreciate it. 1968 & 1969 had been difficult & trying years for me. I lost my mother only 10 months ago. On May 12 my wife was detained indefinitely under the Terrorist Act, leaving behind small chdn as virtual orphans, & now my eldest son is gone never to return. Death is a frightful disaster no matter what the cause & the age of the person affected. Where it approaches gradually as in the case of normal illness, the next-of-kin are at least forewarned & the blow may not be so shattering when it ultimately lands. But when you learn that death has claimed a strapping & healthy person in the prime of his life, then one must actually live through the experience to realise how completely paralysing it can be. This was my experience on July 16 when I was first advised of my son's death. I was shaken from top to bottom & for some seconds I did not know exactly how to react. I ought to have been better prepared for Thembi was not the first child I lost. Way back in the forties I lost a nine months baby girl.[ii] She had been hospitalised & had been making good progress when suddenly her condition took a grave turn & she died the same night. I managed to see her during the critical moments when she was struggling desperately to hold within her tender body the last sparks of life which were flickering away. I have never known whether or not I was fortunate to witness that grievous scene. It haunted me for many days thereafter & still provokes painful memories right up to the present day; but it should have hardened me for similar catastrophes. Then came Sept. 26 (my wife's birthday) when I was advised of my mother's death. I had last seen her the previous Sept. when she visited me on the Island at the ripe age of 76,[iii] having travelled all alone from Umtata.[iv] Her appearance had much distressed me. She had lost weight & although cheerful & charming, she looked ill & tired. At the end of the visit I was

---

i   An isiXhosa reference to royalty.
ii   Mandela's first daughter with his wife Evelyn died of an illness at the age of nine months. She was named Makaziwe. They subsequently had another daughter together to whom they gave the same name.
iii   His mother visited him twice on Robben Island, on 6 March 1966 and on 9 September 1967.
iv   Umtata (now called Mthatha) was the capital of the Transkei homeland and is around 625 miles from Robben Island.

able to watch her as she walked slowly towards the boat which would take her back to the mainland, & somehow the thought flashed across my mind that I had seen her for the last time. But as the months rolled by, the picture I had formed on her last visit began to fade away & was altogether dispelled by the exciting letter she wrote thereafter testifying to her good health. The result was that when the fatal hour struck on Sept. 26[i] I was again quite unprepared & for a few days I spent moments in my cell which I never want to remember. But nothing I experienced in the late forties & in Sept. last year can be likened to what I went through on July 16. The news was broken to me about 2:30 p.m. Suddenly my heart seemed to have stopped beating & the warm blood that had freely flown in my veins for the last 51 years froze into ice. For some time I could neither think nor talk & my strength appeared to be draining out. Eventually, I found my way back to my cell with a heavy load on my shoulders & the last place where a man stricken with sorrow should be. As usual my friends here were kind & helpful & they did what they could to keep me in good spirits. My second son, Kgatho,[ii] sent me a telegram on July 17 & I felt even much better. The telegram from the Chief created a deep impression on me & greatly contributed to my complete recovery from the shock. I should like to assure him that I will always remember his inspiring message of sympathy, as well as the one he sent on the occasion of my mother's death. I feel mighty & strong & confident because of the good wishes & messages of solidarity that have come from my trusted friends, amongst whom I am privileged to include you & the Chief.

My thoughts very often go back to the forties when I lived at Mzilikazi[iii] where I first met your parents. Your father, the son of Mzila, was really a grand old man I admired & respected in all sincerity. He was dignified, courteous & confident & throughout the 4 years of my stay at Mzilikazi we were on friendly terms. The conversations I had with him indicated a man who was proud of the traditions & achievements of his people, & this aspect, more than anything else, fascinated me. But though he loved & respected his own history & culture he was sensitive to modern & progressive ideas & valued education. In this

---

i   Mandela's mother died on 24 September 1968; he received the news on 26 September.

ii   Makgatho Mandela (1950–2005) – see the glossary.

iii   Mandela is referring to a mine compound where he lived while working as a gold mine security guard in the early 1940s. The name Mzilikazi is likely to be a nickname emanating from the surname of the mine compound's manager in charge, Mzila, who was Irene Buthelezi's father. Mandela had known her since she was child.

respect you & your brother should be witnesses. He was often seen at the Bantu Men's Social Centre[i] in his black & gold regalia, decorated with medals & ribbons, playing drafts [*sic*] & other games with remarkable skill against distinguished sportsmen of that city. I will always remember him as a man who gave me much encouragement & help in my struggling days. I have not forgotten the Old Lady & the warm smile with which she always greeted me. I valued it even then, but you have to be behind bars for at least 7 years to appreciate fully just how precious human kindness can be. It gave me much pleasure to be able to act on her behalf when the Old Man's estate was wound up. Always remember that I highly value my association with your family & that I hold the Chief in esteem. My fondest regards to you all & to Dr. Dotwane[ii] & your sister-in-law.

Once again, many thanks to the Chief for his inspiring message.

Yours very sincerely.
Nelson.

MRS IRENE BUTHELEZI
"KWAPHINDANGENE", P.O. BOX 1,
MAHLATHINI, ZULULAND

To Nolusapho Irene Mkwayi, wife of fellow prisoner Wilton Mkwayi[iii]

29.9.69

Our dear Nolusapho,

I was indeed encouraged by the touching message of sympathy you sent me on the occasion of the death of my eldest son, Thembi.[iv] Both the printed text of the condolence card, as well as the soothing senti-

---

i   The Bantu Men's Social Centre (BMSC), founded in Johannesburg, in 1924, was an important cultural, social, and political meeting place for black South Africans. Its facilities included a gym and a library, and it hosted boxing matches, political meetings, and dances. Mandela and others founded the ANC Youth League there in 1944.

ii   Dr. Mafu Dotwana was the husband of Mandela's relative Dili Mtirara.

iii   Wilton Mkwayi (1923–2004), trade unionist, political activist, and political prisoner – see the glossary.

iv   Madiba Thembekile Mandela (1945–69) – see the glossary.

ments you scribbled down next to the text, were singularly appropriate & they did much to inspire me.

I received the tragic news on July 16, & six days thereafter I applied to the Commanding Officer for leave to attend the funeral, at my own cost, & with or without escort. I added that, if Thembi would have been buried by the time my application was received, I should in that event be allowed to visit his grave for the purpose of 'laying the stone' (ukubek'ilitye)[i] – the traditional ceremony that is reserved for those who miss the actual burial.

Ten months before this I had made a similar application when my mother passed away, & though the authorities had then adopted a hard line in refusing what I considered in all the circumstances to be a reasonable request, I nonetheless vaguely hoped that this time the death of two members of the family occurring so soon after the other would probably induce the authorities to give me the one opportunity I had in life of paying my last respects to Thembi. In the letter of application I expressly referred to the fact that I had been refused leave to be present at the graveside when my mother was laid to rest, pointing out at the same time, that approval of that application would have been a generous act on their part and one that would have made a deep impression on me. I drew attention to the fact that I had seen Thembi five years ago, & expressed the hope that they would appreciate how anxious I was to attend the funeral.

I was of course aware that 30 years ago the British had imprisoned a famous freedom fighter in one of the colonies, a man who later became Prime Minister when his country gained full independence in 1947.[ii] He was in jail when his wife's health worsened, & when it became necessary for him to accompany her to Europe for medical treatment.

British imperialism has brought untold misery and suffering to millions of people throughout the world, & when the English with-

---

i   *Ukubek'ilitye* literally means 'to place a stone', and is a ceremony for those who missed the actual burial.
ii   Mandela is referring to Jawaharlal Nehru. Later, in a conversation with Richard Stengel in 1993, he recalled: 'Firstly, I had to pay my respects to my mother's grave, who died in '68 when I was in prison. I had asked the prison authorities to allow me to attend the funeral and I quoted the case of Pandit Nehru, that is before he actually was a prime minister, before independence – before the independence of India. His wife was ill, she had contracted TB, and Nehru was in jail, and he then asked the British for permission to take his wife to Germany which apparently was reputed to . . . have the most advanced methods of curing tuberculosis at the time. The British agreed and he left prison and took his wife to Germany. Unfortunately the wife died but he then returned to jail and the British decided to release him because of the tragedy.' (Conversation with Richard Stengel, 13 January 1993, CD 15, Nelson Mandela Foundation, Johannesburg.)

drew they left behind them countries which had been plundered, and whose people were condemned to many years of poverty, famine, disease and illiteracy. This period forms the black chapter of British history & many historians have justly censured Britain. On the other hand, the English are widely known by friend & foe for their broad outlook & sensible approach to human problems, & for their deep respect for men who are ready to give up their lives for a worthy cause. Often in the course of political conflicts with leaders of national movements in their former colonies, they were able to treat political offenders humanely, & to render them genuine & substantial help whenever necessary. So it was that when the politician referred to above was faced with the problem of the illness of his wife, the English released him to travel abroad. Unfortunately, the wife died after reaching Europe & thereafter the bereaved man returned to his country to serve the balance of his sentence. This is how an enlightened government is expected to treat its citizens, & this is how the British Government responded to an application made on compassionate grounds by political opponents a little more than 30 years ago.

In the case of both my late mother & Thembi, I was faced not with the problem of illness but that of death. I asked for permission not to travel abroad, but to another part of my own country which was under the constant surveillance of a strong & experienced Security Force. In Thembi's case my application was simply ignored & I was not even favoured with the courtesy of an acknowledgement. A further request for permission to obtain copies of press reports on the fatal accident was turned down, & up to now I have no authentic information whatsoever as to how Thembi died. All my efforts to obtain the services of an attorney to investigate the question of legal responsibility for the accident, any claims arising there out & the estate generally, have been unsuccessful. Not only was I deprived of the opportunity of seeing for the last time my eldest son & friend, & the pride of my heart; I am kept in the dark on everything relating to him & his affairs.

On Sept. 6 I received a report on my household affairs which greatly disturbed me. My niece, Nomfundo,[i] who is still in her teens, lives in the house virtually alone, & I believe that the lady who stayed

---

i   Olive Nomfundo Mandela, daughter of Mandela's sister Notancu.

there after Zami's[i] arrest was frightened away. This indifference completely astonished me & kept wide open the painful wounds which the dreadful hands of death had made in my heart.

Your message must be seen in the light of these facts; of the obstacles & frustrations that surround me. Fortunately, my numerous friends here & outside prison have showered me with messages of sympathy & encouragement & the worst is now over. Among these is your own message; you, Nolusapho, the wife of the Amagqunukhwebe,[ii] the children of Khwane,[iii] Cungwa, Pato and Kama.[iv] I should like you to know that I deeply appreciate your wonderful message. Though I have not yet had the privilege of meeting you, I have the picture of one who genuinely loves her people & who always places the welfare & happiness of others above hers. That you were able to send me this message in spite of your own illness & personal problems says a lot more in your favour than language can express. I sincerely wish you a speedy & complete recovery.

Many thanks for the lovely Xmas cards you & Nomazotsho sent me. Love & fondest regards to Georgina,[v] Nondyebo,[vi] Beauty,[vii] Squire,[viii] & Vuyo.

Yours very sincerely,
Nelson

TO: NOLUSAPHO IRENE MKWAYI.
HOUSE NO. 11842 ORLANDO WEST EXTENSION.
JOHANNESBURG.

---

i   One of Winnie Mandela's names.
ii   The Amagqunukhwebe are a sub-group of the Xhosa nation.
iii   Khwane kaLungane, a counsellor and a warrior of King Tshiwo (1670–1702) of amaXhosa, headed the chiefdom of amaGqunukhwebe, and established the Khwane dynasty.
iv   Descendants of Khwane who succeeded him as king.
v   Winnie Mandela's friend who served as one of her bridesmaids.
vi   Nondyebo Jane Bam, a nurse and anti-apartheid activist. She was a sister of Brigalia Bam (1933–), who Mandela later appointed head of South Africa's Independent Electoral Commission when he was president, and Fikile Bam (1937–2011), who was also imprisoned on Robben Island from 1964–75.
vii   Nobantu Mniki, one of Winnie Mandela's sisters.
viii Henry Makgothi (1928–2011), a school teacher who was fired for his political activities. He was elected Transvaal ANC President in 1954 and was an accused in the Treason Trial. He was arrested while trying to leave the country and sentenced to ten years in prison. After his release he lived in exile and worked for the ANC. He returned to South Africa in 1990 and served as ANC chief whip in the National Council of Provinces until 1999.

=====

To Winnie Mandela,[i] his wife

16.11.69

Dade Wethu,[ii]

I believe that on Dec. 21 you and 21 others will appear in the Pretoria Supreme Court under the Sabotage Act,[iii] alternatively, for contravening the provisions of the Suppression of Communism Act.[iv] I am informed that you have all instructed Mr. Joel Carlson to act in the matter.

From the particulars of the charge it would seem that you would require me to give evidence on your behalf & I look forward to an early consultation with you and Counsel. I would certainly consider it irregular & unjust & contrary to the elementary principles of natural justice to force you to start a long and protracted trial on a serious charge without arrangements having first been made for us to meet. We have not seen each other since Dec. last year & a meeting between us would go a long way towards easing the strains & stresses of the last 5 months & putting you in a better physical condition & frame of mind. Only after such a meeting could you have something approximating a fair trial, & I sincerely hope it will be possible to arrange it. I am also keen to discuss the question of how you should conduct your defence & to anticipate the tactics the state will most certainly use. Since our wedding day in June 1958, you have, under some pretext or other, been dragged 3 times before the criminal courts & once before a civil one.[v] The issues involved, at least in part of this litigation, are better forgotten than recalled. They caused much grief & concern.

---

i   Nomzamo Winifred Madikizela-Mandela (1936–2018) – see the glossary.

ii   Normally written as one word, this means 'sister' in isiXhosa.

iii   The General Law Amendment Act, No. 76, is also known as the 'Sabotage Act' of 1962. It provided for ninety days' detention without trial. Mandela's co-accused in the Rivonia Trial, who were arrested in 1963, were held under 'Ninety Days'. It also widened the definition of sabotage to include strikes, making them a capital offence.

iv   An Act passed on 26 June 1950, in which the state banned the South African Communist Party and any activities it deemed communist, defining 'communism' in such broad terms that anyone protesting against apartheid would be in breach of the Act.

v   Winnie Mandela was arrested in October 1958 and held in prison for two weeks for participating in a protest against the extension of pass laws to women. She was arrested in 1963 for attending a gathering and was acquitted. In 1967 she was accused of resisting arrest and was acquitted. She was then sentenced to twelve months' imprisonment for violating her banning order.

16.11.69

Dade Wethu,

I believe that on Dec. 1 you & 21 others will appear in the Pretoria Supreme Court on a charge under the Sabotage Act, alternatively for contravening the provisions of the Suppression of Communism Act. I am informed that you have all instructed me feel Carlson to act in the matter.

From the particulars of the charge it would seem that you would require me to give evidence on your behalf & I look forward to an early consultation with you and Counsel. I would certainly consider it irregular & unjust & contrary to the elementary principles of natural justice to force you to start a long and protracted trial on a serious charge without arrangements having first been made for us to meet. We have not seen each other since Dec. last year & a meeting between us would go a long way towards easing the strains & stresses of the last 5 months & putting you in a better physical condition & frame of mind. Only after such a meeting could you have something approximating a fair trial, & I sincerely hope it will be possible to arrange it. I am also keen to discuss the question of how you should conduct your defence & to anticipate the tactics the state will most certainly use.

Since our wedding day in June 1958, you have, under some pretext or other, been dragged 3 times before the Criminal courts & once before a Civil one. The issues involved, at least in part of this litigation, are better forgotten than recalled. They caused us much grief & concern. This will be the 5th occasion, & I suspect that here there is much that lies beneath the surface & the proceedings are likely to be the bitterest experience of your life to date. There will be those whose chief interest will be to seek to destroy the image we have built over the last decade. Attempts may be made to do now what they have repeatedly failed to achieve in former cases. I write to warn you in time of what lies ahead to enable you to prepare yourself both physically & spiritually to take the full force of the merciless blows that I feel certain will be directed systematically at you from the beginning to the end of the trial. In fact the trial & the circumstances surrounding it, may so far influence your thoughts & actions that it might well constitute an important landmark in your entire career, compelling you to re-examine very carefully values you once firmly cherished & to give up pleasures that once delighted your heart.

Already the months you spent in detention have been a severe test for you & when you come to the end of the case, you will have got a deeper understa—

This will be the 5th occasion, & I suspect that here there is much that lies beneath the surface, & the proceedings are likely to be the bitterest experience of your entire life to date. There will be those whose chief interest will be to seek to destroy the image we have built over the last decade. Attempts may be made to do now what they have repeatedly failed to achieve in former cases. I write to warn you in time of what lies ahead to enable you to prepare yourself both physically & spiritually to take the full force of the merciless blows that I feel certain will be directed systematically at you from the beginning to the end of the trial. In fact, the trial, & the circumstances surrounding it, may so far influence your thoughts & actions that it might well constitute an important landmark in your entire career, compelling you to re-examine very carefully values you once fondly cherished & to give up pleasures that once delighted your heart.

Already the months you spent in detention have been a severe test for you & when you come to the end of the case, you will have got a deeper understanding of human nature & its frailties & what human beings can do to others once their privileged position is endangered. When this threat emerges all the lofty virtues of western democracy about which we read so much in books are brushed aside. Neither the moral standards of modern civilisation, the teachings of the Christian faith, the universal idea of the common brotherhood of men, nor pure sense of honour will deter the privileged circles from applying the multitudinous pressures at their disposal on those who fight for human dignity. Those who are on the front-line should be willing and ready to draw the fire on to themselves in order to inspire their colleagues & make things easier for them. In the battle of ideas the true fighter who strives to free public thinking from the social evils of his age need never be discouraged if, at one & the same time, he is praised & condemned, honoured & degraded, acclaimed as saint & cursed as an irredeemable sinner. In the course of your short but lively political career you have been the object of all these contradictory labels, but you have never wavered; instead you held firmly to your convictions. Today even a bigger test faces you for a conviction will certainly entail many years of sorrow & suffering behind iron doors. But I have not the slightest doubt whatsoever that you will fight to the bitter end with all the tenacity & earnestness that you have shown on previous occasions, for you know only too well that substantial victories will be won by those who stand on their feet & not by those who crawl on their bellies.

In planning your own case & working out your strategy it will be important to bear in mind that you are engaged in a contest with an adversary who possesses vast resources in wealth & means of propaganda & who will be able to give facts any twist which he considers expedient. In such a situation your best defence, & one no power on earth can penetrate, is truth, honesty & courage of conviction. Nothing must be done or said which might imply directly or indirectly a repudiation of your principles & beliefs. The rest I propose discussing with you if & when I see you. That moment may or may never come. I do hope it will. If it doesn't, then I know you will, nevertheless, be in good hands & that you will be able to manage even without my help & advice. For the present, I send you all my good wishes & fondest regards. I will keep my fist clenched, & will do anything to assist you, Ngutyana.[i] How is our dear Nyanya?[ii] Do tell me something about her.

I have just received the tragic news that Cameron[iii] in Botswana had a stroke which resulted in paralysis & the amputation of a leg. To be struck down by such a fatal illness far away from your country & people is a disaster that may well make recovery difficult. I think of just how helpful he has been to you in my absence & regret it very much that we are not in a position to assist him. As far as I know, as an awaiting trial prisoner, you can write as many letters as you please & I suggest that you immediately write to tell him that we wish him speedy recovery. Kgatho[iv] visited me on Oct. 25, following upon Nkosazana Tellie[v] who was here on Sept. 6. On Nov. 8 I received a disturbing letter from her in which she bitterly complains of having been left behind when relatives visited you on Oct. 28. She is very good to us, & is receiving wrong treatment from certain quarters. I hope it will be possible for you to let her know that she means much to us.

I received a stimulating letter from Amina[vi] & she paid you flattering compliments. I am sure you will be happy to know that our friends have not forgotten you. I believe Lily[vii] had at last got my letter. In July she sent me a warm & moving message of sympathy. I

---

i   One of Winnie Mandela's names. She comes from the amaNgutyana clan.
ii   Nonyaniso (Nyanya) Madikizela, Winnie Mandela's youngest sister.
iii   One of Winnie Mandela's brothers.
iv   Makgatho Mandela (1950–2005), Mandela's second-born son – see the glossary.
v   Telia (Telli or Tellie) Mtirara, a relative of Mandela's. *Nkosazana* means 'Miss' or 'princess' in isiXhosa.
vi   Amina Cachalia (1930–2013), friend and anti-apartheid and women's rights activist – see the glossary.
vii   Lilian Ngoyi (1911–80), politician, and anti-apartheid and women's rights activist – see the glossary.

also received an equally inspiring condolence card from Irene.[i] She seems to be a wonderful girl & has built up an impressive image. This month I wrote to Mrs. Adelaide Mase, the wife of Mamqwati's[ii] brother at Engcobo, thanking them for the letter they wrote me in August. Mamqwati also wrote in Oct. in reply to the message I sent to her on behalf of you & I.

The salutation to this letter will not surprise you. In the past I have addressed you in affectionate terms for then I was speaking to Nobandla,[iii] wife of Ama-Dlomo.[iv] But on this occasion, I can claim no such prerogatives because in the freedom struggle we are all equals & your responsibility is as great as mine. We stand in the relationship, not of husband & wife, but of sister & brother. Until you return to 8115, or some other appointed place, this is how I will address you, OK? Perhaps this arrangement will provide room for the legions of students, medical or otherwise, that have crossed the life of one or other of us.

Finally, Mhlope,[v] I do wish you to know that you are the pride of my heart, & with you on my side, I always feel I am part of an invincible force that is ready to win new worlds. I am confident that, however dark & difficult times might seem to be now, one day you will be free & able to see the beautiful birds & lovely fields of our country, bath in its marvellous sunshine & breathe its sweet air. You will again see the picturesque scenery of the land of Faku[vi] where your childhood was spent, & the kingdom of Ngubengcuka[vii] where the ruins of your own kraal are to be found.

I miss you badly! Tons & tons of love & a million kisses.

Devotedly,
Dalibunga.

---

i   Possibly Irene Buthelezi, an old friend and the wife of Chief Mangosuthu Buthelezi, or Irene Mkwayi, wife of fellow prisoner Wilton Mkwayi (see the glossary).
ii   Evelyn Ntoko Mandela (1922–2004), Mandela's first wife (1944–1958) – see the glossary. Maqwati was her clan name, spelled by Mandela here as Mamqati.
iii Nobandla is one of Winnie Mandela's names.
iv   Mandela belonged to the AmaDlomo clan.
v   One of Winnie Mandela's names.
vi   King Faku controlled all of Pondoland. In 1854 he signed a treaty with the British which allowed him to reign supreme. Winnie Mandela's great-grandfather Madikizela was the last chief to sign a treaty with the British.
vii King Ngubengcuka was the great-grandfather of Mandela's father, Nkosi (chief) Mphakanyiswa Gadla Hendry (d. 1930).

NKOSIKAZI NOBANDLA MANDELA.c/o BRIGADIER
AUCAMP.[i]
PRETORIA.
24.3.70: Rewritten & handed in for posting per registered mail.
4.4.70: Registered slip given to me by H/W Joubert.

─────────

**To Thoko Mandela,[ii] his daughter-in-law & the widow of his son
Thembi[iii]**

29.11.69

My dear Thoko,

I have written no less than 7 letters on the death of Thembi either to
express my condolences to members of the family or to thank those
who kindly sent me messages of sympathy. On such an occasion I would
have liked to communicate with you immediately upon receiving the
tragic news, but I could not do so because I did not have your address.

Last July I wrote Kgatho for the address & other essential particulars but he gave me this information only when he visited me on Oct.
25. The previous month I had asked my niece, Tellie,[iv] to apply on
your behalf for a visiting permit, my intention at that time being to
write to you after you had been here. Beryl's[v] letter made me hope that
I would see you today. Instead Lulu[vi] came & although I look forward
to seeing you in December, I feel I can no longer delay this note.

Since the occurrence of the fatal accident, members of the family
& speakers at the graveside as well as friends in various parts of the
country will have said much that helped to raise your spirits & to bring
some sort of peace & hope in your bereavement.

Those who knew Thembi well may have spent the greater part of
their remarks of reminding you of his talents & achievements, his devo-

─────────

i   Brigadier Aucamp, commanding officer of Robben Island – see the glossary.
ii   See the glossary.
iii   Madiba Thembekile (Thembi) Mandela (1945–69), Mandela's eldest son – see the glossary.
iv   Telia (Telli or Tellie) Mtirara, a relative of Mandela's.
v   Beryl Lockman, Walter Sisulu's niece, who was living with Thoko. She later married Thoko's brother,
        Leonard Simelane.
vi   Lulama (Lulu) Mgudlwa was the niece of Mandela's former wife Evelyn Mandela.

tion to you & the children & his parents. Some may have emphasised that he was only 24 years when death claimed him, leaving behind a widow & two very young children to face all alone the grim & tricky world in which we live, & without the help, support & guidance a diligent husband & father would always be ready to give his family.

Others may have stressed the important fact that death comes to each & every family, striking down today either a beloved father or mother or child, brother or sister, [and] that what is essential is not so much the particular calamity that befalls you, but the attitude you adopt towards it. These and many other remarks of a similar nature will have been addressed to you by able & experienced speakers & I do not think it possible to enlarge on them; except to say that I was particularly happy to learn of the contribution made by your parents, the people of Cape Town & Johannesburg, & the large numbers that accompanied our Thembi to eternal rest.

Perhaps some day I will be privileged to meet your parents & thank them personally & directly for the love & help they gave him whilst he lived & for honouring him when he passed away. For the time being I would ask you to acquaint them with these sentiments.

The theme that I wish to discuss with you is one that you may have already thought of & perhaps even started to carry out. Thembi was only 19 when I last saw him, then attending school in Swaziland where I believe you met him. It was a difficult period in the life of any young person when all kinds of ideas were crossing the mind. I had been in jail for almost 2 years & had been unable to help him sort out the numerous problems that he was encountering.

Consequently, I never knew what your ambitions in life were nor am I familiar with your plans at the time of his death nor the resolutions & vows that you may have taken together. But according to Maki's[i] recent letter, both of you aimed high, a statement which confirms similar opinions given me by Mom Winnie. I will always remember him and will reserve July 13 every year as his day. Convey my sympathies to your brother on the death of his wife.

Perhaps the best way to remember Thembi is to do those things which he valued most in life, the things that made life enjoyable & meaningful to him & to carry out any of your joint resolutions as circumstances allow. In my letter to Thembi in '66 or '67, I suggested that both of you

---

i   Makaziwe Mandela (1954–), Mandela's eldest daughter – see the glossary.

should be careful not to neglect your education & that if you found it difficult to go back to boarding school, you should enrol for tuition with a Correspondence College. I want to repeat this suggestion for your consideration. Today there are millions of people throughout the world who are studying privately & who are making excellent progress. By raising their level of education, they increase their knowledge and become more valuable in serving their country & people. For you, Molokazana,[i] advanced studies would serve a double purpose. It would keep your mind engaged in some fruitful occupation which, in turn, will guarantee you some measure of security & independence. Secondly, it would make it easier for you to carry out your life dreams.

But you must bear in mind that this letter comes from one who has been in jail for a little more than 7 years & who is out of touch with developments in the country. You are the best judge & I leave the whole matter in your able hands. Remember that whether or not you accept my advice will not in any way affect my attitude towards you. You are my daughter-in-law of whom I am very proud. You are dear to me & I do look forward to seeing you next month. I hope your arm continues to improve & wish you complete recovery & good luck.

It was very nice for Lulu to motor down all the way from the Reef[ii] to visit me. I had not seen her ever since I was arrested & I spent 60 minutes of real pleasure & joy. In my present circumstances, it is very heartening to know that your relations think of you. I was also happy to have a glimpse of Beryl as she walked out. I was very impressed when I was given the report that she was living with you at this sad moment in your life. From various sources we continue to hear pleasant accounts of her. She seems to have inherited all the good qualities of her late mother who was very close to me[iii] & whose friendship I really valued. Love & fondest regards to Ndindi, Nandi[iv] and your parents. Yours very affectionately, Daddy

MRS LYDIA THOKO MANDELA
"HILLBROW"
SEVENTH AVENUE, RETREAT.

---

i   'Daughter-in-law' in isiXhosa.
ii   The Reef in Johannesburg refers to the gold reef where gold was first discovered by Australian George Harrison in 1896. That gold rush gave birth to Johannesburg, which is now part of Gauteng province.
iii   Rosabella (Barbie) Sisulu, Walter's sister, who married Thomas Lockman.
iv   Ndileka (1965–) and Nandi (1968–) Mandela, the daughters of his late son Thembi (for Thembi Mandela, see the glossary).

◇◇◇◇◇◇◇◇◇◇◇◇

In the following letter to Winnie Mandela, who was then on trial, Mandela reports on a review of a book by a South African author portraying the trial of Christ. According to Winnie Mandela's attorney, Joel Carlson, the first time he got to see her and her twenty-one co-accused, they had not been allowed to take a bath or a shower for 'nearly two hundred days'.[44] *By the time Mandela wrote this letter to her their trial had started. They were accused with furthering the aims of the ANC and conspiring to commit sabotage, although no acts of violence were alleged.*

Mandela was aware that this was quite literally the trial and test of his young wife's life, and his attempt at cheering her saw him dig deep into the story of the injustice of the trial of Christ, and by extension of her and other freedom fighters. If this letter reached her it would indeed have provided strength from an island at the end of the country.

To Winnie Mandela,[i] his wife

466/64 Nelson Mandela [in another hand]

January 1, 1970

Dade Wethu,[ii]

A novel by Langenhoven, *Skaduwees van Nasaret* (Shadows of Nazareth),[iii] depicts the trial of Christ by Pontius Pilate when Israel was a Roman dependency & when Pilate was its military governor. I read the novel in 1964 & now speak purely from memory. Yet though the incident described in the book occurred about 2000 years ago, the story contains a moral whose truth is universal & which is as fresh & meaningful today as it was at the height of the Roman Empire. After the trial, Pilate writes to a friend in Rome to whom he makes remarkable confessions. Briefly this is the story as told by him &, for convenience, I have put it in the first person:

As governor of a Roman province I have tried many cases involving

---

i   Nomzamo Winifred Madikizela-Mandela (1936–2018) – see the glossary.
ii   The usual spelling is Dadewethu, meaning sister.
iii   C. J. Langenhoven, *Skaduwees van Nasaret* (Nasionale Pers, 1927).

all types of rebels. But this trial of Christ I shall never forget! One day a huge crowd of Jewish priests & followers, literally shivering with rage and excitement, assembled just outside my palace & demanded that I crucify Christ for claiming to be king of the Jews, at the same time pointing to a man whose arms & feet were heavily chained. I looked at the prisoner & our eyes met. In the midst of all the excitement & noise, he remained perfectly calm, quiet & confident as if he had millions of people on his side. I told the priests that the prisoner had broken Jewish, & not Roman law & that they were the rightful people to try him. But in spite of my explanation they stubbornly persisted in demanding his crucifixion, immediately realised their dilemma. Christ had become a mighty force in the land & the masses of the people were fully behind him. In this situation the priests felt powerless & did not want to take the responsibility of sentencing & condemning him. Their only solution was to induce imperial Rome to do what they were unable to do.

At festival time it has always been the practice to release some prisoners & as the festival was now due, I suggested that this prisoner be set free. But instead, the priests asked that Barabas, a notorious prisoner, be released & that Christ be executed. At this stage I went into Court & ordered the prisoner to be brought in. My wife & those of other Roman officials occupied seats in the bay reserved for distinguished guests. As the prisoner walked in my wife & her companions instinctively got up as a mark of respect for Christ, but soon realised that this man was a Jew & a prisoner, & whereupon they resumed their seats. For the first time in my experience I faced a man whose eyes appeared to see right through me, whereas I was unable to fathom him. Written across his face was a gleam of love & hope; but at the same time he bore the expression of one who was deeply pained by the folly & suffering of mankind as a whole. He gazed upwards & his eyes seemed to pierce through the roof & to see right beyond the stars. It became clear that in that courtroom authority was not in me as a judge, but was down below in the dock where the prisoner was.

My wife passed me a note in which she informed me that the previous night she had dreamt that I had sentenced an innocent man whose only crime was that of messiah to his people. "There before you, Pilate is the man of my dream; let justice be done!" I knew that what my wife said was quite true, but my duty demanded that I sentence this man irrespective of his innocence. I put the note in my pocket & proceeded with the case. I informed the prisoner what the charge was against him, & asked him to indicate whether or not he was guilty. Several times he completely ignored me & it was clear that he considered the proceedings to be an utter fuss, as I had already made up my mind on the question of sentence. I repeated the question & assured him that I had authority to save his life. The prisoner's gleam dissolved into a smile & for the first time he spoke. He admitted that he was king & with that single & simple answer he totally destroyed me. I had expected that he would deny the charge as all prisoners do, & his admission brought things to a head.

You know, dear friend, that when a Roman judge tries a case in Rome, he is guided simply by the charge, the law & the evidence before the court, & his decision will be determined solely by these factors. But here in the provinces, far away from Rome, we are at war. A man who is in the field of battle is interested only in results, in victory & not in justice, & the judge is himself on trial. So it was, that even though I well knew that this man was innocent, my duty demanded that I give him the death sentence & so I did. The last time I saw him he was struggling towards Calvary amidst jeers, insults & blows, under the crushing weight of the heavy cross on which he was to die. I have decided to write you this personal letter because I believe that this confession to a friend will at least salve my uneasy conscience.

This in brief is the trial of Jesus & comment is unnecessary; save to say that Langenhoven wrote the story in the twenties (?)[i] to arouse the political consciousness of his people in a South Africa where & at a time when, in spite of the formal independence his people enjoyed, the organs of government, including the judiciary, were monopolised by Englishmen. To the Afrikaner, this story may recall unpleasant experiences & open up old wounds, but it belongs to a phase that has passed. To you and I it raises issues of a contemporary nature. I hope you will find it significant & useful, & trust it will bring you some measure of happiness. Molokazana[ii] paid me a visit this Saturday. She is a charming girl & I was really pleased to see her. On 14.1.70 she will be in Johannesburg for the "Kulula" ceremony.[iii] I am writing to

---

i   Mandela's own question mark.
ii   He is most likely referring to Thoko Mandela, his son Thembi's widow – see the glossary.
iii   A ceremony to mark the removal of mourning clothes. It was eighteen months since Thembi Mandela's death.

Ntambozenqanawa[i] to ask him & Jongintaba Mdingi[ii] to help her in this task. Last month I wrote to her, & to Vuyo Masondo[iii] & gave the latter our condolences on the death of her brother at Umtata. Tons & tons of love, Mhlope,[iv] and a million kisses. May good luck be on your side!

Devotedly, Dalibunga.

NKOSIKAZI NOBANDLA MANDELA, C/O BRIGADIER AUCAMP,[v] PRETORIA

To Nkosikazi Nokukhanya Luthuli, widow of former president-general of the ANC Chief Albert Luthuli[vi]

8th June 1970

Our dear Ma,

In July 1967 Major Kellerman, then Commanding Officer of this prison, gave permission for me to write you a special letter of condolence on behalf of all of us here on the occasion of the passing of the late Chief.

Under normal circumstances we would have certainly attended the funeral to pay homage directly to the memory of a great warrior as he passed from the stage into history. A veteran of many campaigns who was deeply loved by his people and respected far and wide as an outstanding champion of those who carried on their shoulders the curse of poverty and want, who were afflicted by disease and ignorance, who never knew real happiness and peace, and to whom opportunities for advancement and fulfilment were beyond reach. For a decade and a half he dominated the country's public life, and led us with great skill during one of the most difficult phases in our struggle for higher

---

i   Mandela's cousin, Chief Ntambozenqanawa Nkosiyane.
ii   The brother of Chief Mdingi who named Mandela's children Zenani and Zindziswa.
iii   The wife of fellow prisoner Andrew Masondo.
iv   One of Winnie Mandela's names.
v   Brigadier Aucamp, commanding officer of Robben Island – see the glossary.
vi   See the glossary.

ideals and a better life. The Chief was in many ways a remarkable man. He was a true nationalist whose feet were firmly planted in his native soil and who drew much strength and inspiration from the traditional background but who, nevertheless, had a progressive outlook and without the slightest trace of racial arrogance or parochialism. His forceful personality and keen brain were tempered by humility, modesty and unequivocal acceptance of the principle of collective leadership. Although he was always calm and restrained, those who came into contact with him were inspired by his warmth and friendship and by his readiness to appreciate other people's good work and talents. He was a national leader in the full sense of the term and especially qualified to lead a broad national movement. He was free of all sectarian tendencies, a dreadful disease which has crippled and even destroyed powerful movements, and which has at various times in our history raised its ugly head. It was a pleasure to watch him in action either as he addressed a public gathering, participated in a committee meeting (or as he gave his memorable evidence in the Treason Trial). His public speeches were simple and frank, and were delivered or expressed without any violent appeal to the emotions of the audience. In committee discussions he had the capacity to listen patiently and carefully to others and when he ultimately spoke he would highlight those issues which would bring about the widest possible measure of agreement. He never fell foul of the temptation of trying to display his knowledge, nor did he ever attempt to prove himself superior to any of his colleagues. Notwithstanding his training as teacher and his former position as tribal Chief, I have never had cause to feel that he approached his public duties with over-caution and conservatism. On the contrary, he consistently gave the impression of a patriot who was moved by radical and advanced ideas and who kept abreast with the most revolutionary of the younger generation.

(His death was a severe setback to our efforts to live decent and honourable lives.) To you it was a disastrous loss for it meant many years of loneliness, of toil and sweat without the expert and experienced help of a life-partner who was deeply attached to you. His death also deprived the children of the guidance of a father who was well-equipped to discharge the duties of parenthood because he was in the centre of public activity and highly sensitive to progressive ideas. We regretted his loss to you and the family and to the community as a whole and gave you our sincere sympathy. We were certain, however, that the immense courage that you had shown throughout the most dangerous period of the Chief's public career, would carry you through that unfortunate experience. We also expressed the hope that the huge crowds that would turn up at the funeral and the numerous messages of condolence that would come from various parts of the world, might serve as a tonic to your wounded feelings.

That letter was in our current circumstances the only means we had of conveying to you and the family the sentiments expressed above, and we did not have the slightest suspicion that you would not receive it. How great was our disappointment when we learnt that it did not reach you! About three months after I had handed in the letter for posting away, I wrote to Alan[i] and gave him our sympathy on the death of his wife. We felt that fate had treated him very savagely in taking away his wife so soon after the death of his friend, the Chief. (We praised the firm stand he had taken on many public questions and thanked him for the evidence in mitigation that he gave on our behalf at the Rivonia Trial[ii]), and concluded the letter by telling him that we were confident that neither family tragedy nor advancing age would induce him to lay down the harness. We now know that Alan's letter never reached also. We cannot imagine that anybody would deliberately interfere with condolence letters and prevent them from reaching the bereaved. I am, however, taking the precaution of having this one registered to ensure its safe arrival. In our present environment kind words achieve an impact that is not easy or wise to analyse. It is sufficient to say that they achieve far more than the mere act of boosting morale. Your short but sweet note of January 1966 exceedingly excited us. It pleased us much to hear that the world, our people and particularly your Ma think of us every day. Your letter is amongst my most treasured possessions. Fondest regards and love to Norman, Fana, Ntombazana, and Kwena, Thandeka and Tulani; Sibongile and Dr Ngobese[iii] and to all the young children.

---

i   Alan Paton (1903–88), author and founder and leader of South Africa's anti-apartheid Liberal Party. He gave evidence in mitigation of sentence for Mandela and his co-accused at the Rivonia Trial – see the glossary.

ii   Alan Paton said that like everyone else, African people aspired 'to live a decent life' and that Mandela was heir apparent to ANC president-general Chief Albert Luthuli. Speaking of the accused, he said, 'I have never had any doubt about their sincerity, their deep devotion to the cause of their people, and their desire to see that South Africa became a country in which all people could participate.' (Joel Joffe, *The State vs. Nelson Mandela: The Trial That Changed South Africa* (London: One World Publications, 2007) p. 249.)

iii   All fellow activists, including Dr. Helen Ngobese, a friend of Winnie Mandela's who was one of her bridesmaids.

Yours very sincerely,
Nelson

Nkosikazi Nokukhanya Luthuli
P.O. Groutville, Stanger, Natal

To Winnie Mandela,[i] his wife

20th June 1970

Dade Wethu,[ii]

Indeed, "the chains of the body are often wings to the spirit." It has
been so long, and so it will always be. Shakespeare in As You Like It[iii]
puts the same idea somewhat differently:
"Sweet are the uses of adversity,
Which like a toad, ugly and venomous,
Wears yet a precious jewel in the head."[iv]

Still others have proclaimed that 'only great aims can arouse great
energies.'
Yet my understanding of the real idea behind these simple words
throughout the 26 years of my career of storms has been superficial,
imperfect & perhaps a bit scholastic. There is a stage in the life of
every social reformer when he will thunder on platforms primarily to
relieve himself of the scraps of indigested information that has accumulated in his head; an attempt to impress the crowds rather than to
start a calm & simple exposition of principles & ideas whose universal
truth is made evident by personal experience & deeper study. In this
regard I am no exception & I have been victim of the weakness of my
own generation not once but a hundred times. I must be frank & tell
you that when I look back at some of my early writings & speeches
I am appalled by their pedantry, artificiality and lack of originality.

---

i   Nomzamo Winifred Madikizela-Mandela (1936–2018) – see the glossary.
ii   Normally written as one word, this means 'sister' in isiXhosa.
iii   This is likely to be Mandela's underlining.
iv   William Shakespeare, As You Like It, Act 2, scene 1.

The urge to impress & advertise is clearly noticeable. What a striking contrast your letters make, Mhlope![i] I hesitate to heap praises on you but you will pardon my vanity and conceit, Ngutyana.[ii] To pay you a compliment may amount to self-praise on my part as you & I are one. Perhaps under the present conditions this type of vanity may serve as a powerful lever to our spirits.

During the 8 lonely years I have spent behind bars I sometimes wished we were born the same hour, grown up together and spent every minute of our lives in each other's company. I sincerely believe that had this been the case I would have been a wise man. Every one of your letters is a precious possession & often succeeds in arousing forces I never suspected to be concealed in my being. In your hands the pen is really mightier than a sabre. Words flow out freely & naturally & common expressions acquire a meaning that is at once challenging & stimulating.

The first paragraph of your moving note, & more especially the opening line, shook me violently. I literally felt every one of the millions of atoms that make up my body pulling forcefully in all directions. The beautiful sentiments you have repeatedly urged on me since my arrest & conviction, & particularly during the last 15 months, are clearly the result more of actual experience than of scholasticism. They come from a woman who has not seen her husband for almost 2 years, who has been excluded from her tender children for more than 12 months & who has been hard hit by loneliness, pining & illness under conditions least conducive for recovery, & who on top of all that must face the most strenuous test of her life.

I understand perfectly well, darling, when you say you miss me & that one of the few blows you found hard to take was not hearing from me. The feeling is mutual, but it is plain that you have gone through a far more ravaging experience than I have ever had. I tried hard & patiently to communicate with you. I sent you a long note on Nov. 16;[iii] thereafter a Xmas card, and again a letter on Jan. 1[iv] – all were written at a time when you were an awaiting-trial prisoner. After Feb. 13 I was informed that I could not communicate with you & my earnest plea for a relaxation of this particular restriction was unsuccessful.

---

i   One of Winnie Mandela's names.
ii   One of Winnie Mandela's names. She comes from the amaNgutyana clan.
iii   See his letter on page 91.
iv   See his letter on page 99.

Your illness has been stubborn & persistent, and I would have expected to be given a proper medical report by the Prisons' Department to help ease my mind. Brig. Aucamp[i] gave me a very generalised account which disturbed me intensely. I was shocked to learn that you had to be hospitalised & to actually see evidence of your present state of health in your sloppy handwriting. I believe you completely when you say that you have shrunk to Zeni's[ii] size. It was some sort of relief to hear that you have been seen by numerous specialists & that blood tests have been taken. But I know, Mntakwethu,[iii] that every piece of your bone, ounce of flesh & drop of blood; your whole being is hewed in one piece out of granite, & that nothing whatsoever, including ailment, can blow out the fires that are burning in your heart. Up on your feet! Onward to duty! My love and devotion is your armour & the ideal of a free South Africa your banner.

A few days after your arrest in May last year I asked for a special letter to my attorney[iv] in connection with the following urgent matters:

1.   The appointment of a caretaker for the house & for the payment of rent;
2.   The appointment of a legal guardian for the children;
3.   The making of arrangements for the maintenance, upbringing & education of the children;
4.   The making of arrangements for the raising of funds for your education, toilet & other requirements in the event of your being found guilty and imprisoned;
5.   The making of arrangements for the raising of funds for my own education, toilet & other requirements during your absence in jail.

Although I have made repeated representations on several occasions, the application was not granted. I have, however, now instructed Mr Brown of the firm of Frank, Bernadt and Joffe[v] in Cape Town to give immediate attention to these matters. I agree with your

---

i   Brigadier Aucamp, commanding officer of Robben Island – see the glossary.
ii   Zenani Mandela (1959–), their eldest daughter, who was then eleven years old – see the glossary.
iii   A term of endearment in isiXhosa.
iv   See his letter to Messrs Frank, Bernadt & Joffe, 20 May 1969, page 61–2, although not all the points he mentions here were actually included in that letter.
v   His attorneys. The instructions were never received.

suggestion that Father Leon Rakale & Uncle Mashumi[i] be appointed joint guardians of the children. I should like to add Uncle Marsh's[ii] name. I wrote him an urgent letter on February 3 in connection with the house. I doubt if he ever received it. He never responded. When Kgatho[iii] visited me on Jan. 31 he indicated that he & Tellie[iv] were in favour of Lulu[v] (Mxolisi's sister) moving into the house. I informed Uncle Marsh of this fact & indicated that I would be happy if she did, provided you approved. Mxolisi visited me last Saturday & she says they have not heard from Marsh. Perhaps you would like to discuss the matter with him & Niki[vi] when they next pay you a visit. I also doubt if Mashumi received my note written on Nov. 19 & rewritten on Apr. 4. I asked him to give me a report on Zeni & Zindzi[vii] and to help get Kgatho to varsity. I received no reply from Mashumi as well. Kgatho is at home and I have no proper information as to why he failed to go to Fort Hare.[viii] I made the necessary arrangements for payment of fees & allowance & when he came down in Jan. he confirmed that everything had been fixed & that he would leave for varsity on Feb. 14. I believe he is not working. My letter to him on March 31st produced no response.

I have written 3 letters to Zeni & Zindzi. I now know that the first 2 never reached them. The 3rd one was written on June 1st. I have received no information whatsoever on them since your arrest save & except the reports you gave me. Of course Niki's letter of Sep. 9 informed me that they were well.

I, however, hope to straighten out the whole affair with Mr. Brown soon & will arrange for you to be regularly informed.

I have raised the question of my paying you a visit once more & I can tell you nothing at present apart from saying that Brig. Aucamp has promised to discuss the matter with the Commissioner. Speaking frankly, I think the Commissioner has been unusually hard & has not shown the consideration & assistance that I normally expect from him in circumstances of this nature.

Dade Wethu, I wish I could have been in a position to tell you

---

i   Winnie Mandela's uncle, Paul Mzaidume.
ii   Marshall Xaba, husband of Niki Xaba, Winnie Mandela's eldest sister (for Niki Xaba, see the glossary).
iii   Makgatho (Kgatho) Mandela (1950–2005), Mandela's second-born son – see the glossary.
iv   Telia (Telli or Tellie) Mtirara, a relative of Mandela's.
v   Lulama (Lulu) was the niece of his former wife Evelyn Mandela.
vi   Niki Xaba (1932–1985), Winnie Mandela's eldest sister – see the glossary.
vii   Zindziswa Mandela (1960–), his youngest daughter – see the glossary.
viii   University College of Fort Hare, Alice in the Ciskei homeland – see the glossary.

something that could gladden your heart & make you smile. But as I see it we may have to wait a long time for that bright & happy moment. In the meantime we must 'drink the cup of bitterness to the dregs.' Perhaps, no I am sure, the good old days will come when life will sweeten our tongues & nurse our wounds. Above all remember March 10. That is the source of our strength. I never forget it.

Tons and tons of love, Mhlope, [i] and a million kisses.
Devotedly.
Dalibunga

Nkosikazi Nobandla Mandela
Pretoria Prison

To Winnie Mandela,[ii] his wife

August 1, 1970

Dade Wethu,[iii]

Can it be that you did not receive my letter of July 1? How can I explain your strange silence at a time when contact between us has become so vital?

In June I learnt for the first time that you had been confined to bed for 2 months & that your condition[iv] was so bad that you did not appear with your friends when the case came up for formal remand. Is your silence due to a worsening of your health or did the July letter suffer the fate of the 39 monthly letters, letters in lieu of visits & specials that I have written since your arrest on May 12 '69, all of which, save 2, seemed not to have reached their destination? Not

---

i   One of Winnie Mandela's names.
ii   Nomzamo Winifred Madikizela-Mandela (1936–2018) – see the glossary
iii   'Sister' in isiXhosa.
iv   Winnie Mandela had a heart condition.

even Kgatho, Maki, Zeni, Zindzi,[i] Tellie,[ii] Ma of Bizana,[iii] Marsh[iv] & Mashumi[v] responded. I am becoming increasingly uneasy every day. I know you would respond quickly if you heard from me & I fear that you have not done so because you either did not receive the letter or you are not fit to write.

The crop of miseries we have harvested from the heartbreaking frustrations of the last 15 months are not likely to fade away easily from the mind. I feel as if I have been soaked in gall, every part of me, my flesh, bloodstream, bone & soul, so bitter am I to be completely powerless to help you in the rough & fierce ordeals you are going through. What a world of difference to your failing health & to your spirit, darling, to my own anxiety & the strain that I cannot shake off, if only we could meet; if I could be on your side & squeeze you, or if I could but catch a glimpse of your outline through the thick wire netting that would inevitably separate us. Physical suffering is nothing compared to the trampling down of those tender bonds of affection that form the basis of the institution of marriage & the family that unite man & wife. This is a frightful moment in our life. It is a moment of challenge to cherished beliefs, putting resolutions to a severe test.

But as long as I still enjoy the privilege of communicating with you, even though it may only exist in form for me, & until it is expressly taken away, the records will bear witness to the fact that I tried hard & earnestly to reach you by writing every month. I owe you this duty & nothing will distract me from it. Maybe this line will one day pay handsome dividends. There will always be good men on earth, in all countries, & even here at home. One day we may have on our side the genuine & firm support of an upright & straightforward man, holding high office, who will consider it improper to shirk his duty of protecting the rights & privileges of even his bitter opponents in the battle of ideas that is being fought in our country today; an official who will have a sufficient sense of justice & fairness to make available to us not only the rights & privileges that the law allows us today, but who will also compensate us for those that were surreptitiously taken away. In spite of all that has happened I have, throughout the ebb & flow of the tides of fortune in the last 15 months, lived in hope &

---

i   His four children.
ii   Telia (Telli or Tellie) Mtirara, a relative of Mandela's.
iii   Nophikela Hilda Madikizela, Winnie Mandela's stepmother.
iv   Marshall Xaba, husband of Niki Xaba, Winnie Mandela's eldest sister (for Niki Xaba, see the glossary).
v   Winnie Mandela's uncle, Paul Mzaidume.

expectation. Sometimes I even have the belief that this feeling is part & parcel of my self. It seems to be woven into my being. I feel my heart pumping hope steadily to every part of my body, warming my blood & pepping up my spirits. I am convinced that floods of personal disaster can never drown a determined revolutionary nor can the cumulus of misery that accompanies tragedy suffocate him. To a freedom fighter hope is what a life-belt is to a swimmer – guarantee that one will keep afloat & free from danger. I know, darling, that if riches were to be counted in terms of the tons of hope & sheer courage that nestle in your breast (this idea I got from you) you would certainly be a million-aire. Remember this always.

By the way, the other day I dreamt of you convulsing your entire body with a graceful Hawaiian dance at the B.M.S.C.[i] I stood at one end of the famous hall with arms outstretched ready to embrace you as you whirled towards me with the enchanting smile that I miss so desperately. I cannot explain why the scene should have located at the B.M.S.C. To my recollection we have been there for a dance only once – on the night of Lindi's[ii] wedding reception. The other occasion was the concert we organised in 1957 when I was courting you, or you me. I am never certain whether I am free to remind you that you took the initiative in this regard.[iii] Anyway the dream was for me a glorious moment. If I must dream in my sleep, please hawaii for me. I like to see you merry & full of life.

I enjoyed reading Fatima's "Portrait of Indian S. Africans"[iv] – a vivid description of Indian life written in a beautiful & simple style. With characteristic modesty she describes the title in the preface as still pretentious for a book that only skims the surface. But the aspects that form its theme are skilfully probed. She raises an issue of wider interest when she points out that "differences that divide are not dif-ferences of custom, of rituals & tradition, but differences of status, of standard of living, of access to power and power-gaining techniques. These are the differences that have at all known times determined the destinies of persons & people, and the same people and the same

---

i   The Bantu Men's Social Centre (BMSC), founded in Johannesburg, in 1924, was an important cultural, social, and political meeting place for black South Africans. Its facilities included a gym and a library, and it hosted boxing matches, political meetings, and dances. Mandela and others founded the ANC Youth League there in 1944.

ii   One of Lionel Ngakane's sisters.

iii   Mandela met Winnie Madikizela when she was consulting with his colleague Oliver Tambo in 1957. They went on their first date on 10 March 1957 and married on 14 June 1958.

iv   Fatima Meer, *Portrait of Indian South Africans* (Durban: Avon House, 1969).

cultures have at one point enjoyed high privilege and at another none."
The book contains chapters which touch on other fundamental matters & I fear that some of her observations on current public questions
may spark off animated debates. I welcome the brutal frankness of her
pen, but it may be that once she elects to raise such matters her duty
is not only to comment but to inspire, to leave her fellow countrymen
with hope & something to live for. I hope you will be able to read the
book before the case ends. It is a brilliant work written by a brilliant
scholar. I thoroughly enjoyed it.

Mr Brown, our Cape Town attorney, should have been here on July
29 in connection with the question of guardianship of the children.[i]
The sea was very rough & this may probably be the reason for his
failure to turn up. I am hoping that he will come soon. In the meantime I am writing to our friend, Duggie Lukhele,[ii] requesting him to
check on them & to give us a detailed report. I shall certainly keep you
informed of developments. Do not allow yourself to be agitated by the
chaos in our household affairs & by the difficulties we are having in
communicating officially & openly with each other. This is a phase in
our life that will pass & leave us still there, & perhaps even growing
stronger. I almost forgot to tell you that my second application to see
you was summarily rejected, notwithstanding the fact that I had cited
your present illness as one reason for renewing the application. The
Commissioner did not even consider it his duty to allay my fears by
giving me a report on your condition.[iii] There was a time when such
experiences would make me wild; now I can take them calmly. I have
become used to them. Keep well, my darling; do not allow yourself
to be run down by illness or longing for the children. Fight with all
your strength. My fist is firm. Tons & tons of love & a million kisses.
Devotedly, Dalibunga

Nkosikazi Nobandla Mandela, Central Prison, Pretoria

---

i This request by Mandela to visit was never received.
ii Douglas Lukhele, Harvard-educated Swazi lawyer who did his articles at Mandela and Oliver Tambo's
   law firm in the 1950s. He was the first Swazi attorney-general and high court judge in Swaziland.
iii Brigadier Aucamp was also in touch with Winnie Mandela as he was in charge of security at all prisons
   where there were inmates held for politically related offences.

To Senator Douglas Lukhele,[i] friend and former colleague

August 1, 1970

My dear Duggie,

Our children, Zeni & Zindzi,[ii] aged 11 & 10 respectively, are at "Our Lady of Sorrows," a Roman Catholic boarding school at Hluti.[iii] We are extremely disturbed because, since Zami's[iv] detention on May 12 last year, we have heard nothing about them. Information reached me that they spend their holidays with Allan.[v] I should have liked to write directly to him & wife, to thank them for the hospitality, but I am not sure whether, having regard to his present position, I am free to do so. I [would] like them to know that Zami & I are sincerely grateful. I believe Mrs Birley,[vi] now lecturing in a British university, had arranged scholarships for the children at Waterford[vii] for next year. I have written them 3 letters & sent a birthday card, but none seems to have reached. Please investigate & give me a detailed report, preferably by registered letter, at your earliest possible convenience. Letters from me hardly ever reach [their] destination & those addressed to me fare no better. I am hoping that the remorseless fates, that consistently interfere with my correspondence & that have cut me off from my family at such a critical moment, will be induced by considerations of honour & honesty to allow this one through. I know that once it reaches your hands my troubles will be virtually over.

You know that I am essentially a rustic like many of my contemporaries, born & brought up in a country village[viii] with its open spaces, lovely scenery & plenty of fresh air. Although prior to my arrest & conviction 8 years ago I lived for two decades as a townsman, I never succeeded in shaking off my peasant background, & now & again I

---

i   Harvard-educated Swazi lawyer Douglas Lukhele did his articles at Mandela and Oliver Tambo's law
     firm in the 1950s. He was the first Swazi attorney-general and high court judge in Swaziland.
ii   Zenani Mandela (1959–) and Zindziswa Mandela (1960–), Mandela's middle and youngest daughters –
     see the glossary.
iii Hluti is in Swaziland.
iv   One of Winnie Mandela's names.
v   Dr. Allen Nxumalo (Mandela misspelled his name 'Allan'), a medical doctor and friend of the
     Mandelas'. Leader of the Swaziland Democratic Party, which was dissolved after independence in 1968,
     and Swaziland's first minister of health.
vi   Lady Elinor Birley (Mandela misspelled her name as 'Eleanor') whose husband Sir Robert Birley
     (1903–82), was the former headmaster of Eton College and at the time the visiting professor of
     education at the University of the Witwatersrand. Whilst there, the Birley's worked to acquire books to
     establish a library in Soweto, which then became known as the Birley Library.
vii Waterford Kamhlaba school in neighbouring Swaziland.
viii Qunu in the Transkei.

spent a few weeks in my home district as a means of recalling the
happy moments of my childhood. Throughout my imprisonment my
heart & soul have always been somewhere far beyond this place, in the
veld[i] & the bushes. I live across these waves with all the memories &
experiences I have accumulated over the last half century – memories
of the grounds in which I tended stock, hunted, played, & where I had
the privilege of attending the traditional initiation school.[ii] I see myself
moving into the Reef[iii] in the early forties, to be caught up in the fer-
ment of the radical ideas which were stirring the more conscious of the
African youth. (Incidentally it was at this stage that I first met Allan,
then a clerk at Union College.) I remember the days when I served
articles, licking stamps daily, running all sorts of errands, including
buying hair shampoo & other cosmetics for white ladies. Chancellor
House![iv] It was there that OR[v] & I became even more intimate than we
were as college mates & as Leaguers.[vi] Around us there developed new
& fruitful friendships – Maindy,[vii] Zubeida Patel & Winnie Mandleni,
our first typists;[viii] the late Mary Anne, whose sudden and untimely
death greatly distressed us, Ruth,[ix] Mavis, Godfrey,[x] boxing Freddy &
Charlie the upright & popular caretaker & cleaner who never missed
a day at Mai-Mai.[xi] For some time you battled almost alone & against
formidable difficulties to keep the firm afloat when OR and I were
immobilised by the Treason Trial. I even recall the strange incident
that occurred when you visited Zami & I at our home in Orlando West
in Dec. '60. As you approached the gate a bolt of lightning split out

---

i   'Field' in Afrikaans.

ii   Mandela describes the importance of initiation into manhood in *Long Walk to Freedom*: 'For the Xhosa
      people, circumcision represents the formal incorporation of males into society. It is not just a surgical
      procedure, but a lengthy and elaborate ritual in preparation for manhood. As a Xhosa, I count my years
      as a man from the date of my circumcision.' (NM., p. 30.)

iii   The Reef in Johannesburg refers to the gold reef where gold was first discovered by Australian George
      Harrison in 1896. That gold rush gave birth to Johannesburg, which is now part of Gauteng province.

iv   Chancellor House was the building in which Mandela and Oliver Tambo started their law practice,
      Mandela and Tambo, in 1952.

v   Oliver Reginald Tambo (1917–93), friend, former law partner, and the president of the ANC – see the
      glossary.

vi   Members of the ANC Youth League established in 1944. More militant African youth like A. P. Mda
      (1916–93), Anton Lembede (1914–47), Walter Sisulu (1912–2003), Jordan Ngubane (1917–85),
      Victor Mbobo, William Nkomo (1915–72), David Bopape (1915–2004), Oliver Tambo (1917–93) and
      Mandela helped to found the organisation proposed by Dr. Lionel Majombozi (d. 1949).

vii   Maindy Msimang (1928–2018), also know an Mendi Msimang, was an administrative officer of the
      ANC in London.

viii For the law firm Mandela and Tambo.

ix   Ruth Mompati (1925–2015) was also one of Mandela and Tambo's typists. She became a member of
      the ANC and was one of the leaders of the 1956 Women's March to protest pass laws for black women.

x   Godfrey Pitje (1917–97), former ANC Youth League president and lawyer who served his articles at
      Mandela and Tambo.

xi   One of the oldest traditional medicine markets in Johannesburg.

with such tremendous force that Zeni, then only 10 months, was flung to the ground where she remained motionless for some seconds. What a relief it was when she came round & started yelling; it was a close shave. Your presence at the D.O.C.C.[i] on that occasion put a new & deeper meaning to your magnificent stand at Winburg[ii] & added more weight & lustre to the eulogies that have since been heaped on you in memory of your outstanding service to the womenfolk.

Lenvick! There you established yourself with Manci as articled clerk & ably assisted by the smooth & energetic Joe Magame. I have not forgotten the good things you did for me personally those days. I was still involved in the T.T.[iii] & during adjournments you kept me busy by giving me work, & it thus became possible for me to assist Zami in some way to keep the home fires burning. I hope one day I shall be able to reciprocate. Anyway I was very happy when I was informed that your fatherland,[iv] the beautiful country which is full of so much promise & potential, could now avail itself of your talents to the fullest extent. I was even more pleased to be told that you were now [a] member of your country's Senate. But I knew at the same time that it must have been a grievous blow for you to sever connections with a country you had chosen to be your permanent home & to be cut off from a community you had served so faithfully & courageously. These & other reminiscences, occupy the long & difficult moments of my present life. Spiritual weapons can be dynamic & often have an impact difficult to appreciate except in the light of actual experience in given situations. In a way they make prisoners free men, turn commoners into monarchs, & dirt into pure gold. To put it quite bluntly, Duggie, it is only my flesh & bones that are shut up behind these tight walls. Otherwise I remain cosmopolitan in my outlook, in my thoughts I am as free as a falcon. The anchor of all my dreams is the collective wisdom of mankind as a whole. I am influenced more than ever before by the

---

i   The Donaldson Orlando Community Centre was a community space in Soweto that hosted dances, concerts, and boxing matches. It was built by the Donaldson Trust, established in 1936 by Lieutenant Colonel James Donaldson D.S.O. to 'advance the status, improve the conditions and remove the disabilities suffered by the black African population of South Africa; and generally to seek their benefit and betterment'. Nelson Mandela used to box there in the 1940s and 1950s and spent many of his evenings training at the gym with his eldest son, Thembi.

ii He is possibly referring to a protest at Winburg in the Orange Free State (now called Free State).

iii The Treason Trial (1956–61) was a result of the apartheid government's attempt to quell the power of the Congress Alliance, a coalition of anti-apartheid organisations. In early-morning raids on 5 December 1956, 156 individuals were arrested and charged with high treason. By the end of the trial in March 1961 all the accused either had the charges withdrawn or, in the case of the last twenty-eight accused (including Mandela), were acquitted.

iv Douglas Lukhele was from Swaziland.

conviction that social equality is the only basis of human happiness. We & the children of Mswati[i] & Mbandzeni[ii] are linked by a million threads. We have a common history & common aspirations. What is precious to you touches our own hearts. It is in this light that we think of Sept. 6[iii] – an historic event that marks the close of an epoch & the rise of a people whose national pride & consciousness helped them to survive the changes of fortune brought by the imperialist era to our Continent. It is around these issues that my thoughts revolve. They are centred on humans, the ideas for which they strive; on the new world that is emerging, the new generation that declares total war against all forms of cruelty, against any social order that upholds economic privilege for a minority & that condemns us the mass of the population to poverty & disease, illiteracy & the host of evils that accompany a stratified society. Remember me to Ntlabati, Leslie's wife, Andrew & wife, Stanley Lollan,[iv] Maggie Chuene, Regina Twala, Wilson & Gladys[v] if they are still around. I am particularly grateful to Wilson for looking after my son, Kgatho,[vi] after he had been expelled from school for organising a strike, & for all the help he & Gladys gave him. Let everyone keep well & be of good cheer; my fist is firm! Yours very sincerely, Nel

Senator D. Lukhele, Parliament, Lobamba, Swaziland

To the minister of justice[vii]

14th September 1970

The Minister of Justice,
Union Buildings
Pretoria.

---

i   Mswati II (c.1820–68), king of Swaziland 1840–68.
ii   Ingwenyama Mbandzeni (1855–1899), the son of Mswati II and Nandzi Nkambule. King of Swaziland, 1875–89.
iii   Swaziland became independent from British rule on 6 September 1968.
iv   A former Treason trialist (for the Treason Trial, see the glossary) who then lived in Swaziland.
v   Friends of Mandela's.
vi   Makgatho Mandela (1950–2005), Mandela's second-born son – see the glossary.
vii   South Africa's minister of justice from 1966 to 1974 was Petrus Cornelius Pelser.

17th September 1970

The Minister of Justice,
Union Buildings
Pretoria.

My wife was detained on May 12, 1970 and has been in custody ever since.

I last saw her in December 1968. Twice after her arrest, I asked the Commissioner of Prisons to make arrangements for me to meet her. The second application was made after I had received information that she had been hospitalised as a result of deteriorating health. Both applications were refused. I now make a special appeal to you to approve the request.

There are important and urgent domestic problems which we cannot properly solve without being together. In examining the matter you will bear in mind that there is nothing in the law or administration of justice to preclude me as husband from having access to her while she is facing trial, political or otherwise. On the contrary it is my duty to give her all the help that she requires. The fact that I am a prisoner ought not of itself to deprive me of the opportunity of honouring the obligations that I owe her. You will also bear in mind that she has been in custody for more than 15 months, 10 of which were spent in solitary confinement — a frightful experience which must have been primarily responsible for the worsening of her condition. I sincerely believe that the pleasure she would derive from a meeting between us would induce a speedy and complete recovery, and put her in a better position to stand trial.

In considering both applications, General Steyn failed to show that high sense of values and human feeling that I have come to associate with him as an individual during the last 8 years. I am willing to hope that you, as executive head of the Department of Justice, are well instructed in the principles of rightness and equity not to turn a deaf ear to this appeal, and that the whole bent of your mind will be used to uphold those virtues that your office symbolises.

NRMandela
NELSON MANDELA: 466/64

Letter to the minister of justice, 14 September 1970, see pages 116–8.

My wife was detained on May 12, 1969 and has been in custody ever since.

I last saw her in December 1968. Twice after her arrest, I asked the Commissioner of Prisons[i] to make arrangements for me to meet her. The second application was made after I had received information that she had been hospitalised as a result of deteriorating health. Both applications were refused. I now make a special appeal to you to approve the request.

There are important and urgent domestic problems which we cannot properly solve without coming together. In examining the matter you will bear in mind that there is nothing in the law or administration of justice to preclude me as husband from having consultations with her while she is facing trial, political or otherwise. On the contrary, it is my duty to give her all the help that she requires. The fact that I am a prisoner ought not of itself to deprive me of the opportunity of honouring the obligations that I owe her. You will also bear in mind that she has been in custody for more than 15 months, 10 of which were spent in solitary confinement – a frightful experience which must have been primarily responsible for the worsening of her condition.[ii] I sincerely believe that the pleasure she would derive from a meeting between us would induce a speedy and complete recovery, and put her in a better position to stand trial.

In considering both applications, General Steyn failed to show that high sense of values and human feeling that I have come to associate with him as an individual during the last 8 years. I am willing to hope that you, as executive head of the Department of Justice, are well instructed in the principle of rightness and equity not to turn a deaf ear to this appeal, and that the whole bent of your mind will be used to uphold those virtues that your office symbolises.

[Signed NR Mandela]
Nelson Mandela: 466/64

◇◇◇◇◇◇◇◇◇◇◇◇

---

i   General Steyn.
ii   Winnie Mandela had a heart condition.

Winnie Mandela was released on 15 September 1970 after 491 days in custody. Two weeks later her banning orders – effective house arrest – were renewed for another five years. She was forced to remain at home from 6 p.m. to 6 a.m. on weekdays and from 2 p.m. to 6 a.m. on weekends. She was not allowed to have visitors other than her own children. She applied for permission to visit her husband in prison whom she had last visited on 28 September 1968 for one hour. The local magistrate rejected her application. She eventually got permission and was allowed to see him on 7 November 1970 for thirty minutes.

────────────

To Winnie Mandela,[i] his wife

October 1, 1970

My Darling,

A respite at last! I received your unexpected telegram in which you informed me of your release. I'm sure you were as surprised to be acquitted as I was when I received the wonderful news. I should have liked to reply also by telegram immediately upon receiving yours, but these conveniences are not available for me even on so important an occasion as an acquittal on a capital charge. I had to wait for 2 weeks before I could send you my warmest congratulations for serving 491,[ii] & still emerge the lively girl you are, & in high spirits.

To you & your determined friends I say welcome back! Were I at home when you returned I should have stolen a white goat from a rich man, slaughtered it & given you ivanya ne ntloya[iii] to down it. Only in this way can a beggar like myself fete and honour his heroes.

You are back & in accordance with my promise I bid good-bye to "dadewethu"[iv] & return to "My darling", to you dear Mhlope.[v] This is

─────────────

i   Nomzamo Winifred Madikizela-Mandela (1936–2018) – see the glossary.
ii   Winnie Mandela had served 491 days in prison.
iii   A traditional southern African welcome drink that is served hot to guests. It is made from the sediment of a traditional maize and sorghum beer, called *umqombothi*, mixed with *intloya*, the watery part of *amasi* (sour milk drink).
iv   'Sister' in isiXhosa. He was making a point of referring to her in this way because he was treating her as a comrade in the struggle against apartheid.
v   One of Winnie Mandela's names.

the salutation I have used since Aug. '62,[i] & I regretted it much when I had to abandon it.

Now that you are back I long for you even much more than I did when you were in. I fought hard to see you in the knowledge that such a meeting would do you a lot of good. But I did so also to save myself from catastrophe. There were times when I felt & responded like one in whom something had suddenly snapped. I could hardly concentrate & the picture of you rotting away in some dingy & isolated apartment with nothing to read & nobody to whom you might talk was unbearable. Your release has relieved me, but it has worsened my pining. I can no longer wait. I want to see you badly; it is now my turn to shrink to a size less than that of Zeni.[ii] When will you come? How I wish I could have a contact visit, where I could hug you, feel the warmth of your blood, smile straight into your eyes, chat to you normally, without having to shout before I could be heard, as happens at present. I long to see you in a peaceful & decent atmosphere, as a man & wife should when discussing tender domestic affairs after a separation of almost 2 years. But those who bear the cross ought never to squeal if the going is uphill, & I shan't. How is your health? Have you seen Zeni & Zindzi?[iii] What news will you bring me?

Incidentally, several hours before I received your exciting message I had handed in a letter addressed to the Minister of Justice asking him to allow us to meet. I imagine me still fighting long after the battle had been won. If your plea had been dismissed by the Court & my application to the Minister refused, I would probably have appealed to a bone-thrower, or beseeched the Divinitus or turned to Marx. Luckily I did not have to choose amongst these alternatives. I was sorry to learn that Ramotse[iv] remained behind. May he also have luck when the case goes to trial.

You have heard by now that our friend Mr Denis Healey,[v] accom-

---

i   Mandela was arrested on 5 August 1962.

ii   Zenani Mandela (1959–), Mandela's middle daughter.

iii Zenani Mandela (1959–) and Zindziswa Mandela (1960–), Mandela's middle and youngest daughters – see the glossary. The girls were at boarding school in Swaziland.

iv   MK activist Benjamin Ramotse was seriously injured in December 1961 in one of the first MK explosions that killed fellow combatant Petrus Molefi. Ramotse was arrested and put on trial but escaped the country while on bail. In his book *No Neutral Ground*, Joel Carson describes how Ramotse 'conducted guerrilla activities on the borders of South Africa for the next eight years when he was kidnapped from Botswana and brought through Rhodesia to South Africa to be tried finally in 1970'. (London: Davis-Poynter Ltd, 1973, p. 117).

v   Denis Healey (1917–2015), British Labour Party politician who Mandela first met during his short visit to London in 1962. Later Healey visited him in prison.

panied by the British ambassador, saw me on Sept. 19. I was pleased to see him again. He told me that you had paid a visit to Helen[i] & Shanti.[ii] He also told me that that evening you would attend a ball given in his honour. I was very happy to hear this because after the ugly experience you had recently, you need relaxation & a lot of fun. Do enjoy yourself but beware of sprees if you can. It is a strange coincidence that you should have chosen to visit the Josephs and the Naidoos at the moment when they were very much in my thoughts. I wish you had met Shanti's father, Naran,[iii] a courageous person who was widely known for his dedication & simplicity. We were arrested together in June 1950 & detained for some hours before we were released. When we reached their Doornfontein[iv] residence we were hungry & tired. Amma,[v] wearing that free and easy smile of hers, presented us with a meal of crab & rice. It was my first time to see these creatures cooked, & the mere sight of them made me sick & everything inside me – my gizzard included – began protesting violently. You know, darling, that I never give up easily on such matters. I tried to be as graceful as was possible in the circumstances & even dared to chew 1 leg or 2. It was a delicate adventure. Thereafter I became much attached to the Naidoos and enjoyed crabs very much. Shanti was then a mere nipper. I was to see her grow into a fearless girl who followed closely on the father's footsteps. But I never suspected that she had such strength of character, pluck & endurance.

As for our friend, Helen,[vi] I believe she is one woman who would continue to swing the sword even beyond the grave; that is if death allows her victims freedom to engage in these posthumous activities. With her background, qualifications, social status & opportunities she hardly had any reason to ruin her brilliant career by following the course she chose.[vii] She had the franchise, could belong to any of the

---

i   Helen Joseph (1905–92), teacher, social worker, and anti-apartheid and women's rights activist – see the glossary.

ii   Shanti Naidoo (1935–), anti-apartheid activist – see the glossary. With another activist, Nondwe Mankahla, she refused to testify against Winnie Mandela and was sentenced to two months in prison. Shanti Naidoo's brother Indres Naidoo (1936–2016) served a long prison sentence on Robben Island – see the glossary.

iii   Thambi Naransamy 'Naran' Naidoo (1901–53), also known as Roy, was the son of an early collaborator of Mahatma Gandhi.

iv   A suburb in downtown Johannesburg.

v   Shanti Naidoo's mother.

vi   Helen Joseph.

vii   British-born teacher Helen Joseph worked in the Women's Auxillary Air Force during World War II and then went to South Africa to work as a social worker. She became aware of the reality of life under apartheid and became politically involved.

respectable parties and express herself fully & freely on any public questions. Only a highly principled person, completely dedicated to the ideals of freedom would make this fatal decision. I have the highest regard for her. She certainly will be one of the very first persons I shall visit when I return, just as you & Nomvula[i] did the day after your release. She can dish out & take punches, & I'm sure she will still be slogging it out when the people of S.A of all races lay her remains to eternal rest. Give her, Amma & Shanti my warmest love. . . .

To come back to you, darling, your friends have impressed me tremendously. I was not the least surprised by David, Elliot, Mqwati, Rita, Douglas, Thoko, Martha, & Livingstone. One day I shall have the opportunity of hearing something on Samson, Jackson, Nomvula, Paulos, Joseph, David Dalton, Victor, George, Joseph Chamberlain, Simon, Owen & Samuel & Peter.[ii] Fondest regards to them all.

I'm proud of you darling & you are more to me than the world. I expect wonderful stories from you when I return home. One day we will pack up. Then we will be free from the troubles of this world. Even then there will be hope for us. I do hope we will be allowed to sleep side by side as we have done in the privacy of our bedroom during the 4 years of our married life that we managed to live together. A million kisses & tons & tons of love.

Devotedly, Dalibunga

Nkosikazi Nobandla Mandela, 8115, Orlando West, J.H.B.

◇◇◇◇◇◇◇◇◇◇◇◇

Joyce Sikhakhane (1943–) was a journalist and anti-apartheid activist who was put on trial with Winnie Mandela and twenty others in 1969. She never received this letter and only heard of it when she was contacted in 2008 by Ruth Muller, then a staff member at the Nelson Mandela Foundation. Sikhakhane hadn't actually met Mandela before he went to prison but had played with the children from his first marriage, as she lived close to them.

Sikhakhane was engaged to marry Samson 'John' Fadana a relative of Mandela's. When they went to the Magistrates Court to be married the

---

i   Joyce Nomafa Sikhakane (1943–), journalist and anti-apartheid activist – see the glossary.
ii   Winnie Mandela's comrades who had been charged with her.

security police threatened to charge her as she was breaking her banning orders to do this. They then 'endorsed' Fadana out of Johannesburg and sent him back to the Transkei. Under apartheid 'influx control' laws, an African person had to have permission to live in a city and authorities had the power to remove anyone from the city by 'endorsing' them out. Fadana later married someone else in the Transkei.

Mandela must have heard that Sikhakhane was a journalist, which is why he refers to a string of well-known journalists in this letter, mostly from the influential Drum *magazine which launched the careers of many black journalists and represented a new black urban identity in contrast to the apartheid regime's tribal and pastoral stereotyping of black people. Sikhakhane had started working as a journalist in December 1963, soon after matriculating.*

––––––––––––

To Joyce Sikhakhane,[i] comrade of Winnie Mandela

PLEASE SEE POSTSCRIPT BEFORE YOU READ THIS LETTER

January 1, 1971

My dear Nomvula,[ii]

Re roba matsoho[iii] for you & John![iv] Is it true? Can you two really do this to me, take such momentous decisions without even as much as giving me a hint? I must have missed heaps of meat & pudding at the engagement party. To your wedding I would have been accepted just as I am, without having to sport a frock coat, starched shirt & top hat. What is even more important to me, your wedding would have been one occasion in which I could have shined at last. I rehearse daily on a penny whistle; everyone around here calls it that though it cost R2.00. I'm still on the d.t.l.-stage but with more practice I could have tried Handel's *Messiah* on it on the great day.

––––––––––––

i   Joyce Nomafa Sikhakhane (1943–), journalist and anti-apartheid activist – see the glossary.
ii   Mandela calls her Nomvula as she was engaged to his relative John Fadana.
iii Meaning 'applause' in Sesotho.
iv   Samson John Fadana whom Mandela had been in prison with.

You have guts in the proper sense of the term. Was it love, love of adventure or both that made you take such a gamble? There is no insurance house anywhere in the country that could secure you against such an obvious risk. One as hopeful & as ambitious as John is will most probably not allow the sweet pleasures of an ordered family life to interfere with his pattern of thoughts and doings. Besides, even at a distance, association with a Nomvula would tend to keep him on the ball most of the time. What do you expect the poor fellow to do when you are actually entrenched right inside his mansion, your ears on the ground and feeling the pulse as usual, now questioning this, condemning that & demanding action all along the line? He will run wild.

They tell the story of a woman (I believe she lives in your street)[i] who has terrific reserves of will-power & initiative, & who made a deal as fatal & remarkably similar to the one you are now contemplating. The going was uphill right from the beginning. Hardly 4 months after the wedding bells had tolled, some hue & cry on the Reef[ii] forced her to live for a fortnight with the matron at Ameshoff St. Yena nowakwakhe[iii] tight-roped for 48 months when their dreams of a well-organised domestic life abruptly ended. Hubby went & real chaos reigned in her soul & everything around her. She now lives like a swimmer in a rough sea, battered & tossed about by giant waves & treacherous currents. Is this the miserable life you now wish to lead?

I suspect you'll immediately retort by pointing out that on questions of this nature I ought to address myself not to your brains but to your breast, persuade not your head but your heart, for it is the latter that John has won; or are you the conqueror? If this be your retort then say I: Hallelujah! benissimo!! Sermons on such matters, even from well-meaning friends, are out of place. What the heart feels may very often be the sole justification for what we do. I have known John since the forties & I regard him very highly. He is human & generous & possesses a lively & sober mind. I sincerely believe that in him you've found an ideal partner who will make life for you happy & enjoyable, & who will encourage you to sharpen the abilities that you undoubtedly possess. You've caught a big fish, little sister! Or are you going to

---

i   He is referring to Winnie Mandela.
ii   A name for the Johannesburg area that refers to the Witwatersrand gold reef where gold was first
        discovered by Australian George Harrison in 1896.
iii   This is isiXhosa for a person and his or her romantic partner.

prove me wrong once again by saying: Buti, I'm a modest person but I can't help thinking that John is a lucky fellow. It's him, not me, who has caught a big fish. I am the creation's rarest fish, the Coelacanth!

This is a duel to be fought between you two & I'll stay out of it. But I do wish you to know that: Siqhwabizandla![i] May the wedding day be bright & lovely & the night lit by a golden moon.

I should have liked to have written to both of you, but I deliberately avoided such a course. John & I are very close & I can speak frankly to him on personal matters without hurting him. If I spoke directly to him I might be tempted to ignore everything I have said here about delivering sermons. My letter might both be congratulations & reprimand, a demand for explanations which might make consciences itch. But to you I can truly speak as I have done here, & this is how I should like things to be. Remember that both of you are very dear to me.

Thanks for the Xmas card you sent in Dec. 69. That I never received it makes no difference whatsoever to my sense of gratitude. My only regret is that I was denied the opportunity of possessing a precious souvenir which would have made John & others shrink with jealousy. It was most kind of you, Thoko,[ii] Rita,[iii] Miriam & our sister to think of me. Give them my fondest regards. Have you seen our sister lately?[iv] I'm worried over hr. I have watched all kinds of storm break loose upon her. The harm occasioned by the ceaseless bombardment to which she has been subjected over a lengthy period is shown by the decline in her health. But it gives me some pleasure to notice that she is taking things well. Give her all my love.

You are probably in touch with an old friend I never forget, Benjy.[v] I have wanted to write to him but on every occasion I have hesitated for reasons you would readily appreciate. He is brilliant & fearless, the type of man who must rise to the top of his profession. His dare-devilry

---

i   'We congratulate you. Literally we are clapping hands' in isiXhosa.

ii   Thoko Mngoma, an ANC activist in Alexandra township. She was also detained and stood trial in what is known as the Trial of the Twenty-two, when Winnie Mandela and twenty-one others were detained and then charged with working for the banned ANC. The trial started on 1 December 1969, and on 16 February 1970 the charges were withdrawn. Before they could leave court they were rearrested. On 3 August 1970 Winnie Mandela and nineteen others were recharged. They were acquitted on 14 September 1970.

iii   Rita Ndzanga (1933–), an ANC activist and trade unionist. She was also one of the accused in the Trial of the Twenty-two. Her husband, Lawrence, was murdered in detention by the security police. Her two sons were in MK but died after 1994.

iv   This is most probably a reference to Winnie Mandela.

v   Most probably this is Benjamin Pogrund (1933–), former deputy editor of the *Rand Daily Mail* and Mandela's friend – see the glossary.

reminds me of another friend for whom I had great admiration, Henry Nxumalo,[i] another go-getter. Give him my greetings.

Do you ever hear of Cecil?[ii] I once wrote to him but he was already settled in New York when my letter reached the Rand.[iii] I'm sorry he had to leave because he played a special role which made him very valuable indeed. In the important media he controlled, he stressed those issues that keep us together as a community. In his office & home he kept a dialogue with those who repeatedly found themselves in disagreement on vital questions & he used his resources to narrow the gaps & to caution against separatism.

Recently I read a stimulating contribution by Lewis Nkosi[iv] on cultural problems & I was happy to note that he is still magnificent. My thoughts immediately went back to the mid-fifties, to other friends in the same profession – the late Can Themba, Todd Matshikiza[v] & Nat Nakasa, to Bloke Modisane, Benson Dyantyi, Robert Resha, . . . Leslie Sehume, Arthur Maimane, Simon Mogapi, Bob Gosani, Harry Mashabela, Casey Motsisi, Ronnie Manyosi, Layton Plata, Doc Bikitsha, Mayekiso & Ikaneng, all of whom we miss.[vi]

Many of them are top chaps & compare very well with their counterparts across the colour line – Ruth First, Stanley Uys, Brian Bunting, Margaret Smith, Charles Bloomberg & others.[vii] Needless to say, I did not agree with everything they said, but I patiently listened to them because they often spoke a language I well understood & drew attention to concrete problems. I hope they still try to uphold these high standards. What new faces are there? How is Owen?[viii] I have seen a couple of your manuscripts.[ix] You'll not feel offended if I tell you that

---

i   Henry Nxumalo (1917–57) was an investigative journalist for *Drum* magazine and wrote stories exposing racial inequality. He was murdered while investigating a story. His killers were never found.

ii   Cecil Eprile (1914–93), friend, journalist, and newspaper editor. Wrote and edited for *Arthur Barlow's Weekly*, the *Sunday Times*, and *Sunday Express*. Editor-in-chief of *Golden City Post* (*Drum* magazine's sister paper), 1955–67, where he trained many prominent black South African journalists.

iii   An abbreviated name for the Witwatersrand, a 56-kilometre-long ridge in the Gauteng province of South Africa where Johannesburg is based.

iv   Lewis Nkosi (1936–2010), South African author who started out as a journalist writing for *Ilanga Lase Natal* (Natal Sun), *Drum* magazine and *Golden City Post*. He criticised the apartheid government and his works were subsequently banned.

v   Todd Matshikiza (1920–68), writer and musician who composed the musical score for the internationally successful South African musical *King Kong* (1960).

vi   Apart from Bob Gosani, who was a photographer, these are mostly South African journalists and editors who worked for *Drum* magazine.

vii   White journalists who were active in or supported the anti-apartheid struggle.

viii   Owen Vanqa, a journalist from the Eastern Cape who was tried with Joyce Sikhakhane, Winnie Mandela, and twenty others in 1969 and 1970.

ix   When Sikhakhane was interviewed by the Nelson Mandela Foundation about this letter in 2008 she said that she thought Mandela was referring to magazine articles published under her byline. ('The Lost Letter', Nelson Mandela Foundation, 22 July 2008, https://www.nelsonmandela.org/news/entry/the-lost-letter).

I was highly impressed. One or two lines caused me concern, but my confidence in you helps me to hope that you would certainly be able to give me an explanation which I could accept.

Re roba matsoho! With love, very sincerely,
Buti[i] Nel

Miss Joyce Sikakane, c/o Nkosikazi Nobandla Mandela, 8115 Orlando West, Johannesburg

Postscript: This letter will amuse you. I received information that you were engaged to one of my great friends, hence this note. Though Zami[ii] corrected the error, I let it go as originally drafted.[iii]

To the commanding officer, Robben Island

[Translated from Afrikaans]

2 January, 1971

The Commanding Officer,
Robben Island.

Attention C/O Fourie

New Year's Day is never an appropriate occasion to announce disappointing news. Unfortunately both of your letters denying my request for a visit and the censoring of the letter from my wife reached me on this significant day.

I don't suppose I'd complain about it, except to say that the guitar player must have a special talent to persuade his listeners to listen

---

i   'Brother' in isiXhosa.
ii   One of Winnie Mandela's names..
iii Sikhakane did marry Samson Fadana but a day later the security police told her that she 'would be charged for entering the Magistrates Court illegally and having been in the presence of more than one person. They told me that my so-called marriage was null and void because it was done illegally. That was the end of the marriage.' ('The Lost Letter', Nelson Mandela Foundation, 22 July 2008, https://www .nelsonmandela.org/news/entry/the-lost-letter).

carefully to him. He must always try to hold the attention of his audience, to draw them unto him. Only a person armed with love for his fellow human beings, and who cares about others, will succeed where force and power will be applied in vain. This simple principle is applicable to ordinary matters also, and is valid even in institutions where strict discipline has to be maintained.

[Signed NR Mandela]
Nelson Mandela 466/64

To Zenani Mandela,[i] his middle daughter

March 1, 1971

My Darling,

Friday the 5th February this year was your 12th birthday and in January I sent you a card containing my congratulations and good wishes. Did you get it? Again I say: many happy returns.

It is not easy for me to believe that our Zeni, who was only a baby when I last saw her, is now a big girl in Standard V at a Boarding School, and doing subjects I never learnt in school, like French, Physical Science and Maths. I still remember clearly the night when you were born in 1959. On February 4th that year I returned home very late and found Mummy highly restless. I rushed for the late Aunt Phyllis Mzaidume, and the two of us drove Mummy to Baragwanath Hospital. There was a remarkable coincidence. Aunt Phyllis herself was born on 5th February and on our way to Bara she hoped you would be born on the same date, and that is exactly what happened. When she heard of the news of your arrival, she was as happy as if she had created you.

Your birth was a great relief to us. Only three months before this, Mummy had spent fifteen days in jail under circumstances that were dangerous for a person in her condition.[ii] We did not know what harm

---

i   Zenani Mandela (1959–) – see the glossary.
ii   Winnie Mandela was arrested in October 1958 and held in prison for two weeks for participating in a protest against the extension of pass laws to women.

might have been done to you and to her health, and were happy indeed to be blessed with a healthy and lovely daughter. Do you understand that you were nearly born in prison? Not many people have had your experience of having been in jail before they were born. You were only 25 months old when I left home and, though I met you frequently thereafter until January 1962 when I left the country for a short period, we never lived together again.

You will probably not remember an incident that moved me very much at the time and about which I never like to think. Towards the end of 1961 you were brought to the house of a friend and I was already waiting when you came.[i] I was wearing no jacket or hat. I took you into my arms and for about ten minutes we hugged, and kissed and talked. Then suddenly you seemed to have remembered something. You pushed me aside and started searching the room. In a corner you found the rest of my clothing. After collecting it, you gave it to me and asked me to go home. You held my hand for quite some time, pulling desperately and begging me to return. It was a difficult moment for both of us. You felt I had deserted you and Mummy, and your request was a reasonable one. It was similar to the note that you added to Mummy's letter of the 3rd December 1965 where you said: "Will you come home next year. My mother will fetch you with her car." Your age in 1961 made it difficult for me to explain my conduct to you, and the worried expression that I saw in your face haunted me for many months thereafter. Luckily, however, you soon cooled down and we parted peacefully. But for days I was lost in thought, wondering how I could show you that I had not failed you and the family. When I returned to South Africa in July 1962 I saw you and Zindzi[ii] twice and this was the last time we met. In 1964 you were brought to the Supreme Court in Pretoria and I was quite disappointed when you were not allowed to see me.[iii] I have been longing to see you ever since. You will be able to pay me a visit me in 1975 when you will have turned sixteen. But I am growing impatient and the coming five years seem longer than eternity. What a lovely letter you wrote me last month! Merci beaucoup! I have started 1971 with a real bang. Yours was the first and only letter I got from the family this year and I read it over and over again. I shall keep it as a souvenir. It pleased me very much to know your subjects for this

---

i   Mandela is referring to the period in 1961 when he was on the run from the authorities and living apart from his family.

ii   Zenani's sister, Zindziswa Mandela (1960–) – see the glossary.

iii   He is referring to the Rivonia Trial – see the glossary.

year and hope you will work hard right from the beginning of the year and pass. French is an important language. On the African continent more people speak French than English. Latin, Zulu, Physical Science, Maths and Geography are also useful and you should pay a great deal of attention to them. I was also pleased to hear that you take walks to the mountains and about the beautiful scenery that you describe.

I saw the note that you wrote at the back of the letter asking the post-man to send the letter away at once and to "be like Elvis, go man, go." The music of Elvis is very lively and popular and I am glad to note that you are fond of it too. I hope that you also love the music of Miriam Makheba [*sic*],[i] Mohapeloa,[ii] Caluza,[iii] Tyamzashe,[iv] Paul Robeson,[v] Beethoven,[vi] Tchaikovsky.[vii] What is even more important, I trust that one day you will be able to compose, sing and play your own music, or do you prefer to be a ballet star in addition to being a scientist, doctor or lawyer?

What games do you play? Basketball, swimming or athletics, espe-cially track events (i.e. running), would keep you healthy and strong, and give you the pleasure of helping your college win victories. Try your luck, darling.

May this letter bring you the same joy and happiness that yours gave me.

Give my love to Zindzi, Maki,[viii] Kgatho,[ix] and abazala[x] Andile, Vuy-ani, Kwayiyo and Maphelo, and of course to you and Mummy.

Lots of love and plenty of kisses.

Yours affectionately,

Tata[xi]

Miss Zeni Mandela, 8115 Orlando West, Johannesburg

---

i   Zenzile Miriam Makeba (1932–2008), South African singer, actor, United Nations goodwill amabassador, and activist.

ii   Joshua Pulumo Mohapeloa (1908–82), a lyricist who worked with Gibson Kente on his musical productions (Sahm Venter, telephonic conversations with Gibson Kente's niece, Vicky Kente, 23 July 2017).

iii   R. T. Caluza (1895–1969), Zulu composer and musician who transcended many musical genres, including hyms, ragtime and vaudeville. He wrote the South African Native National Congress's first anthem, 'iLand Act', protesting against the 1913 Native Land Act.

iv   Benjamin Tyamzashe (1890–1978), South African composer, choir conductor, organist, and teacher.

v   Paul Robeson (1898–1976), American bass singer who was involved with the civil rights movement.

vi   Ludwig van Beethoven (1770–1827), German composer and pianist.

vii   Pyotr Ilyich Tchaikovsky (1840–93), Russian composer of the romantic period.

viii   Makaziwe Mandela (1954–), Mandela's eldest daughter – see the glossary.

ix   Makgatho Mandela (1950–2005), Mandela's second-born son – see the glossary.

x   'Cousins' in isiXhosa.

xi   'Father' in isiXhosa.

To Fatima Meer,[i] friend and comrade

March 1, 1971

My dear Fatima,

This letter should have gone either to Shamim, Shehnaz or Rashid.[ii] To hear directly from them would give me a deeper insight into the shifts in the patterns of thought & outlook amongst the young folk.

My son, Kgatho,[iii] one of my best pals, visits me twice yearly. We seem to be in agreement on major issues, but now & again he clears the cobwebs from my mind by taking a different view on matters which I have come to regard as axiomatic. At times I have suspected that he sees in me something of a useful relic from the past, a sort of souvenir to remind him of the days when he regarded me as knowing everything under the sun, & when he gulped down anything I told him. His independence of mind & fresh ideas have made my conversations with him enjoyable, & this is what I believe that I would get if I spoke directly to the children. You realise now why I prefer Rashid & sisters to you?

I have lived with my generation all these years, a generation that is inclined to be conservative & to lean backwards most of the time. I'm keen to know a bit more about the new ideas stirring among the modern youth. But news about the children tends to remind me of problems about which I prefer never to think. When I'm told that our Shamim is at varsity, constructing beautiful house models, the full weight of my 52 years bears down upon me. She appears on page 70 of the "Portrait[iv] . . ." I suspect Shehnaz to be the second on her left. If I'm wide of the mark let her remember that she was only a little more than a toddler when I last saw her, & her features must have changed a lot after she has grown big enough to be in Standard IX. I have searched in vain for Rashid & have even made wild guesses amongst the boys on page 40. I was very sorry to learn that he could

---

i   Fatima Meer (1928–2010), writer, academic, and anti-apartheid and women's rights activist – see the glossary.

ii   Fatima and Ismail Meer's children.

iii   Makgatho (Kgatho) Mandela (1950–2005), Mandela's second-born son – see the glossary.

iv   *Portrait of Indian South Africans* by Fatima Meer (Durban: Avon House, 1969).

not go to Waterford[i] as he could have acted [as] elder brother to my Zeni & Zindzi.[ii] I have not forgotten about the beautiful face cloth with which they presented me on the last occasion I was there & I should love to hear from them whenever they can spare some time for writing letters.

I could have addressed the letter to Ismail,[iii] my very first friend across the race curtain, comrade of my youth. You know we practically lived together at Kholvad[iv] & it was him who brought me into contact with Dadoo,[v] Naicker brothers,[vi] the Cachalias,[vii] Nana Sita,[viii] Naidoos,[ix] Pahad,[x] Nathie,[xi] the Singhs,[xii] Hurbans,[xiii] Poonen,[xiv] Nair,[xv] Seedat,[xvi] AI Meer[xvii] & other eminent leaders of the Indian community.

---

i   Waterford Kamhlaba school in neighbouring Swaziland.
ii   Zenani (1959–) and Zindzi (1960–) Mandela, Mandela's middle and youngest daughters – see the glossary.
iii   Ismail Meer (1918–2000), Fatima's husband and a lawyer and anti-apartheid activist – see the glossary.
iv   Kholvad House, an apartment block in downtown Johannesburg where Ismail Meer had an apartment. Mandela writes in *Long Walk to Freedom*, 'At Wits I met and became friends with Ismail Meer, J.N. Singh, Ahmed Bhoola, and Ramlal Bhoolia. The centre of this tight-knit community was Ismail's apartment, Flat 13, Kholvad House, four rooms in a residential building in the centre of the city. There we studied, talked and even danced until the early hours of the morning, and it became a kind of headquarters for young freedom fighters. I sometimes slept there when it was too late to catch the last train back to Orlando.' (p. 105.)
v   Dr. Yusuf Dadoo (1909–83), medical doctor, anti-apartheid activist, and orator. President of South African Indian Congress, deputy to Oliver Tambo on the Revolutionary Council of MK, and chairman of the South African Communist Party – see the glossary.
vi   Monty Naicker (1910–78), doctor, politician, and anti-apartheid activist – see the glossary. M. P. Naicker (1920–77), anti-apartheid activist, journalist, leader, and organiser for the Natal Indian Congress, South African Communist Party, and the Congress Alliance. The Naickers were not brothers, but comrades.
vii   Maulvi Cachalia (1908–2003), anti-apartheid activist and leading member of the South African Indian Congress, Transavaal Indian Congress, and ANC – see the glossary. Yusuf Cachalia (1915–95), brother of Maulvi Cachalia. Political activist and secretary of the South African Indian Congress – see the glossary. Their families were also involved in fighting apartheid.
viii   Nana Sita (1898–1969), president of the Transvaal Indian Congress, a follower of Gandhi's philosophy of *satyagraha* (non-violence).
ix   The Naidoo family of Rocky Street, Yeoville, in Johannesburg. Naransamy Roy (1901–53) and Ama Naidoo (1908–93) and the family.
x   Goolam Pahad, executive committee member of the Transvaal Indian Congress and the father of activists Essop (1939–) and Aziz (1940–) Pahad.
xi   Solly Nathie (1918–79), executive committee member of the Transvaal Indian Congress.
xii   J. N. Singh (d. 1996), member of the Transvaal Indian Congress and the Natal Indian Congress. He studied towards his LLB degree with Nelson Mandela at the University of Witwatersrand. His wife was Radhi Singh (d. 2013), anti-apartheid activist, teacher, and attorney.
xiii   Gopal Herbans – treasurer of the Natal Indian Congress and an accused in the Treason Trial (for the Treason Trial, see the glossary).
xiv   George and Vera Poonan.
xv   Billy Nair (1929–2008), comrade and MK member who was charged with sabotage in 1963. He was held in B Section with Mandela on Robben Island and was released in 1984 – see the glossary.
xvi   Dawood Seedat (1916–76) was an accused in the Treason Trial of 1956, and detained in the 1960 State of Emergency (for both the Treason Trial and the 1960 State of Emergency, see the glossary). He was vice-president of the Natal Indian Congress. He and his wife, Fatima, were banned for five years in 1964, then the order was exended to 1974.
xvii   The uncle of I. C. Meer (1918–2000) (for I. C. Meer, see the glossary).

To him I should like to chat freely & openly about the past. But the
trouble, my difficulty is you, behn.[i] I hesitate to put bhai[ii] in a position
where he would have to withhold from you my letters to him, or when
you would feel obliged to rifle his pockets. I've not the slightest doubt
what would happen if you saw any of such letters you would roast
him alive. I often wonder whether you and Radi[iii] ever stop to think
just how much you owe to me for the peace of mind & happiness that
surround you. Remember Ismail, J.N. [Singh] & I have been a solid
trio for almost 30 years. I shall stick to our vow: never, never under
any circumstances, to say anything unbecoming of the other. They
will readily agree that I have not once given away the show. Anyway,
what it is that I could ever think of divulging? Talk of angels! Your
men & I are & have always been. The trouble, of course, is that most
successful men are prone to some form of vanity. There comes a stage
in their lives when they consider it permissible to be egotistic & to brag
to the public at large about their unique achievements. What a sweet
euphemism for self-praise the English language has evolved! Autobiography, they choose to call it, where the shortcomings of others are
frequently exploited to highlight the praiseworthy accomplishments
of the author. I am doubtful if I will ever sit down to sketch my background. I have neither the achievements of which I could boast nor
the skill to do it. If I lived on cane spirit every day of my life, I still
would not have had the courage to attempt it. I sometimes believe
that through me Creation intended to give the world the example of a
mediocre man in the proper sense of the term. Nothing could tempt
me to advertise myself. Had I been in a position to write an autobiography, its publication would have been delayed until our bones had
been laid, & perhaps I might have dropped hints not compatible with
my vow. The dead have no worries, & if the truth & nothing but the
whole truth about them emerged, the image I have helped to maintain
through my perpetual silence was ruined, that would be the affair of
posterity, not ours. You now see what a risk would be entailed in writing to Ismail? Anyway you know he is a heavyweight, moves slowly &
I would probably whistle for a reply.

I can almost hear you ask the pertinent question: Where to does

---

i   'Sister' in Gujarati.
ii   'Brother' in Gujarati.
iii   Wife of J. N. Singh, an activist who was on the executive committees of both the Natal Indian Congress
    and the South African Indian Congress.

this verbosity lead us? Quite a sensible question! The truth is that I am trying to find an excuse for writing to you. How can I resist talking to you, behn, you who has always treated me so kindly? You, Ismail & I have wrenched ourselves free from the inhibitions of our Caucasoid & Negroid ancestries & established firm & warm relations which not even the tempestuous decade of the sixties could shake or chill. We have forged our own kutum: silusapho lendw'enye.[i] Remember the numerous occasions I have lived with you since the early fifties there at Umngeni Road;[ii] were Pamela's parents your next door neighbours then? I moved with you to Sydenham.[iii]

Now & then Zami[iv] tells me some good news about you. Although your application to visit me was refused I was happy to know that I'm in your thoughts. I have read & re-read the "Portrait".[v] Splendid! A moving story & skilfully handled; it is a mine of information for me. The fact that you wrote it obliged me to read it as if you were conversing informally with me. I almost read the 235 pages at one sitting, & it helped me begin the attempt to overcome a weakness which I have never been able to shake off. I'm one of those who possess scraps of superficial information on a variety of subjects, but who lacks depth & expert knowledge in the one thing in which I ought to have specialised, namely the history of my own country & people. I have tried to read anything relating to African history carefully & with real interest, but have tended to neglect that of other national groups. It was when I read the "Portrait . . ." I had the opportunity to appreciate the fascinating human story which begins in 1860.[vi] I asked Zami to try & get the book & indicated to her my own views on the issues raised in Chap. III. Our interpretations may not altogether coincide & I hope to refer to the whole question in my next letter.

In the meantime I say Mubarak![vii]

---

i   An isiXhosa phrase meaning 'We come from one family'. *Silusapho* means 'We are family' and *lendw'enye* means 'one house'.

ii   Where Ismail and Fatima Meer lived from 1951 to 1958 before they moved into their home in Burnwood Road in Sydenham, Durban.

iii   The suburb in Durban to which the Meers later moved.

iv   One of Winnie Mandela's names.

v   *Portrait of Indian South Africans.*

vi   Although there were Indian people in South Africa earlier, between November 1860 and 1911 (when the system of indentured labour was stopped) around 152,000 indentured labourers from across India arrived in Natal. After serving their indentures, the first category of Indians were free to remain in South Africa or to return to India.

vii   'Congratulations' in Gujarati.

With all my love to you, Ismail & kids,[i] Radhi & J.N,[ii] Molly & Monty,[iii] Alan & wife,[iv] G.R.[v] & family, Dawood & Fatima.[vi]

Very sincerely,
Nelson

Mrs Fatima Meer, 148 Burnwood Road, Sydenham, Durban

―――――――――

To Thoko Mandela,[vii] his daughter-in-law and the widow of his son, Thembi[viii]

April 1, 1971

My dear Thoko,

I wish I had some means to influence the invisible force that governs our lives and determines our fortunes and misfortunes.

A broken family, a young widow wrecked by grief and battling all alone against heavy odds, 2 orphaned children deprived of the security of a stable home and father's love, and hungry most of the time are cruel penalties that make life tough and bitter. I have many a time wondered whether the marvellous inventions and progress brought by science make us more secure and happier than were our ancestors a hundred thousand years ago. Sure, there have been significant milestones in man's battle against ignorance, poverty and disease. Means

---

i   Ismail Meer and their children.
ii   J. N. Singh (d. 1996), member of the Transvaal Indian Congress and the Natal Indian Congress. He studied towards his LLB degree with Nelson Mandela at the University of Witwatersrand. His wife was Radhi Singh (d. 2013), anti-apartheid activist, teacher, and attorney.
iii   Monty Naicker.
iv   Alan (1926–2013) and Beata Lipman (1928–2016), their friends. Alan, an architect, designed their house in Sydenham.
v   G. R. Naidoo, a South African photographer. He attended a party at the Meers' home in Durban which Mandela attended the day before he was arrested on 5 August 1962.
vi   Fatima Seedat (1922–2003) was the twin of Rahima Moosa, one of the leaders of the 1956 Women's March. A member of the Natal Indian Congress and ANC, Fatima was jailed for her role in the Passive Resistance Campaign waged by the Transvaal and Natal Indian Congresses from 1946 to 1948 against the Asiatic Land Tenure Act of 1946 which sought to confine Asian ownership of land to particular areas. She was jailed again in 1952 for participating in the Defiance Campaign (for the Defiance Campaign, see the glossary). Natal Indian Congress and ANC member.
vii   See the glossary.
viii Madiba Thembekile (Thembi) Mandela (1945–69), Mandela's eldest son – see the glossary.

are being found to make us less dependent on nature and its moods, to have greater control over our environment and, in the process, we have come to have relatively higher living standards.

But fate continues to be treacherous and to bring us suffering and misery that we do not deserve. The family has had an alarming quantity of catastrophes. Why should Mkozi[i] die so soon after Thembi? During his last visit Kgatho told me that you had attended Kapadika's funeral, one of Thembi's close friends and who spoke on behalf of Cape Town on Aug. 3, 1969.[ii] Why should all these things happen to you at one and the same time? I can imagine the awkward questions Ndindi and Nandi must be asking: Shall we never see our Daddy again? Is he now together with Grandpa of Diepkloof.[iii] Will Tatomkulu[iv] never return from Robben Island? Who will now bring us dresses and chocolates? And many more similarly unanswerable enquiries. The news of your father's death disturbed me. I would have been more troubled if I had not had the privilege of having witnessed how courageous and dignified you can be in the face of personal tragedy. I know that you are not the type of person who will allow sorrow to overwhelm you. In spite of all that has happened you have not lost everything. There are many people who have no mothers, step-fathers, father- and mother-in-laws, no host of relations and friends such as you have, friends and relations who think of you and wish you well. Besides, you have the opportunity to make your future and that of Ndindi and Nandi bright and meaningful. You are young and in good health and full of talent. Do remember this, Thoko.

As you know, I have not met Lennard[v] but all the reports that have reached me indicate that he is equally brave and calm. My deepest sympathy to both of you. Are you sending me a report on the funeral? When did you return from Johannesburg? Are you working?

In March last year I wrote to Lennard and gave him a number of messages. I never heard from him. Perhaps your reply will include this information.

I hope you have not forgotten the matter I raised in my letter of 29th November 1969[vi] relating to your own personal position. I hope at your next visit you will give me some progress report. I

---

i   This is likely to be Thoko Mandela's father.

ii   Mandela must be referring to Thembi Mandela's funeral. His body arrived in Johannesburg from Cape Town on 29 July 1969. (Sophie Tema, 'Mandela's Son's Body Arrives', *The World*, 30 July 1969.)

iii   A suburb in Soweto, Johannesburg.

iv   'Granddad' in isiXhosa.

v   Thoko's brother, Leonard Simelane. Mandela misspelt his name.

vi   See his letter on page 96.

am anxious that you put yourself in a position whereby you will be able to guide the children in the choice of careers and in preparing them for such careers. The home atmosphere must exist which will encourage them to strive for the highest ideals in life, and this depends largely on you. Today your mother and mother-in-law are there to help you bring up Ndindi and Nandi, but sooner or later they will also pass to eternal rest, leaving you to fight all alone, and to face the difficult task of supervising the progress of the children. I shall say more on this matter when you come. In the meantime please read the letter again.

Nandi really looks fine in her maroon and white outfit. The green vegetation that forms the background to the photo is beautiful and reminds me of the happy and romantic days of my childhood. I can almost smell the sweet perfumes that must have filled the area where she posed. I have taken particular note of her mischievous smile. It is a charming picture and I am happy you sent it. I put it alongside that of Zeni and Zindzi[i].

Many thanks for the beautiful Xmas card you sent me. You must have combed the whole of Cape Town to get it. I like its bright red background and its artistic arrangement. I also received Ntombi's with the chocolate belle on the cover. The two of you must be little witches. You seem to know my tastes better than I do. They are really wonderful and I was happy to receive them.

What is happening? Why have you not come? You wrote as far back as November and told me that you had applied for a visiting permit. Four full months have passed and you have not turned up. Did you apply by registered letter? Do know I am looking forward to seeing you soon? Perhaps it may be advisable before you renew your application to phone Mum Winnie, Orlando 113, and find out if she has not already applied to come down.

My fondest regards to your mother and step-father and love to you, Ndindi, Ntombi and Lennard.

Yours affectionately,

Tata[ii]

Mrs Lydia Thoko Mandela, "Hillbrow", 7th Avenue, Retreat

---

i   Zenani Mandela (1959–) and Zindziswa Mandela (1960–), Mandela's middle and youngest daughters – see the glossary..

ii   'Father' in isiXhosa.

To the commanding officer, Robben Island

4 April 1971

The Commanding Officer,
Robben Island

<u>Attention: Lt Badenhorst</u>

Further to my letter addressed to you on the 31st March 1971, I have to advise that yesterday morning I became aware for the first time that two of my foolscap hard cover notebooks, in which I keep copies of my correspondence, had been surreptitiously removed from my cell.

I immediately reported the matter to the Head Warder Carstens in the presence of Warder Meyer. They both emphatically denied that they had searched my cell the previous day and removed the missing notebooks. They further added that they had no information whatsoever as to the identity of the person who removed the books. I asked H/W Carstens to investigate the matter and thereafter acquaint me with his report.

On the night of the 31st March I decided to make a thorough search of my cell to find out what other articles, if any, were missing and I was greatly shocked to observe that my silver Parker T Ball point pen has also disappeared. I had last used it in December 1970 but I continued to see it in the box where I kept it until just the other day. In the morning of the 1st April I reported the fact to Warder Meyer, H/W Carstens being off duty.

I strongly suspect that the person who removed the books from the cell also took the pen and I ask you to investigate the matter and have this article replaced. The disappearance of my pen has greatly disturbed me. Mine is the fifth one to disappear within the first three months of this year. I have lived in the Single Cell section for seven years and this is the first time for us to suffer such losses.

I should also be pleased if you would kindly give me the following information:
1.   The name of the official, if known to you, who removed the notebooks from my cell.

2.   The reason or reasons for removing them
3.   The date when they will be returned to me

I might add that one of the notebooks contains the completed drafts of two of the three letters which I intended to write for this month. The removal of this particular book means that I will have to delay the dispatch of the aforementioned letter until I have access to it.

I should also be pleased if you would allow me to write to Brigadier Aucamp in connection with a letter which I wrote to the Minister of Justice last year[i] relating to my household affairs. Some aspect of the request I made was attended to, and he asked me to raise the matter with him again. In this connection I should like to draw attention to the fact that a copy of this letter, which I should like to consult before I write to Brig Aucamp,[ii] is in one of the missing books, and I should be much indebted to you if you would allow me to have access to it.

[Signed NR Mandela]
NELSON MANDELA: 466/64

To the commanding officer, Robben Island

14th June 1971

The Commanding Officer,
Robben Island

Attention: Major Huisamen

I refer to the letter I addressed to you in March this year, and in which I advised that my preparations for the University of London's Final LL.B Examinations in June 1971 had been hampered by illness which forced me much against my will, to suspend studying completely for several months.[iii]

By February this year my health had improved to such an extent that I

---

i   See his letter from 14 September 1970, pages 116–8.
ii   Brigadier Aucamp, commanding officer of Robben Island – see the glossary.
iii   While on trial in 1962 Mandela had a blackout in prison and was diagnosed with high blood pressure.

resumed preparations for the above examinations, but I discovered that
I had lost my power of concentration and stamina, and the headaches
that had worried me during the second half of 1970 reappeared. I
discussed the matter with Dr Poleksi, the Medical Officer, and it was
after consultation with him that in March I wrote to you and to the
Cultural Attaché. In response to my letter you informed me then that
you had referred the matter to your Headquarters and, at the same
time advised me to continue preparing for the examinations.

I tried hard to comply with your advice and exerted myself to the
utmost, but found that although my health continued to improve the
rate of recovery was not fast and complete enough to enable me to
make satisfactory progress in my work, the main difficulty being, as
always, recurring headaches. Postural hypertension, from which I suffer, is an illness which is aggravated by tension and mental exertion,
both of which naturally follow from concentrated study and preparation. In such circumstances I was compelled to consider the best way
of continuing with the studies without impeding the rate of recovery,
and the obvious answer was to spread the course over two years with
the aim of completing the course in June 1972. Your insistence that I
complete in 1971 was to call upon me to attempt what was entirely
beyond my physical condition.

I might perhaps add that I should have completed in June 1970
and I did not do so because the Prison Department failed to forward
to the university documents which would entitle me to enter for the
above examinations.

The Department sought to justify its action on the ground that my
permission to study with this particular university had lapsed. As you
are aware I was only informed in September that I could resume my
studies. Even if I were in the best of health it would have been quite
difficult for me to obtain a pass with only 8 months of preparation
for a final year course where I had to take 4 wide and complicated
subjects at one sitting.

I must accordingly ask you to allow me a further 12 months to
complete the degree. I should like you to know that, according to the
regulations governing this course, if I fail to satisfy the examiners this
June in any one of the 4 outstanding subjects, I will be forced to repeat
not only these, but also the other 4 that I have completed for Part I of
the Final. A perusal of the General Notes and Reading Lists for the
guidance of students and the syllabus will show that these examina-

tions require prolonged and intensive preparations. I am accordingly most reluctant to tackle the forthcoming examination as my preparations were hampered and I hope you will reconsider your decision and grant the request made above. I need hardly stress that your refusal of my request will involve me in heavy financial loss.

[Signed NRMandela]
NELSON MANDELA: 466/64

[note in Afrikaans in another hand]
21/6/71

Colonel,
His request for extension has already been rejected by Brig. Aucamp. His studies have now ended and his books put with his property.

◇◇◇◇◇◇◇◇◇◇◇◇

In 1971 Winnie Mandela had been sentenced to twelve months in prison for communicating with a banned person in her house. She successfully appealed both the conviction and sentence. The following year she won her appeal against sentences of six and twelve months for receiving visitors.

<hr>

To Winnie Mandela,[i] his wife

[Note in another hand at the top of the letter] 466/64 Nelson Mandela (B Group)

JUNE FIRST 1972

My darling,

Once again your letters are not coming through, and when they do, they are surprisingly late. That of JANUARY 30 was given me on

---

i   Nomzamo Winifred Madikizela-Mandela (1936–2018) – see the glossary.

MARCH 4 whilst that of FEBRUARY 26 I received on APRIL 15.

On FEBRUARY 25 I had discussed the whole question of our correspondence with the Commissioner of Prisons, General Steyn, pointing out to him that I had received only 3 of the 12 you wrote me in 1971, & that you had also got only 3 of the letters I wrote you during the same period.

I told him then that I had had this difficulty since 1969 & that the Commanding Officer had repeatedly explained to me that all my outgoing letters had been sent off & that I had been given all the correspondence that had arrived. The C.O.P.[i] emphatically repudiated my suggestion that our correspondence was being interfered with in the course of transit through the G.P.O.[ii] and promised that he would have the matter investigated.

About a week thereafter I discussed the same matter with Brig Aucamp[iii] to whom it had been referred by the C.O.P. At the end of the discussion he promised that he would instruct the relevant official to tell him (Brig Aucamp) as soon as a letter from you had been received by the prison. This arrangement, he assured me, would solve my difficulties in this particular regard, an assurance which I completely accepted. But now we are exactly where we were before I made these representations to the head of the C.O.P. & to Brig Aucamp. Though on APRIL 8 Lt. Fourie had told me in your presence that he had received your FEBRUARY & MARCH letters only that for FEBRUARY has been delivered & I still await that of MARCH. Those for APRIL & MAY are also overdue. I am disturbed to note that my representations to the head of the Prison Dept & an assurance from Brig. Aucamp, in regard to an issue which they can easily straighten out, should turn out to be fruitless.

One ought not to experience difficulties of this sort in communicating with his family.

As you know none of the birthday cards that you have sent me since 1969 have reached. I have not had the courage to tell you that not even the Xmas cards sent by the children on 1st December arrived. I cannot even be sure that Maki[iv] got the birthday card I sent her last month. I suggest that you urgently communicate with the C.O.P. in

---

i   Commissioner of Prisons.
ii   General Post Office.
iii   Brigadier Aucamp, commanding officer of Robben Island – see the glossary.
iv   Makaziwe Mandela (1954–), Mandela's eldest daughter – see the glossary.

Pretoria, or if he is not there, then through his Cape Town address, and bring the whole matter to his attention again. [?] you register all your letters & you should have little difficulty in finding out from the G.P.O. where they were dispatched, whether they reached their destination, who received them on what date?

It is right that you should know that your letters to me are heavily censored. You do not number the pages and it is often difficult to know whether I have been given the whole letter but lines 43, 44, 45, 46 & 47 on the second page of the letter of January 30 were obliterated. With the exception of the words "lives in prison" the whole of line 12 on the first page of that of FEBRUARY 26 was also obliterated. Lines 30, 31 and 32 on page 2 of this letter were deleted & the last SEVEN lines cut out.

You now keep copies of all the letters you write to me and from now on you will be better able to know what things you must avoid in future letters. My second letter has gone to Thoko[i] & the third to Shadrack & Nyanya.[ii] Please check up whether Uncle Allen got my April letter. Have you now information about the one I wrote to Douglas Lukhele?[iii] It would seem that Lily[iv] plans to visit me this November. She would naturally be free to come down if you approve. I intend writing to her, perhaps next month, care of you again, to indicate that it would be desirable for her to arrange the visit through you. November is, however, not a suitable occasion for her because it is the time when you or the children would like to come along. By the way, last year I asked you to arrange for Kgatho[v] to be here in Dec for I thought you had chosen November because you would not be able to come down on Xmas. Anyway please let me know soon how you feel about the intended visit in November. In November 1970 Joe's mum[vi] P/B 36, Gaborone promised to send me ALBERTI'S ACCOUNT OF THE XHOSA IN 1807.[vii] I wrote back immediately to tell her that the officer in charge of studies then had agreed that I could receive the

---

i Thoko Mandela, his son Thembi's widow – see the glossary.

ii Nonyaniso (Nyanya) Madikizela, Winnie Mandela's youngest sister.

iii Douglas Lukhele, Harvard-educated Swazi lawyer who did his articles at Mandela and Oliver Tambo's law firm in the 1950s. He was the first Swazi attorney-general and high court judge in Swaziland. See Mandela's letter to him on page 113.

iv Lilian Ngoyi (1911–80), politician, and anti-apartheid and women's rights activist – see the glossary.

v Makgatho (Kgatho) Mandela (1950–2005), Mandela's second-born son – see the glossary.

vi This is probably Frieda Matthews (1905–98), friend and wife of his university professor Z. K. Matthews, as she was from Botswana and her son Bakwe Matthews (1929–2010) was also known as Joe – see the glossary for these three individuals.

vii Ludwig Alberti, *Ludwig Alberti's Account of the Xhosa in 1807*, translated by W. Fehr (Cape Town: A.A. Balkema, 1968).

book. I never heard from her again. Are you keeping in touch with Sef & Nali?[i] Remember what they have done for you? Tell Zeni & Zindzi[ii] that I shall write to them soon. In the meantime tons & tons of love and a million kisses, darling.

Devotedly, Dalibunga

Nkosikazi Nobandla Mandela, 8115 Orlando West, Johannesburg

To Helen Suzman,[iii] opposition member of Parliament in South Africa

Nelson Mandela 466/64   A Group   March 1, 1974

Dear Doctor Suzman,

I have just learnt with sincere pleasure that the University of Oxford has honoured you with the Degree of Civil Laws, and I write to give you my warmest congratulations.

I do not exactly know when the degree was conferred, whether you were able to travel there to receive it, nor have I even the faintest idea of the address, if any, which you delivered on that occasion. Of course, views on important questions of principle and method do not always coincide even amongst those who are inspired by the same ideals and whose goal in life is substantially the same. Your reservations in regard to much that I consider natural and inevitable are well-known and even understandable. Nonetheless, yours would be an address which, for obvious reasons, I would have read very carefully. It would attempt to present the point of view of a large segment of liberal opinion that has remained stubbornly vocal. Perhaps one day there will be opportunity to see it.

---

i   Nancy and Sefton Vutela, Winnie's sister and her husband.
ii   Zenani (1959–) and Zindzi (1960–) Mandela, their daughters – see the glossary – who were at boarding
      school in Swaziland.
iii   Helen Suzman (1917–2009), academic, politician, anti-apartheid activist, and MP for the opposition
      party – see the glossary.

In the meantime, I hope you will not consider it out of place for me to say that this is an honour which you thoroughly deserve. A public career such as the one you have chosen, and taking into account all the circumstances, offers many challenges that would deter the average man. It requires a thick skin and strong nerves which you possess in abundance. It means constant hard work, rough passage all along the line, many days, weeks and even months away from your loved ones, and results which, though we hope will come in our lifetime, may in fact be enjoyed only by posterity long after those who laboured for them will have passed from the scene. It is always a source of great comfort to know that your efforts are widely appreciated. Oxford has given you a shot in the arm, an event which must have come as a source of great pleasure to your family and the wider cause that you serve. Perhaps you will permit me a bit of selfishness in hoping that this will even tempt you to cross over to this side more often than you have done in the past.[i]

S.A. has produced a rich crop of eminent women who have played an independent role in our history. At the beginning of the last century 'Manthatisi[ii] rose to command what was by the standards of the time, a powerful army which influenced the course of events in this country, particularly in the Free State and the N.W. Cape. Olive Schreiner[iii] was a militant liberal with a dynamic pen. Even today some of her writings and speeches could turn jelly into solid rock. On the other hand, Cissie Gool[iv] operated within a comparatively narrow compass, but her stand on matters essentially local had repercussions far beyond the W. Cape. A contemporary of yours, Elisabeth Eybers,[v] has written some of the most beautiful poetry in the country and, as "Dertiger", blazed the trail in the sphere of literature. Foremost amongst the women who today are making a significant contribution in the educational, literary, political and sociological field is Fatima Meer[vi] who is attracting atten-

---

i   Suzman continuously raised the issue of political prisoners in Parliament and first met Mandela and his comrades on Robben Island in 1967.

ii   Queen Manthatisi led the Tlôkwa people during the period of the Difiqane/Mefacane wars, 1815–40, until her son, Sekonyela was old enough to rule.

iii   Olive Schreiner (1855–1920), South African author, feminist, socialist, and pacifist.

iv   Cissie Gool was the founder and first president of the National Liberation League, president of the Non-European United Front in the 1940s, and the first coloured woman to graduate from law school in South Africa and be called to the Cape Bar.

v   Elisabeth Eybers (1915–2007), South African poet who mainly wrote in Afrikaans.

vi   Fatima Meer (1928–2010), writer, academic, and anti-apartheid and women's rights activist – see the glossary.

tion from far and wide, whilst Ray Alexander,[i] an active trade unionist since the thirties, has been a commanding figure in the struggle of the workers for a better life.

These are but a few of the many women in S.A. who have made, and are making, a definite mark in public affairs. The link that unites them all is the fine tradition they have built. May be that is that fine tradition which has consciously or unconsciously inspired you to venture out of the sanctuary of your comfortable and happy home into the storms and frustrations of your present life. If today that fine tradition still finds echo inside the most important organ of governance here, it is mainly because you had the courage to step out into the arena when many would prefer to remain on the sidelines.

Perhaps at times you have been driven to near-despair by what seems to be a hopeless endeavour – a task undertaken by a single hand where a whole legion is required. I trust that any doubts you might have entertained have now been completely dispelled, that you will consider both the honour, as well as the numerous messages of congratulations I assume you received, as a tangible expression of the crucial value of your efforts. You have many friends and well-wishers.

Once more, my warmest congratulations! May the coming month be a day of joyful occurrence for you and colleagues. Fondest regards to you and family.

Yours very sincerely,
[Signed NR Mandela]

Dr Helen Suzman, M.P., c/o Nkosikazi Nobandla Mandela, House no 8115, Orlando West, P.O. Phirima, Johannesburg

1/3/74

SECRET[ii]

LETTER FROM PRISONER MANDELA TO MRS H SUZMAN, MP.

---

i   Ray Alexander was born in Latvia and arrived in South Africa on 6 November 1929 where she joined the Communist Party of South Africa at age sixteen.

ii   It is not immediately clear why the official marked this cover note as 'Secret' other than that he intended for it to remain secret that it was not sent.

THE HONOURABLE THE DEPUTY MINISTER OF PRISONS.

1. Attached hereto is a typewritten copy of a letter from prisoner Nelson Mandela, addressed to Mrs. H Suzman, MP. Via Nkisikazi[i] [sic] Nobandla Mandela[ii] of Orlando West, for your information.
2. As the letter does not convey any domestic affairs, but is dressed with political suggestions and ideas, it has not been released

JC STEYN

COMMISSIONER OF PRISONS
CHIEF DEPUTY COMMISSIONER (FUNCTIONAL)

Copy for your information

[Signed]

COMMISSIONER OF PRISONS

[Stamp dated] 3-4-1974

◇◇◇◇◇◇◇◇◇◇◇◇

Throughout much of Mandela's time in prison he was forced to write to various government bodies from the police to the minister of justice in a desperate attempt to protect his wife. From the time he was imprisoned right up until he was released, Winnie Mandela was the subject of a sustained campaign of abuse by the apartheid state. Her husband could only learn of attacks on his wife through some of the letters from her that reached him, from lawyers and later through the media. His sense of powerlessness must have been overwhelming at times when he could do little to assist her and could only imagine what she had to endure. To add to his anxiety was the question of the safety of their children.

---

i   Correct spelling should be *Nkosikazi*, meaning 'Mrs.' in isiXhosa.
ii   Nobandla is one of Winnie Mandela's names.

To the minister of justice

[Message in another hand in Afrikaans at the top of the letter] 466/64
N. Mandela. Special letter to Commissioner about how his wife is
being handled

13 May 1974

The Honourable Advocate J Kruger,[i]
Minister of Justice
Pretoria.

Dear Sir,

I should be pleased if you would treat this matter as one of the utmost
urgency. I should have liked to have made these representations more
than three months ago, but due to my current circumstances and the
measured pace at which government departments are accustomed to
move, it has not been possible for me to write earlier than today.

1

In this connection, I should be grateful if you would:

a) grant my wife, Mrs Winnie Mandela, House no 8115 Orlando West,
   Johannesburg, a permit to acquire a firearm for purposes of self-
   defence;
b) request the Minister of Police to order members of the South African Police in dealing with my wife to confine themselves strictly to
   the execution of their duties according to law.
c) use your influence with the City Council of Johannesburg to relax
   their influx control regulations and to allow my brother-in-law Mr
   Msuthu Thanduxolo Madikizela,[ii] and his wife to live permanently
   with my wife at 8115 Orlando West, Johannesburg.
d) arrange with the Minister of Police for members of the South Afri-

---

i   James (Jimmy) Kruger (1917–87), minister of justice and police, 1974–79 – see the glossary.
ii   One of Winnie Mandela's brothers.

466/64 N. Mandela. A/B. aan Kmva od oy wan as behandl g.

Robben Island Prison.
Robben Island
13 May 1974.

The Honourable Advocate J Kruger,
Minister of Justice
Pretoria.

Dear Sir,

I should be pleased if you would treat this matter as one of the utmost urgency. I should have liked to have made these representations more than two months ago, but due to my current circumstances and the measured pace at which government departments are accustomed to move, it has not been possible for me to write earlier than today.

1

In this connection, I should be grateful if you would:
(a) grant my wife, Mrs Winnie Mandela, House no 8115 Orlando West, Johannesburg, a permit to acquire a firearm for purposes of self-defence;
(b) request the Minister of Police to order members of the South African Police in dealing with my wife to confine themselves strictly to the execution of their duties according to law
(c) use your influence with the City Council of Johannesburg to relax their influx control regulations and to allow my brother-in-law, Mr Msuthu Thanduxolo Madikizela, and his wife to live permanently with my wife at 8115 Orlando West, Johannesburg.
(d) arrange with the Minister of Police for members of the South African Police to guard the house daily from 7 p.m. to 6 am until my brother-in-law and his family join my wife.
(e) to request the minister of Interior to furnish my wife with a passport to enable her to holiday abroad.
(f) grant my wife and me a two hour contact visit for the purpose of discussing the special problems outlined here.

2

My wife is a person upon whom notice has been served under the provisions of the Suppression of Communism Act, 44 of 1950. I have not had the opportunity of seeing the actual text of the above-mentioned notice, but to the best of my knowledge and belief, she is prohibited from

CPS-17-5

Page from a letter to the minister of justice, 13 May 1974, see pages 148–55.

can Police to guard the house daily from 7 pm to 6 am until my brother-in-law and his family join my wife.

e) to request the Minister of Interior to furnish my wife with a passport to enable her to holiday abroad.

f) grant my wife and me a two-hour contact visit for the purpose of discussing the special problems outlined here.

2

My wife is a person upon whom notice has been served under the provisions of the Suppression of Communism Act, 44 of 1950. I have not had the opportunity of seeing the actual text of the abovementioned notice, but to the best of my knowledge and belief, she is prohibited from attending gatherings, entering a factory, an educational centre or similar places. Though she is free to take up employment within the urban area of Johannesburg, she is otherwise confined to Orlando township and is not permitted to enter the rest of the area in Johannesburg known as Soweto.

3

In terms of the abovementioned notice, and with the exception of our two daughters now aged 15 and 13 respectively, no person is allowed to visit the house during certain specified hours. As the children were then and still are, away at a boarding school for the greater part of the year, this meant that she had to live all alone in the house.

4

Towards the end of 1970 and again on 27 May 1971 I wrote to your predecessor, Mr P.C. Pelser,[i] requesting him to grant me an interview to enable me to discuss with him my wife's house-arrest and its implications. In this connection I wish to refer you to the following passage in my letter of 27 May 1971:

> "I consider it dangerous for a woman and detrimental to her health to live alone in a rough city like Johannesburg. She suffers from an illness which is caused by worry and tension and which has on occasions rendered her unconscious. Believe me when I say that I have since September

---

i   See his letter on pages 116–8.

last year lived in a real nightmare. She has visited me thrice since her release from prison, and the harmful effects of many nights of loneliness, fear and anxiety are written across her face. She looks pale and spent. I am further told that her hardships have been carefully and fully explained to you, without success, by herself as well as her legal representative. I cannot get myself to accept that you could remain indifferent where the very life of another human being is actually involved, and I ask you to relax the notice to enable her to live with friends and relatives."

In addition, I raised other family problems which I considered serious and repeated the request for an interview.

5

I was informed by the Commanding Officer at the time, and by Brigadier Aucamp,[i] that both letters had been forwarded to your predecessor. I regret to advise you, however, that Mr Pelser did not even favour me with the courtesy of an acknowledgement to say nothing of a reasoned reply.

However, some time after the May 1971 letter had been forwarded my wife informed me that the notice had been relaxed and that she could now live with such relatives or friends as were qualified to remain within the urban area of Johannesburg in terms of its influx control regulations. She further informed me that although the terms of the notice were still restrictive, some of the problems about which I had complained in my second letter had somewhat eased.

6

In pursuance of the abovementioned relaxation our friends, Mr and Mrs Madhlala, came to live with my wife. To the best of my knowledge and belief, the Madhlalas were not associated with any of the political organisations that fight against racial oppression generally and the policy of separate development in particular. In spite of this, the Security Police repeatedly dragged them to their headquarters and subjected them to gruelling interrogation. As a result of this harassment they were reluctantly compelled to leave our place. The news of the experiences of the Madhlalas at our house spread far and wide

---

i   Brigadier Aucamp, commanding officer of Robben Island – see the glossary.

and people, including close friends who would readily agree to reside with my wife, took fright and are now unwilling to do anything that may attract the attention of the Security Police, so much so that today there is hardly any person who is willing to share the type of life my wife is forced to lead.

7

The one and only person who is still prepared to live with my wife is Mr Madikizela, and I must request you to use your influence with the City Council of Johannesburg to give him permission to live at 8115 Orlando West. I must add that prior to his endorsement out of the urban area of Johannesburg, Mr Madikizela stayed with my wife.

8

The fears I expressed in my letters to your predecessors were not unfounded. On several occasions my wife has been the subject of brutal night attacks from criminals whose identity is unknown to us. In this connection I wish to quote from a letter she wrote me on 6 December 1972:

> "You must have perhaps heard from our mutual informer of the serious events which have left me quite shaken. Briefly, the house was broken into whilst I went home with the children to see my sick father. All our little valuable possessions were taken, the strange thief did extensive damage to the house, smashed to pieces what he could not take, tore down paintings from the walls, broke our glass partition, smashed the glass doors, removed books and personal documents . . .[i]

> "Then at 3.30 am Sunday morning two weeks ago, three black man gained entry into the house through the same window which I had not fixed because the police had not taken the statement of the burglary. They tried to strangle me with a cloth. Had he not taken a deep breath as he bent over my neck to tie the cloth I would not have heard anything. I did not know I could scream so much, they switched off the light & fighting them off in the dark saved

---

i   Mandela's own ellipsis.

me. I sustained slight injuries. I was given police protection for a few days whilst an urgent application was made
for someone to stay with me. My attorneys applied for
Msuthu & Nonyaniso[i] and her husband temporarily whilst
the Minister is deciding on Msuthu. However I was subsequently granted permission for a Mr & Mrs Ntsokonsoko
whom I met at work, they have been given 7 days at a time
and their permit is expiring tomorrow. Our problem is that
no one is prepared to share my kind of life, the situation is
far worse now."

I also quote from her letter of 20 March 1974:

"The last attempt on my life on the 9th (i.e. 9 February)
has left me quite speechless . . . The damage to the house
was quite extensive. I have been battling to repair what can
be repaired, the garage doors need complete replacement.
The hatred with which iron doors were torn apart, like
pieces of wood is indescribable. It is a mystery to me how
the house doors took so long to give in with such heavy
impact on them."

These events show that the effects of the restrictions placed upon my
wife, and the persistent refusal of the Johannesburg City Council to
allow Mr Madikizela to stay with her, have made her an easy target to
a mysterious type of thugs. An Alsatian dog, which she acquired at the
end of 1970, was poisoned and killed quite obviously by a person who
has considerable experience in dealing with dogs that are trained to do
police duties and to accept food from one person only.

All the fears I expressed to your predecessor have been confirmed
and today my wife lives in perpetual danger and acute anxiety. I am
reluctantly compelled to request you to give her a permit to acquire a
firearm for purposes of self-defence, a request which I hope you will
consider fair and reasonable, having regard to all the circumstances. I
might add, that last year a man attempted to stab her in the streets of
Johannesburg in broad daylight and she was saved only by the intervention of friends. The man was subsequently arrested, but I have been
told that the charge was later withdrawn.

---

i   Nonyaniso (Nyana) Madikizela, Winnie Mandela's youngest sister.

9

In the light of my wife's experiences I must ask you to arrange for the house to be guarded by members of the South African Police daily from 7 pm to 6 am. Until Mr Madikizela moves in.

I must point out that from all the reports I have received the Security Police have acted towards my wife in a manner which I cannot accept as a proper execution of their duties. She is shadowed wherever she goes, taxi men whom she hires to convey her to and from work are frequently interrogated, and those who come to stay with her persistently harassed. Generally their attitude is hostile and on occasions positively provocative. Your intervention could give her some respite and ease the strain.

10

In spite of all her bitter experiences my wife has no intention whatsoever of leaving the house. But I think it advisable for her to be furnished with a passport to enable her to travel abroad on holiday. Getting away from Orlando for a month or two might ease the strain and benefit her health immensely.

11

I must add that although I have now completed eleven years of my sentence, and although I have reached 'A' Group, the highest classification a prisoner may attain, I have never been given the privilege of a contact visit with my wife. I have been forced to discuss serious domestic problems across a glass partition, and under difficult conditions where I have to shout to be heard even in regard to highly confidential matters. Moreover, the one hour allocated for the visit is too short a period, if account is taken of our special problems. I must accordingly ask you to allow me a two-hour contact visit, with all the normal liberties and courtesies associated with such visits, for the purpose of discussing these special problems.

12

I am quite certain that if you think that my representations are reasonable and substantial, and you consider it your duty to help, all red tape will be brushed aside and our problems could be solved with the stroke of a pen.

13

It would be quite easy for you to reject each and every one of the requests I have made. You could, for example, point out that the question of the relaxation of influx control regulations is a matter outside your competence and within the jurisdiction of the Johannesburg City Council. You could adopt the same attitude towards my request in regard to the South African Police and passports, and tell me that my wife and I should apply directly to the appropriate authorities. You could even go further to rub it in by adding that my wife, in fighting racial oppression, had deliberately invited all the troubles she is now experiencing, and that the Security Police, in giving more than ordinary attention to her movements and activities, are carrying out their normal duties under the law.

14

I am well aware that, in view of all the circumstances, my representations will have to be approached cautiously and carefully, and that a decision either way will carry a heavy responsibility. Your official capacity may demand that you should pay attention to policy and security considerations which will result in grave injustices to specific individuals. I am also aware that the decisions you arrive at in your Ministerial capacity may frequently clash with your own personal feelings in matters of this nature.

15

The representations contained in this letter are made in the knowledge and certainty that they can be approved in such manner and under such conditions as will not endanger the security of the State or the public interest.

Above all, is the fact that the central issue in this matter is that the life of another human being, of a citizen, is at stake. I feel confident that in examining my requests you will allow humanitarian considerations to override all others, and do everything in your power to enable my wife to lead at last a normal and happy life.

Yours faithfully,
[Signed NRMandela] .
NELSON MANDELA 466/64

To Winnie Mandela,[i] his wife

[Note in Afrikaans in another hand] Keep 913 [the number of Mandela's file]

Nelson Mandela 466/64   A Group   1.2.75

Dadewethu,[ii]

This is the 5th & last letter I'll write to you before you leave jail.[iii] I fear that the March letter may reach Kroonstad after you'll have been drafted & I'll accordingly send it straight home. I'll do the same with that of Apr. My other letters for Feb have gone to Zeni,[iv] Ndindi[v] (Thembi's[vi] eldest daughter who will be 9 on 20/2), Sisi Phathiwe & Florence Matanzima.[vii] Sisi Phathiwe is Mrs Nkala & now matron of the Mditshwa High School in Ncambele[viii] & probably the first in the Dalindyebo[ix] family to qualify as a teacher. She was at Shawbury.[x] As you know, Florence is our Molokazana.[xi]

I told Judy[xii] in my Nov letter to her that I should like to see Zeni alone as soon as she turns 16. I would suggest that for her 16th birthday you attempt something a little more than usual, say, slaughter a sheep & call together AmaDlomo[xiii] & friends. You should consult

---

i   Nomzamo Winifred Madikizela-Mandela (1936–2018) – see the glossary.
ii   'Sister' in isiXhosa.
iii   Winnie Mandela was still serving her six-month sentence in Kroonstad Prison for being in the presence of another banned person.
iv   Zenani Mandela (1950–), their eldest daughter – see the glossary.
v   Ndileka Mandela (1965–), Mandela's eldest grandchild.
vi   Madiba Thembekile (Thembi) Mandela (1945–69), Mandela's eldest son – see the glossary.
vii   A wife of K. D. Matanzima (for K. D. Matanzima, see the glossary).
viii   A village about 20 km outside Mthatha in the Transkei (now Eastern Cape province).
ix   Chief Jongintaba Dalindyebo (d. 1942), the chief and regent of the Thembu people. He became Mandela's guardian following his father's death – see the glossary.
x   A high school run by Methodists.
xi   'Daughter-in-law' in isiXhosa.
xii   Nombulelo Judith Mtirara is a sister of Sabata Jonguhlanga Dalindyebo (for Sabata Jonguhlanga Dalindyebo, see the glossary).
xiii   Mandela was part of the AmaDlomo clan.

Kgatho,[i] Jongintaba, Ntatho,[ii] Lily,[iii] Dorcas,[iv] Marwede & others. Such an affair may give her a lot of pride, self-confidence & joy. But you should keep it within bounds. There's still the more important 21st birthday when you'll have to go all out to launch the girl into a new life as an independent person.

Visits from across the Kei[v] affect me in a special sort of way. Seeing the old lady,[vi] Mabel,[vii] Luvuyo, Bambilanga,[viii] Chief of the Qulunqu,[ix] Mbuzo, George[x] & others revived many fond memories. But there is a gap which has not been filled. One of the fervent hopes I have nursed these last 10 yrs is that of seeing Amangutyana[xi] from Mbongweni, a hope which was kindled by Manyawuza's[xii] visit & by C.K.[xiii] himself in the one & only letter I ever received from Bizana (dated 12/3/68). Of course Niki, Nali & Bantu[xiv] have been here, but they are all townsmen to whom the approach & idiom of people from the village has now become foreign. I was tempted to believe that Nyawuza's visit would be the first in a series that would come from Amangutyana. I also thought that 14/10 would shake up Ma[xv] & bring her over there & here at once. Maybe she is well aware of our almost expectations but I suspect that the poor soul is experiencing pretty formidable problems. I've never received a single line from her & Mpumelelo in spite of several letters I've written home. But it would be unwise, & even unfair, to suggest that she should come. The beauty about these things is the knowledge that your people think of you on their own.

A million thanks for the beautiful Xmas card, almost identical with that of Alan Paton[xvi] which arrived the same day. The rest came from

---

i   Makgatho Mandela (1950–2005), Mandela's second-born son – see the glossary.
ii   Nthato Motlana (1925–2008), friend, medical doctor, businessman, and anti-apartheid activist – see the glossary.
iii   Lilian Ngoyi (1911–80), politician, and anti-apartheid and women's rights activist – see the glossary.
iv   Possibly Dorcas Nongxa, an ANC Women's League activist.
v   Kei River in the Transkei.
vi   Possibly he means his mother.
vii   Mabel Notancu Timakwe (1924–2002), Mandela's sister.
viii Bambilanga (also known as Nxeko) is the brother of King Sabata Jonguhlanga Dalindyebo, paramount chief of the Transkei homeland.
ix   The Qulunqu people were from the district of Engcobo in the Transkei.
x   George Matanzima (1918–2000), K. D. Matanzima's brother, Transkei leader and chief. While Mandela was at University College of Fort Hare with KD, George studied at nearby Lovedale College.
xi   Members of Winnie Mandela's family who come from the amaNgutyana clan.
xii   Sibali Nyawuza. Mandela confused his clan name and referred to him as Manyawuza. *Sibali* means 'brother-in-law' in isiXhosa.
xiii Columbus Kokani Madikizela, Winnie Mandela's father – see the glossary.
xiv   Three of Winnie Mandela's sisters.
xv   He is most likely referring to Nophikela Hilda Madikizela, Winnie Mandela's stepmother.
xvi   Alan Paton (1903–88), author and founder and leader of South Africa's anti-apartheid Liberal Party.

Judy, Rochelle & sisters,[i] Tellie[ii] & Mafu,[iii] Leabie & hubby,[iv] Nolusa-
pho, Gwen Curry, Anne & Benjie,[v] Phyllis & kids, Mkentane family,
Monica Kobus, Euphemia Mhlatuzana.[vi] Nothing from the chdn &
Thoko.[vii] Apart from yours, which I hope you've got, I sent cards to
the ff.[viii] Kgatho & Reyne,[ix] the girls, Maki, Ma & Camagu,[x] Ndindi
& Nandi,[xi] Thoko,[xii] Buyelekhaya,[xiii] Judy & kids, Bantu & Earl,[xiv] Lily,
Fatima & Ismail,[xv] & Tim. By the way, in my last letter I spoke of
Esther,[xvi] instead of Jane, to whom I intend writing in March.

The discreetness of Hans St[xvii] in regard to family matters impresses
me very much. There have been a few notable occasions in which
caution has been thrown to the winds. But I have the hope & confidence that this will be avoided in future. There are affairs in life
where third parties, no matter who they are, should not be let in at
all. Incidentally, you may find that the cell is an ideal place to learn
to know yourself, to search realistically & regularly the process of
your own mind & feelings. In judging our progress as individuals we
tend to concentrate on external factors such as one's social position,
influence & popularity, wealth & standard of education. These are, of
course, important in measuring one's success in material matters & it
is perfectly understandable if many people exert themselves mainly
to achieve all these. But internal factors may be even more crucial
in assessing one's development as a human being. Honesty, sincerity,

---

He gave evidence in mitigation of sentence for Mandela and his co-accused at the Rivonia Trial – see
    the glossary.
i   Nombulelo Judith Mtirara's daughters.
ii   Telia (Telli or Tellie) Mtirara, a relative of Mandela's.
iii   One of Winnie's brothers.
iv   Leabie Makhutswana Piliso (1930–97), Mandela's sister, and her husband.
v   Anne Sassoon and Benjamin Pogrund (1933–), friends. Anne is an artist and Benjamin was former
    deputy editor of *the Rand Daily Mail* – see the glossary.
vi   A friend of Mandela's.
vii Thoko Mandela, his son Thembi's widow, and their two daughters.
viii 'And the following'.
ix   Makgatho (Kgatho) Mandela (1950–2005), Mandela's second-born son – see the glossary – and his
    then wife, Rose Rayne Mandela, known as Rennie.
x   Makaziwe Mandela (1954–), Mandela's eldest daughter – see the glossary – and her husband.
xi   Ndileka (1965–) and Nandi (1968–) Mandela, the daughters of his late son, Thembi (for Thembi
    Mandela, see the glossary).
xii Thoko Mandela, the daughter of his late son, Thembi.
xiii Buyelekhaya Dalindyebo (1964), son of Sabata Jonguhlanga Dalindyebo – see the glossary.
xiv Winnie Mandela's sister Nobantu and her husband Earl Mnki.
xv Fatima (1928–2010) and Ismail Meer (1918–2000), friends. Fatima was a professor, author, and anti-
    apartheid activist and Ismail was a lawyer and anti-apartheid activist – see the glossary for both these
    individuals.
xvi Esther Maleka, an ANC activist who worked in the underground.
xvii Hans Street is where the Helping Hand boarding house was located. Winnie Mandela stayed there when
    she arrived in Johannesburg in 1953.

simplicity, humility, pure generosity, absence of vanity, readiness to serve others – qualities which are within easy reach of every soul – are the foundation of one's spiritual life.

Development in matters of this nature is inconceivable without serious introspection, without knowing yourself, your weaknesses & mistakes. At least, if for nothing else, the cell gives you the opportunity to look daily into your entire conduct, to overcome the bad & develop whatever is good in you. Regular meditation, say about 15 minutes a day before you turn in, can be very fruitful in this regard. You may find it difficult at first to pinpoint the negative features in your life, but the 10th attempt may yield rich rewards. Never forget that a saint is a sinner who keeps on trying.

You should also think seriously about the new life you'll have to lead after Apr. 13. The bit of warm sunshine in which you once bathed may be gone & the atmosphere more chilly & glum than you may imagine. There certainly will be no trumpets to announce your return & perhaps there'll hardly be a soul to meet you at the Fort, & sharp arrows may come from unexpected quarters, even from those who adore you. Maybe that even resuming old jobs may be a milestone in your life in which the most elaborate explanations to those who have been on your side would be pointless.

But even on such occasions the opportunities for challenge, initiative & success are tremendous. Difficulties break some men but make others. No axe is sharp enough to cut the soul of a sinner who keeps on trying, one armed with the hope that he will rise & win in the end. I have every reason to love you. There are treasures buried deep inside you & I live in the hope that you'll be able to unlock them some day. My most tender thoughts centre always on you. A million kisses & tons & tons of love.

Devotedly,
Dalibunga

Your Dec letter never arrived. Have written to you monthly since Oct. Nkosikazi Nobandla Mandela, C/o Major Van Zyl, Women's Prison, Kroonstad (9500)

To Adelaide Joseph,[i] a friend

Nelson Mandela 466/64   A Group   1 March '75

Our dear Adie,

There are few people I have wronged as much as you, Paul,[ii] Zoya, Tania & Nadia, the late Anand[iii] also. That you have never written to me either is hardly any excuse for my long silence. You should have been among the very first persons to hear from me. You & Paul, Zami[iv] & I have had many hrs of pleasure together &, in your company, one felt had access to all the good things in life. The last dys we spent together were in many ways the end of an era in our life &, to this dy, serve as a source of inspiration at groovy moments. Perhaps that is one reason I miss you so much.

Do you still remember Aug – Oct '62 when you would visit me almost dyly at Ameshoff St,[v] carrying a pantry of tasty curries in your hands? Perhaps there have been times when you were tempted to think I have forgotten all that. I should like you to know that I have repeatedly asked Zami about you & even sent you a birthday card which I hope you received. I lap up every bit of news about you & have even mastered sufficient courage to study your man's hieroglyphics with which I am now fairly familiar. I tried to follow the news of Zoya's movements & was happy to hear good accounts from those who met her. I am told that she is as beautiful & relaxed as Lord Rama.

Does she still remember the first time she met Zeni[vi] at Zeni's second birthday party. A friend here always reminds me of that amusing occasion. Whenever he feels homesick he grabs the guitar & harps merrily away. When he picks the strings he does reasonably well. But let him strum to the accompaniment of his own voice, then a whirlwind of discordant sounds begin crashing around the building, the instrument tuned on G

---

i   Adelaide Joseph (1932–) and Paul Joseph (1930–), were South African political activists who went into exile in London in 1965. When Mandela was arrested in 1962 Adelaide brought him food in prison.
ii   Paul Joseph, Adelaide Joseph's husband.
iii   Adelaide and Paul Joseph's children. Zoya and Anand were twins born in 1959. Anand died in 1970. Tanya (Mandela misspelled her name as 'Tania') (1963–), and Nadia (1966–).
iv   Another name for Winnie Mandela.
v   Ameshoff Street is close to the Fort Prison where Mandela was then being held.
vi   Zenani Mandela (1959–), Mandela's first-born daughter to his second wife, Winnie – see the glossary.

Nelson Mandela 466/64   A Group   1 March '75
                          221/75
Our dear Arlie,

There are few people I have wronged as much as you, Paul, Zami, Tanya & Nadia, the late Amaud aka that you have never written to me either is hardly any excuse for my long silence. You should have been among the very first persons to hear from me. Yours Paul, Zami & I have had many hrs of pleasure together &, in your company, one felt he had access to all the good things in life. The last days we spent together were in many ways the end of an era in our life &, to this day, serve as a source of inspiration at groovy moments. Perhaps that is one reason I miss you so much.

Do you still remember a Sep-Oct '62 when you would visit me almost daily at Aimeshoff St. carrying a panful of tasty curries in your hands? Perhaps there have been times when you were tempted to think I have forgotten all that. I should like you to know that I have repeatedly asked Zami about you & even sent you a birthday card which I hope you received. I lap up every bit of news about you & have even mastered sufficient courage to study your man's hieroglyphics with which I am now fairly familiar. I tried to follow the news of Zoya's movements & was happy to hear good accounts from those who met her. I am told that she is as beautiful & pleasant as Lord Rama.

Does she still remember the first time she met Zeni at Zeni's second birthday party. A friend here always reminds me of that amusing occasion. Whenever he feels home-sick he grabs the guitar & taps merrily away. When he picks the strings he does reasonably well. But let him stream to the accompaniment of his own voice, then a whirlwind of discordant sounds begin crashing around the building, the instrument tuned in G & the guitarist croaking dolefully in a different key. When the girls met at the Orlando party they did something much the same, one chatting away in English & the other in Xhosa. Nevertheless, they seem to understand each other well. By the way, Zeni turned 16 on Feb. 5 & I plan to see me in May. I have waited an eternity for that moment.

I often think of the flutter Zoya & I caused at Baia. The day I drove you & Amaud to see a specialist. I left you & Amaud at the Outpatients. A dog & showed Zoya round the place, canvassing freely as we went along, the reaction of those we met was quite amusing. Some were somewhat puzzled but held their tongues. Others were more daring & chose to probe a bit. "Your child?" asked a sister, quite politely first. I let her imagination run wild. Is the mother this or that? she added. I told her I was a bit blind & could not answer the question. This time she was sharp: "Indeed you must be." & I walked away. Zoya was hardly 3 then but was quite philosophical about the incident. I am pleased to know that she has grown to become a charming & warm lady. I once hoped that I would have the pleasure of handing her over to the groom at a wedding & perhaps even naming her first-born. Maybe I will!

You will have to introduce me to both Tanya & Nadia & hope they will be equally friendly & warm. There is a group photo here in which Tanya appears. She looks a chip of the old block. I look forward to seeing all of them some day. In the meanwhile, you should know that you are ever in my thoughts & those days we spent together in Fordsburg & Orlando have become even more precious now & help to brighten each day.

We learnt of the death of Amaud & of your struggle to save his life & are really sorry to hear that he had left us. Perhaps the blow would have been easier to take if we had all been there. I well remember how Zoya used to play with him while lying on his back in the cot, & how he would giggle away as you tickled him with your fingers. Our deepest sympathy, & die, even at this late hr. I hope Jack was encouraged to hear from us & to know that he is constantly in our thoughts. He is both tough & optimistic & has held on most of the time, I suspect, through sheer will power. With all this, a woman like Rica on his side plays such abundant goodwill to draw on, he should be able to get up & move around as before. Did Mike's Barbara receive my letter of condolence written on 11/11/74? I should also

& the guitarist croaking dolefully on a different key. When the girls met at the Orlando party, they did something much the same, one chatting away in English & the other in Xhosa. Nevertheless they seemed to understand each other well. By the way, Zeni turned 16 on Feb. 5 and plans to see me in May. I have waited an eternity for that moment.

I often think of the flutter Zoya & I caused at Bara.[i] The dy I drove you and Anand to see a specialist. I left you & Anand at the Outpatients Dept and showed Zoya around the place, conversing freely as we went along. The reaction of those we met was quite amusing. Some were somewhat puzzled but held their tongues. Others were more daring & chose to probe a bit. "Your child?" asked a sister, quite politely at first. I let her imagination run wild. Is the mother this or that? she added. I told her I was a bit blind & could not answer the question. This time she was sharp: "Indeed you must be." I walked away. Zoya was hardly 3 then but was quite philosophical about the incident. I am pleased to know that she has grown to become a charming & warm lady. I once hoped that I would have the pleasure of handing her over to the groom on her wedding day & perhaps even naming her first-born. Maybe I will!

You will have to introduce me to both Tanya & Nadia & hope they will be equally friendly & warm. There is a group photo here in which Tanya appears. She looks a chip off the old block. I look forward to seeing all of them some dy. In the meantime you should know that you are ever in my thoughts & those dys we spent together in Fordsburg & Orlando have become even more precious now & help to brighten each day.

We learned of the death of Anand & your struggle to save his life & were really sorry to hear that he had left us. Perhaps the blow would have been easier to take if we had all been there. I well remember how Zoya used to play with him while lying on his back in the cot, & how he would giggle away as you tickled him with your fingers. Our deepest sympathy, Adie, even at this late hr. I hope Jack[ii] was encouraged to hear from us & to know that he is constantly in our thoughts. He is both tough and optimistic & has held on most of the time I suspect, through sheer willpower. With all this, a woman like Rica[iii] on his side plus such abundant goodwill to draw on, he should be able to get up & move around as before. Did Mike's Barbara[iv] receive my letter of condolence

---

i   Baragwanath Hospital in Soweto, Johannesburg.

ii   Percy John 'Jack' Hodgson (1910–77), a member of the armed wing of the ANC living in exile in London.

iii   Rica Hodgson (1920–2018), an activist living in exile in London.

iv   Michael Harmel (1915–74), a leading member of the Communist Party, and his daughter, Barbara (1942–2018).

on 1/10/74? I should also like to write a similar letter to Jimmy's Barbara[i] but do not have her present address. Have they any other children apart from Tanya? I also think of Anne-marie & Harold[ii] & will be writing to them as soon as I can. In the meantime I send them my fondest regards.

I enjoyed Willie's letter to which I shall certainly reply. But I am 2 yrs behind schedule at present.

[This part is written inside an accompanying birthday card.]

I am busy attending to the '73 correspondence. That letter took me back to '61 when I saw him almost daily.[iii] In fact I was thinking whether I should not hire a ground floor flat in Ophirton, Fordsburg or Hillbrow where he & I could move in and pick up the old threads again. I miss Ruth's[iv] notes of the century[v] to Das.[vi] Invariably thorough in her accounts & neat in expression, her notes tell more about mother earth than all the unique harvest of data gathered by Skylab. I miss her & her lord[vii] a great deal. Find out from your namesake[viii] & Maggie[ix] whether they receive my letters & give fondest regards to OR,[x] Mota,[xi] Rusty & Hilda[xii] & Reggie.[xiii]

---

i   James Kantor's wife, Barbara. For James Kantor, see the glossary.

ii   Annemarie (1930–2018) and Harold Wolpe (1926–96). Harold Wolpe had been arrested at Liliesleaf Farm and named as a co-conspirator in the Rivonia Trial. They went into exile in London after Harold Wolpe escaped from police detention with Mosie Moolla, Arthur Goldreich and Abdullay Jassat in 1963.

iii Mandela is referring to his friend and comrade Wolfie Kodesh (1918–2002). Mandela had stayed for a time at Kodesh's flat in Yeoville, Johannesburg, when he was in hiding. (Mac Maharaj in a conversation with Sahm Venter, 11 December 2018.)

iv   Ruth First (1925–82), journalist and Communist Party and ANC activist. An accused in the 1956 Treason Trial (for the Treason Trial, see the glossary). She went into exile in 1964 and was killed by a parcel bomb sent by apartheid agents while she was living in Mozambique.

v   Mandela's reference to Ruth First's 'notes of the century' refers to her editorship of *Fighting Talk* during the mid-1950s, a monthly magazine which provided information on resistance by South Africans to the suppressive actions and legislation of the National Party Government. (Mac Maharaj in a conversation with Sahm Venter, 11 December 2018.)

vi   A name used by Mac Maharaj while he was in the German Democratic Republic (GDR) in 1961, where he had been sent by the South African Communist Party (SACP) to undertake military training. (Mac Maharaj in a conversation with Sahm Venter, 11 December 2018.) For the South African Communist Party (SACP), see the glossary.

vii 'Her lord' refers to Ruth First's husband, Joe Slovo. Mandela would not have been able to send this letter if it had been clear whom he was referring to. (Mac Maharaj in a conversation with Sahm Venter, 11 December 2018.)

viii Must be Adelaide Tambo (1929–2007), wife of Mandela's former law partner and president of the ANC, Oliver Tambo – see the glossary.

ix   Magdaline 'Maggie' Resha (1923–2003), nurse and anti-apartheid activist who was living in London at the time. (Mac Maharaj in a conversation with Sahm Venter, 11 December 2018.)

x   Oliver Tambo (1917–93), Mandela's friend, former law partner, and the president of the ANC – see the glossary.

xi   Dr. Yusuf Dadoo (1909–93), medical doctor, anti-apartheid activist, and orator. President of the South African Indian Congress, deputy to Oliver Tambo on the Revolutionary Council of MK, and chairman of the South African Communist Party – see the glossary.

xii Rusty Bernstein (1920–2002), architect and anti-apartheid activist, and his wife, Hilda, who went into exile after his acquittal in the Rivonia Trial – see the glossary.

xiii Reggie September (1923–2013), a political activist accused in the 1956 Treason Trial (for the Treason Trial, see the glossary). He left South Africa to live in exile in 1963, first in Tanzania and then in London.

I am busy attending to the '73 correspondence. That letter took me back to '61 when I saw him almost daily. In fact I was thinking whether I should not hire a ground floor flat in Osterton, Fordsburg or Hillbrow where he & I could move in & pick up the old threads again. I miss Ruth's notes of the century to Das. Invariably thorough in her accounts & neat in expression, her notes tell more about the mother earth than all the unique harvest of data gathered by Skylab. I miss her & her lord a great deal. Find out from your namesake & Maggie whether they receive my letters & give fondest regards to DR, Meta, Rusty & Hilda & Reggie.

I sincerely hope that everything is going well with you on the mainland & that a letter from across the waves gives you as much pleasure as those from your side. Hawzile!

            Very sincerely,

                Nel.

Miss Adie Zoya Macikizela, c/o Nkosikazi Nobandla Mandela, 8115 Orlando West, P.O. Phirima Lisbon / HB.

The back of a birthday card enclosed with a letter to Adelaide Joseph, 1 March 1975, see previous pages 163–5.

I sincerely hope that everything is going well with you on the mainland & that a letter from across the waves gives you as much pleasure as those from your side. Hantle!ⁱ

Very sincerely,
Nel

Miss Adie Zoya Madikizela,ⁱⁱ
c/o Nkosikazi Nobandla Mandela,
8115 Orlando West,
P.O. Phirima [1848] JHB

To Yusuf Dadoo,ⁱⁱⁱ comrade in exile in London

NELSON MANDELA 466/64   A. GROUP.

1.11.75

My dear Motabhai,ⁱᵛ

Since Jan. '73 I've written the family, relatives & friends 190 letters &, during the past 13 yrs have amassed a precious fortune of 199 letters that contain inspiring sentiments of love & devotion, solidarity & hope. Some of these are disturbingly realistic & sober whilst others are highly idealistic.

Do you still remember the '52 D.C.ᵛ with its apostolic themes of "Crossroads" and "in our lifetime"? Of course you do. I can still see

---

i 'Well' in Sesotho, usually accompanied by the word 'sala' to read 'Sala hantle', meaning 'stay or keep well'.

ii Mandela has deliberately made up the name 'Adie Zoya Madikizela' from Adelaide Joseph's first name (Adie), her daughter's name (Zoya), and Winnie Mandela's maiden name (Madikizela), probably in an effort to fool the authorities into allowing the letter to be posted.

iii Dr. Yusuf Dadoo (1909–83), medical doctor, anti-apartheid activist, and orator. President of South African Indian Congress, deputy to Oliver Tambo on the Revolutionary Council of MK, and chairman of the South African Communist Party – see the glossary.

iv 'Big brother' in Gujarati. *Mota* means someone older than you – a sign of respect – and Dadoo was known as Mota.

v Initiated by the ANC in December 1951, and launched with the South African Indian Congress on 26 June 1952 against six apartheid laws, the Defiance Campaign Against Unjust Laws (known as the Defiance Campaign for short) involved individuals breaking racist laws such as entering premises reserved for 'whites only', breaking curfews, and courting arrest. Mandela was appointed national volunteer-in-chief and Maulvi Cachalia as his deputy. Over 8,500 volunteers were imprisoned for their participation in the Defiance Campaign.

[word very difficult to read] as black as nicotine in khaki outfit & with baton in hand, singing with his congregation those thrilling hosannas & ready to foot it all the way to heaven. My letters are rich with such sentiments.

My aunt, who is fond of me & whom I last saw 20 yrs ago, writes lively letters. "A hothead is tamed by his own people," says she in one of them & then goes on to urge perfect submission on my part in the hope that such an attitude will lead to a change of heart in relevant quarters. Others turn to the last weapon of those who have no concrete suggestion to offer & advise that we pray hard & sincerely because, so they argue, the divinities can never let down those who seek their protection. The third category stresses while you've repeatedly urged on formal & informal occasions in the past & what has influenced me in the last 30 yrs. This is the rich harvest I've gathered in the last decade. But none of these letters contains a note of despair or pessimism & all of them assume that one day we'll be back to share all the pleasures of a free life. Each one of them is a powerful tonic that keeps my blood clean & my head clear. Each one that comes makes me feel stronger & more confident than the day before.

It is mainly for this reason that Saturdays are so important here. Our post is always delivered on this day. Almost all eyes are usually fixed on the main gate to the Section, & officials that bring the letters are for the moment as popular as film stars. When they appear, otherwise ponderous fellows & who normally move around like confident pontiffs, suddenly become alert ready to dart forward to find out whether there's something for them. Smiles immediately light the faces of those who are lucky, whilst a few amongst them even hum a ditty out of pure joy. The rest stroll away bravely hoping for better luck next time. If Matlala,[i] Reggie,[ii] Muggie, Adie & Barbra knew all this, they would long have acknowledged my letters. Did Ruth[iii] receive hers?

A substantial percentage of my outgowing correspondence consists of condolence letters. It may well be that death has always been as common as it is at this distance & that in the old days pressure of work gave me little time to think about such matters. It is also possible that my

---

i   A nickname for Adelaide Tambo (1929–2007), friend, anti-apartheid activist, and wife of Oliver Tambo, Mandela's former law partner and president of the ANC – see the glossary. The Tambos were living in exile in London.

ii   Oliver Tambo's middle name was Reginald and Mandela referred to him as Reggie.

iii He could be referring to anti-apartheid and women's rights activist Ruth First (1925–82) who was also in exile in London.

present circumstances have made death appear far more tragic than I saw it before I was jailed. Certainly the death of members of the family & other relatives has hit me very hard. I was equally shaken by that of friends like A.J.,[i] Amina, Debi, Hymie, Jimmy, Mike, Miriam, Molly & your successor, Nana, Z.K.[ii] & others I remember with fond memories. Such losses inevitably make one feel alone when one has become thoroughly accustomed to group life. I've found it hard to live away from old friends & even harder to be away from those I'll never see again.

I told Amina in a letter to her today that I remember all the memorable days from 52 onwards. Of course I've nothing to prod the memory – photos. I can pull out of the drawer, records I can consult & landmarks that show the future direction of affairs. Nevertheless I often think of '46 the year when Ismail introduced me to you. By the way, he & I still keep together as we did during our varsity days.[iii] Fatima[iv] writes regularly & even visited me in '73. I think of 47, the yr of the medical congress in which you, Xuma[v] and Monty[vi] prominently featured.[vii] Does James still remember that occasion? I also remember the day in the Broadway Cinema in '52 when we gave you & Dave[viii] a boisterous send-off & everything that followed thereafter. You know the score quite well.

I think much of the days to come, the problems of adjustment, & of picking up the old threads. It is mainly in this regard that I never really live on this island. My thoughts are ever travelling up & down the country, remembering the places I've visited. The *Oxford Atlas* in spite of its old age – having acquired it in '63 – is one of my greatest companions, & in the process I've come to know the world & my country far better than when I was free.

But the purpose of this note is not to talk about correspondence, past memories or the *Oxford Atlas*, but to tell you that I never forget

---

i   Chief Albert Luthuli (1898–1967), president-general of the ANC, 1952–67 – see the glossary.
ii   Professor Z. K. Matthews (1901–1968), academic, politician, anti-apartheid activist, and ANC member – see the glossary.
iii   He is indicating to Dadoo who was in exile that he is still close to Ismail Meer.
iv   Ismail Meer's wife.
v   Albert Xuma (1893–1962), first black South African to become a medical doctor, president-general of the ANC 1940–49.
vi   Monty Naicker (1910–78), doctor, politician, and anti-apartheid activist – see the glossary.
vii   He is mostly likely referring to 'The Doctors' Pact' of 1947 signed by Dr. Yusuf Dadoo, Dr. Alfred Xuma, and Dr. Monty Naicker about cooperation between the ANC, the Transvaal Indian Congress, and the Natal Indian Congress and calling for the right of freedom of movement, education, the right to vote, and equal opportunities for all 'non-European' South Africans.
viii David Bopape (1915–2004), ANC and South African Communist Party member.

Sept 5[i] to wish you many happy returns. We think of you with far more pride than words can express. The birthday parties we used to hold for you are amongst the memorable occasions Ahmed[ii] and I often talk about. We realise only too well that perhaps now it may not be possible for you to celebrate in the usual way. But even so I hope you'll at least find time to gather a few friends and have a bit of relaxation. In particular I hope that you, the 2 Reggies[iii] and Toni's Pa[iv] are keeping together like quadruplets. I always think of you in this way.

For god's sake don't tell me that you gave up indlamu[v] which you used to dance so well in Soweto in the fifties. It's a typical S. African dance – as typical as "daar kom die Alabama",[vi] the tickiedraai[vii] & the Bharat natium.[viii] But I'd like to try the very oldest of our traditional dances: the Basaxwa[ix] ceremonial hunting dance & the Khoikhoi askoek.[x] Not only will they keep you as fit & fearless as one strives to be, but will give you a more realistic insight into why the aborigines loved life so intensely & why they defended themselves so stubbornly & long against the vicissitudes of nature & of human folly.

Finally, I wish to remind you of the many ties that hold us together, not the least of which is the Winnies on our side[xi] – the most wonderful creatures on earth. Once more many happy returns. I look forward to seeing you some day. In the meantime I send you fondest regards & my very best wishes to your Winnie, Shireen[xii] & everybody.

Sincerely, Nelson

Mr Mota D, Mothabhai,[xiii] c/o Mrs Amina Cachalia, PO Box 3265, Johannesburg

---

i   Yusuf Dadoo's birthday.
ii   Ahmed Kathrada (1929–2017), leading member of the ANC and South African Communist Party, and fellow Rivonia trialist who was imprisoned with Mandela – see the glossary.
iii   These are likely Oliver Reginald Tambo (see the glossary) and Reggie September (1923–2013), a political activist accused in the 1956 Treason Trial (for the Treason Trial, see the glossary). He left South Africa to live in exile in 1963, first in Tanzania and then in London.
iv   Mandela is possibly referring to comrade Rusty Bernstein (1920–2002) – see the glossary – who was acquitted in the Rivonia Trial. His daughter's name was Toni.
v   A traditional Zulu dance.
vi   An Afrikaans folk song.
vii   A traditional Afrikaans dance.
viii   A genre of classical Indian dance.
ix   A ceremonial hunting dance perfomed by the Basarwa people.
x   A dance step of the San people.
xi   Both their wives were named Winnie.
xii   Yusuf and Winnie Dadoo's daughter.
xiii   By using Dadoo's nickname, Mandela is trying to disguise his identity.

◇◇◇◇◇◇◇◇◇◇◇◇

The year 1976 in South Africa was marked by a growing unease among young people frustrated by their parents' lack of resistance to apartheid.

The clampdown of the 1960s, which followed the arrest and imprisonment of a range of freedom fighters, was intended to have permanently suppressed opposition to the regime. The rise of Black Consciousness from the late sixties culminated in the student uprising in Soweto on 16 June 1976 against a plan to have black students taught in Afrikaans, the language of the oppressor. The police responded to the peaceful protests with live ammunition, killing hundreds. Hundreds more were arrested, many of them ending up as sentenced prisoners; even more fled the country to swell the ranks of the exiled armies of the liberation movements. Cut off from news media until 1980, the prisoners on Robben Island only became aware of what had happened in August 1976 when the first of the young people began arriving with sentences to serve.

The following long letter to the prison authorities detailing the continuing abuses of authority can also be read as Mandela's way of trying to improve conditions for all prisoners, including the new group of angry young men. He and his comrade Walter Sisulu[i] *stood out for their efforts to talk down the firebrands and advise them on a better path to survival in prison.*[45]

To the commanding officer, Robben Island

12 July 1976

The Commanding Officer
Robben Island

<u>Attention: Col. Roelofse</u>

The attached letter is for the personal attention of the Commissioner of Prisons, General Du Preez, and I should be pleased if you would approve and forward it to him.

---

i   Walter Sisulu (1912–2003), ANC and MK activist and fellow Rivonia trialist who was imprisoned with
      Mandela – see the glossary.

I am putting it in a sealed envelope addressed to you and marked "Confidential and for the personal attention of Col. Roelofse." But once I hand it over to the official-in-charge of the section, I have no further control over it and cannot guarantee that it will reach you in the condition in which it left me.

[Signed NRMandela]

To the commissioner of prisons

12 July 1976

The Commissioner of Prisons
Pretoria

Attention: General Du Preez

I must draw your attention to the abuse of authority, political perse-cution and other irregularities that are being committed by the Com-manding Officer of this prison and members of his staff. Although this letter raises complaints of a personal nature, some of them affect other prisoners as well and it may, therefore, be necessary to mention certain names by way of illustration of these irregularities.

During the past 14 years of my incarceration I have tried to the best of my ability to cooperate with all officials, from the Commis-sioner of Prisons to the Section warder, as long as that cooperation did not compromise my principles. I have never regarded any man as my superior, either in my life outside or inside prison, and have freely offered this cooperation in the belief that to do so would promote harmonious relations between prisoners and warders and contribute to the general welfare of us all. My respect for human beings is based, not on the colour of a man's skin nor authority he may wield, but purely on merit.

Although I did not agree with the approach of General Steyn on the country's major problems and the policy of the Department of Prisons I, nevertheless, respected him as head of this Department and as an individual and have never had occasion to question his integrity.

Even though I think he could have done more that he did to promote the welfare of prisoners here and elsewhere in the country, his genial and unassuming manner made it easy for me to discuss with him otherwise delicate matters and, in spite of many disagreements I had with him from time to time on the actual decisions he made on specific issues, he was often prepared to give a reasoned motivation for his actions.

I met your immediate predecessor Gen Nel, when he came to the Island in 1970 with Mr Dennis [sic] Healey[i] and, bearing in mind the few remarks we exchanged on that occasion, I have no reason to think that as head of this Department he fell short of the standard set by his predecessor in regard to the manner in which he handled problems I brought to his attention. Unfortunately I have not had the pleasure of an interview with you but I have assumed throughout this letter that you would do everything in your power to improve prisoner-warder relations and to promote our welfare.

I have now had no less than 3 interviews with Brigadier Du Plessis, head of the security section and, in spite of the fact that every one of my complaints was not rectified, he nevertheless tried to give reasonable explanations for his actions and outlined the policy of the Department on the matters we discussed as patiently as time allowed.

As I understand it, one of the principal functions of this Department is to maintain good order, discipline and the proper administration of the prison. In terms of the Prison Rules, special attention shall be accorded to the preservation of good relationships between a prisoner and his relatives in the best interests of both parties. This object is normally attained through visits, letters, telegrams, birthday, Easter and Christmas cards.

A public department is a creation of a law and should be run in accordance with the governing legal rules. The actions of both the officials and prisoners in every field of activity should be based on rules that can easily be ascertained and, even where officials are given a wide discretion on a particular point, respect for the principles of natural justice would demand a clear indication of the considerations that will be taken into account in the exercise of that discretion. This rule is observed in many countries throughout the world by public

---

i   Denis Healey (1917–2015), British Labour Party politician who Mandela first met on a short visit to London in 1962. Later Healey visited him in prison.

bodies which deal with human problems so as to remove or minimize the dangers of injustice though malice, caprice, arbitrariness, corruption, pettiness and other improper motives.

The actions of the Commanding Officer and his staff that are mentioned below have nothing to do with the maintenance of good order, discipline and the proper administration of the prison, nor with the promotion of harmonious relations between prisoners and officials, such actions are incompatible with the preservation of good relations between a prisoner and his relatives and constitute abuse of authority, political persecution and vindictiveness.

The absence of clearly defined rules that lay down how the discretion enjoyed by local officials is to be exercised in the particular cases indicated below has given them wide scope for malice, arbitrariness and other improper motives.

On several occasions I have tried in vain to draw the attention of Col. Roelofse to these problems and it is because he and the head of the prison Lt. Prins, and the official in charge of censoring, W/O Steenkamp have fallen short of the high standard of morality required from those who are entrusted with the running of a public department that I now feel compelled to place the whole matter before you.

1. Abuse of authority
    (a) On December 27, 1974 the Minister of Prisons, Advocate J. T. Kruger, in the presence of the C.O.;[i] granted me permission to purchase Piet Meiring's "Ons Ses Eerste Premiers" and, at the same time, informed the C.O. that there was nothing in the book he considered objectionable. In pursuance of this permission I ordered the book, but, as it was out of print at the time, it only arrived on the Island on February 16 this year. In spite of the fact that permission to acquire the book was given by the Minister himself, and in spite of repeated efforts on my part to get it, the C.O. failed to release the book until April 27, exactly 2 months 11 days after it had arrived. I probably would not have got it if Brigadier Du Plessis had not intervened on my behalf.
    (b) Both Col. Roelofse and Lt Prins have been systematically practicing racialism to prisoners in the Single Cell Section and trying to foment feelings of hostility among us.

---

i   Commissioner of Prisons.

(i)   At the meeting of the Prison Board this year, the C.O. asked a coloured prisoner from this section what he thought of the level of civilisation of the 'Bantu' in the section and how the coloured prisoners were getting on with the 'Bantu'.[i] When this particular prisoners replied that his African colleagues in this section were educated and cultured men for whom he had good respect and that we all got on with one another, the C.O. made disparaging remarks describing Africans as being from a low level of civilisation and as people who walked about the country half naked.

(ii)   On two previous occasions W/O Prince, as he then was, made remarks to 2 Indian prisoners, speaking to each one on a different occasion, to the effect that Africans were uncivilized and that when they were in power they would attack whites, coloured and Indians alike, and stressed that the best course for Indians would be to join whites. To one of them he added that he always thought politically on these matters.

It is dangerous to entrust the task of promoting the welfare of prisoners to officials who hold racialistic views, and it is an abuse of authority to take advantage of their official positions to try and create feelings of hostility amongst prisoners of different population groups. We totally reject apartheid in all its forms and the C.O. had no right whatsoever to attempt to sell us an idea we regard as diabolical and dangerous.

In this connection, I should like to add that the conduct of these officials is not only improper but also contrary at least to the avowed official policy. Government spokesmen, including the present Premier, have repeatedly repudiated the idea that any particular population group in the country is superior to others.

2.   Improper interference with Social Relationships
(a) My youngest daughter, Zindziswa,[ii] sent me photographs on 3 different occasions, one of which I actually saw in my file in 1974 when W/O Du Plessis and I were looking for the copy of a

---

i   While the word 'Bantu' comes from 'Abantu' meaning people, it can be seen as offensive in a context such as this one where the speaker is using it as a racial description. It was used under apartheid to refer to Africans.

ii   Zindziswa Mandela (1960–), Mandela's youngest daughter – see the glossary.

letter I had written to a former Minister of Justice. When I asked for the photo, he told me we should deal with one thing at a time and, for that day, I left the matter there. When I subsequently asked for it, the photo had disappeared.

I mentioned the matter to Lt. Terblanche then head of the prison, who told me he would investigate it. Later, I received 2 other letters in which my wife reported that my daughter had sent other photos. As I had not received them, I immediately placed the matter before Lt Prins. Although I mentioned it to him twice thereafter, I have never heard from him again.

I might add that I had no trouble with letters from my daughters until Zindziswa complained to the United Nations about the systematic persecution of her mother by the Government and I believe that the difficulties that have since arisen with her correspondence with me and that of her elder sister, Zenani,[i] is a pure act of vindictiveness from the C.O. acting in collaboration with the Security Police.

(b) In January this year my 2 daughters wrote me letters which they sent by registered post. Although both Lt Prins and Sgt Fourie of the Censors Office have assured me that they have not been received, I have been given the same information before and later discovered that in actual fact, the letters had already been received when such assurances were given.

(c) Two children who live with my wife also sent me 2 registered letters about the same time. A month or so after that, my wife advised me of this fact and Sgt Fourie assured me as usual that they had not been received. I warned him of the seriousness of telling me an untruth in regard to letters sent by registered post and asked him to make further investigation. He later informed me that he had checked as requested but reiterated his earlier assurance.

I then reported the matter to Lt Prins who subsequently acknowledged that the letters had been received some weeks before I spoke to Sgt Fourie. Lt Prins than formally advised me that the letters would not be given to me because they were militant and written by children who did not know me. One is related to my wife and I was already in prison when she was born. The

---

i   Zenani Mandela (1959–), Mandela's middle daughter – see the glossary.

other was only 5 when I was sentenced. Lt Prins refused to tell me why I was given untruthful explanations about the letters by Sgt Fourie. *Precisely the same thing happened with the letters from Mrs Adelaide Joseph[i] and again the abovementioned 2 officials were involved.

(d) Letters written by my wife to her relative, Mr Sandi Sejake, also in this section and those written by him to her do not reach their destination.

(e) There are many cases of this nature, but I should like to cite that of my fellow prisoner Theophilus Cholo, who was convicted in 1973 and who has not received a visit from his wife since then, their only means of contact being through letters. He last received one from her in February this year and in May Lt. Prins refused to give him a 3 page letter from her on the ground that its contents were objectionable, and at the same time prohibited him from telling her that her letter was withheld from him. I now consider the untruthful explanations that are repeatedly made by the local officials about our correspondence and the so-called objection either to the contents of the letter or person who wrote it as a mere technique to deprive us of the legal right of preserving good relationships between ourselves and our relatives and friends.

3. Censorship of outgoing mail

The following examples will demonstrate to you the type of difficulties we are having due to over-suspicion on the part of your officials and maybe even to their difficulty of understanding the language and its idiom.

(a) On July 1, 1975 I sent a birthday card to a friend who is in his early thirties and ended the message of felicitations with the greeting in phonetic script: "Me-e-e-e-i Bra-a-a!" which is a corruption of the Afrikaans "My Broer" and which form of greeting is commonly used by today's urban youth. I was told to rewrite the whole birthday message and to leave out the words quoted above. I was asked for no explanation and put to the unnecessary expense of using another card.

---

i   Adelaide Joseph (1932–) and Paul Joseph (1930–), were South African political activists who went into exile in London in 1965. When Mandela was arrested in 1962 Adelaide brought him food in prison.

(b) As has often happened in the past, the birthday card I sent to my daughter Zindziswa, on December 1 last year did not reach her. On February 1 I wrote to my wife:

"These are the only occasions when I sometimes wish science could invent miracles and make my daughter get her missing birthday cards and have the pleasure of knowing that her Pa loves her, thinks of her and makes efforts to reach her whenever necessary. It is significant that repeated attempts on her part to reach me and the photos she has sent have disappeared without trace whatsoever."

Again I was ordered to omit this passage and when I asked Sgt Steenkamp, as he then was, for an explanation he discourteously told me that the letter would not go if I did not rewrite it.

c) My daughter Zindziswa plays rugby at school and has openly discussed her sport interests both during her visits and in her letters. In her letter of February 8 this year which came through the normal official channels, she complained about loss of weight. On April 15 I wrote back to her:

"But if you really want to be in top condition for such strenuous games as rugby, which require tremendous reserves of energy and speed, you'll have to pay due attention to your diet – eat well, I repeat, eat well! Although I do not know where Mum will raise all the cash for that."

The passage was disallowed and Lt Prins refused to give me any explanation about the matter.

(d)   My grandniece, Xoliswa Jozana,[i] wishes to study LL.B with a view of practising as a lawyer and the parents asked for my advice as to whether it would be wise for her to do law. On April 15 I wrote back to them encouraging my grand-niece to proceed as she wished, but at the same time advised the parents that I have been out of practice for 16 years and would accordingly

---

i   Xoliswa Jozana, daughter of K. D. Matanzima (1915– 2003), Mandela's nephew, a Thembu chief, and chief minister for the Transkei – see the glossary. His middle name was Daliwonga.

consult Mrs F Kentridge, who formerly practised at the Johannesburg Bar. On May 9 I wrote to Mrs Kentridge along the lines indicated above and, on June 4, Lt Prins arrogantly told me that I should rewrite the letter and leave out the facts mentioned above, adding that the Matanzimas could get the advice from somebody else.

It was the hostility with which he spoke more than his unreasonable explanation that struck me. In addition, I wondered what had happened to my letter of April 15. Whatever they did with it they acted improperly. If they sent it to the Matanzimas then they allowed me to make a promise to my relatives which they knew in advance they would not permit me to fulfill. If the letter was held back, I should have been told about the matter, which was not done.

To prevent me from telling my wife that I sent my daughter a birthday card which did not reach her, that I always think of her and that the photos she had posted to me had disappeared is an unreasonable act based neither on security considerations nor on the desire to maintain good order and discipline nor to promote my welfare. The same applies to my letter to Mrs Kentridge in which I requested her to advise my grandniece on her desire to become a lawyer.

4. Censorship of incoming correspondence

But the worst abuses in regard to the censoring of letters are committed in regard to incoming correspondence and, in this connection, the C.O. and his staff have gone rampant. The censoring is malicious and vindictive and again is motivated by considerations of security and discipline not the desire to promote our welfare.

I regard it as part of a campaign of systematic political persecution and an attempt to keep us in the dark about what goes on outside prison & about our own family affairs. What the C.O. is trying to do is not only to cut us off from the powerful current of goodwill and support that has ceaselessly flown in during the 14 years of my incarceration in the form of visits, letters, cards and telegrams, but also to discredit us to our family and friends by presenting us to them as irresponsible people who neither acknowledge letters written to them nor deal with important matters referred to us by our correspondents.

In addition the double standards used in censoring letters is cowardly and calculated to deceive the public into the false impression that our outgoing mail is not censored. In the case of outgoing letters we are required to rewrite them whenever there is any matter to which the prison authorities object, so as to remove any evidence that they have been heavily censored whilst incoming ones are badly cut or scratched out as the censors please. Nothing will best convey to you the extent of the damage caused to our incoming mail more than an actual inspection by you in person. Many of the letters from my wife consist of strips of incoherent information that are difficult to keep together even in a file.

My wife has been in prison several times and not only knows the relevant Prison Rules well, but also the sensitivity of your local officials to anything they might consider objectionable. She makes a conscious effort to confine herself to family affairs, yet hardly a single one of her letters escapes mutilation.

On November 24 1975 she wrote me a 5-page letter and only the remains of 2 pages finally reached me. The censorship policy adopted here is not followed even by your own officials in other jails. As you are aware, my wife has recently served a 6 months sentence in Kroonstad. Some of her letters were passed by the C.O. of that prison but heavily censored this end.

But what I intensely detest is to force us to be parties to a practice based on plain falsehood. It is immoral for the C.O. to destroy or withhold letters from our families and friends and at the same time prevent us from telling them about what he does with them. I consider it callous to allow our people to continue wasting money, time, energy, goodwill and love by sending us letters and cards which the C.O. knows will never be given to us.

Between December 1974 and April 1976 no less than 15 letters for Mr A Kathrada were withheld. Among them were those from members of his family, from Prof Rampol, Messrs Ismail Bhoola, Essop Pahad[i] and Navraj Joseph.[ii] Lt Prins refused Mr Kathrada permission to tell his people to stop writing to him, adding that he found their letters interesting. When Mr Kathrada said he supposed the security police were also interested, Lt. Prins, although

---

i   Essop Pahad (1939–), political activist in exile in London.
ii   Paul Joseph (1930–), a friend and anti-apartheid activist who went into exile in London in 1965.

he did not say so categorically, indicated that they would be so interested. This is a clear case of abuse of authority and you ought to issue a public statement in which you clearly define the policy of your Department, and set out, more particularly, what you consider objectionable and the categories of persons who may not write or send us money or messages of goodwill.

5. Disappearance of letters in transit

The number of letters that disappear in transit is far too large to be explained on the basis of the inefficiency of the Post Office Department and, from the unreasonable and persistent refusal of the C.O. to allow us to register our letters, I must draw the inference that their disappearance is not accidental. In this regard the C.O. recently made a bad mistake which confirmed my suspicion that in these matters he and subordinates are not acting openly.

On March 1 I wrote to Mr Q Mvambo, care of my wife, and at the same time advised her about it. She replied that she had not received the letter to Mr Mvambo and the C.O. had that information cut out from my wife's letter so as to keep me in the dark about the fact. If the C.O. were not implicated about the disappearance of this particular letter why did he deliberately try to conceal the fact?

The registration of outgoing mail will partly solve this particular problem and the introduction of this practice will not increase the work of the local officials at all. A post office book for the bulk registration of mail can be used as in all big firms and we are prepared to do the secretarial work under the supervision of the Sgt in charge of the section and all that the censors would be required to do would be exactly what they are doing now, namely, to enter the letters in the official records and post them away.

6. Visits

Even here the measures taken by the C.O. in supervising conversations between prisoners and their visitors go beyond the security requirements. To put four and sometimes even six warders on duty to one visitor, breathing into her face or staring threateningly at her is a blatant form of intimidation.

It is my duty to tell you that there is a widespread belief amongst my fellow prisoners that at these visits there is a listening device that records all conversations, including confidential matters between husband and wife. If this be the case there is hardly any justification for the show of force now generally displayed during such visits. I might add that I encountered repeated opposition from the warder-in-charge when, during one of her visits, I kept on reminding my daughter not to allow herself to be distracted by these strong-arm tactics. For several years in the past only one or two warders were on duty during these visits and I request you to reintroduce this system.

In addition, we were also allowed to use memory aids to make certain that nothing of importance would escape attention and to deny us that privilege after we have enjoyed it for more than a decade is to deprive us of all the advantages of a planned and systematic conversation. We have repeatedly assured the C.O. that we would be prepared to submit these aids for inspection before and after the visit. Moreover, as there are always warders on duty, the danger of passing on objectionable information does not exist at all.

7. Language qualifications of the censors

The man who is directly in charge of censoring of our mail and magazines is W/O Steenkamp who was previously in charge of this section. Although he may have passed matric English, he is certainly no more proficient in that language than I am in Afrikaans and I doubt if Sgt Fourie is any the better in this regard. I would certainly consider it an injustice to entrust me with the task of censoring Afrikaans letters. Neither of the officials in the Censors Office is properly qualified for the job.

Even the C.O. finds it difficult to express himself in English. In fact, during the 14 years of my imprisonment I have met no C.O. whose English is as poor as that of Roelofse; who commands a prison where the overwhelming majority of prisoners are English-speaking and who have no knowledge of Afrikaans at all.

The poor language qualifications of the local officials, especially in the Censors Office, may be one of the contributing factors to the unreasonably heavy censoring of our letters and it is proper for you to review the whole position and appoint censors who are thoroughly conversant with English, Herero, Ovambo,[i] Sotho, Tswana, Xhosa and Zulu.[ii]

---

i   Herero and Ovambo are languages from Namibia.
ii   Sesotho is the language of the Sotho people, Setswana is the language of the Tswana people, isiXhosa is the language of the Xhosa people and isiZulu is the language of the Zulu people.

8. Ban on correspondence with political supporters

Lt Prins has now told me that we are no longer allowed to communicate with any people known to the Department to be our political associates nor to relatives of other prisoners, irrespective of the contents of the letter. He accordingly refused me permission to write a condolence letter to Mrs N Mgabela, wife of a fellow prisoner on this island, who lost a grandchild. He also did not allow a letter to Mrs Lilian Ngoyi,[i] a lifelong friend, who helped look after the house and the children when my wife was jailed. A letter I wrote to her on January 1, 1975 and in which I thanked her for her gesture never reached. The failure of all my attempts to acknowledge the help she freely gave and her hospitality to the children is a constant worry to me and I must request you to allow me to send her a copy of the letter of January 1. I am equally anxious to send Mrs Mgabela my condolences and undertake not to say anything in the letter to which any reasonable objection might be made by the C.O.

9. Telegrams and Easter Cards

(a) the C.O. has introduced a new practice of not allowing us to see the actual telegrams sent to us. He has given us no reasons for departing from a practice that has been followed for many years. But I have had two experiences in which the local officials have been quite negligent and failed to deliver telegrams punctually.

(i) In 1972 when Col Willemse was C.O., I expected a visit on a Saturday from my eldest daughter, Makaziwe.[ii] That Saturday I was actually taken to the visiting rooms but she did not arrive. Later she wrote and referred me to a telegram she had sent postponing the visit. In response to my enquiry, the telegram was delivered two weeks after it had been received here. Col Willemse, however, gave me an explanation which exonerated him from any blame in his personal capacity and we settled the matter amicably.

(ii) Last year I was given a telegram announcing the death of the brother of the Paramount Chief Sabata Dalindyebo[iii] and

---

i   Lilian Ngoyi (1911–80), politician, and anti-apartheid and women's rights activist – see the glossary.
ii   Makaziwe Mandela (1954–), Mandela's eldest daughter – see the glossary.
iii   King Sabata Jonguhlanga Dalindyebo (1928–86), paramount chief of the Transkei homeland and leader of the Democratic Progressive Party, the opposition party in Transkei which opposed apartheid rule – see the glossary.

advising me of the day when he would be buried. Although the telegram was received before the funeral, it was given to me about 6 days after the burial and I now strongly protested at what I considered to be plain irresponsibility.

What happens now is that we are given a message scrawled on a piece of paper, sometimes in writing that is difficult to read, and without the date when the telegram was sent and received as well as other essential information. Again the current belief is that some of these telegrams are first referred for scrutiny to the Security Police before delivery to the addressee and in order to cover up the delay in handing over, the C.O. has introduced this practice.

The people who send these telegrams pay more money in order to ensure a speedy transmission of the message and it is a matter of public concern when a government department deliberately frustrates the smooth and efficient operation of a public service for which citizens pay an appropriate fee.

(iii) For several years now I have received Easter cards from a number of friends but this year none arrived. Last month and again in response to my enquiries Lt. Prins told me that one had arrived but that he objected to the person who sent it and refused to disclose the identity of the sender. Against the background set out above I did not find it easy to accept the truthfulness of that statement.

10. Money received for prisoners

There is a general impression amongst prisoners here that the C.O. and the Security Police are running a racket with our moneys. Although I have no evidence to substantiate this allegation, I should like to draw your attention to the following aspects:

(a) Last December my wife told me that our friends, Mr and Mrs Matlhaku, from Botswana,[i] had sent me R20.00. I immediately enquired from Lt Prins and on several occasions this year he assured me as usual that the money had not been received. Early in May the accounts section, in response to an earlier request,

---

i   Ishmael and Martha Matlhaku, friends of Mandela. Martha had worked as Mandela's personal secretary; Ishmael often transported comrades or activists to the Botswana border and on occasion had been entrusted with the transportation of ANC leadership, including Mandela.

furnished me with my balance and statement of moneys credited to my account[i] as from February 1975 to this year.

On May 31 Lt Prins sent a message to the effect that an amount of R30.00 was received from the Matlhakus on November 5 1975. No explanation as to why this year he repeatedly told me that the money had not been received nor why the money was not shown as having been credited to my account in the statement supplied to me by the accounts sections, nor about the covering letter from the Matlhakus. I assume that in due course I will be given the usual flippant excuse that the C.O. objects either to the Matlhakus or the contents of the letter.

(b) I have repeatedly complained about the amount of R40.00 which, according to my wife, was sent to me by my nephew from Cape Town and even mentioned the matter to Brigadier Du Plessis on April 28, as I had done with that of the Matlhakus. Lt Prins asked me to produce proof that this amount had been sent by my nephew and I showed him one letter from my wife and promised to produce a second one, also from my wife, which was not immediately available when I gave him the first. Early in May I offered to show him the second letter and he indicated that he would tell me when he wanted. To the best of my knowledge and belief the matter has received no further attention.

(c) For several years now, Mr G Mlyekisana and friends in Cape Town have been sending me and some of my fellow prisoners Christmas presents in the form of small amounts. None of us received any of these sums last year. This cannot be a pure coincidence. I believe the C.O., acting in consultation with the Security Police, has done something to prevent us from getting the moneys which he does not wish us to know.

(d) My friend, Mr Robert Matji, from Lesotho wrote some time last year and promised to send me and another fellow prisoner money for study purposes and, despite repeated enquiries, I have not been told whether or not that money came.

---

i   Upon entering prison, a list was made of the belongings a prisoner had with them. Details of the amount of cash a prisoner may have brought with them were recorded in an individual account under the name of the prisoner (this was not a bank account but simply a separate bookkeeping record). Thereafter, any funds reaching the prison in the name of that prisoner were recorded in that account and so too were any disbursements made in the name of the prisoner. When they were discharged from prison, the prisoner was given what remained in the account.

I must tell you that in the negligent manner in which my complaints have been investigated and the lengthy delays involved in extracting simple information on what are essentially trust moneys, is a matter of serious concern which you ought to investigate as soon as you can to clear the reputation of your Department at least in this particular respect. In the light of my experiences with the amount from the Matlhakus, you will readily appreciate my present state of mind on this question.

11. Problems relating to health matters

(a) About July last year and as a result of a knee injury I sustained last year whilst working at the seaside,[i] Dr Edelstein recommended that I should be provided with a sanitary pail lighter than the standard one I am presently using. Sgt Schoeman of the local hospital duly communicated the doctor's recommendation to the head of the prison. When difficulties arose, I personally interviewed Lt Prins on the matter. Although the injury has now healed, I was never provided with the pail as recommended by the doctor.

(b) On July 17 this year and again on health grounds, Dr Edelstein recommended that I could acquire at my own cost a pair of pyjamas and this recommendation by a competent medical practitioner was turned down by the C.O. on the ground, I learn, that prisoners are only allowed to buy sports equipment. With due respect to the C.O., it seems to me ridiculous to allow us to buy outfits for mere recreation, a concession we naturally appreciate, and refuse us permission to buy nightwear recommended by an experienced doctor.

As a matter of fact the C.O. knows only too well that his decision is arbitrary and inconsistent with a practice he himself has followed. My skin is sensitive to brackwater[ii] used on the Island, and on the recommendation of [the] doctor, I have been using a special cream since the Sixties to keep the skin soft.

On July 5 I discussed the matter with Dr Edelstein and he was surprised that I encountered difficulties in this matter and promised to take up the issue with the C.O. directly. I have since been informed that he could not move Col Roelofse. With his surprisingly backward views on race relations, I believe the C.O.

---

i   The prisoners collected seaweed.
ii   Brackish water – fresh water mixed with saltwater.

fears that if I acquire the pair of pyjamas as recommended by Dr Edelstein, the Senior Medical Officer on the Island, I will virtually become a white man.

In this country only white prisoners have the right to sleep in pyjamas with the exception of those fellow prisoners who are hospitalised locally and who are provided with a nightshirt which in many cases barely reaches ones knees. Black prisoners here sleep naked with only blankets as a cover. This is the real reason for the unusual step of a mere layman vetoing the considered decision of a competent professional man in his own field. When I saw Dr Edelstein on June 17 Sgt Schoeman had suggested that the prison hospital could provide me with a nightshirt which the doctor found unsuitable. It was after this offer that had been made that Dr Edelstein made his recommendation.

For 13 years I have slept naked on a cement floor that becomes damp and cold during the rainy season. Although I am physically fit and active, such unhealthy conditions have caused some damage. I will certainly not embarrass Dr Edelstein who has treated me well by discussing the matter with him again. But I need the outfit urgently and I must request you to allow me to purchase the recommended pyjamas at the earliest possible convenience.

I hope, General, you will not consider it as a threat directly or indirectly when I say that I have the legal right to take measures to protect my health and, once the medical officer is of the opinion that these measures will best improve a man's health, the C.O. has no jurisdiction whatsoever in the matter.

13. Political discussions at the sittings of the Prison Board[i]

It has been the practice for several years now at the sittings of the Prison Board for its members to engage prisoners in political discussions. Political discussions are welcome and may even be fruitful if they are properly arranged by the right people. The correct premise for any such discussions is the clear recognition that we are loyal and disciplined members of political organisations that have definite policies, and that on fundamental political problems we cannot act as individuals but as representatives of our organisations.

Secondly, if the discussions are to be profitable, we must be

---

i   Point 12 of Mandela's original letter was missing, he must have mis-numbered when writing it.

told about them beforehand, be furnished with the actual topic
for discussion, the names of the persons who will conduct such
discussions with us and their principal aim. It is certainly not the
function of the Board to conduct discussions of a political nature
and I consider the whole practice improper and request you to stop
it. Its function is to submit reports to the C.O.P. on the conduct,
training, aptitude and maturity of a prisoner and to make recom-
mendations for his classification, release without conditions, or on
probation or parole.

It is also the firm opinion of my fellow prisoners that these
discussions are used by the Board for the purpose of victimising
those who are opposed to the policy of separate development by
not upgrading them.

14. Other acts of victimisation
Throughout our stay here we have been constantly subjected to
various forms of victimisation for a variety of reasons connected
with political events outside the prison or with the usual tensions
that characterise relations between prisoners and warders. Many
examples can be quoted to illustrate the point, but for purposes of
this letter, it is sufficient to mention 3 of the current or recent cases.

(a)   As you are aware the churches have provided us with an
      inter-communication system to supply us with music from
      records bought by ourselves. Since the installation of the service
      we have invested in more than R1,000 worth of records. The
      service has been out of action for about 5 months now and we
      do not accept the explanation that the main difficulty in restor-
      ing it is the C.O. cannot obtain the necessary spare parts.

(b)   On July 3 we expected to see a film in accordance with a pro-
      gramme which has been in operation for some time now. It was
      not shown and the only explanation given by W/O Du Plessis
      was that it was not worth seeing.

(c)   A hot water system was installed last year and, on several
      occasions since its installation, the electric geyser failed but the
      electrician was able to fix it in a matter of minutes. For more than
      a week now, it has been out of order and the 'breakdown' coin-
      cides with a spell of cold weather on the Island. The remarkable
      thing about the matter is that, although we repeatedly reported
      the matter to the authorities, the electrician has not even come

to examine the apparatus to see what is wrong with it, with the result that we have been deprived[i] of hot water at the one time of the year when it is most needed.

The coincidence between the disorder in the geyser and the spell of cold weather becomes even more significant when considered against the surrounding circumstances. The general practice in the past has been to keep the span[ii] inside on rainy days but on July 7 the span was sent out to pull out bamboo[iii] from the sea although it was raining. They returned about lunchtime all wet and cold. By the morning of July 8 a few had contracted a cold. With the possible exception of the severe winter of 1964, this was certainly the coldest day on the Island in the last 12 years. Nevertheless the span was again sent out to the same spot which was the most exposed in the whole of this area from about 8am to 3.30 pm. The span shivered from cold and many were almost numb on their return. On July 9 a delegation consisting of Messrs Billy Nair,[iv] John Pokela and JB Vusani discussed the whole matter with Lt. Prins who promised that throughout the winter the span would not again be sent to work on that spot. He also arranged for hot water to be brought in drums from the kitchen.

15. Complaints against juniors

Lt. Prins, W/O Du Plessis and Steenkamp and Sgt. Fourie are all too junior to be expressly mentioned in a letter from me to you. But they are the officials in charge of our affairs and it is through them that the C.O. abuses his authority and persecutes us.

I have repeatedly brought to his attention most of the complaints discussed above without success. It is clear that he considers it his duty to support almost everything done by his officials against prisoners, however wrong that official may be, and I see no useful purpose whatsoever in pursuing these issues with him any longer.

---

i   Mandela includes a note in the margin to see footnote 22 and writes at the end of the letter: 'In regard to this matter I speak purely as a layman and from experience of what actually happened in the past when the geyser was out of order. It may well be that the electrician has some more reliable means of identifying the fault without actually inspecting the apparatus itself.'

ii   Afrikaans word for 'team' that was used in prison.

iii This is actually a type of seaweed which had the Afrikaans name of *bambous*. (Christo Brand, *Doing Life with Mandela* (Johannesburg: Jonathan Ball, 2014, p. 38.)

iv   Billy Nair (1929–2008), comrade and MK member who was charged with sabotage in 1963. He was held in B Section with Mandela on Robben Island and was released in 1984 – see the glossary.

As already indicated, I have had no less than 3 interviews with Brigadier Du Plessis and, in spite of his friendliness and courtesy it is clear that the situation is in many respects beyond his control, and what has happened since his last visit and my interview with him seems to have fanned the abuse of authority and political persecution.

Had I not been a Black prisoner born and brought up in South Africa, and who has been subjected in his daily life to all the excesses of racial prejudice, I would not have believed that normal human beings could be associated with such a mania for persecuting their fellow men. It is a mean type of cowardice to wreak vengeance on defenceless men who cannot hit back. An honourable warrior is no peacetime hero who concentrates his attacks on those who carry no weapons and he prefers to use his sword against those who are similarly armed.

16. The C.O.P.'s failure to visit political prisoners on Robben Island
The abuses described above are aggravated by your failure personally to visit the Island and to give us the opportunity to discuss these problems directly with you. The C.O. told us in the course of an interview with him early this year, that Gen Nel's term as C.O.P. would be expiring soon and that he was not likely to visit the Island before his retirement. This was unfortunate because regular visits by the C.O.P. are in themselves a means of checking abuses by subordinates and the knowledge that he would not be coming down made the C.O. unrestrained in his actions.

When Gen. Steyn was C.O.P. he visited us at least once a year and listened to complaints and requests. Then he brought Col. Badenhorst who tried to terrorise us and, in order to give him a free hand to transgress the law, Gen. Steyn stayed away from the Island whilst we were being persecuted, tortured, beaten up and humiliated in various ways. In 1972 I gave judges Steyn, Theron and Corbett,[i] in the presence of Gen. Steyn and Col. Badenhorst, details of the persecution we had received whilst the latter was C.O., stressing that in spite of my repeated requests to Gen Steyn to continue visiting the prison regularly he had kept away. I told the judges that he had stayed away because he realised that he could

---

i   Justice Michael Corbett (1923–2007) was the judge who administered Mandela's oath of office when he became president of South Africa in 1994.

not defend the illegalities that were being committed by his subordinates. I got the distinct impression that the judges were as much concerned about the General's failure to carry out his duties in this particular regard as I was.

A visit by other officials from Headquarters, whatever their ranks may be, can be no substitute for a visit by the Department Head in person. As already indicated, our treatment here is much influenced by political events outside prison and, in a way, the C.O. treats us like hostages. Whenever South Africa is under heavy attack for its racial policies, prison officials try to vent their anger and frustration on us.

In addition, any substantial complaint from a political prisoner, however genuine, tends to be regarded as a threat to the survival of the white man and even high ranking officials consider it their duty to resist it at all costs. In the prevailing political atmosphere in which it is being denounced by the whole world, no officials from Headquarters who still look forward to promotions and other lucrative benefits after retirement, are to burn their fingers by checking the abuses of a C.O. and upholding the complaints of the men who have played a part in mobilising opposition to apartheid. Only you and you alone, is in a position to take a bold line and confine the actions of the C.O. within the four corners of the law.

It is my earnest opinion that his actions fall outside the scope of the Prison Rules. A C.O. and Head of the Prison who still try today to perpetuate the myth of the superiority of the white man, who equate civilisation with a white skin and the clothing one wears, are not the fit and proper persons to be in charge of an institution, one of whose principal aims is the promotion of the welfare of Black prisoners.

One of the main causes of the friction here is the link between this Department and the Security Police and one of the first steps in your attempt to redress our grievances is to cut out that link completely. Honest officials from the Department frankly admit that in many respects we, as political prisoners, fall outside the scope of the Department and are the responsibility of the Security Police. The latter have no legal right to interfere in the internal administration of this institution and I hope that, in this regard, you will be able to assert yourself far more than your predecessors were able to do, and stop this unwarranted practice. Our treatment should be the responsibility of your Department not just in theory but in actual practice as well. The duty of the Security Police is to ensure that we are kept in a maximum security prison and their authority should go no further.

Many prisoners regard the C.O.P. in relation to all matters concerning us as a mere figurehead, and that the real boss is the Chief of the Security Police who order the C.O.P. not only what to do but how to do it. It is the Security Police that have induced your Department to want to isolate us from the people outside prison, to deny us the love of our wives and children and the good wishes from our friends by cutting down visits to the so-called first degree relations, trying to terrorise our visitors, not allowing us to use notes at visits, through malicious censoring of letters, cards and other material, false information in regard to letters, cards and money received on our behalf and the unprecedented 'disappearance' of letters in the post.

I have been wondering for some time now whether I should continue to be party to a practice I consider unethical and which gives the impression that I still enjoy rights and privileges which have been whittled away so much so that they have become practically useless. In particular, I have considered the question whether I should allow my wife and children to come down the 1000 miles from Johannesburg at great expense only to see me under such humiliating conditions, whether I should allow them to waste time, energy and money to write letters that 'disappear' in transit and whose remains that reach me are quite disconnected and meaningless. I resent the fact that before every visit they should receive lectures from swaggering and vindictive officials as to what they may or may not say when they talk to me.

Since January 1973 to June this year I have received 42 letters from my wife. Of the 6 I got in 1973 only 3 were mutilated. Of the 11 which came in 1974 7 were heavily censored and in 1975 6 out of the 16. But the picture for 1976 is totally different. Of the 9 I have received since the beginning of the year only 1 reached me unscathed. It is this situation that makes me wonder whether I should continue enduring these indignities.

But I still believe that you, as Head of this Department, who holds the rank of General, will not allow or condone these underhand methods and, until your actual decision on the matter proves me wrong, I shall continue to act in the belief that you are not aware of what is going on in this prison.

It is futile to think that any form of persecution will ever change our views. Your Government and Department have a notorious reputation for their hatred, contempt and persecution of the Black man, especially the African, a hatred and contempt which forms the basic principle of a multiplicity of the country's statutes and cases. The cruelty of this Department in subjecting our people to the indecent practice of thawuza according to which a prisoner was required to strip naked and display his anus for inspection by an official in the presence of other prisoners, the equally obscene practice of a warder poking a finger into a prisoner's rectum, of brutally assaulting them daily and without provocation, was curbed by the Government after it had erupted in a national scandal.

But the inhumanity of the average South African warder still remains, only now it has been diverted into other channels and has taken the subtle form of psychological persecution, a field in which some of your local officials are striving to and becoming specialists. You are no doubt aware that many psychologists regards psychological persecution in circumstances such as ours as more dangerous than plain assault. I have the hope that a man of your rank and experience will immediately grasp the gravity of this dangerous practice and take adequate measures to stop it.

It is pointless and contrary to this country's historical experience to think that our people will ever forget us. Although 160 years have passed since the Schlachters Nek executions,[i] 74 since the internment camps of the Anglo Boer War[ii] and 61 since Jopie Fourie[iii] made his last speech, I will certainly never believe you when you tell me that you have now forgotten those Afrikaner patriots, the men whose sacrifices helped to free you from British Imperialism and to rule the country, and for you in particular to be Head of this Department.

It is certainly quite unreasonable for any man to expect our

---

i   In 1815 a Boer farmer named Bezuidenhout refused to answer to charges of having mistreated his workers. He was shot by a British soldier when they came to arrest him. His supporters attempted to have revenge and were arrested. Six were executed by hanging at Schlachters Nek.

ii   The British ran concentration camps for Boer women and children during the South African War (1899–1902) and separate ones for black prisoners.

iii 'Jopie' Fourie (1879–1914), an Afrikaner rebel, was the last person to be put to death by firing squad in South Africa after he rebelled against the government which had chosen to support the British in the First World War rather than the Germans.

21.

P.21 81/143198

life. Of the 6 I got in 1973 only 3 were mutilated. Of the 11 which came in 1974 7 were heavily censored and in 1975 6 out of 16. But the picture for 1976 is totally different. Of the 9 I have received since the beginning of the year only 1 reached me unsealed. It is this situation that makes me wonder whether I should continue enduring these indignities.

But I still believe that you, as Head of this Department who holds the rank of General, will not allow this dubious practice to ~~continue~~ these underhand methods and, until your actual decision on the matter proves me wrong, I shall continue to act in the belief that you are not aware of what is going on in this prison.

It is futile to think that any form of persecution will ever change our views. Your Government and Department have a notorious reputation for their hatred-contempt and persecution of the Black man, especially the African, a hatred and contempt which forms the basic principle of a multiplicity of the country's statutes and cases. The cruelty of this ~~practice~~ Department in subjecting our people to the indecent practice of thawuza in which a prisoner was required to display his anus for inspection by an official in the presence of other prisoners, the equally obscene practice of a warder poking a finger into a prisoner's rectum, of brutally assaulting them daily and without provocation, was curbed by the Government after it had erupted into a national scandal.

But the inhumanity of the average South African warder still remains; only now it has been diverted into other channels and has taken the subtle form of psychological persecution, a field in which some of your local officials are showing to become specialists. You are no doubt aware that many psychologists regard psychological persecution in circumstances such as ours as even more dangerous than plain assault. I have the hope that a man of your rank and experience will immediately grasp the gravity of this ~~practice~~ dangerous practice and take adequate measures to stop it.

It is pointless and contrary to this country's historical experience to think that our people will ever forget us. Although 160 years have passed since the Slachter's Nek executions, 74 since the internment camps of the Anglo-Boer War and 61 since Jopie Fourie made his last speech, I will certainly never

I believe ...

Page from a letter to the commissioner of prisons, 12 July 1976, see pages 170–93.

people, to whom we are national heroes, persecuted for striving to win back our country, to forget us in our lifetime at the height of the struggle for a free South Africa. Your people are slaughtering mine today and not a century and a half ago. It is present South Africa that is a country of racial oppression, imprisonment without trial, of torture and harsh sentences and the threat of internment camps lies not in the distant past but in the immediate future. How can our people ever forget us when we fight to free them from all these evils?

In South Africa, as in many other countries, various issues divide prisoners and officials. I do not agree with the policy of the Department of which you are the Head. I detest white supremacy and will fight it with every weapon in my hands. But even when the clash between you and me has taken the most extreme form, I should like us to fight over principles and ideas and without personal hatred, so that at the end of the battle, whatever the results might be, I can proudly shake hands with you because I feel I have fought an upright and worthy opponent who has observed the whole code of honour and decency. But when your subordinates continue to use foul methods then a sense of real bitterness and contempt becomes irresistible.

[Signed NRMandela]
NELSON MANDELA

To Winnie Mandela,[i] his wife

Nelson Mandela, 466/64   Aug 19, '76

Dadewethu,[ii]

Yesterday I'd just finished writing & explaining to you the position relating to my studies & giving you a brief account of the representa-

---

i   Nomzamo Winifred Madikizela-Mandela (1936–2018) – see the glossary.
ii   'Sister' in isiXhosa.

tions I'd made in regard to the restrictions previously imposed on you as well as about Msuthu[i] when I learnt from the Commanding Officer that you'd been arrested, but gave me no further information.

Up to now I don't know where & when you were apprehended, the law under which you're held in custody, where you're kept & the charge, if any, against you. What I do know now is that the brief spell of [freedom] you've enjoyed for just 10 mnths in 13 yrs has come & gone barely 2 mths before your birthday; gone in '76 less than a ¼ century to 2000 which you'll see certainly in your lifetime. I've, however, requested the Commissioner of Prisons to give me information on your arrest.

In my letter of Aug. 1, which I doubt if you received, I warmly thanked you for joining me on my birthday & tried to entice you to come down by reminding you that Sept 25 & 26, just like July 17 & 18,[ii] would fall on a Saturday & Sunday & I'd vaguely hoped that you might bite, funds being available. I now know that that is not possible. Still & especially because of that, it's always a dy to which I look forward very keenly as if you're still coming. For me it's always a dy I value & honour more than all the dys in the history of this world. I'll remember you more than you shook me that March 10.[iii]

It's always given me plenty of satisfaction & joy to write to you. I sincerely don't know whether you'll ever get this particular one nor those of July 18, Aug 1 & 18 &, if you do, when that'll be. Nonetheless, the act of writing to you at this moment removes all the tensions & impurities in my feelings & thoughts. It's the only time I ever feel that some dy in the future it'll be possible for humanity to produce saints who will really be upright & venerable, inspired in everything they do by genuine love for humanity & who'll serve all humans selflessly. Since yesterday I feel closer & more proud of you than ever before & I'm sure the girls also feel the same.

I've no false illusions whatsoever, my darling Mum, & know only too well the ghastly shocks you've had in the past 14 yrs & the lurid accounts that've been repeatedly blazed about you & that'd completely shattered another woman. Do you think I've forgotten '63/'64, May 13 & the 18 months that followed, Oct '70 in particular, April '75 to last mth, the venemous telegrams, reports, some sent anonymously,

---

i   Msuthu Thanduxolo Madikizela, Winnie Mandela's brother.
ii   He is referring to their birthdays – 26 September for Winnie Mandela's and 18 July for Mandela.
iii   The date of their first date.

Nelson Mandela, 466/64   Aug. 19, '76

Dadewethu,

Yesterday I'd just finished writing & explaining to you the position relating to my studies & giving you a brief account of the representations I'd made in regard to the restrictions previously imposed on you as well as about Msuthu whom I learnt from the Commanding Officer that you'd been arrested, but gave me no further information.

Up to now I don't know where & when you were apprehended, the law under which you're held in custody, where you're kept & the charge, if any, against you. What I do know now is that the brief spell you've enjoyed for just 10 mths in 13 yrs has come & gone barely 2 mths before your birthday; gone in '76 less than a ¼ century to 2000 which you'll see certainly in your lifetime. I've, however, requested the Commissioner of Prisons to give me information on your arrest.

In my letter of Aug. 1, which I doubt if you received, I warmly thanked you for joining me on my thirty & tried to entice you to come down by reminding you that Sept 25 & 26, just like July 17 & 18, would fall on a Saturday & Sunday & I'd vaguely hoped that you might bite, funds being available. I now know that that is not possible. Still I especially because of that, 18 is a day to which I look forward very keenly as if you're still coming. For me it's always a day I value & honour more than all the days in the history of this world. I'll remember you more than you should me that March 10.

It's always given me plenty of satisfaction & joy to write to you. I sincerely don't know whether you'll ever get this particular one nor those of July 18, Aug 1 & 18 &, if you do, whom that'll be, none the less, the act of writing to you at this moment removes all the tensions & impurities in my feelings & thoughts. It's the only time I ever feel that some day in the future it'll be possible for humanity to produce saints who will really be upright & venerable, inspired in everything they do & by genuine love for humanity & who'll serve all humans selflessly. Since yesterday I feel closer & more proud of you than ever before & I'm sure the girls also feel the same.

I've no false illusions whatsoever, my darling mum & know only too well the ghastly schemes you've faced in the past 14 yrs & the lurid accounts that've been repeatedly blazed about how & that'd completely shattered another woman. Do you think I've forgotten '63/64, May '63 & the 18 mths that followed, Oct. '70 in particular, Apr. '73 to Aug last mth, the venomous telegrams, reports, some sort anonymously by others from well-meaning people known to both of us, all full of alarming & vile information?

It has been valuable experience for me to watch powerful organisations & highly-placed individuals clubbing together for the specific purpose of destroying a relatively innocent woman; how all these can stoop so low as to bring to my notice all sorts of details

Page from a letter to Winnie Mandela, 19 August 1976, see pages 193–7.

& others from well-meaning people known to both of us, all full of alarming & vile information?[i]

It has been a valuable experience for me to watch powerful organisations & highly-placed individuals clubbing together for the specific purpose of destroying a virtually widowed woman; how all these can stoop so low as to bring to my notice all sorts of details calculated to dim the clear image I have about the most wonderful friend I have in life completely baffles me. My consolation has always been that you've kept your head, held the family tight together & made us as happy & optimistic as circs.[ii] would allow a girl who's lived under heavy & sustained pressure from all directions. Of course, dear Mum, we're but human – Zeni, Zindzi[iii] & I & we'd like you to be highly praised by all & all the time, just like the lady who rose from the valley of the Caledon in the 1820's. But the more you're slandered, the more attached to you do I become. These are not the things we should even mention in our correspondence to each other. But we live 1000 miles apart, see each other rarely & for short periods & with all the jazz around your ears you may even wonder what Madiba thinks. Only because of this do I think I should, nevertheless, hint to you that I LOVE YOU ALWAYS.

Strength of affection & rising admiration for you, Mhlope,[iv] create stalemate situations. Concern & adoration frequently intermingle & at times I'm not at all certain which is dominant. Your health, the intense longing for & anxiety about the girls, the many hrs, mths & even yrs living alone for the one who loves the open air & the warm sunshine in which she was brought up, who likes the company of others & can laugh very well, who has lost a comfortable job, the chance to write a university exam for which so much money had been sunk, hard work, energy & precious time had been spent, the uncertainty when I'll see you again, all make the heart heavy. As to why I adore you particularly at this hr you know exactly why. Do you still remember when I first addressed you as Dadewethu[v] & why I've stubbornly stuck to it all

---

i   Mandela may be referring to such events in *Long Walk to Freedom* when he writes: 'Some of the nastiest items were known to me because when I would return from the quarry, I would often find neatly cut clippings about Winnie that had been anonymously placed on my bed by the warders.' (p. 504) and 'I had also learned from a newspaper clipping that a Special Branch officer broke into our Orlando house while Winnie was dressing and she reacted angrily, pushing the officer out of the bedroom.' (p. 505.)

ii   Circumstances.

iii Zenani Mandela (1959–) and Zindziswa Mandela (1960–), Mandela's middle and youngest daughters – see the glossary.

iv   One of Winnie Mandela's names.

v   'Sister' in isiXhosa.

these yrs? Yes, yes, you do, Ngutyana.[i] Your optimism & wonderful smile have put more steel in me than all the famous classics of this world. You're my darling & in moments such as these, it's reasonable to speak frankly & sincerely. Although I can't be certain, my own hope is that these 2 letters will reach you duly & in the form in which I've written them.

I'm writing to the girls to put them at rest & to assure them that you're now a veteran who can take care of herself & to wish them good luck in the exams. I believe Zeni & Bahle still hold on each other but that Zeni has broken with poor Fidza & has had a new gold strike in Mafuta oupa about whom she says you'll tell me a lot. I don't know who to suggest about where they'd spend their Dec. holidays in your absence. There's of course Kgatho & Rennie,[ii] the ever-willing Fatu,[iii] Niki[iv] and Bantu.[v] But I'll wait until I've had a clearer picture of the situation before I make positive suggestions. Who did you leave behind with the chdn? You told me the name of Zizwe's Mum but [I] have now forgotten it. I'll also ask Ntatho & Sally[vi] to visit you if they can get permits & to look after the house & kids. On Aug. 1. I wrote to your sister Connie a condolence letter[vii] & asked you to redirect it to her. I'll now ask Rennie to do so. Devotedly, Dalibhunga.
I LOVE YOU ALWAYS!

Nkosk Nobandla Mandela, c/o Commissioner of Prisons. Pretoria

---

i   One of Winnie Mandela's names. She comes from the amaNgutyana clan.
ii   Makgatho (Kgatho) Mandela (1950–2005), Mandela's second-born son – see the glossary – and his then wife, Rose Rayne Mandela, known as Rennie.
iii Fatima Meer (1928–2010), writer, academic, and anti-apartheid and women's rights activist – see the glossary.
iv   Niki Xaba (1932–1985), Winnie Mandela's eldest sister – see the glossary.
v   Nobantu Mniki, Winnie Mandela's sister.
vi   Nthato Motlana (1925–2008), friend, medical doctor, businessman, and anti-apartheid activist – see the glossary, and his wife Sally.
vii This was probably a condolence letter on the death, in 1976, of Connie Njongwe's husband Dr. James 'Jimmy' Njongwe (1919–76), medical doctor, ANC leader, and organiser of the Defiance Campaign (for the Defiance Campaign, see the glossary) in the Eastern Cape – for Jimmy Njongwe, see the glossary.

To Advocate Duma Nokwe (Gcwanini Miya)[i]

Nelson Mandela 466/64   1.1.77

Our dear Gcwanini,

When I was free as an eagle it wasn't easy for me to keep track of developments in the field of music & drama.

I attended a few of the most colourful shows, hurriedly read the reviews in between court sessions & the more serious commitments & thereafter forgot about the matter. Now it's even more difficult to follow cultural events on the mainland & even cautious comment would literally be to rush in where angels fear to tread. But perhaps to you & Radebe I may risk & speak freely about things where my information is dangerously thin, knowing that you'd keep them to yourselves, [and] supply me with the relevant material I need to talk more confidently.

The only aspect which makes me hesitant is your closeness to Ishy & Mohla[ii] &, having once had [the] frightening experience of seeing you & AP flexing your muscles at dawn some yrs back outside Dila's lodge,[iii] I'm not so sure whether after spending a whole night at Ishy's, you may not feel like singing your favourite Ch's song[iv] of the rising star & thereafter loose and reveal things about which you should be silent.

Anyway 3 musicals seem to have attracted a lot of attention recently, namely *Umabatha*,[v] *Ipi-Tombi*[vi] & *Meropa*.[vii] All of them seem tremendous on print, so much so that I was even tempted to wonder whether the claim that Africans are natural actors may not be true after all.

The first is Welcome Msomi's adaptation of Shakespeare's *Macbeth*

---

i   Advocate Duma Nokwe (1927–78), political activist and advocate – see the glossary. Mandela is addressing Nokwe by two of his clan names so that the officials don't know who he is writing to and will post his letter.

ii   Ishmael and Martha Matlhaku, friends of Mandela. Martha had worked as Mandela's personal secretary; Ishmael often transported comrades or activists to the Botswana border and on occasion had been entrusted with the transportation of ANC leadership, including Mandela.

iii   Dr. Diliza Mji, a friend and neighbour of Mandela's from Orlando West, Soweto.

iv   This may be a coded reference to the Communist Party with which Duma Nokwe was affiliated.

v   A Zulu version of *Macbeth* written in 1970 by South African playwright Welcome Msomi and performed by Zulu actors.

vi   A musical written by Bertha Egnos Godfrey and her daughter Gail Lakier in 1974.

vii   A musical produced by Candian producer Clarence Williams in 1974, which toured to Japan and the Far East. It was adapted from a musical called *Isintu* created by Cocky Thlotothlamaje, and after being redeveloped as *Meropa*, its name was changed to *Kwazulu*.

& is cast in indigenous music, tradition & dancing. This is clearly a promising playwright who has gathered around him a group of talented and versatile players. I believe in England the play impressed a galaxy of stars like Peter Ustinov,[i] Sidney Poitier,[ii] Rex Harrison,[iii] ballerina Margot Fonteyn[iv] & other artist[s] & public figures. *Ipi-Tombi* attempts to portray the social forces that influence the life of the African & again, from the pictures & scattered clues I've seen, the actors seem to be boys & girls of ability. It's said to have broken all records in JHB[v] when it ran for 122 weeks & was seen by about 500,000 people. I also understand that in London it had similar success & that 3 companies are presently performing in several continents.

Meropa is yet another attempt to depict the African background by means of drums, music & dancing. In all these plays the scenes are exciting & arouse feelings I've rarely experienced when attending the more sophisticated functions of the Western type. You must have seen the reviews & probably even spoken to some of the leading actors.

However, all of them have major themes that are disturbing & that dwarf the beautiful play acting on the stage. In addition, it's not clear who the real bosses are & who holds the purse strings. Whilst Msomi was assisted by Prof E. Sneddon,[vi] P. Scholtz[vii] & the Englishman P. Daubeny,[viii] Bertha Egnos, Sheila Wartski & Liz MacLeish worked together on *Ipi-Tombi*. The latter & *Meropa* were quite obviously written by persons who are familiar neither with our life & culture nor who are fully aware of our aspirations.

There's much praise for Bra Gibbs[ix] as a playwright & I believe some of his works have drawn full houses for many wks. Unfortunately, I've not been so lucky to see any of his scripts nor write-ups. I would also like to have seen the productions of the Music, Drama & Literature

---

i   Peter Ustinov (1921–2004), Russian-English actor, writer, filmmaker, and theatre director.
ii   Sidney Poitier (1927–), Bahamian-American actor, film director, author, and diplomat. He played Mandela in the 1997 television film *Mandela and De Klerk*.
iii   Rex Harrison (1908–90), English stage and screen actor.
iv   Margot Fonteyn (1919–91), English ballerina who danced with the British ballet company, the Royal Ballet.
v   Johannesburg.
vi   Elizabeth Sneddon, head of the department of speech and drama at the University of Natal and director of the Natal Theatre Workshop Company. She commissioned Welcome Msomi to write *Umabatha*.
vii   Pieter Scholtz who directed *Umabatha* at the University of Natal and translated the play from Zulu into English.
viii   Peter Daubeney (1921–75), British theatre impresario who brought *Umabatha* to London where it was performed to sell-out audiences as part of his World Theatre Sessions.
ix   Gibson Kente (1932–2004), playwright, composer, and director. Like Mandela, he was from the Madiba clan, so Mandela referred to him as a nephew – see the glossary.

Institute & those of the other young black artists I believe are now coming forward. I envy you very much. Do you still see Bakwe[i] & Dan[ii]? I hope Mabhomvu[iii], Alfie, Tom, John, Gabula & your colleague, Joe[iv], are all keeping well & fit. I've also written to Thorobetsane.[v]

I think of you all & sincerely wish that today we could be together & as in older dys, sit down & tell stories, tall & otherwise. What a moment that could be! The varied experiences each one of us has had during the past 15 yrs add up to real life. All the same fond memories & warm thoughts have pulled the world with its sunshine into my quarters. That's why you're all so near; with me on this Island. Perhaps one dy I'll hear you singing and dancing, this time not only to the rising star, if you please, but also from songs from the soil[vi], accompanied by the brass band with its trumpets & bugels, drums & all. Merry Xmas & happy new yr to Radebe,[vii] the kids, you & all our friends. Very sincerely, Nel.

Mr Gcwanini Miya, c/o Nkosk Nobandla, P.O. Box 2947, JHB, 2000

◇◇◇◇◇◇◇◇◇◇

On 25 April 1977 the authorities famously brought a selected group of reporters on a tour to the island as a response to rumours of unforgiving conditions. As part of a manufactured spectacle for the media, the guards put the men to work in the 'garden' near the cell block. It was a far cry from their daily grind, by then at the shoreline pulling up seaweed.

Photographs were taken of Mandela and his comrades. His response was a furious written charge against the prison head for the creation of the photo opportunity.

At the end of the year, Mandela and Ahmed Kathrada had their study

---

i   Bakwe (Joe) Matthews (1929–2010), political activist and son of Frieda and Z. K. Matthews – see the glossary for these three individuals.

ii   Dan Tloome (1919–92), leader of the ANC and the South African Communist Party who was working for the ANC in Botswana, and who spent many decades in exile in Zambia.

iii   A code word for the Communist Party. *Bhomvu* means red in isiXhosa and ANC members attached 'Mabhomvu' when referring to a person regarded as Communist. (Nomvuyo Nokwe in an email to Sahm Venter, 11 December 2017.)

iv   Members of the ANC leadership

v   Made-up name for Adelaide Tambo (1929–2007), friend, anti-apartheid activist, and wife of Oliver Tambo, Mandela's former law partner and president of the ANC – see the glossary. The Tambos were living in exile in London.

vi   ANC freedom songs

vii   Vuyiswa Nokwe (Radebe is her clan name), Duma Nokwe's wife.

privileges revoked when it was discovered that Mandela had been secretly writing his autobiography with the help of a handful of trusted comrades.

To the head of prison, Robben Island

[Typed]

19 May 1977

The Head of Prison
ROBBEN ISLAND

We strongly protest against the purpose for and manner in which the visit to this prison of the local and overseas press and television men on the 25th April was organised and conducted by the Department of Prisons. We resent the deliberate violation of our right of privacy by taking our photographs without our permission, and regard this as concrete evidence of the contempt with which the Department continues to treat us.

On the 26th April fellow prisoner Nelson Mandela was informed by Major Zandberg that the Minister of Prisons had finally agreed to the repeated requests by the press over the years to visit Robben Island. We also learnt that the minister had authorised the visit provided no communication whatsoever would take place between pressmen and prisoners.

The Minister planned the visit in the hope that it would whitewash the Prisons Department; pacify public criticism of the Department here and abroad; and counteract any adverse publicity that might arise in the future. To ensure the success of the plan we were not given prior notice of the visit, on that particular day the span[i] from our Section was given the special work of "gardening" instead of pulling out bamboo from the sea[ii] as we normally do when we go to work. Some 30 litres of milk was placed at the entrance to our Section,[iii] quite

---

i   Afrikaans word for 'team' that was used in prison.

ii   This is actually a type of seaweed which had the Afrikaans name of *bambous*. (Christo Brand, *Doing Life with Mandela* (Johannesburg: Jonathan Ball, 2014. p. 38.)

iii   A handwritten note in the margin, presumably from a prison official, reads: 'Not true. I didn't even see the milk (JM)'.

obviously to give the impression that it was all meant for us, whereas in truth we receive only 6½ litres a day.

Most of us know that a section of the press here and abroad is sympathetic to our cause, and that they would have preferred to handle the operation in a dignified manner. Nevertheless, the Minister's disregard for our feelings has led to the situation where total strangers are now in possession of photographs and films of ourselves. The impropriety of the Minister's action is sharpened by the Department's persistent refusal to allow us to take and send our photographs to our own families.

We stress the fact that the way in which the Minister planned this visit in no way differs from previous ones. In August 1964 reporters from the "Daily Telegraph"[i] found those of us who were here at the time "mending clothes" instead of our normal work at the time of knapping stones with 5 lb. hammers. As soon as the reporters left we were ordered to crush stones as usual. At the end of August 1965 Mrs Ida Parker from "The Sunday Tribune" found us wearing raincoats on our way back from the lime quarry – raincoats which were hurriedly issued to us at work on the very day of her visit, and which were immediately taken away when she left. The rain coats were not issued to us again until a year or so later.

We emphatically state that under no circumstances are we willing to co-operate with the Department in any manoeuvre on its part to distort the true state of affairs obtaining on this island. With few exceptions our span has been kept inside for several months now, but our normal work is still that of pulling seaweed, and the Department has given no assurance that we will never be sent out to the quarry again.

We also cite the example of the cupboards we have in our cells. Any television viewer is likely to be impressed with this furniture and would naturally give all the credit to the Department. It is unlikely that such television-viewers and newspaper readers would be aware that the cupboards have been painstakingly built with crude tools in a crude "workshop" from cardboard cartons and from driftwood picked up on the beaches by prisoners, that the costs for beautifying them have been borne by the prisoners themselves[ii] and that they have

---

i   It was actually the *Daily Express*, identified by photographer Cloete Breytenbach (who accompanied writer John Rydon to the Island) in an interview with Sahm Venter, Johannesburg, 30 June 2013.

ii   A handwritten note in the margin reads 'Rubbish!'.

-2-

take and send our photographs to our own families.

We stress the fact that the way in which the Minister planned this visit in no way differs from previous ones.   IN August 1964 re= porters from "The Daily Telegraph" found those of us who were here at the time "mending clothes" instead of our normal work at the time of knapping stones with 5 lb. hammers.   As soon as the re= porters left we were ordered to crush stones as usual.   At the end of August 1965 Mrs. I.≠da Parker from "The Sunday Tribune" found us wearing raincoats on our way back from the lime quarry - raincoats which were hurriedly issued to us at work on the very day of her visit, and which were immediately taken away when she left.   The rain coats were not issued to us again until a year or so later.

We emphatically state that under no circumstances are we willing to cooperate with the Department in any manoeuvre on its part to distort the true state of affairs obtaining on this island.   With few exceptions our span has been kept inside for several months now, but our normal work is still that of pulling sea-weed, and the Department has given no assurance that we will never be sent out to the quarry again.

We also cite the example of the cupboards we have in our cells. Any television-viewer is likely to be impressed with this furniture and would naturally give all the credit to the Department.   It is unlikely that such telefision-viewers and newspaper readers would be aware that the cupboards have been painstakingly built with crude tools in a crude "workshop" from cardboard cartons and from driftwood picked up on the beaches by prisoners, that the costs for beautifying them have been borne by the prisoners themselves, and that they have been built by a talented fellow prisoner, Jafta Masemola, working approximately 8 hours a day on weekdays at the rate of R1,50 (One Rand fifty Cents) a month.

Rubbish!

The same for other prisoners

At all times wer are willing to have press and television inter= views, provided that the aim is to present to the public a balanced picture of our living conditions.   This means that we would be allowed to express our grievances and demands freely, and to make comments whether such comments are favourable or otherwise to the Department.

We are fully aware that the Department desires to protect a favourable

3/......

Page from a letter written by prisoners to the head of the prison complaining about the journalists' visit of 1977 and the inherent abuse of their rights. Note the comments in the margin: "Rubbish!" and "The same for other prisoners" (see pages 201–6).

been built by a talented fellow prisoner, Jafta Masemola,[i] working
approximately 8 hours a day on weekends at the rate of R1.50 (One
Rand fifty Cents) a month.[ii]

At all times we are willing to have press and television interviews,
provided that the aim is to present to the public a balanced picture of
our living conditions. This means that we would be allowed to express
our grievances and demands freely, and to make comments whether
such comments are favourable or otherwise to the Department.

We are fully aware that the Department desires to project a favourable image to the world of its policies. We can think of no better way
of doing so than by abolishing all forms of racial discrimination in
the administration, by keeping abreast of enlightened penal reforms,
by granting us the status of political prisoners, and by introducing a
non-racial administration throughout the country's prisons. With few
or no skeletons to hide the Department will then no longer stand in
any need for resorting to stratagems.

The actual execution of the plan was entrusted to Gen Roux[iii] and
in his presence, the reporters and cameramen stormed down upon
us like excited visitors to an agricultural show.[iv] For all that we have
seen of Gen Roux, we are convinced that he has no respect whatsoever for our feelings and dignity. The way he handled the visit is
no different from his conduct when he visited this prison on the 15
November 1976. On that occasion he conducted his interviews with
us individually in a cloak-and-dagger fashion in the hope of finding us
at a complete loss when confronted with the unexpected. That there
were no ugly incidents as a result of the provocative action on the 25th
April was due solely to our sense of responsibility.

We are fully aware that we cannot prevent the publication of such
articles on prison conditions here as the Minister might authorize. But
we are equally aware that, whatever the law might be, the taking of
our photographs by the press for publication purposes or otherwise
without our consent, constitutes an invasion of our privacy. That privacy has been blatantly violated by the very people who, within the
framework of the law, are considered to be its guardians. And, having

---

i   Jafta Kgalabi 'Jeff' Masemola (1929–90), teacher, member of the ANC Youth League, member of the
        Pan Africanist Congress, and political prisoner – see the glossary.
ii   A handwritten note in the margin reads, 'The same as other prisoners'.
iii   General Jannie Roux was then the commissioner of prisons and accompanied the journalists on the
        visit.
iv   A handwritten note in the margin reads: 'Very interesting'.

violated that privacy, the Department had the temerity to ask us for permission to make us objects of public scrutiny.

We stress that we are not chattels of the Prisons Department. That we happen to be prisoners in no way detracts from the fact that we are, nevertheless, South African and Namibian citizens, entitled to protections against any abuses by the Department.[i]

Finally, we place on record that we cannot tolerate indefinitely any treatment we consider degrading and provocative and, should the Minister continue to do so, we reserve to ourselves the right to take such action as we deem appropriate.

F. Anthony[ii]

J.E. April[iii]

L. Chiba[iv]

T.T. Cholo[v]

E.J. Daniels[vi]

T.L. Daweti[vii]

M.K. Dingake[viii]

M.S. Essop[ix]

J. Fuzile[x]

K. Hassim[xi]

T.H. Ja-Toivo[xii]

A.M. Kathrada[xiii]

N.R. Mandela[xiv]

J. Masemola[xv]

---

i   A handwritten note in the margin reads: 'I suppose all other SA citizens are also entitled to protections against them!'

ii   Frank Anthony, African People's Democratic Union of South Africa prisoner.

iii   James April (1940–), ANC prisoner.

iv   Laloo Chiba (1930–2017), ANC prisoner – see the glossary.

v   Theophilus Cholo (1926–), ANC prisoner.

vi   Eddie Daniels (1928–2017), African Resistance Movement prisoner – see the glossary.

vii   Thompson Daweti, ANC prisoner.

viii   Michael Dingake (1928–), ANC prisoner.

ix   Salim Essop, ANC prisoner.

x   Jackson Fuzile, ANC prisoner.

xi   Kader Hassim (1934–2019), African People's Democratic Union of South Africa prisoner.

xii   Namibian prisoner Andimba Toivo ya Toivo (1924–2017), South West African People's Organisation.

xiii   Ahmed Kathrada (1929–2017) – Rivonia trialist and ANC and South African Communist Party prisoner – see the glossary.

xiv   Nelson Mandela. (1918–2013) – Rivonia trialist and MK prisoner.

xv   Jafta Kgalabi 'Jeff' Masemola (1929–90), teacher, member of the ANC Youth League, member of the Pan Africanist Congress, and political prisoner – see the glossary.

G. Mbeki[i]
R. Mhlaba[ii]
K. Mkalipi[iii]
W.Z. Mkwayi[iv]
A. Mlangeni[v]
E. Motsoaledi[vi]
J. Mpanza[vii]
P. Mthembu[viii]
B. Nair[ix]
J.N. Pokela[x]
S. Sijake[xi]
W.U. Sisulu[xii]
M.M. Siyothula[xiii]
J.B. Vusani[xiv]
R.C. Wilcox[xv]

To the head of prison, Robben Island

[Note in another hand in Afrikaans] Letter to head approved

Robben Island
18th September 1977

---

i   Govan Mbeki (1910–2001), Rivonia trialist prisoner – see the glossary.
ii   Raymond Mhlaba (1920–2005), Rivonia trialist and MK prisoner – see the glossary.
iii   Kwedi Mkalipi, PAC prisoner.
iv   Wilton Mkwayi (1923–2004), Little Rivonia trialist and MK prisoner – see the glossary. The Little Rivonia Trial took place in November 1964, five months after the Rivonia Trial (see the glossary) ended, after Laloo Chiba, Mac Maharaj, Wilton Mkwayi, Dave Kitson and John Matthews were charged with sabotage for their activities on behalf of MK. The former three were sent to Robben Island and the other two, being white, were held in Pretoria.
v   Andrew Mlangeni (1925–), Rivonia trialist and MK prisoner – see the glossary.
vi   Elias Motsoaledi (1924–94), Rivonia trialist and ANC prisoner – see the glossary.
vii   Justice Mpanza, (1937–2002), ANC prisoner.
viii   Peter Mthembu, ANC prisoner.
ix   Billy Nair (1929–2008), MK prisoner – see the glossary.
x   John Pokela (1922–85), Pan Africanist Congress prisoner.
xi   Sandi Sijake, ANC prisoner.
xii   Walter Sisulu (1912– 2003), Rivonia trialist and MK prisoner – see the glossary.
xiii   Mannert Siyothula, Pan Africanist Congress prisoner.
xiv   Joseph Bransby Vusani.
xv   Robert Wilcox, African People's Democratic Union of South Africa (APDUSA) prisoner

The Head of Prison,

I protest in the strongest terms against the unethical conduct of the Department of Prisons in violating my right of privileged communication with my legal representatives.

The persistent infringement of the law and flouting of the principles of justice by officials are some of the factors that have destroyed harmonious prisoner-warder relations throughout the country, and that make it difficult for us to accord to such officials the respect and courtesy we should like to give to those who are entrusted with our welfare as prisoners. The manner in which the Department encroached on this right tends to show that the use of <u>improper methods in dealing with us forms an inseparable part of prison policy.</u>[i]

On 12th September 1977 I was brought before the Officers' Court on a charge in which Lt. Prins was the complainant, and that had been remanded several times since January this year. The prosecutor, W/O Bierenbroodspot, withdrew the charge in terms, I believe, of Section 6 of the Criminal Procedure Act. As the court adjourned and in the presence of the prosecutor, W/O Olchers, seized my file which contained privileged papers relating to the case. Amongst those documents was a 7-page statement in which I gave reasons why I believed that the building where consultations between prisoners and lawyers are held had a secret device by means of which officials could listen to consultations. There was also a 40-page document with annexures, in which I set out the issues involved, my defence to the charge and the names of prisoners and non-prisoners I considered material witnesses.

I pointed out to both officials that the right they were violating was permanent and protected privileged communications not only during, but also after the disposal of the proceedings. I further told them that right formed the foundation of the administration of justice throughout the enlightened world, and that I expected any prosecutor, worth the name, to respect it both in theory and practice. I added that nothing would stop the institution of fresh proceedings against me after the complainant had studied my statements, that by taking away my papers they were attacking not only the principles of natural justice, but were <u>acting in contravention of an express provision of their own regulations.</u>

---

i   The underlining in this letter doesn't appear to be Mandela's as it is not his usual neat, straight underlining.

It soon became clear, however, that the 2 officials were carrying out instructions from their superiors and that no amount of persuasion would convince them not to interfere with the right. The prosecutor kept on telling me that, since he had withdrawn the charge, he no longer had jurisdiction because the matter was now purely administrative. W/O Olchers was even more taciturn and all that he could say in reply to my arguments was that he wanted the file. In the course of the discussion I said, for all I knew, the Security Police, who are the real people who run this prison, might be waiting for the papers somewhere in the same building. By way of a compromise, I suggested that I destroy the papers in their presence. They rejected the suggestion and, in spite of my protests, seized the file, promising to return it later during that day. I then asked them to give me an inventory of all the papers in the file. This request was also refused.

My legal representatives could not have been aware of this manoeuvre. I even suspect that when the Department advised me last week that the court would convene on 12th September, and that permission had now been given for me to hand over my statement to my lawyers, prison officials already knew that the case would be withdrawn. I further suspect that the real purpose of giving me this information was to induce me to load the file with illegal messages which, it was hoped, the lawyers would then smuggle out.

My experience during the last 15 years of my imprisonment has taught me that, when dealing with prisoners, the average prison official does not at all consider it improper to transgress the law, to plot secretly and to brush aside the moral code.[i] There have been notable exceptions of officers who have tried in difficult situations to carry out their duties fairly and justly and who tempered the strict letter of the law with a bit of humanism. But such men have been few and far between. Clearly the Department prefers that political prisoners, in particular, should be handled by men who are not strongly committed to any exemplary standard of conduct.

It has been disconcerting for us to see the tragedy of otherwise gifted and friendly young men who, on arrival here, worked quite well with us, but who were later forced to do many things which conflicted with their own feelings and views.

W/O Bierenbroodspot is a case in point. In the early stages of the

---

i   A vertical line has been made in the margin from here until the end of the paragraph.

case, he made a good impression on me and his sense of fairness and impartiality was striking. But within 8 months of his arrival his whole personality has changed, the idealism with which he began his work has disappeared and the role he has played in the case makes it now difficult for him to face me. Like many other young people, he has been forced to pursue a line which clashes with his principles as an individual and as an official. I have known several officers of higher ranks than he who found themselves in a similar predicament.

I regret that in a letter of this nature I should even mention his name and that of his colleague, W/O Olchers. I know that the strategy in regard to the conduct of this case was probably all worked out to its finest details in higher quarters, and that the 2 officials were merely functionaries who had no choice but to carry out instructions from above.

In due course the Department may be asked to justify its conduct in this matter. I hope when that happens Government propagandists will resist the temptation to mislead the public by claiming that subversive documents were found in the file whose contents cannot be published on "security grounds". No illegal material can be produced because there was none in fact.

I further hope the Minister of Prisons, Mr J.T. Kruger, now that my confidential papers are in the possession of his officials will be big enough to acknowledge his mistake and to apologise to my legal representatives, Mr Kawalsky,[i] Mr Ismail Ayob[ii] and to advocate George Bizos[iii] for questioning their integrity. The privileged papers could only have been taken away on the ground that they contained communications that had nothing to do with the case, and which the lawyers would smuggle out, an act which would make them guilty of unprofessional conduct.

Finally, I must ask you to return all the papers at once and to allow me to report the whole matter to my legal representatives without further delay.

Meantime, I should like you to acquaint the Commissioner of Prisons, through your Commanding Officer, with the contents of this letter.

[Signed NRMandela]
NELSON MANDELA

---

i   Stanley Kawalsky (1946–2018), attorney at Frank, Bernadt and Joffe.
ii   Ismail Ayob (1942–), Mandela's attorney – see the glossary.
iii   George Bizos (1927–), defence lawyer in the Rivonia Trial – see the glossary.

To Amina Cachalia,[i] his friend and comrade

Special letter[ii]   Nelson Mandela 466/64

12.12.77

Vahali Aminaben,[iii]

I've been given special permission to write to you in connection with
an album for a photo of 21 x 27 centimetres. The Mother City[iv] cannot
supply me with that size & I should like you to enquire from Juta &
Co or Van Schaik's Bookstore, Pretoria, whether they have that size in
stock; the price & postage. These 2 book firms are the approved stores
from which we can order & if they've not got the right size in stock,
they can get it from other firms. You in person should not buy & send
it as that would be a waste of your fortune. Regulations expressly pro-
hibit the receipt of articles from outside that are not ordered directly
by the Prisons Dpt. We will then order it from this end.

Perhaps I could exploit this chance & ask you to send a family photo
so that I could have the pleasure of seeing how Kaene & Nomente[v]
are maturing & how you & Yusuf are struggling to hide the marks of
creeping age. Your letter of 18/7/75, the last I received from you, gave
me the hope that I might see Miss Johannesburg, you Amina, & I said
so in so many words in my reply of 1/11 that yr, adding that out of the
much sought-after school of snoek[vi] fish that milled around F. Square[vii]
in Fordsburg those exciting days, you looked the right one to handle
such delicate negotiations. I am still convinced that there's no one in
S.A. who can rival him in that field & he could only fail in getting you
permission to come down if he himself does not wish you to do so. To
make sure that you got the message, I wrote to Zami[viii] to let you know

---

i   Amina Cachalia (1930–2013), friend and anti-apartheid and women's rights activist – see the glossary.
ii   Special letters were not deducted from a prisoner's quota.
iii   *Vehalie* means 'dear' in Gujarati. Mandela probably would have consulted with one of his fellow
       prisoners who was fluent in Gujarati, such as Laloo Chiba, about how to write it. Mandela spelled it
       various ways including as *wahalie*. *Ben* means 'sister' in Gujarati.
iv   Cape Town.
v   Mandela's names for Amina and Yusuf Cachalia's son, Ghaleb, and daughter, Dilshan.
vi   A South African name for barracouta.
vii   Freedom Square in the suburb of Fordsburg, Johannesburg, was a popular location for political
       meetings during the 1940s and 1950s.
viii   One of Winnie Mandela's names.

that I would never excuse you & Yusuf if you aroused in me expectations you could not fulfil. But the poor girl has been so hard-pressed in my absence that she often overlooks or finds it difficult to attend to matters affecting even those, like you & Yusuf, she loves very much.

In your last letter you remarked that the children were growing, that you intended visiting them that August for a few mnths & rightly complained of loneliness. I fully understand your difficulties. But my friend who can prepare a dove meal so beautifully knows only too well that, apart from Yusuf, few men in this country know her as much as I do. I've no doubt that she'll always welcome the chance to be all alone with her man; that when she says they are lonely the pen is putting words into her mouth. Her heart & the whole of her system feel differently. Do you realise how hard it is to rub off images that friends write into our minds during trying & blissful moments?

Still I must admit that seeing Kaene & Nomente must have been a great moment for all of you. In that environment they must be as bright & resourceful as their Mum & Dad. At 20 & 19 respectively they should be writing interesting letters which bring you much joy. You'll probably be surprised to know that the picture of them that stands out clearly in my mind is when I last saw them in Jeppe in May '61. I still recall how Nomente rushed into the sitting room & asked for your attention, claiming that some object had bumped her smooth forehead. From the way she looked, one would have thought she had collided with a goods train; & for all I know an innocent butterfly might have touched her face. When she got what she wanted she melted at once & romped away beaming & bright like an iris in good soil & in good weather. So are all kids & that's one reason why we love them so much.

Sometimes I come across familiar names in approved publications circulating here. Just the other day I discovered that Effie's husband[i] was busy doing research on renin, cholesterol & the like & I really wished I could read the results of his investigations. From all that I am able to read, unfortunately in popular & not professional journals, it would appear that heart diseases, from which Blacks were once thought to be immune, are now deadly killers. I used to enjoy reading the British Medical Journal, *The Lancet*. I was wondering whether

---

i   Effie Schultz's husband, Professor Harry Seftel.

Effie was also doing research.[i] As student, houseman & practitioner she was non-conformist. Perhaps she still is, or maybe pressure of patients hardly give her time to breathe. I hope sincerely that Yusuf's eye troubles have cleared & that he still spends the greater part of each day praising your face, one of his precious treasures. It will not be easy for you to find parking space at Jutas & trust that your mini legs are still as strong & reliable as they were in the early 60s, & that they'll be able to carry you from Ferreirastown[ii] (or is it Oriental Bazaar?).[iii] I miss both of you & the children. Love & fondest regards, Very sincerely, Nelson

Mrs Amina Cachalia, P.O. Box 3265, Johannesburg

To Helen Joseph,[iv] a friend

[Prison censor stamp dated 19-10-78]

Nelson Mandela 466/64   15.10.78

Our dearest Helen,

Yes, I got your terrific letter. How you can inspire others! Your congratulations & good wishes had a tremendous effect on me. They wrenched me off this island, out of my cell & put me right in the centre of the Golden City,[v] in Soweto, in Gould[vi] & Pritchard,[vii] on the road to Pretoria & back, & into the lovely cottage at 35 Fanny Avenue.[viii]

My mind carries a picture that never fades in spite of the yrs that have passed since I last saw you. You were standing in front of the

---

i   Effie Schultz was a medical doctor and activist.
ii   A suburb in inner-city Johannesburg.
iii   Mandela is probably referring to the Oriental Plaza, which was established in the 1970s.
iv   Helen Joseph (1905–92), teacher, social worker, and anti-apartheid and women's rights activist – see the glossary.
v   Johannesburg.
vi   Gould Street, a street in Mogale City, Gauteng, located west of Johannesburg (formerly known as Krugersdorp).
vii   Pritchard Street in the Johannesburg city centre.
viii Helen Joseph's address, 35 Fanny Avenue, Norwood.

house, like one waiting for the chickens [to] come home to roost. Zami[i] & Co. were outside the gate talking lively to one another. There has always been something of the British isles in that home, serving as a crossroad in a vast sea. Few were surprised to see them there. At that time I was travelling, worried that I had left behind Zami all alone. Strange as that may sound in the circs,[ii] the fact that you were still there comforted me. I was confident that you would always play the role of guardian angel to her. Perhaps that is one of the reasons why the picture is unforgettable.

But not even in my wildest dream did I ever suspect that I would again hear from you. Least of all, that I would have the opportunity of including your picture in the family album. Of course, Zami & the children often speak of you, especially after May last yr.[iii] In her June letter she mentioned Zazi's[iv] christening ceremony & your special flight to Bloemfontein for the great occasion. She left the fuller description to Zindzi[v] who tenderly referred to you in some detail. But the real surprise was yours which came 2 wks later, followed by several photos from Muzi.[vi]

I immediately spotted a tall lady[vii] who stood upright like a field marshal.[viii] From her defiant & graceful pose, she seemed to enjoy carrying her 73 yrs. I got the snaps on 30/7 & you will be interested to know that they have reached my cell the other day. Old friends in my Section[ix] have not forgotten her & were just as keen to keep them. But now they are back in the cell & make me feel that I also witnessed the Christening ceremony.

It is fitting that you should be godmother to Zazi & for Dr Moroka[x] to be godfather. Helen and Rra;[xi] that is a tremendous combination. I sincerely hope that when Zazi grows up, that combination will be one

---

i   Another name for Winnie Mandela.

ii   Circumstances.

iii   Winnie Mandela was banished to the Free State town of Brandfort in May 1977.

iv   Zaziwe (1977–), the first child of Zenani Mandela and her husband Prince Thumbumuzi 'Muzi' Dlamini.

v   Zindziswa (Zindzi) Mandela (1960–), Mandela's second-born daughter to his second wife, Winnie – see the glossary.

vi   Zenani Mandela's husband Prince Thumbumuzi 'Muzi' Dlamini, a son of King Sobhuza of Swaziland.

vii   Helen Joseph (1905–92), teacher, social worker, and anti-apartheid and women's rights activist – see the glossary.

viii   She served in the Women's Auxiliary Air Force in World War II.

ix   B Section, Robben Island.

x   James Moroka (1892–1985), medical doctor, politician and anti-apartheid activist, president of the African National Congress, 1949–52.

xi   'Sir' in Setswana.

of the driving forces in her life. No wonder Zami was so 'radiant & beautiful'.

I am sorry that Zindzi has to live so far from you. My wish has always been that she should be near you, so that you can help Zami in guiding her. This is especially the case at her present age[i] & with her ambitions. She & Zeni were too young when we parted & Zami's kind of life has brought a lot of emotional suffering on them. I always encourage them to come over to you whenever they can.

It must have been a terrible blow for you to lose the old cat. I know how you loved it & how it was attached to you. I hope Lolita is equally attached & gives you the same pleasure as the old one. German Shepherds are considered intelligent & reliable animals. I trust that Kwacha represents the breed well. That you have some company in the house is a source of comfort to me.[ii]

Cape Town cannot supply me with a photo album of at least 24 x 30 cm to hold one of Zami's portraits. Please check whether that size is available there.[iii] But on no account should you buy one because it will not be given to me. I have enough funds to order it from this end.

Finally, Helen, I should like to take this opportunity to thank you & all those who look after Zami & the children in my absence. The heat of the summer & the winter colds would have been difficult to bear without you all. I am keeping my right hand clean & warm because it has an important duty to perform, i.e. to hold yours very firmly. Meantime, your message of congratulations & good wishes has cut down my age by half. Perhaps, if I had received from JHB more than your message & that of Ismail Ayob, I would feel even younger. Never mind, I feel & move like a lightweight in spite of the 76 kg I carry.

Love from Nelson.

Mrs Helen Joseph,
35 Fanny Avenue, Norwood 2192,
Johannesburg

---

i   Zindzi was then aged seventeen.
ii   Helen Joseph was the first person to be put under house arrest in South Africa under the Sabotage Act which was promulgated in 1962. The order was made on 13 October 1962.
iii   Johannesburg.

To Ndileka Mandela,[i] his granddaughter and eldest daughter of his late son, Thembi[ii]

Nelson Mandela 466/64   21.1.79

My darling Zukulu,[iii]

It seems it was only yesterday when, on February 19 last year, I sent you a card on your 13 birthday. Again I say "Many Happy Returns and a wonderful year!"

I hope you and Nandi[iv] got the Xmas cards I sent you and that you enjoyed your Xmas. I also hope you will write and tell me everything about it. Will you?

I am told that you passed your Form I. Aunt Rennic wrote to me from Inanda[v] to say that this year you will be doing Form II there. I don't know whether you have succeeded in doing so. My warmest congratulations!

If you are at Inanda, please tell me about the total amount of fees to be paid so that I can arrange for a scholarship. In your last letter you asked that I send you a leather jacket with a fur neck. I passed on your request to Khulu,[vi] Winnie. She has many problems and easily forgets. But she is a very kind person & loves you & Nandi very much. Although she is out of work, she will struggle and send you the things you want.

I keep on thinking of 1981 which is only 2 years from now, and when you will be able to visit me. I am dying to see you, and I cannot wait at all for that day.

Give my love to Mum Thoko[vii] and Tata Phineas.[viii]

What is his surname and address in Claremont?[ix] I wanted to send them a Xmas card, but I could not do so because I do not know their Claremont address.

---

i   Ndileka Mandela (1965–) – see the glossary.
ii   Madiba Thembekile (Thembi) Mandela (1945–69), Mandela's eldest son – see the glossary.
iii   Mzukulu is 'grandchild' in isiXhosa. Zukulu is a diminutive of mzukulu.
iv   Nandi Mandela (1968–), his granddaughter and youngest daughter of his late son, Thembi.
v   Inanda Seminary, a prestigious boarding school in Durban, KwaZulu-Natal.
vi   'Grandparent' in isiXhosa.
vii   Thoko Mandela, wife of Thembekile Mandela and mother of their two daughters – see glossary.
viii   Thoko's second husband, Phineas Nkosi. *Tata* means 'father' in isiXhosa.
ix   A suburb in Durban.

Meantime I wish this year will bring you a lot of joy & good luck. A million kisses and tons and tons of love, darling.

Affectionately, Khulu To Ndindi Mandela. Inanda Seminary

Miss Ndileka Mandela
c/o Mrs Rennie Mandela
Inanda Seminary
Private Bag X54105
DURBAN
4000

To Winnie Mandela,[i] his wife

Nelson Mandela 466/64   21. 1. 79

Mntakwethu,[ii]

There are very few occasions in which I have actually feared to write to you as I now do. I cannot excuse myself for my failure to find out about your exam results on 26/12.

My sense of guilt is sharpened by the fact that a few dys before you came, I congratulated several colleagues who had passed the same exam & I sympathised with those who failed; good friends [of] mine they all are, but just friends. That is a relationship that can be valuable & which it pays to cultivate & nurse. But however strong it may be, it lacks the tenderness & intimacy that exist between a man & his mum, dade[iii] & the special friend that you are. This particular relationship carries with it something that cannot be separated from self. It imposes on one certain elementary decencies of which the failure to carry out is well-nigh inexcusable. Are you cursing me for this [?] slip-up? [?], Ngutyana![iv] Is it too late for me to ask? Last yr I collected another harvest of 15 visits and 43 letters. Of these letters 15 came from you.

---

i   Nomzamo Winifred Madikizela-Mandela (1936–2018) – see the glossary.
ii   A term of endearment in isiXhosa.
iii   'Sister' in isiXhosa. In this context it means Winnie Mandela.
iv   One of Winnie Mandela's names. She comes from the amaNgutyana clan.

There were 7 birthday cards & the birthday message from Helen[i] was in the form of a letter. I had more visits than in '77 but, although the letters were more than the previous year, I have not reached the record number of 50 that I got in '75. Those wonderful visits and lovely letters make the atmosphere around me relatively pleasant and the outlook bright.

Though cheerful on 19/2 you, nonetheless, looked a bit ill, and the tiny pools of water in your eyes drowned the love and tenderness they always radiate; the love and tenderness that always pulls me so close to you. But the knowledge of what I have enjoyed in the last 20 years made me feel the force of that love even though physically dimmed by illness. On 29/10 you were even more queenly and desirable in your deep green dress and I thought you were lucky that I could neither reach [?] nor confide to you how I felt.

Sometimes I feel like one who is on the sidelines, who has missed life itself. Travelling with you to work in the early morning, phoning you during the dy, touching your hand or hugging you as you moved up & down the house, enjoying your delicious dishes, the unforgettable hrs in the bedroom, made life taste like honey. These are things I cannot forget. On 2/12 Zindzi[ii] hinted that she & you planned to be here on her birthday. I looked forward to that dy as if I would be seeing both of you for the first time. But on the morning of that dy I prayed that you might not come.

Unconsciously during the previous dy & night I worked a little harder than I realised. I thought the eyes might betray me again, much to your concern as when Zindzi visited me on 21/10. I was, therefore, much relieved when you did not turn up. I was, however, certain that you would be here in a few dys' time. What a moment that turned out to be, mntakwethu!

The only thing that worried me was to note that you have over-scaled your weight to the extent of endangering your health. In spite of the fact that several people thought you looked like Nobandla's[iii] daughter, which is very encouraging, you frightened me. Frankly I don't want to see you again so starved & bony. Fortunately your elegant outfit & matching headgear saved the occasion. An otherwise

---

i   This is most likely his friend Helen Joseph (1905–92), teacher, social worker, and anti-apartheid and women's rights activist – see the glossary.

ii   Zindziswa Mandela (1960–), his and Winnie Mandela's youngest daughter.

iii   Nobandla is one of Winnie Mandela's names.

enjoyable yr would have ticked off on an anti-climax. By the way, I liked the khaki garments you & Zindzi wore on 27/8. You looked really fresh like isidudu brewing in yeast. Your love & devotion has created a debt which I will never attempt to pay back. So enormous is it that even if I were to continue paying regular instalments for another century, I would not settle it. All I can say Mum is, Nangomso![i]

In regard to Zeni's[ii] education, I was perhaps very rash with my advice because of anger. We should constantly consult with her as to how the matter should be handled. Everything should be done to get her away even if alone, if Muzi[iii] is not ready to leave. Keep on putting the pressure on Douglas, Ismail[iv] & on Muzi.

I hope Zindzi's health has improved. In regard to her bronchitis I would suggest that she should use no anti-biotics but very hot tea. In addition she should use Mendel's throat paint with throat brush. That is how Mohammed Abdula cured mine. Bronchitis troubled me here for several mnths in '70 but once I used hot water or tea & Mendel's paint it completely disappeared to this dy. Do let me know if Lady Eleanor[v] has cleared the question of her registration for the exams.

If you can raise the money a car would definitely be a good investment for Zindzi even though fuel is becoming more scarce & dear. I fully approve of your stand in regard to the suggestion or veiled hint that you should shift to Welkom. You were deported to that place & there you should remain. Even though Brandfort is no more than a farming village, you have now found your feet there & paid heavily for doing so. I don't want you to start all over again trying to turn a cave into a habitation. After my arrest you had a difficult time in J.H.B.[vi] & later things improved. As your legal representatives have told the court & Brig Coetzee,[vii] your arrival in Brandfort was followed by unusual experiences which made your life difficult. Even in Brandfort conditions are improving. If you go to Welkom the same process will

---

i   'Nangomso' is an isiXhosa word that expresses deep gratitude to a person who has gone beyond the call of duty. Mandela sometimes spelled it nangomso.

ii Zenani Mandela, his and Winnie's eldeset daughter – see the glossary.

iii Zenani's husband, Prince Thumbumuzi Dlamini, a son of King Sobhuza of Swaziland.

iv Douglas Lukhele, Harvard-educated Swazi lawyer who did his articles at Mandela and Oliver Tambo's law firm in the 1950s, and Ismail Meer (1918-2000), Fatima's husband and a lawyer and anti-apartheid activist – see the glossary.

v   Lady Elinor Birley whose husband Sir Robert Birley (1903–82) was the former headmaster of Eton College and at the time the visiting professor of education at the University of the Witwatersrand. Mandela misspelled her name as 'Eleanor'.

vi Johannesburg.

vii Head of the security police.

start all over again. I repeat you should stay where you are. Neither Kgatho[i] nor Maki[ii] has turned up.

With regard to my health I feel fine both physically & spiritually. I keep fit through indoor & outdoor exercises. The B.P.[iii] is under control. You see me often & rumours that I am ill ought not to worry you. Zwangendaba[iv] is such a conscientious nephew that I am surprised that up to now he has not helped Zindzi in her attempt to write the family history. You ought to find out what his difficulties are before the child thinks we are indifferent to her request. Lack of co-operation from us can discourage her. I still have not got Oupa's[v] birth date. Again a million thanks for your warm love & tender care. I LOVE YOU Devotedly, Dalibhunga

Nkosk. Nobandla Mandela, 802 Phathakhahle Location, P.O. Brandfort 9400

To Makaziwe Mandela,[vi] his eldest daughter

Nelson Mandela 466/64   13.5.79

To my darling Maki
    On your 25th birthday.
    MAY 1st
    Many Happy Returns!

How does it feel to be 25? I still remember that when I was 8 I was in a hurry to get old, to have a grey patch on my head like my father. But now I am battling to keep young & even try to compete with young people in various kinds of indoor & outdoor games. Though not so easy it's a challenge I thoroughly enjoy. All that you need with only ¼ century behind you is to use the amount of energy you possess in such

---

i   Makgatho Mandela (1950–2005), Mandela's second-born son – see the glossary.
ii   Makaziwe Mandela (1954–), Mandela's eldest daughter – see the glossary.
iii   Blood pressure.
iv   A nephew.
v   Zindzi's partner, Oupa Seakamela.
vi   Makaziwe Mandela (1954–) – see the glossary.

a way as to keep you in good health & to enjoy living almost every day in your life.

You must be wondering just why I have taken so long to send you a birthday card. For the last 2 months I had a persistent conjunctivitis inflammation of the conjunctiva. I had good treatment & soon I will see an eye specialist. I had a similar problem in '76 and he prescribed then the same treatment that I use now. He thought that for my age my eyesight was quite good. Naturally I always feel good. My worry throughout this period has been you, darling, & your birthday. It's such a relief for me to be able to say at last: Happy Birthday! Ukhule ude Ukhokhobe![i] Aunt Helen[ii] is now 74 but still fairly active. Perhaps you may live longer than herself. Again: Many Happy Returns! About your school work I was happy to know that you got 58% in your first Sociology test. I know Prof Hough[iii] and Mr. Somhlahlo[iv] well from the Jan Hofmeyr School of Social Work in JHB. But I have not had the pleasure of meeting Miss Mabete.[v] Please give all of them my best regards. I was also pleased to hear that Aunt Helen & Uncle Steve wrote to you and I hope you have answered both of them punctually. Giving attention to matters which seem to many people small is normally one of the marks of a good sense of responsibility. You should cultivate that habit carefully by having a particular day of the week or month reserved for writing letters. It's always better to draft a letter & then go over it to check its mistakes & to improve your formulations.

I hope you have already written to the secretary of the Memon Bursary Fund[vi] to thank his organisation for helping you to pursue one of your most fervent ambitions in life. Tell him that without their help, it would have been well-nigh impossible for you to further your university studies. Let them know that you intend seeing them in June when you will thank them directly.

You should also thank Aunt Helen for all her efforts. Tell her that you would like to spend your June holidays with a sociologist or sociol-

---

i   An isiXhosa saying which means 'Wishing you a long life'.

ii   Helen Joseph (1905–92), teacher, social worker, and anti-apartheid and women's rights activist – see the glossary.

iii   Professor Hough taught Winnie Mandela at the Jan Hofmeyr School of Social Work.

iv   A former classmate of Winnie Mandela at the Jan Hofmeyr School of Social Work, who later became a lecturer at the University College of Fort Hare.

v   A friend.

vi   The Memon Association of South Africa was established in 1965 and provides funding to tertiary students.

ogy student where you can pick up in this subject as well as in your English.

You could perhaps ask her to give the task of getting a suitable person in this regard to ILONA[i] or her (Aunt Helen's) neighbour, Sheila. Dr. Fatima Meer's address is 141 Burnwood Rd, Sydenham (4091) Durban. She would be delighted to hear from you, but my only fear is that she might ask you to go over to the Natal University where she is a lecturer.

You are also quite mistaken in thinking I am the person who got you the bursary. All that I did was to ask Aunt Helen to get in touch with some of my JHB friends. I was certain that they would raise the necessary funds. But by then Mum Winnie had already contacted the Memon Bursary Fund through our attorney Mr. Ismail Ayob,[ii] himself a Memon.[iii] That is the true story. That is the person who, more than any other one, deserves your thanks. Whether or not you will do what every decent beneficiary would do in your circs.[iv] is, of course, entirely your affair.

Concerning Dr. Vilakazi's[v] efforts your sharp reaction equally surprised me. Both Mum Winnie and he are only trying to help you and not to dictate to you. I agree that you should complete your first degree at F.H.[vi] and then go abroad for Honours and Masters. All that you should do is to inform her accordingly, sign the forms & return them to her at once; and ask her to postpone the particular bursary for 1982 when you will be able to take it.

I am also pleased to know that Maureen is your friend. I used to know a grand old man, Mr. Pike, who lived next to the Orlando East Communal Hall. I wonder if Maureen knew him. Perhaps he was her grandfather. Please give her my love.

Zeni's[vii] address is P.O. Box 546 Mbabane, Swaziland. Her official name is Princess La Mandela Dlamini and she and her husband intend leaving for studies in the U.S.A. in this yr. You are right when you say

---

i   Ilona Kleinschmidt, a friend and the wife of Horst Kleinschmidt, an activist who worked for the South African Christian Institute. The Kleinschmidts provided financial assistance when Winnie Mandela was in prison, and Mandela appointed Kleinschmidt to be the legal guardian of Zenani and Zindzi Mandela when Winnie Mandela was in prison in 1974.

ii   Ismail Ayob (1942–), Mandela's attorney – see the glossary.

iii   Mandela's use of the word Memon possibly refers to a subgroup of Muslims who descend from the western part of South Asia.

iv   Circumstances.

v   Herbert Vilakazi (1943–2016), professor of sociology.

vi   University College of Fort Hare, Alice in the Ciskei homeland – see the glossary.

vii   Zenani Mandela (1959–), Mandela's middle daughter and Makaziwe's half-sister.

that she is a kind person. Have you read Zindzi's[i] anthology?[ii] It is now being sold by S.A. book firms. Unfortunately I have not seen it and do not know its title. I am looking forward to seeing you this June. Meantime, do study hard and know that we are holding up thumbs for you. Above all, we love you & once again, wish you a very very Happy birthday & the best of luck.

Tons and tons of love and a million kisses
Your loving Tata[iii]

Miss Makaziwe Mandela, Elukhanyisweni, P.O. Alice.
P.S. Send me your latest photo of not more than 15 x 20 centimetres. Treat the matter urgently.
By the way, aunt Helen is herself a well-qualified sociologist with an Honours Degree from the University of London.

[words printed in card:]
However you
May celebrate
Here's hoping
You will find
Your special day
In every way

Will be
The perfect kind

―――――――

To Peter Wellman,[iv] a friend and journalist

Nelson Mandela 466/64

27-5-79

―――――――

i   Zindziswa Mandela (1960–), Mandela's youngest daughter and Makaziwe's half-sister.
ii   Zindzi Mandela's book of poetry, *Black As I Am* (Los Angeles: Guild of Tutors Press, 1978).
iii   'Father' in isiXhosa.
iv   Peter Wellman (1941-2001) was a journalist on the *Rand Daily Mail* when he met Mandela. He used to drive Mandela's daughters Zenani and Zindziswa to school in Swaziland.

My dear Peter

I was quite flattered to receive your telegram &, even more, by the knowledge that I am godfather to the chdn.

To be godparent is always an intimate honour.[i] For one thing it makes one virtually a member of the family & the fulfilment of its responsibilities is a challenge that affords plenty of joy & satisfaction in my current circs.[ii] The honour has a wider significance which I hope I deserve. A million thanks, Peter!

My present position will of course make it quite difficult, in certain cases even impossible, for me to do what I would have liked to do. But I will always try to let the chdn know that I love them & always think of them. I sincerely hope that soon you will send me a group photo not more than 10 x 15 cms. If I cannot give them chocolates,[iii] put them on my lap, talk, play & sing with them at least they, Pa & Mom can all appear in the family album. Naturally I expect you to give me their full names & dates of birth & a bit of family history. You & Winnie may have tried in the past to tell me that I am godfather & to give me all the relevant information. But your telegram was the very first hint of the fact. Once more, many thanks!

I like you to know that throughout the many yrs of incarceration numerous messages of good wishes & hope sent by people from different walks of life, have cut through massive iron doors & grim stone walls, bringing into the cell the splendour & warmth of springtime. No two messages are ever the same & each one has struck a special note. Yours was typical. Frankly, there are moments, like now, when I feel as if the whole world, or at least the greater part of it, has been squeezed into my tiny cell. I have comparatively more time to think & dream; obsessed with a sense of involvement & with far more friends than ever before. Your telegram pulled me across these waves towards the Golden City[iv] which, from many photographs I have seen, appears to have in many ways changed from the town I once knew so well.

A few slums have been cleared away & the underlying social problems transported elsewhere.[v] In the process beloved nooks & dens cherished

i   Wellman sent Mandela a telegram asking him to be godfather to his daughter Emily.
ii   Circumstances.
iii   When Emily Wellman met Mandela after his release he told her that he was sorry he did not send her
        the chocolates. (Emily Welman in an email to Sahm Venter, 6 September 2017.)
iv   Johannesburg is called the Golden City due its origins as a gold-mining town in the nineteenth century.
v   In order to separate people according to their race, the apartheid government enacted a range of laws
        including the Group Areas Act which separated residential areas. From the 1950s and right through
        until the early 1980s, areas were designated for white occupation and black people were forcibly moved

in fond memories have been destroyed, & those who once hoped for the day when shacks would become hallowed monuments must start building new shrines.

On the cleared areas modern buildings & skyscrapers, all glittering in wealth & power dominate the scene, while spacious highways crisscross the City bringing widely separated outskirts closer than ever before. In the field of economics, govt, education, and many arts, new faces, eager to live in unconventional ways, have come to the fore, sharpening the generation gap. Aging pessimists may be looking around constantly lest carrion birds notice that death is about to strike.

Thinking about J.H.B.[i] reminds me of my return in '55 to the country village across the Kei[ii] where I grew up. During our young days there was a thick bush that covered a mountain slope. In the valley below, especially on the river banks, there were several imposing trees I thought would stand for all time. Apart from Zami's[iii] love and affection that bush was to me as a child the nearest thing to paradise I ever experienced. Have you ever been out on a fox hunt, togged out in smart riding breeches, shining boots & spurs, with the ponies at full gallop & the hounds yelling? Then you have an idea of how we felt in that bush. Full of wild fruit, a variety of small game & bird life, wild honey, plenty of fresh water & parlangs, the bush attracted almost all the boys in the village.

We hunted rabbits, polecats, partridges & doves & pulled fish from the water. Even when I was at boarding school I returned to the bush during the holidays & enjoyed the chase even more. My early crowded programme in J.H.B. & its attractions never wiped off the mind the pleasant memories of my youth & I thought often of the bush & veld.[iv] After an absence of 15 yrs I returned home & one of the first places I visited was that bush. It was springtime & the vegetation was green. The bush had lost most of its picturesqueness. The once imposing trees on the river bank had either disappeared or withered away & those that were still healthy no longer looked so swaggering. All over the valley vigorous young bushes were asserting themselves. I recalled the words

from those areas. One of the most well-known of these moves was of the people of Sophiatown, a mixed suburb close to the CBD of Johannesburg. Thousands of people in Johannesburg were moved to the new township of Soweto.

i   Johannesburg
ii   'River'.
iii   One of Winnie's names.
iv   'Field' in Afrikaans.

of an English poet who once said ". . . changeth, yielding place to new, & God fulfils himself in many ways, lest one good custom corrupts the world."[i] I have not seen this poem for almost 40 yrs & may have mixed up the lines.[ii] But that is what went through my mind as I surveyed my boyhood paradise. Similar memories, though not so nostalgic, transport me to a world that once was when I see pictures of J.H.B.

I am looking forward to seeing you & family one day. Meantime, my thoughts are in Main Street[iii] particularly after receipt of your telegram.

Hazel once worked with you. If you still see her & Hymie give them my fondest regards. I shake your hand very firmly. Sincerely Nelson

Mr Peter Wellman, 171 Main St, Johannesburg

◇◇◇◇◇◇◇◇◇◇◇◇

In 1975 Walter Sisulu and Ahmed Kathrada approached Mandela and suggested that he secretly write his autobiography in prison and smuggle it out for publication in time for his sixtieth birthday in 1978. He agreed and began writing. In Long Walk to Freedom, *the book it eventually became, he recalled: 'I would write most of the night and sleep during the day. During the first week or two I would take a nap after dinner, wake at 10 p.m. and then write until it was time for breakfast. After working at the quarry, I would then sleep until dinner, and the process would begin again. After a few weeks of this, I notified the authorities that I was not feeling well and would not be going to the quarry. They did not seem to care, and from then on I was able to sleep most of the day.'[2a] Each day Mandela would pass what he had written to Kathrada who commented in writing and handed it to Sisulu. After Mandela had made the corrections, the pages were given to fellow prisoners Isu 'Laloo' Chiba and Mac Maharaj to transcribe into tiny handwriting. In an interview in 2010, Chiba described how he and Maharaj transcribed the 600 pages of manuscript into about sixty pages. That manuscript was then divided into cocoa containers and buried in the garden of B Section, Robben Island.[3a] In this letter to Alan Paton, author*

---

i   Alfred Lord Tennyson's poem 'Morte d'Arthur' written in 1838.
ii   His quotation is actually very close. The original lines read: 'The old order changeth, yielding place to new. / And God fulfils himself in many ways. / Lest one good custom should corrupt the world.'
iii   A street in Johannesburg.

of the famous South African novel Cry, the Beloved Country, *Mandela focuses on the literary talents of his youngest daughter.*

To Alan Paton,[i] author and leader of the Liberal Party who gave evidence in mitigation of sentence in the Rivonia Trial

Nelson Mandela 466/64   29.7.79

[Note at the top of the letter in Afrikaans] Rejected. Objections to Alan Paton]

Dear Dr Paton,

This is my third attempt to reach you during the last 15 years. I first wrote to you immediately I could send out more than just two letters a year, and I thanked you for your courageous response of June 1964.[ii] It was not so easy those days to come forward as you did and few people are likely to forget that inspiring gesture.

In the second letter I expressed my sympathies on the passing away of your first wife. I pointed out that the tragedy, coming so soon after the death of your friend, Chief Luthuli, must have been exceptionally difficult to endure. I mentioned the Browns,[iii] Kupers[iv] and the late Dr Edgar Brookes[v] and asked you to give all of them my fondest regards.

I hope the letters reached you and that your long silence is due to pressure of engagements. If they did not, then I will hardly blame you if you think our sense of gratitude is not very high. I have taken the precaution of registering this particular one to make sure that it reaches you.

When I and a friend visited their house, Mrs Brown served us with coffee and buttered scones so fresh and soft that they went down before one could chew. Almost two decades have passed since that day, yet the memory of that visit has not faded. I also met the Kupers only

---

i   Alan Paton (1903–88) – see the glossary.
ii   A reference to the evidence in mitigation of sentence that Paton gave for Mandela and his co-accused at
        the Rivonia Trial (for the Rivonia Trial, see the glossary).
iii   The Browns were members of the Liberal Party.
iv   Hilda Kuper (1911–92), social anthropologist. Her husband, Leo Kuper (1908–94) was a sociologist.
        They helped to found the Liberal Party in Natal (now KwaZulu-Natal).
v   Edgar Brookes (1987–79), South African Liberal Party politican, professor of history, and author.

once; in their house in Durban. Although I am confident that they will never cease burrowing wherever they may be, I was sorry to hear that they had emigrated. Their contribution in the fields of education and literature has been impressive and their exit must have weakened their school of thought in several directions. As a matter of fact, I first heard of their emigration when I was trying to order their work on the African bourgeoisie.[i] Unfortunately, the book was unknown to the firms approved by this Department.[ii] Though I have never had the honour of meeting Dr Brookes, our generation of students in Native Administration,[iii] as the subject was then known, knew of him quite well. He was widely acknowledged as the leading authority on that topic. I was sorry to learn of his death and would be pleased if you would kindly give my condolences to his family.

In March last year my wife told me that you had visited her in Brandfort. Even at our best moments in Johannesburg, such visits always left us with a tremendous feeling. Today they assume a special significance and I was happy to know that many of our friends could have the courage and time to travel to Brandfort[iv] bringing good wishes to the family. I was also pleased to know that you made it possible for my daughter-in-law, Rayne,[v] to return to college. I saw her only once when she came down in 1974. She struck me as a sweet and ambitious child who is keen on education. I hope she will not disappoint those who love and wish her well. The other day I read your article in *Fair Lady*[vi] of January 31 on your visit to Zindzi[vii] in Brandfort. Unfortunately I could neither keep it nor make notes. Still it struck me as a powerful story and a shot in the arm for the young lady. To be introduced to the readers of *Fair Lady* by a well-known and experienced writer is a flattering compliment to Zindzi. When I reached the last line "joy was great and sorrow small."

A few days before I saw your review I had read an article in this month's issue of the *Reader's Digest*. It attempted to analyse the problems facing amateur writers in the country. To illustrate the point,

---

i   Leo Kuper, *African Bourgeoisie: Race, Class and Politics* (New Haven, Yale University Press, 1965). The
      book was banned by the apartheid government.
ii   The book was banned in South Africa.
iii   Mandela is referring to a subject that he possibly studied at the University College of Fort Hare, which
      he attended from 1939 to 1940 until he was expelled for embarking on protest action.
iv   Brandfort is around 350 km from Johannesburg by car.
v   Rose Rayne 'Rennie' Mandela, the wife of his son Makgatho.
vi   *Fair Lady* is a South African women's magazine.
vii   Zindziswa Mandela, Mandela's youngest daughter – see the glossary.

the writer referred to the number of manuscripts received by various publications and the number accepted by each. Among the magazines mentioned in the article is *Fair Lady* which in 1977 received about 700 fiction manuscripts. According to the writer, it published only fifty of these most from overseas. In the light of these, I thought it significant that Zindzi's efforts had attracted the attention of such a selective magazine. I will try to keep my hand clean so that I can give you a firm handshake when we meet.

It is because we have many good friends whose support and encouragement has been a source of tremendous inspiration that Zindzi has been inspired to urge the tomorrow to "increase your speed, I eagerly await you."

The family has experienced a lot of problems, some of which you are aware. In my current position it is difficult to handle even such personal problems. It is much more difficult to intervene when such problems go beyond first degree relatives. But if the road between Hillcrest[i] & Brandfort should cave in on the sides & develop potholes, I would do everything in my power to repair it, to clear any debris that might block the free passage of the love and goodwill that characterises the relations between our respective families. Particularly at this moment, I like you never to forget that.

I do not know what works you published during the last 17 years, and I have no means of knowing. All I can tell you is that I am confident that you have not been idle. In fact, last year I heard that an American university had awarded you an honorary doctorate.[ii] Although I have no other information on the matter, I was happy to receive the news. Such an honour was well-deserved. That award has a personal and wider significance. For one thing it shows that your labours have not been in vain, that in spite of persistent droughts and choking weed, you sowed on good ground, that "the harvest is late; has not failed." My love and fondest regards to you and your wife, and to all the friends mentioned above.

Sincerely,
[Signed NR Mandela]

Dr Alan Paton, P.O. Box 278 Hillcrest 3650, Natal.

---

i   Paton lived in Hillcrest, Natal (now KwaZulu-Natal).
ii   Paton received twelve honorary doctorates during his life, including from Yale University and the Univeristy of Michigan.

◇◇◇◇◇◇◇◇◇◇◇◇

This letter to Mandela's youngest daughter, Zindziswa, was never sent. It was discovered in the National Archives and Record Service of South Africa with a note from prison officials reading: 'The attached piece that prisoner Mandela included with his Christmas card will not be sent. The card will be sent. The prisoner has not been informed that this piece has been rejected. He does not have permission to include it with the card. I discussed this on 20 December 1979 with Brigadier du Plessis and he agrees with the decision. Keep it in his file.'

═══════════════

To Zindzi Mandela,[i] his youngest daughter

Nelson Mandela 466/64   9.12.79

My darling Zindzi,

I sometimes wonder what happened to our boxing gym at what used to be called St Joseph's in Orlando East. The walls of that school and of the D.O.C.C.[ii] are drenched with sweet memories that will delight me for yrs. When we trained at the D.O.C.C. in the early 50s the club included amateur & professional boxers as well as wrestlers. The club was managed by Johannes (Skip Adonis) Molosi, a former champ & a capable trainer who knew the history, theory and practical side of the game.

Unfortunately, in the mid-50s he began neglecting his duties and would stay away from the gym for long periods.

Because of this, the boxers revolted. Twice I settled the matter, but when Skip failed to pay heed to repeated protests from the boxers, things reached breaking point. This time I was totally unable to recon-

---

i   Zindziswa Mandela (1960–) – see the glossary
ii   The Donaldson Orlando Community Centre was a community space in Soweto that hosted dances, concerts, and boxing matches. It was built by the Donaldson Trust, established in 1936 by Lieutenant Colonel James Donaldson D.S.O. to 'advance the status, improve the conditions and remove the disabilities suffered by the black African population of South Africa; and generally to seek their benefit and betterment'. Nelson Mandela used to box there in the 1940s and 1950s and spent many of his evenings training at the gym with his eldest son, Thembi.

cile the parties. The boxers left the D.O.C.C. & opened their own gym at St Joseph's. Thembi[i] and I went along with them. Simon Tshabalala, who is now abroad, became the manager, & the star boxer was, of course, still Jerry (Uyinja) Moloi who later became the Tvl[ii] lightweight champ and leading contender for the national title. Apart from Jerry we produced 3 other champs: Eric (Black Material) Ntsele who won the national bantamweight from Leslie Tanjee, Freddie (Tomahawk) Ngidi who became Tvl flyweight champ, a title which was later held by one of our gym mates, Johannes Mokotedi. There were other good prospects like Peter, the flyweight, who built our garage at home. He hailed from Bloemfontein & was a student at the Vacation School in Dube. Thembi himself was a good boxer & on occasions I sat until very late at night waiting for him to return from a tournament in Randfontein, Vereeniging[iii] or other centres. I and my gym mates were a closely knit family and when Mum came into the picture that family became even more intimate. Jerry & Eric even drove Mum around when I could not do so and the entire gym turned up at our engagement party.

By the way, Freddie worked for our firm as a clerk. He was quiet & reliable and the entire staff was fond of him. But on one Xmas eve I returned to the office & who did I find lying flat & helpless in the passage just outside the general office? Freddie. His appearance so shocked me that I rushed him to a doctor. The quack gave him one quick look & assured me that the champ was O.K. but that he needed more sleep. He had succumbed to the usual Xmas sprees & over-indulged himself. I drove him to his home at OE[iv] quite relieved. Incidentally, I should have told you that during the dispute at the D.O.C.C. Skip accused Jerry of stabbing him in the back just as Mark Antony betrayed his friend Caesar. Thembi asked who Antony & Caesar were. At the time Thembi was only 9. Skip explained, * "Don't tell us about people who are dead." If I had not been there Skip would have pulled out the child's bowels, so furious he was. He bitterly complained to me about what he considered to be discourtesy on the part of the boy. I reminded him that in my house I was the patriarch & ruled over the household. But that I had no such powers in the gym; that Thembi had paid membership fees, we were perfect equals & I could give him no instructions.

---

i   Madiba Thembekile (Thembi) Mandela (1945–69), Mandela's eldest son – see the glossary.
ii   Transvaal.
iii   Both places are between 50 to 60 km from Johannesburg.
iv   Orlando East.

We would spend about 1½ hrs in the gym & I was at home about 9 pm. Tired & with hardly a drop of water in my body. Mum would give me a glass of fresh and cold orange juice, supper served with well-prepared sour milk. Mum was gloweth with good health & happiness those dys. The house was like a beehive with the family, old school friends, fellow workers from Bara,[i] members of the gym & even clients calling at the house to chat with her. For more than 2 yrs she and I literally lived on honey-moon. I quietly resisted any activity that kept me away from home after office hrs. Yet she & I kept warning each other that we were living on borrowed time, that hard times would soon knock at the door. But we were having a great time with good friends & we did not have much time for self-pity. It is more than 2 decades since then, yet I recall those dys so clearly as if everything happened yesterday.

But this letter, darling is not about old boxing mates, school friends and social workers or even about Mum. It is meant for a lovely young lady whose picture is always in my mind, a go getter who makes Mum & me dangerously proud of being parents. As I write this letter, her photo and that of her sister are on the book case on my left with the frames of the 2 photos touching each other & with a simple blue rosary strung on them for ornament. It has a sentimental value as it reminds me of our connection with the Catholic church through "Our Lady of Sorrows".[ii] That young lady is none other than our lady Mantu Nobutho Zindzi, you Nkosazana.[iii]

On the 23/12 you will be 19 & I send you my love and congrats. Mum tells me that you will be here on that Sunday & I am looking forward to it with great expectation. Until then, I will keep my fingers crossed. Someone once said that happy couples get happy children & happy children make happy families and happy nations. May you be blessed with all these, Mantu.

Again, Many Happy Returns & the best of health.

Tons and tons of love and a million kisses, darling. Affectionately, Tata.[iv]

---

i   Baragwanath Hospital in Soweto, Johannesburg, where Winnie Mandela worked as a social worker.
ii   Our Lady of Sorrows was the Roman Catholic boarding school in Swaziland that Zindziswa was attending.
iii   *Nkosazana* means 'Miss' or 'princess' in isiXhosa.
iv   'Father' in isiXhosa.

Miss Zindzi Mantu Nobutho Mandela
802 Phathakahle, P.O. Brandfort 9400, OFS

* your brother hit back

――――――――――

To Winnie Mandela,[i] his wife

466/64: Nelson Mandela   30.7.80

My darling Mum.

How dare you send me a mere telegram on the occasion of my 62nd
birthday! I was tempted to let it go up in flames, if only I could destroy
the paper on which it is written without doing so to the message, & if
only I could make you feel the pain there in Brandfort. You have now
forgotten that I always want to feed my vanity for displaying the affectionate messages on the bookcase long enough to attract my inmates
without any formal invitation from me.

Do you realise that this yr I did not even get the wedding anniversary card you occasionally send? Of course both cards would, like all
your letters & telegrams, be subjected to the usual censorship; but
unlike the type of telegram I receive this end, they can be preserved so
as to remind our chdn of these hectic dys, especially your harrowing
problems in that backveld.[ii]

Never mind, darling Mum, your love & affectionate messages always
lift me in whatever form they come. I was delighted to get the telegrams
after spending the 19/7 with Mantu.[iii] Coming at the same time with the
visits on 13 & 19/7 it made me feel ever more certain that the springs in
you that have flown so strong all these yrs & whose waters are so cool
& sweet, will never dry. This is the case even though you did not look so
well. The fire that usually glows so brilliantly in you was missing. May
be the pains on your back had not eased much & that the rough seas

――――――――――

i   Nomzamo Winifred Madikizela-Mandela (1936–2018) – see the glossary.
ii   Winnie Mandela was still living in the rural township of Brandfort in the Orange Free State (now Free
      State), where she had been banished in 1977. She lived there until 1985. Veld means 'field' in Afrikaans.
iii   Their younger daughter, Zindzi.

466/64 Nelson Mandela   30 · 7 · 80

My darling Mum,

How dare you send me a mere telegram on the occasion of my 62 nd birthday. I was tempted to let it go up in flames, if only I could destroy the paper on which it is written without doing so to the message, & if I could make you feel the pain out there in Brandfort. You have now forgotten that I always want to feed my vanity by displaying your affectionate messages on the book case long enough to attract to attract my inmates without any formal invitation from me

Do you realise that this yr I did not even get the wedding anniversary card you occasionally send? Of course both cards would, like all your letters & telegrams, be subjected to the usual censorships; but unlike the type of telegram I receive this end, they can be preserved so as to remind our children of these hectic days, especially your harrowing problems in that backveld.

Never mind, darling Mum your love & affectionate messages always lift me in whatever form they come. I was delighted to get the telegrams after spending the 19/7 with Maki. Coming at the same time with the visits on 13 & 19/7 it made me feel ever more certain that the springs in you that have flown so strong all these yrs & whose waters are so cool & sweet, will never dry. This is the case even though you did not look so well. The fire that usually glows so brilliantly in you was missing. May be the pains on your back had not eased much & that the rough seas may have unconsciously affected you. I hope you will continue to do your regular exercises, darling. The only answer is to develop the back muscles & make them strong enough to hold the backbones in position. Take it easy, however, especially while the pain still lingers.

Apart from your telegram I received 2 cards both from Zeni & Muzi & from Zozi & Swati. I believe that those of Maki are in the pipeline. There were 3 other telegrams, one from JHB's Israel, Mkentane's Kepu & Mangosuthu. So far I have received not a single one of the multitude that friends have sent from all over the world. Nevertheless, it is very comforting to know that so many friends still think of us after so many yrs.

As far as the illness of Mati is concerned, I sincerely hope nothing will happen to her. Such a tragedy would open up a wound that would be difficult to heal. We love her & the children so much. I would have preferred her to remain in JHB & get some work. There she would at least be sure of the best medical care in the country & would also be nearer the children. Were it not for the scarcity of doctors & work in Brandfort I would have strongly advised that she should stay with you. Life in Brandfort would be as tough & depressing as it has been for Kungie &, if possible, we should try to help her. Niki & Marsh may find it very difficult to assist in view of the distance

_____

Our darling Matlala, I miss you, Reggie & the children very badly & hope you are all well. Both you & Reggie do need a holiday & a complete rest for a couple of mths. That's absolutely necessary. Zami tells me that you are very angry with her for using part of the money you sent me. In actual fact she consulted me before hand & I authorised her to use it. You are of course aware that circs have reversed the roles in this may have unconsciously affected you. I hope you will continue to do your regular exercises, darling. The only answer is to develop the back muscles & make them strong enough to hold the backbones in position. Take it easy, however, especially while the pain still lingers.

Apart from your telegram I received 2 cards both from Zeni & Muzi[i] and from Zazi & Swati.[ii] I believe that those of Mantu are in the pipeline. There were 3 other telegrams, one from J.H.B.'s[iii] Ismail, Kentane's Kepu[iv] and Mangosuthu.[v] So far I have received not a single one of the multitude that friends have sent from all over the world. Nevertheless, it is very comforting to know that so many friends still think of us after so many yrs.

As far as the illness of Nali[vi] is concerned, I sincerely hope nothing will happen to her. Such a tragedy would open up a wound that would be difficult to heal. We love her & the chdn so much. I would have preferred her to remain in J.H.B. & get some work. There she would at least be sure of the best medical care in the country & would also be nearer the chdn. Were it not for the scarcity of doctors & work in Brandfort, I would have strongly advised that she should stay with you. Life in Pondoland[vii] would be as tough & depressing as it has been for Lungile[viii] &, if possible, we should try to help her. Niki & Marsh[ix] may find it difficult to assist in view of the disturbing report you have given me on what they recently went through. I would certainly have no objection to the 2 of them going over to Zeni. It would mean a great deal to her to have them nearby.

It pleased me to hear that Lungile is now in J.H.B. for treatment. Staying a while with his niece may alone benefit his health. But I think he probably would have been more happy with you & Nyanya.[x] If you still have some of my clothing I wouldn't mind giving them to him as a present, provided that you have no objection. . . .

---

i   Their older daughter, Zenani, and her husband, Prince Thumbumuzi Dlamini, a son of King Sobhuza of Swaziland. They married in 1977.

ii   Zenani Mandela's children, Zaziwe (1977–) and Zamaswazi (1979–).

iii   Johannesburg.

iv   Kepu Mkentane, the wife of Lincoln Mkentane, a former university classmate of Mandela's who became a lawyer.

v   Chief Mangosuthu Gatsha Buthelezi (1928–), Zulu prince, member of the ANC until the relationship deteriorated in 1979, chief minister of KwaZulu 1972–94, founder and president of the Inkatha Freedom Party in 1975 – see the glossary.

vi   Winnie Mandela's sister.

vii   The district in the Transkei where Winnie Mandela grew up.

viii   Winnie Mandela's brother.

ix   Winnie Mandela's eldest sister Niki and her husband Marshall Xaba (for Niki Xaba, see the glossary).

x   Nonyaniso (Nyanya) Madikizela, Winnie Mandela's youngest sister.

You heard about the sudden death of Sanjay[i] in a private plane accident & I do hope that you sent a message of condolence to his mother.[ii] Nothing could ever excuse our failure to do so. If you have not yet done so, Mum, I would suggest that you dispatch a message immediately. It will also be proper for the chdn to leave a wreath on his "grave" when they go over for the ceremony.[iii] I hope there will be coordination between you and Reggie[iv] about the proposed trip.

You will not believe me when I tell you that apart from the long letter I received from Muzi,[v] he also followed with a beautiful postcard sent from Mombasa.[vi] He says his return has been postponed by 1½ wks. I am writing to him via Mbabane[vii] lest I should miss him if I direct it to Kenya. I am also writing to Zeni. I forgot to tell you during the last visit that Dr. Phatudi[viii] visited the Island last mnth & asked to see me. I wrote him a short note in which I pointed out that I could not acede to his request. But I added that my refusal to see him should not be regarded as a discourtesy to him.[ix]

I came out empty-handed with Mantu. She suggested bringing Oupa[x] along so that the 3 of us could put our heads together. But she added that it will not be so easy to discuss the problem with me in my present circs.[xi] I am, nevertheless, keen to see them & hope they have applied.

The family is growing fast, Mum, & in spite of our present position, it is of some importance that we try to acquire a proper home. It is far better that we work on the idea of buying a house in Soweto &

---

i Sanjay Gandhi (1946–80), a son of India's prime minister Indira Gandhi, was killed in an airplane accident on 23 June 1980.

ii Mandela did not meet Indira Gandhi but he had been impressed by India's stand against apartheid since 1946.

iii Fatima Meer wrote to Indira Gandhi in 1979 suggesting she put Mandela forward for the Jawaharlal Nehru Award for International Understanding. He was awarded the prize in 1979 and when Winnie Mandela was denied a passport to attend the ceremony on 14 November 1980, he was represented by Oliver Tambo. Mandela's middle daughter, Princess Zenani Dlamini, also attended the ceremony.

iv Oliver Reginald Tambo (1917–93), Mandela's friend, former law partner, and the president of the ANC – see the glossary. His middle name was Reginald and Mandela referred to him as Reggie.

v Prince Thumbumuzi Dlamini, a son of King Sobhuza of Swaziland and Zenani Mandela's husband.

vi A city on the coast of Kenya.

vii The largest city in Swaziland.

viii Cedric Phatudi, chief minister of the Lebowa homeland, Transvaal. An article in the *Citizen* newspaper dated 28 June 1980 reports that he was to ask Prime Minister P. W. Botha to release Mandela and that he had visited Robben Island that week but that he did not meet Mandela. ('Phatudi to Ask PM to Free Nelson Mandela', *The Citizen*, 28 June 1980.)

ix Just as Mandela had refused to be released to the Transkei homeland, he also refused to recognise the Lebowa homeland.

x Zindzi's partner, Oupa Seakamela.

xi Circumstances.

abandon the plan of extending the present one. The entire stand is too small for our purpose. There Mantu can never get the privacy needed for her studies & writing. My suggestion is that the R10,000 should be invested in such a project. I would have liked to exchange views on the matter with someone like Marsh or Ntatho[i] if they could come down. The other matter that worries me presently is the fact that you are now staying alone. I am wracking my brains for a solution. It is something for which we should find a way out without delay. We both know how your being alone will be adversely exploited. Meantime, I miss you a lot & hope you will look far better when I see you again. I LOVE You! Devotedly, Madiba.

Nkosk. Nobandla Mandela, 802 Phathakahle.

[At the bottom of each page of this letter there is a note to Adelaide Tambo.[ii] It could be that he tried to sneak it into this letter to his wife.] 'Our darling Matlala,[iii] I miss you, Reggie & the chn very badly & hope you are all well. Both you & Reggie do need a holiday & a complete rest for a couple of mths. That's absolutely necessary. Zami[iv] tells me that you are very angry with her for using part of the money you sent me. In actual fact she consulted me beforehand & I authorised her to use it. You are of course aware that circs. have reversed the roles in this family & that Zami has established herself as the undisputed kraal-hand,[v] so much so that I doubt it if, on my return, I will be able to dislodge her from that position. She is generally a frugal person & I depend entirely on her in matters of this kind. Again I miss you & even this pen that I am using is full of nostalgic memories. We all love you, Matlala. Very sincerely, Bhuti.[vi] P.S. A million thanks for the cash & for everything else. Bhuti.

---

i   Nthato Motlana (1925–2008), friend, medical doctor, businessman, and anti-apartheid activist – see the glossary.

ii   Adelaide Tambo (1929–2007), friend, anti-apartheid activist, and wife of Oliver Tambo, Mandela's former law partner and president of the ANC – see the glossary for both these individuals. The Tambos were living in exile in London.

iii   A nickname for Adelaide Tambo.

iv   One of Winnie Mandela's names.

v   A *kraal* is an Afrikaans word for a traditional collection of huts surrounded by a fence for enclosing cattle. A *kraal*-hand would be a worker who provided assistance.

vi   'Brother' in Afrikaans.

To Zindzi Mandela,[i] his youngest daughter

[Note in another hand] Censored original letter 10.2.81

466/64: Nelson Mandela   1.3.81

My darling,

Prison, <u>especially for those who stay in single cells</u>,[ii] provides many moments of reflection on problems too numerous to be listed down on paper. Often as I walk up & down the tiny cell, or as I lie on my bed, the mind wanders far & wide, recalling this episode & that mistake. Among these is the thought whether in my best days outside prison I showed sufficient appreciation for the love & kindness of many of those who befriended & even helped me when I was poor & struggling.

The other day I was thinking of the Xhomas in 46 – 7th Avenue, Alexandra Township, where I lived on my arrival in JHB.[iii] At that time I was earning the mthly wage of £2 (R4.00)[iv] & out of this amount I had to pay the mthly rent of 13/-4d plus bus fare of 8d a day to town & back. It was hard-going & I often found it quite difficult to pay the rent & bus fare. But my landlord & his wife were kind. Not only did they give me an extension when I could not raise the rent, but on Sundays they gave me a lovely lunch free of charge.

I also stayed with Rev Mabuto of the Anglican Church in 46 8th Avenue in the same township & he & Gogo,[v] as we fondly called his wife, were also very kind, even though she was rather strict, insisting that I should take out only Xhosa girls. Despite the fact that my political outlook was still formative, Healdtown & Fort Hare[vi] had brought me into contact with students from other sections of our

---

i   Zindziswa Mandela (1960–) – see the glossary.
ii   This underlining has most probably been done by a prison censor.
iii   Mandela fled an arranged marriage in 1941 after his expulsion from the University College of Fort Hare and went to Johannesburg where he lodged with the Xhoma family in Alexandra.
iv   He was an articled clerk at the law firm Witkin, Sidelksy & Eidelman.
v   'Granny' in isiZulu and isiXhosa.
vi   Mandela attended the Wesleyan College Healdtown in Fort Beaufort in 1937 and then the University College of Fort Hare, in Alice, in 1939 – see the glossary.

people, & at least I had already developed beyond thinking along ethnic lines. I was determined not to follow her advice on this particular matter. But she & husband played the role of parents to me rather admirably.

Mr Schreiner Baduza,[i] originally from Sterkspruit,[ii] lived as tenant with his wife in 46 7th Avenue. He & Mr J.P. Mngoma,[iii] although much older than myself, especially the latter, were among some of my best friends of those days. Mr Mngoma was a property owner & father to Aunt Virginia, one of Mum's friends.[iv] Later I was introduced to Mr P. Joyana, father-in-law to the brother of the late Chief Jongintaba Mdingi.[v] He (Mr Joyana) was a clerk at the Rand Leases Mine. I used to travel there on Saturdays to collect his rations – samp,[vi] rice, mealie meal,[vii] meat, peanuts & other items.

Much later my financial position slightly improved, but I hardly thought of those who had stood on my side during difficult times, nor did I ever visit them except once or twice only. Both the Mabutos[viii] & the Baduzas subsequently came to live in Soweto & I visited the Mabutos on a few occasions. I met both Messrs Joyana & Baduza on many occasions, but not once did I even think of returning their kindness. Both in the late forties & early fifties Mr Baduza became a very prominent figure in the civic affairs of Soweto & our association was limited to that level.

I was deeply upset when one day early in 1953 the Old Lady, Mrs Xhoma, once a lively & beautiful person, shuffled into my office at Chancellor House looking quite aged & broken. The old man had passed away & she wanted me to wind up his estate. I had hardly known about his illness, to say nothing of his death & funeral, an occasion I had no right not to know.

---

i   One of Mandela's best friends who, with his wife, lodged in the same house as him in Alexandra. After
        he moved to Soweto he became a prominent figure in civic affairs.
ii   A town in the Transkei homeland.
iii   Mandela's friend in Alexandra. A property owner and the father of Aunt Virginia, a friend of Winnie
        Mandela's.
iv   Winnie Mandela.
v   This is most likely Chief Mdingi, a relative of Mandela's and the Thembu Chief who named Mandela's
        two younger daughters. The eldest he named Zenani, meaning 'What have you brought?', and the
        Madikizelas (Winnie Mandela's family) named her Nomadabi Nosizwe, meaning 'battlefield of the
        nation'. Chief Mdingi named the youngest daughter Mantu Nobutho Zindziswa.
vi   A porridge made of coarsely ground corn.
vii   An ingredient made from ground maize, also known as maize meal, which is combined with boiling
        water to make a porridge.
viii   A friend of Mandela's.

Even to my beloved Old Lady[i] I was not as attentive as I should have been. I rarely wrote to her, except to try to persuade her to come up to live with me in J.H.B.[ii] There are many other examples I could give & these are but a few which I give by way of illustration.

My arrest for treason on 5/12/56[iii] & the lengthy proceedings that followed, worsened the position. The world around me literally crumbled, income disappeared & many obligations could not be honoured. Only the coming of Mum[iv] into the picture helped to bring about a bit of order in my personal affairs. But the chaos had gone too far even for herself to bring back the stability & easy life I had only just begun to taste when misfortune struck.

It is all these things which keep turning up as the mind strays over my days in the Golden City.[v] But this soul-searching melts away altogether when I think of Mum & all the chdn, of the pride & joy you all give me. Among us is Nobutho,[vi] the beautiful Mantu whose love & loyalty, visits, letters, birthday & Xmas cards are an essential part in the efforts of the family to help me endure many of the challenges of the past two decades. Nobutho is a Capricorn & according to astrologers the stars last mth foretold a period of pleasure & excitement that awaited the Capricorns, that you are likely to have many visitors, many invitations & that health should be excellent. It is a carefully worked out superstition & which is attractively presented. It has fascinated mankind from the dawn of history & has even inspired many people, who believe in it, to excel themselves in many fields. Indeed many Capricorns may have felt flattered when they read these fantastic predictions. But let us leave superstitions & close this note with an observation that is based on facts. It is my real message to you, darling – your ability to appreciate the love & kindness of others. It is a precious virtue to try to make others happy & to forget their worries. It is a quality which you & Zeni[vii] seem to have inherited from Mum. My wish is that it may deepen as you

i   His mother, Nosekeni Mandela.

ii   Johannesburg.

iii   Mandela is referring to the Treason Trial (1956–61), which was a result of the apartheid government's attempt to quell the power of the Congress Alliance, a coalition of anti-apartheid organisations. In early-morning raids on 5 December 1956, 156 individuals were arrested and charged with high treason. By the end of the trial in March 1961 all the accused either had the charges withdrawn or, in the case of the last twenty-eight accused (including Mandela), were acquitted.

iv   Winnie Madikizela whom he married in 1958.

v   Johannesburg is called the Golden City due its origins as a gold-mining town in the nineteenth century.

vi   One of Zindzi's names.

vii His middle daughter.

grow so that more & more people may benefit from it. Love to you, Oupa[i] & Zobuhle.[ii]

Affectionately, Tata.[iii]

Miss Zindzi Mandela, 8115 Orlando West, JHB [1804]
What is the address of Nozizwe Mvembe?

_____

To Winnie Mandela,[iv] his wife

466/64   26.4.81

My darling Mum.

I continue to dream, some pleasant, others not. On the eve of Good Friday you & I were in a cottage on the top of a hill overlooking a deep valley & with a big river coursing the edge of a forest. I saw you walk down the slope of the hill, not as erect in your bearing as you usually are & with your footsteps less confident. All the time your head was down, apparently searching for something a few paces from your feet. You crossed the river & carried away all my love, leaving me rather empty & uneasy. I watched closely as you wandered aimlessly in that forest keeping close to the river bank. Immediately above you there was a couple which presented a striking contrast. They were obviously in love & concentrating on themselves. The whole universe seemed to be on that spot.

My concern for your safety & pure longing for you drove me down the hill to welcome you back as you recrossed the river on your way back to the cottage. The prospect of joining you in the open air & in such beautiful surroundings evoked fond memories & I looked forward to holding your hand & to a passionate kiss. To my disappointment I lost you in the ravines that cut deep into the valley & I only met

_____

i   Zindzi's partner, Oupa Seakamela.
ii   Zindzi's daughter Zoleka Mandela (1980–).
iii   'Father' in isiXhosa.
iv   Nomzamo Winifred Madikizela-Mandela (1936–2018) – see the glossary.

you again when I returned to the cottage. This time the place was full of colleagues who deprived us of the privacy I so wanted to sort out so many things.

In the last scene you were stretched out on the floor in a corner, sleeping out depression, boredom & fatigue. I knelt down to cover the exposed parts of your body with a blanket. Whenever I have such dreams I often wake up feeling anxious & much concerned, but I immediately become relieved when I discover that it was all but a dream. However, this time my reaction was a mixed one.

On 23/4 I was called by the Head of the Prison, something quite routine in this set-up & to which I am used. Suddenly I felt he had unpleasant news for me. When I reached the interview room, I saw him talking to some staff members in the reception office across the passage with a telegram in his hand. This deepened my anxiety. He could not have remained there for more than a minute when he walked towards me, but the tension from anxiety was so distressing that it seemed I had waited for a whole hr. "I have bad news for you" he said as he gave me the telegram. It was from Ismail[i] & reported the death of Samela. I was shocked because I always think of her as a young, strong & healthy girl. To the best of my memory I last saw her on the day we were convicted 17 yrs ago & she was then working at NEH. I was immediately in difficulties & did not know to whom I should send a message of sympathy. Her father, Mehthafa, during his lifetime chief of Sithebe, died in the late thirties already & buried her mother NoFrance. Her brother Zwelizolile, is also late. Her eldest sister, who did Std VI with me at Qokolweni[ii] in the mid-thirties, got married, but I have now forgotten her address & even her husband's surname. Equally regrettable, is the fact that I don't even know whether Samela was now married. In the circumstances I thought it better to wait in the hope that I will get the necessary details in due course. Sometimes I pause to reflect on the countless relatives & friends we have lost over the last 18 yrs of my imprisonment, the tragedy of being unable to nurse those who mean so much to us & of being unable to pay our last respects when they die. Feelings of shock & grief for the death of a relative or close friend are perfectly understandable – CK,[iii] the Old

---

i   He may be referring to Ismail Ayob (1942–), one of his attorneys while he was in prison – see the glossary.

ii   The primary school Mandela attended in Qokolweni in the Transkei.

iii   Columbus Kokani Madikizela, Winnie Mandela's father – see the glossary.

Lady,[i] Thembi,[ii] Nali,[iii] NoEngland,[iv] Nqonqi,[v] Connie & several others too numerous to mention. But there are many other acquaintances who never did anything particularly significant for us other than a warm handshake or pleasant smile when we met, but whose death touched us all the same. But when it is close relatives like Samela, & when you receive the tragic news in the circumstances in which they reached me, without the slightest clue as to the cause of death, then the blow becomes particularly brutal. I sincerely hope that when the fatal hr struck she was at least surrounded by those who could give her love & whose deep concern could assure her efforts were fully appreciated. May be that I will get further details some day.

. . . Yesterday, I also received an equally beautiful letter from Amina[vi] with two lovely photos. She & her Yusuf have kept their ages very well & they both look very impressive indeed. She has all the reason to claim, as she does, that "Yusuf [vii] doesn't look like a sucked orange, but he does not look like an overfed puppy either.". . .

Perhaps one day I will be able to know whether Zindzi[viii] got my telegram re the Durban boarding school which Fatima[ix] undertook to arrange. I am thinking of sending another telegram to her (Fatima) to find out whether Zindzi is now there. Age seems to have affected Zindzi's capacity for writing letters, not even about such essential matters as her education. But she is a good & responsible girl & I am always prepared to give her the benefit of the doubt.

It would appear that a friend has made a press statement that your husband may be suffering from cancer. I have assumed that the statement was made in good faith by one who believes the allegation. But I must at once allay your fears, for I have no reason whatsoever to suspect that any part of my body is cancerous. I can only think the rumour was sparked off by the operation on the right heel in Nov. 79. It has healed beautifully & no longer gives me trouble. I have, however, a lingering pain on the inside part of the left knee. But I feel

---

i   This is likely to be his mother, Nosekeni Fanny Mandela, who died in 1968.

ii   Madiba Thembekile (Thembi) Mandela (1945–69), Mandela's eldest son – see the glossary.

iii   Nali Nancy Vutela, Winnie Mandela's sister.

iv   Wife of the regent Chief Jongintaba Dalindyebo who was Mandela's guardian after his father died when he was twelve (see the glossary).

v   Nqonqi Mtirara, a cousin of Mandela's.

vi   Amina Cachalia (1930–2013), friend and anti-apartheid and women's rights activist – see the glossary.

vii   Yusuf Cachalia (1915–95), Amina Cachalia's husband, political activist and secretary of the South African Indian Congress – see the glossary.

viii   Zindziswa Mandela (1960–), his and Winnie Mandela's youngest daughter – see the glossary.

ix   Fatima Meer (1928–2010), friend, professor, author, and anti-apartheid activist – see the glossary.

it only when I climb or go down some steps & on some nights it has rather been painful; not so much though as to induce me to take any pain tablets. Up to now I have successfully resisted using any of that junk. Earlier in the year I took the precaution of having a blood test & the medical report was negative. The present pain is receiving attention & apart from distance running, it has not affected my exercises very much. I still do quite a lot of leg exercises including station [*sic*] running. Please tell the chdn & all those who may inquire that I feel tremendous. Devotedly, Madiba. I LOVE YOU!

Nkosk. Nobandla Mandela, 802 Phatakahle, P.O. Brandfort, 9400

———————————

To Petronella Ferus, widow of ex–political prisoner Hennie Ferus[i]

466/64: Nelson Mandela   3.5.81

Dearest Sussie,[ii]

The sudden death of your beloved husband, Hennie,[iii] deeply shocked me and my family and I send our deepest sympathy to you, Henshil, Wilna, Peter and Aunt Stienie.

I live in the hope that one day I may be privileged to meet you and family in order to speak more freely and fully on those aspects of Hennie's life which impressed me most. All I can say here is that I spent three years with him on this Island & I look back to that period with fond memories.

I still clearly remember the day when he was released from here on January 22nd, a departure I accepted with mixed feelings. I was sorry to part with such a good and loyal comrade, but I shared the happiness which freedom and reunion with his family would bring him.

During those three years Hennie was highly active in sports, music and other activities which looked after the welfare of his fellow prisoners. One year he became the table-tennis champion of the single cell

---

i   Hennie Ferus (1940–81), anti-apartheid activist who had been a political prisoner on Robben Island.
ii   'Sister' in Afrikaans.
iii   He died in a car accident on 20 April 1981.

section, and was a dangerous opponent in chess. He was a key member of both the quartet and the bigger choir we formed in this Section. Both music groups played an important role in the entertainment of his fellow-prisoners.

His entire life was that of a man who lived in a world of reality, who could think clearly and act correctly. In this regard he was largely influenced by Aunt Stienie, herself a person of strong character and equally clear vision, who will always be remembered for her love of and loyalty to the family and community at large.

It is never easy to close the gap left by a man like Hennie, but I sincerely hope that it was a source of real comfort to you that he was accompanied to his resting place by a crowd of more than 4 000 mourners, four television crews and several press men.[i] That demonstration was but a small measure of the high esteem in which he was regarded by the people.

Again, my family and I send you our deepest sympathy and love, Sussie. We hope that time will in due course heal your painful wounds, and that the children will follow on the father's footsteps and bring a lot of pride and joy to you and Aunt Stienie. Josephine and her elder sister, Susan, are included in this message of sympathy. Very sincerely,
[Signed NR Mandela]

Mrs Petronella Ferus, c/o Mrs Hadjie, 45 Le Seur Street, Worcester, 6850

To Ayesha Arnold[ii]

466/64: Nelson Mandela   15.11.81

Our dearest Ayesha,

---

i   Mourners at Hennie Ferus's funeral in Worcester wore ANC colours and khakis and raised the illegal ANC flag. It is widely perceived as being a 'political funeral' that motivated activists to become more defiant (Pippa Green, *Choice Not Fate: The Life and Times of Trevor Manuel* (Johannesburg: Penguin Books, 2008). p. 166.

ii Dr. Ayesha Arnold was a medical doctor in Cape Town whom Mandela's wife and children would stay with when they visited him in prison. She was a friend of Fatima Meer's (see the glossary).

You will certainly be able to smell the feeling of guilt & shame that has seized me since I received your invitation to attend your 50th natal Day, plus the flattering, if amusing, birthday card you sent me.

Although I received your letter long after 6/8 & should have brushed aside everything & written this letter on the spot, so that you could get my best wishes before the heady effects of champagne & halal had cleared away. Perhaps you are aware that over the last 3 or 4 months I endured an ever-growing pressure which made it difficult for me to write even to you & Zami[i] – two women whose love & affection has been such a source of strength to me, & who I would never like to disappoint.

The moment the pressure eased I reached out for pen & paper & here is your letter, Ayeshaben. It brings to you my warmest love & congratulations on hitting the half-century. My sincere wish is that you should live to be a centurion spanning 2 centuries, & continue to be a source of strength & hope to Ameen,[ii] Shukri & Mymoena[iii] & to your multitude of friends. I have included the 6/8 in the growing list of family birthdays & will not forget it. By the way, the date is so remarkably close to the 5/8 – the day on which I was arrested – that I regard the two dates as one & the same. Once again my warmest congratulations, Ben.[iv]

The birthday card was so smart that I even thought that it was designed & its message drawn up by Muhammad Ali, so full of punch & wit it was. The affectionate sentiments you added made me feel as strong as a tank & full of expectation as a bridegroom on the eve of [his] wedding day. You certainly will be able to congratulate me personally one day & I look forward to it very eagerly.

Zami had earlier told me about the beautiful present from you. Despite the fact that she described it rather elaborately, I had no idea of just how beautiful it actually was until I tried it on. It fitted well & I immediately felt twice as tall & half my age. I hug you. Zami also told me that Ameen had given up General Practice & gone back to hospital for paediatrics. Although his patients will certainly miss him, & despite the disparity in salaries, I think his decision has much to commend itself. With his background, training & experience he should be an

i   One of Winnie Mandela's names.
ii   Ameen Arnold, her husband, was also a medical doctor.
iii   The Arnolds' children.
iv   'Ben' means sister in Gujarati.

exceptionally valuable medical guru. The treatment of children's diseases is an essential part of the medical profession. One eventually learns to endure disease, pain & suffering on the part of adults, but it is, to say the least, very disturbing to see an innocent child in any form of physical or mental disability or distress. Although I am not conversant with the complex problems in this field, I assume that as a hospital doctor &, apart from his actual studies in paediatrics, he will relatively speaking, have more time for theory than was the case as a busy doctor in General Practice.

The other dy I was paging through the family album & particularly looked at the photo where you appear with Ameen & the chdn. He looks sharp & professional. Written across his face is the expression of a man who has been steeled by the tough sport of karate & who knows how to enjoy success in life without ostentation. I wish him well in his new venture & his decision should bring a lot of joy to both the patients & staff of the Red Cross Hospital.[i] There he will probably work together with Mrs Monica Kobas, an old friend from Fort Hare.[ii] If so, please ask him to give her & family our fondest regards.

Thinking about you hitting a century, I was listening to a radio tape on longevity a few dys ago, particularly on people who had reached 100 yrs of age. The speaker dealt with the position in England & stressed that the number of these people had increased substantially, especially after the introduction of the National Health Scheme in that country. I was somewhat surprised, even though pleasantly, to hear from the speaker that senility is a problem that can be medically controlled even at such an advanced age in a man's life. I had all along equated it with old age & assumed that one's mental faculties must inevitably deteriorate as he ages. But apparently it is not necessarily so.

But to come back to Mother Earth, it pleases me to hear that Mymoena & Shukri are making good progress at school. From the photo, they seem to be growing very fast & the difference between their pictures taken at Burnwood Rd & the one you sent me is quite remarkable. I wish I could see them face to face & chat to them at their present age. It would be such a pleasure to do so & this is an aspect I miss very badly. Kindly give them my love.

I thought I had written sometime this yr to assure you that, con-

---

i   Red Cross Children's Hospital in Cape Town.
ii   University College of Fort Hare, which Mandela attended in 1939 until 1940 when he was expelled for embarking on protest action.

trary to press reports during the April General Election to the effect that I was ill, in fact I felt quite well. But on checking through my letter-book, I could find no evidence that I had actually written to you.

Even as I read the press statements that sparked off the speculation & disturbed Zami & the children, I was almost overwhelmed by a feeling of well-being, nevertheless, Dr Coetzee, the District Surgeon, gave me what I, as a layman, considered a thorough examination. Shortly thereafter, Dr Le Roux, who also lectures to medical students at Tygerberg,[i] gave me an even more exhaustive check-up. Both of them cleared me. On [?]/8, the day after I received your invitation & birthday card, their finding was confirmed by Dr Jorg Nagel of the I.R.C.[ii] I believe that such illness can be treacherous & eat you away without betraying its presence to both victim & quack. Subject to that I feel quite well & in high spirits.

Many thanks for the beautiful photos you sent me; they were all well-taken & I loved each & every one of them. But why should a generous person be so stingy this time? I thought you would send me quite a batch. Except for the one in which you appear with Ameen & the chdn, they have all disappeared. I couldn't even save the one in which you appeared with Zami.

Finally, Ayeshaben, I like you to know that it is always a pleasure to think of you, Ameen & the chdn. It gives me even more pleasure & joy to write to you. Tons & tons of love & a million kisses.

Very sincerely, Nelson

Dr Ayesha Ahmed, Cor. 39th Avenue & Connaught Rd, Elsies River, 7460

---

i   Tygerberg Hospital in Cape Town.
ii   Possibly this stands for 'International Red Cross'.

POLLSMOOR
MAXIMUM SECURITY
PRISON

||||||||||||

MARCH 1982–AUGUST 1988

Nelson Mandela, Walter Sisulu, Raymond Mhlaba, and Andrew Mlangeni[i] were transferred on 31 March 1982 from Robben Island to Pollsmoor Maximum Security Prison on the mainland, where they were held in a large communal cell. They were joined in Pollsmoor Prison by Ahmed Kathrada on 21 October 1982. Mandela said he was never told why they were all transferred. He asked the commanding officer who replied that he could not say.

'I was disturbed and unsettled. What did it mean? Where were we going? In prison, one can only question and resist an order to a certain point, then one must succumb. We had no warning, no preparation. I had been on the island for over eighteen years, and to leave so abruptly?

'We were each given several large cardboard boxes in which to pack our things. Everything that I had accumulated in nearly two decades could fit into these few boxes. We packed in little more than half an hour.'[46]

A large face-brick prison complex nestling at the foot of the mountains outside Cape Town, with beds and better food, Pollsmoor was in a way a tougher existence for the men. Gone was the open space they had walked in from the cell block to the lime quarry; or down to the seashore to harvest seaweed. Separated from the rest of the prison population, they were held in a rooftop cell and could only see the sky from their yard.

---

i   For notes on these individuals, see the glossary.

To Helen Joseph,[i] a friend

[Prison censor stamp dated 83.04.13]

D220/82: N. MANDELA   28.3.83

Our dear Helen,

It may well be that my experience is no more than a peculiar feeling
confined to just one individual living under extraordinary conditions
far away from home & friends. But I find that as I grow older the
keener do I become to see the places where I spent my childhood,
particularly the thatched-roof school where I learned my ABC, the
plains & hills where I shepherded livestock & hunted all kinds of small
game, the muddy pools & shallow streams where I used to swim with
other boys, unmindful of cholera bacteria & the bilharzia worms & you
name it. We occasionally invaded the mealie[ii] fields where we pinched
mealies for roasting in secluded valleys. In my current situation, & as
fully occupied as I always am, it is never easy to suppress this longing
for those romantic days.

It is precisely in this regard that I often think of you, of just how you
feel after an absence of so many yrs from your birthplace.[iii] Although
you are now permanently rooted to Fanny Ave, & although I am confident that you would never like to exchange that place with any other
in the world, I believe at the same time that you probably would have
liked to land, whenever necessary, at Heathrow, each time to be welcomed by admiring crowds – by friends of your childhood days, varsity
class & former college mates, miners straight from the pits, comrades
who have been with you through storms & calamity, those with whom
you have tasted the sweetness of victory & accomplishment,[iv] & by
many who have never even had the pleasure of seeing you, all of which
would have cut down your age by half, leaving you feeling twice as tall
& with an irrepressible urge to attempt the gumboot dance right there
before the crowds.

---

i   Helen Joseph (1905–92), teacher, social worker, and anti-apartheid and women's rights activist – see the
      glossary.
ii   Corn.
iii   Helen Joseph was born in Sussex, England in 1905 and in 1927 left for India and then South Africa in
      1931.
iv   He is probably referring to their comrades living in exile in England.

I can picture you moving through the corridors of London University,[i] strolling along the banks of the Thames, visiting old friends & even the golf course where you used to hit the air with your club, gossiping with the Adelaides,[ii] Hilda[iii] & others, all of which would leave you feeling refreshed & bright. But with your tight programme you probably have no time even for such fond memories.

While on this topic, I would like to remind you that, although now & again you have volunteered something current about yourself, hardly anything is ever said about the past. Searching questions are often asked on this aspect by those who had every reason to know. But, as you would expect, memories are fading with time & details which were once so clear in one's mind are being lost. I do so look forward to this sketch in 2 or 3 pages. Clearly related to this aspect is the hope that 35 F. Av[iv] will ever remain open to the numerous friends & descendants who have been in & out of it over the yrs. May well be that there are many who sincerely hope that one day the house will be raised to the status of a monument. On several occasions it has been a significant first.

About your life expectation, I suspect that you are not praying hard enough & the gods are not prepared to grant your wish. As I have pointed out several times before, you once told me that you do not want to live as long as Dr Moroka.[v] It seems you will. It is now almost 5 yrs since you volunteered that horrible wish. But you seem to be growing stronger and [more] mobile with yrs. Despite fractures your legs are not giving in,[vi] the growing strains do not appear to weigh heavily on your heart & the mind appears to be as keen as ever. May your health continue to be good & your heart stouter. It is in this spirit that your friends will think of you as you celebrate your birthday in a few days' time. From all I hear you are strong enough to blow out 77 candles simultaneously on the birthday cake. I only wish I could be there as you do so, to shake your hand directly & to wish you a Happy Birthday & the best of luck. I will also think of you at Easter in the knowledge

---

i   She graduated with a degree in English from London University in 1927.
ii   Friends and comrades Adelaide Tambo and Adelaide Joseph, both in exile in London.
iii   Hilda Bernstein (née Watts) (1915–2006), author, artist, and anti-apartheid and women's rights activist. She was a founding member of the South African Peace Council and of the Federation of South African Women. After her husband, Lionel (Rusty), was acquitted in the Rivonia Trial, they crossed into neighbouring Botswana on foot. They were living in exile in London.
iv   Her house, 35 Fanny Avenue, Norwood.
v   James Moroka (1892–1985), medical doctor, politician and anti-apartheid activist, president of the African National Congress, 1949–52, was then aged 92.
vi   In 1981 she slipped and broke her leg.

that your larder will be full of delicious hot buns as usual. Early that morning I will stand outside the cell, face north & try & catch the smell of those lovely buns. Meanwhile I send you my love & good wishes.

Very sincerely,
Nelson.

P.S. You probably have heard that I had an op early in Feb. one at the back of the head and the other involved the removal of the big toe nail for a medical test. The head op was as minor as removing a pimple but the lifting of the nail necessitated a general anesthetic. The result of the test was negative & I feel tremendous. Only I miss you all & wish I could see you. Please tell Zindzi[i] that I love & miss her always & that I look forward to seeing her on the 1st & 2nd of May. Again, Happy Birthday, dear Helen!

Nelson.

═══════════

To Adele de Waal, a friend of his wife, Winnie Mandela

D220/82: NELSON MANDELA

29.8.83

Dear Adele,

[Written in Afrikaans] My knowledge of Afrikaans is very bad and my vocabulary leaves a lot to be desired. At my age I am struggling to learn grammar and to improve my syntax. It would certainly be disastrous if I wrote this letter in Afrikaans. I sincerely hope you will understand if I change to English.

[Written in English] Zami[ii] has told me several times of the interest you and Piet[iii] have shown in her problems over the past 6 years.

---

i   Zindziswa (Zindzi) Mandela (1960–), Mandela's second-born daughter to his second wife, Winnie – see the glossary.
ii   One of Winnie Mandela's names.
iii   Petrus Johannes de Waal (1932–2001), a lawyer, had a legal practice in Brandfort where he met Winnie

Although I have on each occasion requested her to convey my appreciation to you, the beautiful and valuable present of books you sent me has given me the opportunity of writing to thank you directly for your efforts.

It was certainly not so easy for her at middle-age to leave her home and to start life in a new and strange environment and where she has no means of earning a livelihood. In this regard, the response of friends has, on the whole, been magnificent, and it made it possible for her to generate the inner strength to endure what she cannot avoid. We were particularly fortunate to be able to count on the friendship of a family that is right on the spot and to whom she can turn when faced with immediate problems. [Written in Afrikaans] You and Piet have contributed significantly to her relative safety and happiness. [Written in English] I sincerely hope that one day I will be able to join you in your village and shake your hands very warmly as we chat along.

[Written in Afrikaans] Schalk Pienaar's book *Witness to Great Times* is one of the books on the shelf. On page 13 there is a reference to a farmer,[i] Pieter de Waal, who participated in the 1938 oxwagon trek to Monument Hill. According to the story he succeeded to calm a group of restive trekkers in Oggies in the Free State. Perhaps he was Piet's father or grandfather.

[Written in English] Whenever Piet's name is mentioned, especially when I receive a letter from him, I instinctively think of a friend, Mr Combrink, from that world who probably is now running a flourishing legal firm. I last saw him about 30 years ago when he used to work in a dairy during the night and as an articled clerk during the day. Perhaps Piet will be able to give him my regards if and when he meets him.

Meantime, I send you, Piet and the children my fondest regards, and hope that your daughter is doing well in England.

Sincerely,
Nelson.

Mrs Adele de Waal, Duke Street, P.O. Brandfort, 9400.

Mandela who had been banished to the town. They became friends. He was a friend of justice minister Kobie Coetsee. The couple's friendship with Winnie Mandela is said to have made an impact on Coetsee who later visited Mandela in hospital in late 1985. Mandela then contacted him about talks with the government which began the following year.

i   The Afrikaans word Mandela used is *uitsaaiman*, which can mean farmer or broadcaster.

To Ismail Meer,[i] friend and comrade

D220/82: NELSON MANDELA   29.1.85

Dear Ismail,

I have missed you so much these 22 yrs that there are occasions when I even entertain the wild hope that one good morning I will be told that you are waiting for me in the consultation room downstairs.

As I watch the world ageing, scenes from our younger days in Kholvad House[ii] & Umngeni Rd[iii] come back so vividly as if they occurred only the other day – plodding endlessly on our text books, travelling to & from Milner Park,[iv] indulging in a bit of agitation, now on opposite sides & now together, some fruitless polemic with Boola[v] & Essack,[vi] & kept going throughout those lean yrs by a litany of dreams & expectations, some of which have been realised, while the fulfilment of others still eludes us to this day.

Nevertheless, few people will deny that the harvest has merely been delayed but far from destroyed. It is out there on rich & well-watered fields, even though the actual task of gathering it has proved far more testing than we once thought. For the moment, however, all that I want to tell you is that I miss you & that thinking of you affords me a lot of pleasure, & makes life rich & pleasant even under these grim conditions.

But it is about that tragic 31 October[vii] that I want to talk to you. You will, of course, appreciate that my present position does not allow me to express my feelings & thoughts fully & freely as I would have

---

i   Ismail Meer (1918–2000), a lawyer and anti-apartheid activist – see the glossary.
ii Kholvad House, an apartment block in downtown Johannesburg where Ismail Meer had an apartment. Mandela writes in *Long Walk to Freedom*, 'At Wits I met and became friends with Ismail Meer, J.N. Singh, Ahmed Bhoola, and Ramlal Bhoolia. The centre of this tight-knit community was Ismail's apartment, Flat 13, Kholvad House, four rooms in a residential building in the centre of the city. There we studied, talked and even danced until the early hours of the morning, and it became a kind of headquarters for young freedom fighters. I sometimes slept there when it was too late to catch the last train back to Orlando.' (NM, *Long Walk to Freedom*, p. 105.)
iii Where Ismail and Fatima Meer lived in the 1950s.
iv Location of the University of the Witwatersrand where Mandela and Ismail Meer met.
v   Ahmed Bhoola, a Durban lawyer who wrote for the *Leader* newspaper.
vi Abdul Karrim Essack, African People's Democratic Union of Southern Africa and Natal Unity Movement leader who went into exile in the 1950s and died in Tanzania in 1997.
vii Indian prime minister Indira Gandhi (1917–84) was assassinated on 31 October 1984.

liked. It is sufficient to say that when reports reach us that Indiraben[i] had passed away, I had already exhausted my 1984 quota of outgoing letters. This is the only reason why it took me so long to respond.

Even though Zami[ii] may have already conveyed our condolences (please check) I would like Rajiv[iii] to know that he & family are in our thoughts in their bereavement, that on occasions of this nature it is appropriate to recall the immortal words which have been said over & over again: When you are alone, you are not alone, there is always a haven of friends nearby. For Rajiv now to feel all alone is but natural. But in actual fact he is not alone. We are his friends, we are close to him & we fully [share] the deep sorrow that has hit the family.

Indira was a brick of pure gold & her death is a painful blow which [we] find difficult to endure. She lived up to expectations & measured remarkably well to the countless challenges which confronted her during the last 18 yrs.

[There] must be few world leaders who are so revered but who are lovingly [referred] to by their first name by thousands of South Africans as Indira. [People] from different walks of life seemed to have accepted her as one of [them] &, to them, she could have come from Cato Manor,[iv] Soweto,[v] or District [Six].[vi] That explains why her death has been so shattering.

[I] had hoped that one day Zami and I would travel all the way to India to meet Indira in person. That hope became a resolution especially after 1979. Although the yrs keep on rolling away & old age is beginning to threaten, hope [never] fades & that journey remains one of my fondest dreams.

[We] wish Rajiv well in his new office[vii] & we sincerely hope that his youth & good health, his training & the support of friends from far & wide will enable him to bear the heavy work load with the same strength & assurance as was displayed by his famous mother over the past 18yrs. Again, our sincerest sympathies to Rajiv, Sonia[viii] & Maneka.[ix]

I must repeat that I miss you badly & I hope you are keeping well. I do look forward to seeing you some day. Until then our love & fondest

i   Indira Gandhi.
ii   His wife, Winnie Mandela.
iii   Rajiv Gandhi (1944–91), one of Indira Gandhi's sons.
iv   A working-class area outside of Durban, Natal (now KwaZulu-Natal).
v   Township in Johannesburg.
vi   Working-class area in Johannesburg.
vii   He succeeded his mother as prime minister of India.
viii   Rajiv Gandhi's wife Sonia.
ix   The widow of Sanjay Gandhi, Rajiv's brother who died in a plane crash in 1980.

regards to you, Fatima,[i] the children & everybody. Please do tell me about Nokhukhanya[ii] & her children.

Very Sincerely,
Nelson

Mr Ismail Meer, 148 Burnwood Rd, Sydenham, 4091

To Adelaide Joseph,[iii] a friend

[A note at the top reads: Please pass the enclosed letter to Thembi's mum][iv]

25.2.85

D220/82: NELSON MANDELA

Our dear Adie,

The love, affection and support which you and Paul have given me and Zami[v] throughout these years have been a source of so much strength and hope and, in addition, they have helped us to face countless difficulties in the knowledge that we are not alone. Zami never stops talking about you and the many good things you do for her.

We have always valued friendship and have tried to the best of our ability to strengthen and deepen such relationships. But to appreciate just how very precious friendship can be you must be in prison and cut off from your beloved wife and children, unable to rejoice with them on important family days, to give them presents on such occasions, to help your wife when ugly problems outside her experience occur, when you cannot guide the children as they grow up, or help them to take advantage of whatever opportunities are available in our

---

i   Fatima Meer, Ismail Meer's wife.
ii   Nokhukhanya Luthuli, widow of Chief Albert Luthuli.
iii   Adelaide Joseph (1932–) and Paul Joseph (1930–), were South African political activists who went into exile in London in 1965. When Mandela was arrested in 1962 Adelaide brought him food in prison.
iv   Mandela is referring to Adelaide Tambo, who was also in exile in England.
v   Another name for Winnie Mandela.

closed society. On such occasions, life becomes torture in the proper sense of the term. Against this background, I must leave it to you to guess just how I feel whenever Zami mentions you and Paul. In a letter of this kind I cannot expand on this aspect; it is sufficient for me merely to say that you are among those we will never forget.

The close contact between you and Zami for so long tended to make me forget that the Joseph family is big. Of course, I thought and even heard now and again about your late mother-in-law, Mr and Mrs Pillay in Verulam, Violet and the charming young lady whose name I am ashamed to have forgotten, Dasu and Sally.[i] But I had rarely ever thought about Peter[ii] until one day Zindzi told me "Uncle Peter is for all practical purposes our father and one of my best friends." And then she excitedly recounted how he regularly drives to Orlando with the panel van loaded with this and that. I know that this is exactly what you would have done if you were still in the country. Peter has stepped into your shoes and is apparently doing very well.

I got the beautiful picture of the children and want to thank you for sending it. Zoya[iii] is really striking with a face which bristles with charm and awareness. Alan[iv] appears, quite apart from his rising fame as a musician, to be an impressive and cheerful young man; a perfect match for Zoya. Please give them my congratulations and best wishes.

I must add that it is a source of joy to know that Zeni and Zoya are still so very close to each other, and I was really happy to note that Zeni and Muzi were able to attend the wedding. I was equally pleased to hear that Nomadabi[v] is doing the 3rd year at the LSE [London School of Economics], and to her as well I send my best wishes. History and French are both important subjects and I hope she is enjoying them. There are more French-speaking African states than the English-speaking countries. A good command of the language will certainly be of great benefit to her.

Our love also goes out to Nadia and I hope she will do as well as her sisters. I hope she enjoyed her NY visit. In this regard, I wish to compliment you and Paul for managing, in spite of the numerous difficulties of adjusting to a new environment, to give the children a sound education.

---

i   Paul and Adelaide Joseph's daughter.
ii   Paul Joseph's brother, Peter.
iii   Paul and Adelaide Joseph's daughter.
iv   Alan Gruner, Zoya's husband at the time.
v   Tanya Joseph, Paul and Adelaide Joseph's daughter, who was studying at the London School of Economics. Madiba sent her the name Nomadabi from prison.

Please pass the enclosed letter to Zindzi's mum.
N.   25. 2. 85

D220/82: NELSON MANDELA

Dear dear Adie,

The love, affection and support which you and Paul have given me and Zami throughout these years have been a source of so much strength and hope and, in addition, they have helped us to face countless difficulties in the knowledge that we are not alone. Zami never stops talking about you and the many good things you do for her.

We have always valued friendship and have tried to the best of our ability to strengthen and deepen such relationships. But to appreciate just how very precious friendship can be you must be in prison and cut off from your beloved wife and children, unable to rejoice with them on important family days, to give them presents on such days occasions, to help your wife when ugly problems outside her experience occur, when you cannot guide the children as they grow up, or help them to take advantage of whatever opportunities are available in our closed society. On such occasions, life becomes torture in the proper sense of the term. Against this background, I must leave it to you to guess just how I feel whenever Zami mentions you and Paul. In a letter of this kind I cannot expand on this aspect. It is sufficient for me merely to say that you are among those we will never forget.

The close contact between you and Zami for so long tended to make me forget that the Joseph family is big. Of course, I thought and even heard now and again about your late mother-in-law, Mr and Mrs Pillay in Verulam, Violet and the charming young lady whose name I am ashamed to have forgotten, Dasu and Sally. But I had rarely ever thought about Peter until one day Zindzi told me "Uncle Peter is for all practical purposes our father and one of my best friends." And then she excitedly recounted how he regularly drives to Orlando with the panel van loaded with this and that. I know that this is exactly what you would have done if you were still in the country. Peter has stepped into your shoes and is apparently doing very well.

I got the beautiful picture of the children and I want to thank you for sending it. Zoya is really striking with a face which bristles with charm and awareness. Alan appears, quite apart from his rising fame as musician, to be an impressive and cheerful young man, a perfect match for Zoya. Please give them my congratulations and best wishes.

A letter to Adelaide Joseph, 25 February 1985, see pages 257–61.

I would love to see all the girls and I suggest that one should apply. But I must warn that it will not be so easy to get a permit. Local friends, like Fatima Meer and Amina Cachalia, have for quite some time been battling without success for a visiting permit. I last saw Fatima in 1973 but they will not allow her to return. Incidentally, the other day I received a 9 page letter from her which made me really homesick and I have not fully recovered, even now. She visited my home at Umtata and actually saw the hut where I used to sleep and the primary school where I was taught, together with a mass of pleasant and unpleasant information dug up from the family. She has a lot of energy and drive.

Your mother-in-law lived to a ripe age and she must have been in her 80s or 90s when she passed away. She was always cheerful, with a wonderful sense of humour. In normal times Zami and I would certainly have been at the graveside to pay our last respects to her. Our deepest sympathies to you, Paul and the rest of the family.

The death of Mota[i] was very shattering and, again, we were very sorry that we neither could be at the graveside nor be able to send a timely message of condolence on the death of such an esteemed comrade. About three years before his death I sent him a long letter in which I wished him well on his birthday. I only hope he received it. We loved and respected him years before the 1948 Pact[ii] was signed. By then already his influence had gone far beyond the ranks of a single ethnic group. He possessed excellent gifts and made enormous sacrifices which became more evident because of his courtesy and humility, qualities which inspired respect even from his enemies. I sincerely hope that the pains he endured on his death bed were made tolerable by the knowledge that the vast majority of our people hailed him as one of those who blazed the trail and made us heirs to a rich heritage. I asked a friend to pass our condolences to Winnie,[iii] Shireen and Roshan[iv] to whom I sent my fondest regards.

Paul wants to know about Sanna Teyise, the lady who used to run

---

i   Dr. Yusuf Dadoo (1909–93), medical doctor, anti-apartheid activist, and orator. President of the South African Indian Congress, deputy to Oliver Tambo on the Revolutionary Council of MK, and chairman of the South African Communist Party – see the glossary.

ii   Known as the 'Doctor's Pact', it was signed on 9 March 1947 (it is unclear why Mandela wrote 1948) as an agreement of cooperation by the ANC's Dr. Alfred Bitini Xuma with Dr. Yusuf Dadoo of the Transvaal Indian Congress and Dr. Monty Naicker of the Natal Indian Congress. Dr. Alfred Bitini Xuma (1893–1962) was the first black South African to become a medical doctor and president-general of the ANC (1940–49). For Dr. Yusuf Dadoo and Dr. Monty Naicker – see the glossary

iii   Dr. Yusuf Dadoo's wife.

iv   Yusuf and Winnie Dadoo's daughters.

the Blue Lagoon in Von Weillich St. She died about 7 years ago. But it is a strange coincidence that your letter should come when I am trying to trace members of her family. I used to handle her affairs and she must have left behind quite an estate. She was unmarried but had a number of sisters and cousins, and I am keen to know whether they got their respective bequests.

I am sorry to hear that Mary[i] had had an op recently. She means a lot to many of us and I will appreciate it if you will be kind enough to give me more details. What is she doing in the Caribbean? Material for yet another book?

It was fortunate that Paul's hernia was discovered in time and attended to. With all the sophisticated developments in medical science today, such problems can easily be controlled and even cured.

You say that you are plagued by illness. Again, you have given me no details and I hope that it is nothing very serious. One thing I know about you is your strength of character and optimism. I believe that you are one of those who can frighten away even death. Your letter suggests that you have lost none of these over the years. It expresses the feelings and thoughts of a happy woman with a healthy mind. No wonder; you have Paul and three beautiful and enterprising girls around you. That alone means health and nothing will happen to you.

As far as books are concerned, I need relaxation in the form of novels and autobiographies, but no useful purpose will be served by sending them here or the records you mentioned. They will not be allowed. In any case, your love is all that I need and I have all of it. Why should I care about fiction? My fondest regards to Rusty & Hilda,[ii] Vela,[iii] Mac,[iv] Indres[v] and their wives, Brian and Sonia,[vi] MD,[vii] Mary and Ben, Anne-marie and Harold,[viii] Paul and the children and above all, to you, Adie.

Sincerely,
Nelson

---

i   Mary Benson (1919–2000), friend, author, journalist, and anti-apartheid activist – see the glossary.
ii   Rusty & Hilda Bernstein, friends and comrades in exile in London. For Rusty Bernstein, see the glossary.
iii   Vela Pillay.
iv   Mac Maharaj (1935–) fellow Robben Island prisoner and former comrade – see the glossary.
v   Indres Naidoo (1936–2016) fellow Robben Island prisoner – see the glossary.
vi   Brian and Sonia Bunting.
vii   M. D. Naidoo, a member of the South African Communist Party and the South African Indian Congress who was in B Section with Mandela on Robben Island – see the glossary.
viii Annemarie and Harold Wolpe. Harold Wolpe had been arrested at Liliesleaf Farm and named as a co-conspirator in the Rivonia Trial. They went into exile in London after Harold Wolpe escaped from police detention with Mosie Moolla, Arthur Goldreich and Abdullay Jassat in 1963.

To P. W. Botha, president of South Africa

13 February 1985

The Commissioner of Prisons,
Pretoria.

The subjoined letter is for the attention of the State President,
Mr P. W. Botha :

"The State President,
Cape Town

Sir,

Copies of the *Hansard* parliamentary record to 25 January to 1 February were delivered to us on 8 February.

We note that during the debate in the House of Assembly you indicated that you were prepared to release prisoners in our particular category provided that we unconditionally renounce violence as a means of furthering our political objectives.

We have given earnest consideration to your offer but we regret to inform you that it is not acceptable in its present form. We hesitate to associate you with a move which, on a proper analysis, appears to be no more than a shrewd and calculated attempt to mislead the world into the belief that you have magnanimously offered us release from prison which we ourselves have rejected. Coming in the face of such unprecedented and widespread demand for our release, your remarks can only be seen as the height of cynical politicking.

We refuse to be party to anything which is really intended to create division, confusion and uncertainty within the African National Congress at a time when the unity of the organisation has become a matter of crucial importance to the whole country. The refusal by the Department of Prisons to allow us to consult fellow prisoners in other prisons has confirmed our view.

Just as some of us refused the humiliating condition that we should be released to the Transkei,[i] we also reject your offer on the same

---

i   A homeland which was absorbed back into the Eastern Cape province in 1994.

GEHEIM
SECRET   13 February 1985

The Commissioner of Prisons
PRETORIA

THE SUBJOINED LETTER IS FOR THE ATTENTION OF THE STATE PRESIDENT,
MR P W BOTHA :

"The State President,
CAPE TOWN

Sir,

Copies of the Hansard parliamentary record of

25 January to 1 February 1985 were delivered to us on

8 February.

We note that during the debate in the House of Assembly you

indicated that you were prepared to release prisoners in our

particular category provided that we unconditionally renounce

violence as a means of furthering our political objectives.

We have given earnest consideration to your offer but we

regret to inform you that it is not acceptable in its present

form. We hesitate to associate you with a move which, on a

proper analysis, appears to be no more than a shrewd and

calculated attempt to mislead the world into the belief

that you have magnanimously offered us release from prison

which we ourselves have rejected. Coming in the face of such

unprecedented and widespread demand for our release, your

remarks can only be seen as the height of cynical politicking.

We refuse to be party to anything which is really intended to

create division, confusion and uncertainty within the

Page from a letter to the commissioner of prisons, 13 February 1985, see opposite.

ground. No self-respecting human being will demean and humiliate himself by making a commitment of the nature you demand. You ought not to perpetuate our imprisonment by the simple expedient of setting conditions which, to your own knowledge, we will never under any circumstances accept.

Our political beliefs are largely influenced by the Freedom Charter,[i] a programme of principles whose basic premise is the equality of all human beings. It is not only the clearest repudiation of all forms of racial discrimination, but also the country's most advanced statement of political principles. It calls for universal franchise in a united South Africa and for the equitable distribution of the wealth of the country.

The intensification of apartheid, the banning of political organisations and the closing of all channels of peaceful protest conflicted sharply with these principles and forced the ANC to turn to violence. Consequently, until apartheid is completely uprooted, our people will continue to kill one another and South Africa will be subjected to all the pressures of an escalating civil war.

Yet the ANC has for almost 50 years since its establishment faithfully followed peaceful and non-violent forms of struggle. During the period 1952 to 1961 alone[ii] it appealed, in vain, to no less than three South African premiers to call a round-table conference of all population groups where the country's problems could be thrashed out, and it only resorted to violence when all other options had been blocked.

The peaceful and non-violent nature of our struggle never made any impression to your government. Innocent and defenceless people were pitilessly massacred in the course of peaceful demonstrations. You will remember the shootings in Johannesburg on 1 May 1950[iii] and in Sharpeville in 1960.[iv] On both occasions, as in every other instance of police brutality, the victims had invariably been unarmed and defenceless men, women and even children. At that time the ANC

---

i   A statement of the principles of the Congress Alliance (see the glossary), adopted at the Congress of the People in Kliptown, Soweto, on 26 June 1955. The Congress Alliance rallied thousands of volunteers across South Africa to record the demands of the people. The Freedom Charter espoused equal rights for all South Africans regardless of race, along with land reform, improved working and living conditions, the fair distribution of wealth, compulsory education, and fairer laws. It was a powerful tool used in the fight against apartheid.

ii   Mandela wrote twice to Prime Minister H. F. Verwoerd, calling on him to set up a national convention on a non-racial and democratic constitution for South Africa. His letters were ignored.

iii   On 1 May 1950, eighteen people were shot dead by police during a strike over the apartheid regime's plans to ban the Communist Party.

iv   On 21 March 1961 in Sharpeville, police shot and killed sixty-nine unarmed people protesting against having to carry identity documents which controlled where they could live and work.

had not even mooted the idea of resorting to armed struggle. You were the country's Defence Minister when no less than 600 people, mostly children, were shot down in Soweto in 1976. You were the country's premier when the police beat up people, again in the course of orderly demonstrations against the 1984 coloured and Indian elections,[i] and 7000 heavily armed troopers invaded the Vaal Triangle to put down an essentially peaceful protest by the residents.[ii]

Apartheid, which is condemned not only by blacks but also by a substantial section of the whites, is the greatest single source of violence against our people. As leader of the National Party, which seeks to uphold apartheid through force and violence, we expect you to be the first to renounce violence.

But it would seem that you have no intention whatsoever of using democratic and peaceful forms of dealing with black grievances, that the real purpose of attaching conditions to your offer is to ensure that the NP should enjoy the monopoly of committing violence against defenceless people. The founding of Umkhonto weSizwe was designed to end that monopoly and forcefully bring home to the rulers that the oppressed people were prepared to stand up and defend themselves and to fight back if necessary, with force.

We note that on page 312 of *Hansard* you say that you are personally prepared to go a long way to relax the tensions in inter-group relations in this country but that you are not prepared to lead the whites to abdication. By making this statement you have again categorically reaffirmed that you remain obsessed with the preservation of domination by the white minority. You should not be surprised, therefore, if, in spite of the supposed good intentions of the government, the vast masses of the oppressed people continue to regard you as a mere broker of the interests of the white tribe, and consequently unfit to handle national affairs.

Again on pages 318–319 you state that you cannot talk with people who do not want to cooperate, that you hold talks with every possible leader who is prepared to renounce violence.

---

i In 1984 Prime Minister P. W. Botha established a tricameral parliament with separate chambers for Indians, coloureds, and whites. The United Democratic Front, which was formed in 1983, mounted nationwide protests against this parliament and its elections. All the protests were met with a violent response by police.

ii In September 1984 the townships of Boipatong, Bophelong, Evaton, Sebokeng, and Sharpeville in the area known as the Vaal Triangle exploded in protests against rent increases proposed by the black-run town councils. Three township councillors, including the deputy mayor of the Vaal Triangle, Kuzwayo Jacob Dlamini, were killed in mob violence on this day. Five men and one woman who became internationally known as the 'Sharpeville Six' were tried, convicted, and sentenced to hang for the killings.

Coming from the leader of the NP this statement is a shocking revelation as it shows more than anything else, that there is not a single figure in that party today who is advanced enough to understand the basic problems of our country, who has profited from the bitter experiences of the 37 years of NP rule, and who is prepared to take a bold lead towards the building of a truly democratic South Africa.

It is clear from this statement that you would prefer to talk only to people who accept apartheid even though they are emphatically repudiated by the very community on whom you want to impose them, through violence, if necessary.

We would have thought that the ongoing and increasing resistance in black townships, despite the massive deployment of the Defence Force, would have brought home to you the utter futility of unacceptable apartheid structures, manned by servile and self-seeking individuals of dubious credentials. But your government seems bent on continuing to move along this costly path and, instead of heeding the voice of the true leaders of the communities, in many cases they have been flung into prison. If your government seriously wants to halt the escalating violence, the only method open is to declare your commitment to end the evil of apartheid, and show your willingness to negotiate with the true leaders at local and national levels.

At no time have the oppressed people, especially the youth, displayed such unity in action, such resistance to racial oppression and such prolonged demonstrations in the face of brutal military and police action. Students in secondary schools and the universities are clamouring for the end of apartheid now and for equal opportunities for all. Black and white churchmen and intellectuals, civic associations and workers' and women's organisations demand genuine political changes. Those who "co-operate" with you, who have served with you so loyally throughout these troubled years have not at all helped you to stem the rapidly rising tide. The coming confrontation will only be averted if the following steps are taken without delay.

1. The government must renounce violence first;
2. It must dismantle apartheid;
3. It must unban the ANC;
4. It must free all who have been imprisoned, banished or exiled for their opposition to apartheid;
5. It must guarantee free political activity.

On page 309 you refer to allegations which have regularly been made at the United Nations and throughout the world that Mr Mandela's health has deteriorated in prison and that he is detained under inhuman conditions.

There is no need for you to be sanctimonious in this regard. The United Nations is an important and responsible organ of world peace and is, in many respects, the hope of the international community. Its affairs are handled by the finest brains on earth, by men whose integrity is flawless. If they made such allegations, they do so in the honest belief that they were true.

If we continue to enjoy good health, and if our spirits remain high it has not necessarily been due to any special consideration or care taken by the Department of Prisons. Indeed it is common knowledge that in the course of our long imprisonment, especially during the first years, the prison authorities had implemented a deliberate policy of doing everything to break our morale. We were subjected to harsh, if not brutal, treatment and permanent physical and spiritual harm was caused to many prisoners.

Although conditions have since improved in relation to the Sixties and Seventies, life in prison is not so rosy as you may suppose and we still face serious problems in many respects. There is still racial discrimination in our treatment; we have not yet won the right to be treated as political prisoners. We are no longer visited by the Minister of Prisons, the Commissioner of Prisons and other officials from the headquarters, and by judges and magistrates. These conditions are cause for concern to the United Nations, Organisation of African Unity,[i] Anti-apartheid Movement[ii] and to our numerous friends.

Taking into account the actual practice of the Department of Prisons, we must reject the view that a life sentence means that one should

---

i   Formed in 1963 in Addis Ababa, Ethiopia, with thirty-two signatory governments and eventually including all of Africa's fifty-three states excluding Morocco, which withdrew in 1984. It aimed to eradicate all forms of colonialism and white minority rule on the African continent. It also aimed to coordinate and intensify the cooperation of African states to achieve a better life for the people of Africa and to defend the sovereignty, territorial integrity, and independence of African states. It was disbanded on 9 July 2002 by its last chairperson, South African President Thabo Mbeki, and replaced by the African Union.

ii   Originally called the Boycott Movement, the British Anti-Apartheid Movement (AAM) was established in London in 1959 and opposed South Africa's system of apartheid. It demanded international sanctions against apartheid South Africa and called for its total isolation. In 1988 the AAM organised a pop concert, known as the Free Nelson Mandela Concert, at Wembley Stadium, London, to celebrate Mandela's seventieth birthday. A second concert, Nelson Mandela: An International Tribute for a Free South Africa, took place there in 1990, two months after Mandela's release from prison, and was attended by him.

die in prison. By applying to security prisoners the principle that "life is life" you are using double standards, since common law prisoners with clean prison records serve about 15 years of a life sentence. We must also remind you that it was the NP whose very first act on coming to power was to release the traitor Robey Leibbrandt[i] (and others) after he had served only a couple of years of his life sentence. These were men who had betrayed their own country to Nazi Germany during the last World War in which South Africa was involved.

As far as we are concerned we have long ago completed our life sentences. We're now being actually kept in preventative detention without enjoying the rights attached to that category of prisoners. The outdated and universally rejected philosophy of retribution is being meted out to us, and every day we spend in prison is simply an act of revenge against us.

Despite your commitment to the maintenance of white supremacy, however, your attempt to create new apartheid structures, and your hostility to a non-racial system of government in this country, and despite our determination to resist this policy to the bitter end, the simple fact is that you are South Africa's head of government, you enjoy the support of the majority of the white population and you can help change the course of South African history. A beginning can be made if you accept and agree to implement the five-point programme on pages 4–5 of this document. If you accept the programme our people would readily cooperate with you to sort out whatever problems arise as far as the implementation thereof is concerned.

In this regard, we have taken note of the fact that you no longer insist on some of us being released to the Transkei. We have also noted the restrained tone which you adopted when you made the offer in Parliament. We hope you will show the same flexibility and examine these proposals objectively. That flexibility and objectivity may help to create a better climate for a fruitful national debate.

Yours faithfully,

NELSON MANDELA

---

i   Sidney Robey Leibbrandt (1913–66), the South African heavyweight boxing champion, was led by the German military intelligence under the pseudonym 'Robert Leibbrand'. He was a South African Boer of German and Irish descent.

WALTER SISULU

RAYMOND MHLABA

AHMED KATHRADA

ANDREW MLANGENI[i]

[Each one signed above their name]

◇◇◇◇◇◇◇◇◇◇◇◇◇

From time to time in the latter years of his imprisonment, Mandela received letters from people he had never met – ordinary members of the public who knew of him and wrote to show that he had support outside of his normal circle of friends and family. Mrs Ray Carter, a British-born nurse married to an Anglican bishop, John Carter, was one such supporter. This letter was provided by her family who said that she and Mandela had struck up a pen-pal relationship after she telephoned the head of Pollsmoor Prison saying she wanted to bring a birthday gift to Nelson Mandela. She promptly dropped off a paperback, called Daily Light, *containing Biblical texts, two readings a day. Some months later a registered letter arrived from Mandela.*

To Ray Carter, a supporter

4.3.85

D220/82: NELSON MANDELA

Our dear Ray,

The picture on the outside cover of *Daily Light* has upset me beyond words. Although I spent no less than two decades on the Rand[ii] before

---

i   Rivonia trialists imprisoned with Mandela. See the glossary for notes on the individuals other than Mandela. Each prisoner signed their name twice.

ii   An abbreviated name for the Witwatersrand, a 56-kilometre-long ridge in the Gauteng province of South Africa where Johannesburg is based.

I was arrested, I am still essentially a peasant in outlook. I am intrigued by the wilds, the bush, a blade of grass and by all the things which are associated with the veld.[i]

Every time I look at the book – and I try to do so every morning and evening – I invariably start from the cover, and the mind immediately lights up. Long-forgotten scenes come back as fresh as dew. The thick bush, the ten fat sheep on a green field remind me of my childhood days in the countryside when everything I saw looked golden, a real place of bliss, an extension of heaven itself. That romantic world is engraved permanently in the memory and never fades, even though I now know as a fact that it is gone never to return.

Fourteen years after I had settled in Johannesburg I went back home[ii] and reached my village in early evening. At sunrise I left the car behind and walked out into the veld in search of the world of my youth, but it was no more.

The bush, where I used to pick wild fruits, dig up edible roots and trap small game, was now an unimpressive grove of scattered and stunted shrubs. The river, in which I swam on hot days and caught fat eels, was choking in mud and sand. I could no longer see the blazing flowers that beautified the veld and sweetened the air.

Although the sweet rains had recently washed the area, and the rising sun was throwing its warmth over the entire veld, no honey bird or skylark greeted me. Overpopulation, overgrazing and soil erosion had done irreparable havoc, and everything seemed to be crumbling. Even the huge ironstones which had stood out defiantly for eternity appeared to be succumbing to the total desolation which enveloped the area. The cattle and sheep tended to be skinny and listless. Life itself seemed to be dying away slowly. This was the sad picture that confronted me on my return home almost 30 yrs ago. It contrasted very sharply with the place where I was born. I have never been home again, yet the romantic years of my youth remain printed clearly in the mind. The cover picture in *Daily Light* calls forth those wonderful times.

Where does this picture come from? It looks so familiar.

How long it has taken for a parcel or message from you to come through! It was some time in 1982, I think, that Zami (Winnie) asked

---

i   'Field' in Afrikaans.
ii   Mandela is referring to Qunu, Transkei, where he grew up.

whether I had received a postcard from you. My enquiries from the Commanding Officer drew a blank. You have to be a prisoner serving a life sentence to appreciate just how frustrating and painful it can be when the efforts of friends to reach and encourage you are blocked somewhere along the line.

But as I look back now, that frustration was not without value. You have turned it into triumph. Your determination to break through the barriers is a measure of the depth of your love and concern. The three-word inscription in the book makes it a precious possession indeed. I sincerely hope that Zami and I will prove to be worthy of that love and support. I look forward to seeing you and John[i] one day. Meantime, I send you my love and best wishes.

Sincerely,
Nelson

Mrs Ray Carter, 51 Dalene Rd, Bramley, 2192

To Lionel Ngakane,[ii] a friend and filmmaker

1.4.85

D220/82: NELSON MANDELA

Dear Lionel,

The world we knew so well seems to be crumbling down very fast, and the men and women who once moved scores of people are disappearing from the scene just as quickly. Lutuli,[iii] Dadoo,[iv] Matthews,[v] Kotane,[vi]

---

i   Her husband, the Anglican bishop John Carter.

ii   Lionel Ngakane (1928–2003), filmmaker, actor. He went into exile in the 1950s and returned to South Africa in 1994.

iii   Chief Albert Luthuli (1898–1967), president-general of the ANC, 1952–67 – see the glossary. Mandela spelt his name 'Lutuli'.

iv   Dr .Yusuf Dadoo (1909–83), medical doctor, anti-apartheid activist, and orator. President of the South African Indian Congress, deputy to Oliver Tambo on the Revolutionary Council of MK, and chairman of the South African Communist Party – see the glossary.

v   Professor Z. K. Matthews (1901–68), academic, politician, anti-apartheid activist, and ANC member – see the glossary.

vi   Moses Kotane (1905–78), ANC member and secretary-general of the South African Communist Party.

Harmel,[i] Gomas, the Naickers,[ii] Marks,[iii] Molema,[iv] Letele,[v] Ruth First,[vi] Njongwe,[vii] Calata,[viii] Ngoyi,[ix] Peake,[x] Hodgson,[xi] Nokwe[xii] and many others now sleep in eternal peace; and all this happens in less than two decades.

We will never see them again, exchange views with them when problems arise, or exploit their immense influence in the struggle for the South Africa of our dreams. But few people will deny that in their lifetime they made a magnificent achievement and, in the process created a rich tradition which serves as a source of pride and strength to those who have now stepped into their shoes.

We were so busy outside prison that we hardly had time to think seriously about death. But you have to be locked up in a prison cell for life to appreciate the paralysing grief which seizes you when death strikes close to you. To lose a leading public figure can be a painful blow; but to lose a lifelong friend and neighbour is a devastating experience, and sharpens the sense of shock beyond words.

This is how I felt when Zami[xiii] gave me the sad news of the death of your beloved mother, adding that at that time your father was under detention and had to attend the funeral under police escort. I thought of you, Pascal,[xiv] Lindi, Seleke, Mpho, Thabo[xv] and, of course, your

---

i   Michael Harmel (1915–74), a leading member of the Communist Party. He died in exile in Prague.

ii   Monty Naicker (1910–78), doctor, politician, and anti-apartheid activist – see the glossary. M. P. Naicker (1920–77), anti-apartheid activist, journalist, leader, and organiser for the Natal Indian Congress, South African Communist Party, and the Congress Alliance. The Naickers were not brothers, but comrades.

iii   J. B. Marks (1903–72), ANC member and a leader in the 1952 Defiance Campaign (for the Defiance Campaign, see the glossary).

iv   Dr. Silas Modiri Molema (1891–1965), medical doctor and ANC activist.

v   Dr. Arthur Elias Letele (1916–65), medical doctor and ANC activist. An accused in the 1956 Treason Trial (for the Treason Trial, see the glossary).

vi   Ruth First (1925–82), journalist and Communist Party and ANC activist. An accused in the 1956 Treason Trial (for the Treason Trial, see the glossary). She went into exile in 1964 and was killed by a parcel bomb sent by apartheid agents while she was living in Mozambique.

vii   Dr. James Jimmy Njongwe (1919–76), medical doctor, ANC leader, and organiser of the Defiance Campaign (for the Defiance Campaign, see the glossary) in the Eastern Cape – for Jimmy Njongwe, see the glossary.

viii   Rev. James Arthur Calata (1895–1983), a teacher and a priest in the Anglican Church, he was a leading member of the ANC.

ix   Lilian Ngoyi (1911–80), politician, and anti-apartheid and women's rights activist – see the glossary.

x   George Edward Peake (1922–1981), founding member of the South African Coloured People's Organisation. Was an accused in the 1956 Treason Trial (for the Treason Trial, see the glossary). He was jailed for two years in 1962 for his involvement in a sabotage plot. He was forced into exile in 1968, where he died.

xi   Percy John 'Jack' Hodgson (1910–77), an accused in the 1956 Treason Trial and a founding member of the ANC's armed wing, Umkhonto weSizwe. He died in exile.

xii   Advocate Duma Nokwe (1927–78), political activist and advocate – see the glossary.

xiii   One of Winnie Mandela's names.

xiv   Pascal Shaudi Ngakane (1930–2015), one of Lionel Ngakane's siblings who was in prison with Mandela.

xv   William Barney (1902-88), ANC activist and Monzondeki Ngakane's children. Siblings of Lionel Ngakane.

father. I sent him a letter of condolence which I hope he also conveyed to you all.

The death of your father was equally devastating, and particularly so because I learnt about it from press reports as I was about to reply to his last letter which I had received on 31 December 1984. That shock unlocked a corner of my mind and I literally re-lived the almost 40 years of our friendship.

I particularly recalled an occasion at the Bantu Men's Social Centre[i] when we were addressed by Dr Yergan[ii] towards the end of the Defiance Campaign.[iii] Attendance was by invitation only and the City's top brass was all there – Xuma,[iv] Mosaka, Rathebe, Denelane, Madibane, Ntloana, Xorile, Twala, Rezant, Mali, Nobanda, Magagane, Mophiring and so on. The audience had been made specially receptive by the D.C.[v] and Yergan, who gave an outstanding review of the national movements on our continent, was in terrific form. You could hear a pin drop. He closed that brilliant speech with a concerted attack on Communism – and drew prolonged ovation from that elitist audience.

There followed a chorus of praises for Yergan until your father took the floor. He could not match Yergan in eloquence and in the vast amount of scientific knowledge the American commanded. But he spoke in the simple language we all understood and drew attention to issues we deeply cherished. He made pertinent observations on Yergan's deafening silence on our struggle generally and on the current D.C. in particular. Pressing his attack he challenged our guest speaker to speak about the giant American cartels, trusts and multi-national corporations that were causing so much misery and hardship throughout the world, and he foiled Yergan's attempt to drag us into the cold war. The same people who had given the speaker such a prolonged

---

i   The Bantu Men's Social Centre (BMSC), founded in Johannesburg, in 1924, was an important cultural, social, and political meeting place for black South Africans. Its facilities included a gym and a library, and it hosted boxing matches, political meetings, and dances. Mandela and others founded the ANC Youth League there in 1944.

ii   Dr. Max Yergan (1892–1975), the grandson of a slave in the United States, he was stationed in South Africa for eighteen years after World War II as senior secretary of the International Committee of the YCMA.

iii   Initiated by the ANC in December 1951, and launched with the South African Indian Congress on 26 June 1952 against six apartheid laws, the Defiance Campaign Against Unjust Laws (known as the Defiance Campaign for short) involved individuals breaking racist laws such as entering premises reserved for 'whites only', breaking curfews, and courting arrest. Mandela was appointed national volunteer-in-chief and Maulvi Cachalia as his deputy. Over 8,500 volunteers were imprisoned for their participation in the Defiance Campaign.

iv   Dr. Alfred Bitini Xuma (1893–1962) was the first black South African to become a medical doctor and president-general of the ANC (1940–49).

v   Defiance Campaign.

ovation now applauded your father just as enthusiastically. I must confess that I was more than impressed.

During the 1960 state of emergency,[i] we spent several months with him in the Pretoria local prison. Again he showed special qualities of leadership and was of considerable help in the maintenance of morale and discipline. There are many aspects of his life that flashed across the mind on that unforgettable day when I learnt of his death. But a restricted prison letter is not a suitable channel to express my views frankly and fully on such matters. It is sufficient for me to say that Zami and I will always treasure the memory of our friendship with your parents. Please convey these sentiments to Pascal, Lindi, Seleke, Mpho and Thabo. The attached cutting from the *Sowetan* is hopelessly inadequate and inaccurate and I sincerely hope that you or Lindi will in due course record the story of his life and make it available to a wider audience. That is a challenge to you all, but especially to Lindi,[ii] who has special qualifications, both academically and from her actual role in the struggle, to undertake such an important task.

Turning now to more lighter matters, I must confess that I am keen to hear more about your personal affairs. I know a direct question will not ruffle you. Are you married? If so, who is the fortunate young lady? How strong is your manpower? I must add that I never forget the day we spent together in London, and it pleased me tremendously to know that around O.R.[iii] there were talented young men of your calibre. You may not be aware that that discovery made me even more attached to your parents.

Pascal and I spent a lot of time together at home, and when I visited Durban in 1955 I made a special point to see him. But it was the three years that we spent together somewhere[iv] that made an even greater mark on me. I have not heard of him for some time now and would like to have his address. It was a pleasant surprise to me to learn that Clifford[v] is now Lesotho's ambassador in Rome.[vi] Until I saw press

---

i   Declared on 30 March 1960 as a response to the Sharpeville Massacre, the 1960 State of Emergency was characterised by mass arrests and the imprisonment of most African leaders. On 8 April 1960 the ANC and Pan Africanist Congress were banned under the Unlawful Organisations Act.

ii   One of Lionel Ngakane's sisters.

iii   Oliver Reginald Tambo (1917–93), Mandela's friend, former law partner, and the president of the ANC – see the glossary. His middle name was Reginald and Mandela referred to him as Reggie.

iv   Mandela is referring to when they were in prison together on Robben Island.

v   Clifford Morojele was married to Lindi, Lionel Ngakane's sister.

vi   Clifford Morojele worked for the United Nations in Addis Ababa and in Rome, but was not an reports to that effect, I had been under the impression that he was a UNO official. I will be quite happy if these reports are correct. I have a lot of admiration for Chief Leabua and, from this distance, he seems to be playing the trump cards exceptionally well.

Seleke[i] was a mere teenager when I last saw her, but I was later told that she was happily married to a medical practitioner in Maseru. I look forward to seeing all of you some day. Meantime I send you my fondest regards and best wishes.

Sincerely,
Madiba

Mr Lionel Ngakane, c/o Mr Paul Joseph, London

P.S. If you find time to reply to this note, please register your letter.

———

To Sheena Duncan,[ii] president of Black Sash

D220/82: NELSON MANDELA   1.4.85

Dear Mrs Duncan,

In my current position it is by no means easy to keep abreast of the course of events outside prison. It may well be that the membership of the B-Sash has not grown significantly over the last 30 years and that, in this respect, this pattern of development is not likely to be different in the immediate future at least.

But few people will deny that, in spite of its relatively small numbers, the impact of the Sash is quite formidable, and that it has emerged as one of the forces which help to focus attention on those social issues which are shattering the lives of so many people. It is giving a bold

---

ambassador. That fact was incorrectly reported in the newspapers at the time. (Sahm Venter in conversation with Clifford's son, Morabo Morojele, 14 October 2017.)

i   One of Lionel Ngakane's sisters.

ii   Sheena Duncan (1932–2010), member of Black Sash, an organisation of white middle-class women who protested against apartheid laws and assisted its vicims. Sheena's mother, Jean Sinclair, had been one of its founding members in 1955.

lead on how these problems can be concretely tackled and, in this way, it helps to bring a measure of relief and hope to many victims of a degrading social order.

The ideals we cherish, our fondest dreams and fervent hopes may not be realised in our lifetime. But that is besides the point. The knowledge that in your day you did your duty, and lived up to the expectations of your fellowmen is in itself a rewarding experience and magnificent achievement. The good image which the Sash is projecting may be largely due to the wider realisation that it is fulfilling these expectations.

To speak with a firm and clear voice on major national questions, unprotected by the shield of immunity enjoyed by members of the country's organs of government, and unruffled by the countless repurcussions of being ostracised by a privileged minority, is a measure of your deep concern for human rights and commitment to the principle of justice for all. In this regard, your recent comments in Port Elizabeth,[i] articulating as they did, the convictions of those who strive for real progress and a new South Africa were indeed significant.

In spite of the immense difficulties against which you have to operate, your voice is heard right across the country. Even though [it is] frowned upon by some, it pricks the conscience of others and is warmly welcomed by all good men and women. Those who are prepared to face problems at eyeball range, and who embrace universal beliefs which have changed the course of history in many societies must, in due course, command solid support and admiration far beyond their own ranks.

In congratulating you on your 30th birthday,[ii] I must add that I fully share the view that you "can look back with pride on three decades of endeavour which now, at least, is beginning to bear fruit."

In conclusion, I must point out that I know so many of your colleagues that if I were to name each and every one in this letter, the list would be too long. All I can do is to assure you of my fondest regards and best wishes.

Sincerely,
[Signed NRMandela]

---

i   City in the Eastern Cape province.
ii   Black Sash's thirtieth anniversary.

◇◇◇◇◇◇◇◇◇◇◇◇

This letter to anti-apartheid activist and lawyer Archie Gumede demon-strates the difficulties and frustrations of writing and receiving letters in prison, and the lack of information about what happened to them. In 1985 Mandela rewrote the letter that he had first sent to Gumede ten years ear-lier in 1975, as he suspected it had never reached him.

To Archie Gumede,[i] comrade & friend

D220/82: NELSON MANDELA

8.7.85

Phakathwayo! Qwabe![ii]

The other day I was going through the notebook in which I keep the record of my outgoing letters, and I came across the copy of the attached letter, which I wrote to you on Jan 1, 1975. As you have never responded, and in view of the peculiar problems we were experiencing with our post at the time, I have assumed that it never reached you.

Although more than 10 years have passed since it was written, and although some of its contents are now hopelessly outdated I, nonetheless, thought you should get it. The letter was written when Mphephethe,[iii] Sibalukhulu, Danapathy[iv] and Georgina's husband from Hammarsdale were all with you over there[v] and fairly active. One of the aims of the letter was to make them aware that there was deep appreciation for their work.

You will also bear in mind that, at that time, the relations between Khongolose[vi] and Shenge[vii] were good, and there was cooperation in many areas. In addition, he and I had been in contact since the late 60's, and he still sends me goodwill messages on specific occasions.

---

i   Archibald Jacob Gumede (1914–98) – see the glossary.
ii   Archie Gumede's clan names.
iii   Harry Gwala's clan name.
iv   The middle name of M. D. Naidoo who was in prison with Mandela on Robben Island.
v   Mandela is most likely referring to Natal.
vi   Mandela is referring to the African National Congress – *khongolose* for 'congress'.
vii   Chief Mangosuthu Buthelezi (1928–), Zulu prince, chief minister of KwaZulu 1972–94, and founder and president of the Inkatha Freedom Party in 1975 – see the glossary. His clan name is Shenge. Mandela is talking about relations with the ANC and Inkatha.

On the Island we fully discussed the matter in a special meeting of reps from all sections, and it was felt that it would be a mistake to ignore his gestures. I accordingly continued to respond.

Last year he sent me another telegram on a personal matter and my colleagues and I exchanged views. Again it was felt that, subject to what you might advise, I should write and thank him. But by the time the note reached the family you could no longer be reached. The note was ultimately forwarded to him.

At this stage I would like to digress a bit and tell you about a young lady, Ms Nomsa Khanyeza, 3156, Nkwazi Rd, Imbali, whose letter I received in Nov '82 and to which I immediately replied. I never heard from her again. I would like you to visit her home when you are in the area. In particular I would like to know whether she is still at school, and whether her parents have the funds for her education. From her letter she appears to be a child of ability.

Perhaps Thozamile and Sisa are aware that <u>Between the Lines: Conversations in SA</u>[i] by Harriet Sergeant has been published. She has some interesting observations to make on a wide variety of interviews. But a young lady of 26 can often be outspoken, and she seems to have recorded intimate sentiments and reactions which were not meant for public consumption. Although she is forthright in her manner, in my opinion, she has said nothing really damaging about the trade unionists she met. I am keen to know who Connaugh is. This is apparently the cover name of the bearded white man with jeans, earphones on his head, microphone in hand and a recording machine at the EL[ii] trade union meeting. Please get me this information if they already have the book.

In conclusion, I would like to draw your attention to a letter in a JHB[iii] daily which dealt with the case of 9 men who were condemned to death by Queen Victoria for treason. As a result of protests from all over the world the men were banished. Many years thereafter, the Queen learned that one of these men had been elected PM[iv] of Australia,[v] the second was appointed Brigadier-General in the U.S.A.

---

i   Harriet Sergeant's *Between the Lines: Conversations in South Africa* (London: J. Cape, 1984) was a book that explored the effect of apartheid on South Africans in the 1980s.

ii   This most likely stands for 'East London', a city in the Eastern Cape province.

iii   'Johannesburg.'

iv   'Prime minister'.

v   Charles Duffy (1816–1903) was not the prime minister of Australia but the eighth premier of the Australian state of Victoria. Historical information about Duffy doesn't suggest that he was sent into exile, and the article Mandela is referring to may be incorrect.

Army,[i] the third became Attorney-General for Australia,[ii] the fourth succeeded the third as A.G.,[iii] the fifth became Minister of Agriculture for Canada,[iv] the sixth also became Brigadier-General in the U.S.A.,[v] the seventh was appointed Governor-General of Montana,[vi] the eighth became a prominent New York politician,[vii] and the last was appointed Governor-General of Newfoundland.[viii]

It is a relevant story which, although you are probably aware of it, I think it proper to remind you of it. Fondest regards and best wishes to you and all your colleagues. Remember that you are all in our thoughts.

Sincerely, Madiba.

P.S. Nomsa was at the time of writing the letter a pupil at the Georgetown High School.

To Victoria Nonyamezelo Mxenge,[ix] lawyer and political activist

8.7.85

D220/82: NELSON MANDELA

Our dear Nonyamezelo,

---

i Patrick Donahue.
ii Morris Leyne.
iii Michael Ireland succeeded Morris Leyne as attorney-general of Australia.
iv Thomas Darcy McGee (1825–68) became the minister of agriculture, immigration, and statistics.
v Thomas McManus.
vi Thomas Francis Meagher (1823–67) became a cattle baron and the governor of Montana following the American Civil War.
vii John Mitchel (1815–75), Irish nationalist, author, and journalist who supported the Confederate States of America during the American Civil War. His son, John Purroy Mitchell (1879–1918), later served as mayor of New York City.
viii Richard O'Gorman.
ix Victoria Nonyamezelo Mxenge (1942–85), lawyer and anti-apartheid activist. Her husband and law partner Griffiths Mxenge was assassinated in 1981 and days after speaking at the funeral of four United Democratic Front activists killed by the police, she was murdered outside her home on 1 August 1985, less than a month after this letter was written. The Truth and Reconciliation Commission (TRC) report on the assassination of Victoria Mxenge documents that one Marvin Sefako (alias Bongi Raymond Malinga) was allegedly recruited by the security branch and that Brigadier Peter Swanepoel was his handler. Malinga confessed that he had killed Mxenge, claiming that he shot her five times in the chest, but she never fell and that he followed her with an axe and chopped her next to her dining room door. The TRC report contains no indication whether any person had applied for or had been granted amnesty in relation to her murder. (TRC Final Report, volume 2, chapter 3, subsection 28, p. 227.)

I believe that one of you has already visited Ntobeko at Mgungun-dlovu,[i] and I sincerely hope that his preparations are proceeding smoothly. Far more is involved in his case than the simple legal issues set out in the pleadings, and I felt that once you, Pius,[ii] Louis, Boyce, Yunus and others become consciously aware of its wider implications, you would immediately rally to his assistance. In this connection, I trust that you will be good enough to remind attorneys Ismail Meer, Verulam,[iii] and JN Singh, Durban, of my message in which I outlined how they could team up on an important aspect of this matter. It will be a splendid victory if Ntobeko will still be on the roll after Aug 9. But if friends rise to the occasion, as I expect they will, it can still be a resounding triumph even when we lose the actual court battle. Do you meet Poswa[iv] and Kall? Do give my fondest regards and best wishes to all of them for the excellent work they are doing all over the country.

Turning now to you, I must tell you that when an inmate discovered that I intended writing to you, he remarked that I was wasting energy and time, as you are reputed to be a bad correspondent, I brushed him aside by pointing out that those who failed to get your response obviously had nothing worthwhile to say, that even if the rumour were true, this time you would put everything aside and reply.

First, I would like to know just how you have managed over these last three years. I believe that the firm had already grown immensely. I accordingly imagined that you were stretched out almost to the limit when you suddenly found yourself all alone; without the skill and vast experience GM[v] commanded. Having spent a few years with him on Robben Island, I have a fairly good idea of the precious talents which he so richly possessed. But – from all the accounts I have received, it seems that you are a tough and determined girl, a go-getter. I am confident that you are not only equal to the task of running a big firm, but that you have by now succeeded in expanding it to a legal giant.

The news of your Cape Town adventure with Allan and others will have caught many people unawares. It is the last place where I

---

i   A place in Natal.
ii   Pius Nkonzo Langa (1939– 2013), lawyer who was a founding member of the National Association of Democratic Lawyers. In 1994 Mandela appointed him a justice of the Constitutional Court of South Africa. He became deputy chief justice in 2001 and was elevated to chief justice in 2005 by President Thabo Mbeki. He retired in October 2009.
iii Town in KwaZulu-Natal where Mandela's friend Ismail Meer lived.
iv   Mandela is most likely referring to Ntsikelelo Poswa, who was a lawyer and is now a judge.
v   Nonyamezelo's husband, Griffiths Mxenge.

8507080

Pollsmoor Maximum Prison,
P/BX 4, TOKAI, 7966   51

11220/82 NELSON MANDELA   8   7   85

Our dear Nonyamezelo,

I have that one of you has already decided Ntobeko at Ngqungushcon, and I sincerely hope that his preparations are proceeding smoothly. Far more is involved in his case than the simple legal issues set out in the pleadings, and I felt that once you, Plus Lewis, Boyce, Mervis and others become consciously aware of its wider implications, you would immediately rally to his assistance. In this connection, I trust that you will be good enough to remind attorneys Ismail Meer, Vimlam, and N Singh, Durban, of my message in which I outlined how they could team up on an important aspect of this matter. It will be a splendid victory if Ntobeko will still be on the roll after Aug. 9. But if friends rise to the occasion, as I expect they will, it can still be a resounding triumph even when we lose the actual court battle. Do you meet Swa and Kati?
Do give my fondest regards and best wishes to all of them for the excellent work they are doing all over the country.

Turning now to you, I must tell you that when an inmate discovered that I intended writing to you, he remarked that I was wasting valuable time energy and time, as you are reputed to be a bad correspondent. I brushed him aside by pointing out that those who failed to get your response obviously had nothing worthwhile to say, that even if the rumour were true, this time you would put everything aside and reply.

First, I would like to know just how you have managed over these last three years. I believe that the firm had already grown immensely. I accordingly imagined that you were stretched out almost to the limit when you suddenly found yourself all alone, without the skill and vast experience GM commanded. Having spent a few years with him on Robben Island, I have a fairly good idea of the precious talents which he so richly possessed. But from all the accounts I have received, it seems that you are a tough and determined girl, a go-getter. I am confident that you are not only equal to the task of running a big firm, but that you have by now succeeded in expanding it to a legal giant.

The news of your Cape Town adventure with Allan and others will have caught many people unawares. It is the last place where I expected you to become involved, and I was happy indeed when I heard that you did not have to travel down again. Nevertheless, the incident beautifully confirmed the image you have projected in my mind

Page from a letter to Victoria Nonyamezelo Mxenge, dated 8 July 1985, see pages 279–83. Various names mentioned in the letter have been highlighted in yellow highlighter by another hand.

expected you to become involved, and I was happy indeed when I heard that you did not have to travel down again. Nevertheless, the incident beautifully confirmed the image you have projected in my mind all these years.

Are the children well, and how are they faring with their school work? Where and when did you spend your last holiday? An overseas vacation, if you have a passport, would certainly be a refreshing experience both from the point of view of your own health, and that of the firm. The batteries that keep you going require to be constantly charged and recharged, if you are going to maintain a high standard of performance on professional and wider issues. It would also be an unforgettable experience for you to visit some of the big USA legal firms, some of which have not less than 100 partners each, with computers and well-stocked libraries. Do consider that.

I notice that we now have several lawyers' organisations: Lawyers for Human Rights,[i] Black Lawyers Association[ii] and the Democratic Lawyers Association.[iii] To which do you belong? Can you give me some information on the DLA?[iv]

Now I would like you to put a few telephone calls on my behalf to some friends over there: my sympathy to Chief Lutuli's[v] son, Sibusiso, and his wife, Wilhelmina, who were attacked at their Gledhow store recently. We wish them a speedy and complete recovery. Last year I wrote to the Old lady, Nokhukhanya;[vi] I don't know whether she ever received the letter as she never responded. Fondest regards to Diliza Mji, Senior,[vii] whose impressive contribution in the late 40s and early 50s can never be forgotten. The same sentiments to Diliza Mji, Junior[viii] in regard to his current efforts. We are particularly proud of him. Assure attorney Vahed that although I have not seen him for 30 yrs, I think of him and his wife. To Billy Nair[ix] just say, "Madiba sends

i   A non-government, non-profit organisation established in 1979.
ii   Established in 1976 to oppose the Group Areas permit system.
iii   The National Association of Democratic Lawyers was established in 1987 (note that Mandela's letter to Victoria Mxenge was written in 1985) and was established by the Black Lawyers Association.
iv   Democratic Lawyers Association.
v   Chief Albert Luthuli (1898–1967), president-general of the ANC, 1952–67 – see the glossary – who was killed by a train in July 1967. Mandela also spelt his name 'Lutuli'.
vi   Nokhukhanya Luthuli, Chief Luthuli's widow.
vii   Dilizantaba Mji, physician and president of the Transvaal ANC Youth League in the early 1950s.
viii Son of Diliza Mji, also a medical doctor and one-time president of the South African Students' Organisation.
ix   Billy Nair (1929–2008), comrade and MK member who was charged with sabotage in 1963. He was imprisoned in B Section with Mandela on Robben Island and was released in 1984 – see the glossary.

warmest greetings to Thambi and Elsie" and to attorney Bhengu I say "Halala Dlabazana!"[i]

In conclusion I want to tell you that Zami[ii] and I love you, and we often talk about you when she visits me. We sincerely look forward to seeing you one day. Hope and the future are always before us, mainly because S.A. has produced many men and women of your calibre, who will never allow the flames to die down. Our love and best wishes to you and the children.

Kindly register your reply.

Sincerely, 'Madiba'

Mrs Nonyamezelo Victoria Mxenge, 503 Damjee Centre, 158 Victoria St, Durban, 4001

◇◇◇◇◇◇◇◇◇◇◇◇

The first two paragraphs in this, one of Mandela's most seminal prison letters, signals his absolute faith in his chosen path of political activism and becoming a freedom fighter to win change in the country of his birth. He would have been writing this letter to Joy Motsieloa in his small single cell at Pollsmoor Prison, aware that outside its walls the country was in many parts literally burning.

Since September 1980 he and his comrades had been allowed access to newspapers and radio news, and by the mid-1980s they would have been fully informed of the events unfolding in South Africa. An upsurge in anti-apartheid activity in response to President P. W. Botha's establishment of a tricameral parliament with separate chambers for whites, coloureds and Indians – and nothing for Africans – in 1983 had given birth to a powerful new organisation, the United Democratic Front.

In 1985 the ANC in exile called upon South Africans to make black neighbourhoods 'ungovernable'. In July the same year the 'Pollsmoor March' was planned for activists to march on the prison and to 'free' Nelson Mandela. Although thousands of protesters set off from Cape Town on the march to Pollsmoor Prison on 28 August 1985, the iron fist of the apartheid regime crushed this march before it got anywhere near the prison and that day nine activists were killed, with a further nineteen people dead by the

---

i   'Halala' is a greeting and Dlabazana is probably Bhengu's clan name.
ii   One of Winnie Mandela's names.

*end of the week. This led to widespread protests throughout Cape Town for
the rest of the year.*

*As Mandela was writing this letter activists were being detained en masse,
kidnapped, and murdered. Six months earlier, Victoria Mxenge, one of the
friends he wrote to from prison (see his letter from 8 July 1985, pages 279–83)
was assassinated by a man paid by apartheid security forces. The country was
under a State of Emergency, in effect martial law. Severe restrictions were in
place to prevent the media from reporting on the action of the security police.*

To Joy Motsieloa, his friend

D220/82: NELSON MANDELA

17. 2. 86

Dear Joy,

When a man commits himself to the type of life he has lived for 45
years, even though he may well have been aware from the outset of all
the attendant hazards, the actual course of events and the precise manner in which they would influence his life could never have been clearly
foreseeable in every respect.

If I had been able to foresee all that has since happened, I would
certainly have made the same decision, so I believe at least. But that
decision would certainly have been far more daunting, and some of
the tragedies which subsequently followed would have melted whatever traces of steel were inside me. The death of your beloveds and
your intimate friends to whom you are linked by countless ties, some
going back for several decades; the wide variety of problems to which
your family would be exposed in your absence, are personal disasters
which are often difficult to endure and, on most occasions, leaving you
wondering whether in this kind of life one should have a family, raise
children and make firm friendships.

There have been many occasions on which such thoughts have
crossed the mind. The death of your brother, Gabula,[i] was one of

---

i   Gabula Mahlasela, Joy Motsieloa's brother, who visited Mandela at the Fort Prison in Johannesburg
     while he was awaiting trial in 1962.

those painful moments. The report literally paralysed me; I could write neither to you or to Zozo, I was not certain whether the old people were still alive or not and, if so, what their address was. All that I could do in my circumstances was to retire to the privacy of the cell, heavily stunned by the knowledge that I would never see him again. I, however, felt relieved when I thought of the happy days we spent together and his wonderful sense of humour.

Later as the turmoil inside me slowly began clearing away, I succeeded in rationalising the situation, and consoled myself with the belief that a man of his positive outlook would like to be remembered through his constructive efforts, which were fairly substantial, and for the joy and laughter he brought to those around him. I have missed him ever since.

Kepu,[i] who has been corresponding with me since our Robben Island days, informed me by telegram about the death of Thandi,[ii] and I sent a message of sympathy to the family.

Last year Vuyiswa sent me a birthday telegram and, in response to my letter of thanks, she wrote me a [?] letter which I value very much. She wrote on a piece of paper she probably retrieved from a waste paper basket. On the reverse side it was criss-crossed by untidy roneoed[iii] particulars. But the actual letter was, notwithstanding, warm and sweet, and its total lack of formality made it somewhat unique. She seems to be a tremendous person and I look forward to seeing her in the flesh one day.

When I visited London in June 1962 I thought of you and Jimmy,[iv] but the visit was a secret and highly packed one and I was unfortunately unable to contact many people I would have liked to see. Until I got Vuyiswa's letter I did not know that you were in Mogadishu[v] and Jimmy in Scandinavia. I hope you find a lot of pleasure and satisfaction in your respective occupations, although I imagine that you probably do a lot of travelling. How many children have you got and what are they doing? When last did you come home? Remember that we think of you and your Jimmy. Meantime, we send you our fondest regards and best wishes.

---

i   Kepu Mkentane, the wife of Lincoln Mkentane, a friend and former university classmate of Mandela's who became a lawyer.

ii   Vuyiswa Mhasela, one of Joy Motsieloa's relatives.

iii   Copies made on a Roneo duplicating machine.

iv   Jimmy Njongwe (1919–76), medical doctor, ANC leader, and organiser of the Defiance Campaign (for the Defiance Campaign, see the glossary) in the Eastern Cape – for Jimmy Njongwe, see the glossary. He was a relative of Joy Motsieloa's.

v   The capital of Somalia.

Sincerely,
Madiba

P.S. Should you ever forget the above address or wish not to use it, send the letters by registered post to P.O. Box 728 Johannesburg, 2000

[Envelope]
Mrs Joy Motsieloa,
United Nations High Commissioner for Refugees,
P.O. Box 2925.
MOGADISHU
Somalia

<hr />

To Michael Dingake,[i] friend, comrade and former fellow prisoner

D220/82

24.4.86

Dear Tlou,[ii]

This letter to Rakgadi[iii] was returned by the Post Office in Gaborone[iv] marked "Box Closed". Please ensure that it reaches her, and thereafter kindly inform me by registered letter of the results of your efforts.

This is a special letter strictly confined to the above message. But I must, at least, tell you that you, Edna[v] and the young lady[vi] are always in my thoughts. When Ntatho[vii] came last year I literally interrogated him on you. I sincerely hope that your health is sound and that you still find some time for jogging. Do let me know about the university and the young lady in your reply.

<hr />

i   Michael Dingake (1928–), ANC member who was convicted for sabotage and imprisoned on Robben Island – see the glossary.
ii   Tlou is Michael Dingake's clan name.
iii   'Sister' in Setswana. He is referring to Frieda Matthews (1905–98), friend and wife of his university professor Z. K. Matthews – see the glossary for both individuals.
iv   Capital of Botswana where the Matthewses lived.
v   Edna Dingake (d. 2009), Michael Dingake's wife.
vi   The Dingakes' daughter Goseo Dingake.
vii   Nthato Motlana (1925–2008), friend, medical doctor, businessman, and anti-apartheid activist – see the glossary. He was Edna Dingake's brother-in-law.

Fondest regards and best wishes to Quett,[i] Gaositwe,[ii] Sefton,[iii] Tloome,[iv] Martha, Ishy,[v] Nana & hubby,[vi] Dan, Edna & last, but not least, to you.

Very sincerely,

Madiba

―――――――

To K. D. Matanzima,[vii] his nephew, a Thembu chief, and chief minister of the Transkei

D220/82: NELSON MANDELA

19.5.86

Ngubengcuka,[viii]

The Department of Prisons informs me that you will in no circumstances come to Cape Town to see me, because I grossly insulted you when I refused your request to visit me last year.

I have on several occasions in the past expressly warned you against using our relationship to involve me and my organisation in Bantustan politics, and I will not allow you to do so.

But I am disturbed by recent press reports which indicate the existence of a tragic turmoil in family affairs.[ix] It has distressed me even more to discover from your reaction that this state of affairs no longer moves you. I sincerely hope that wiser counsels will ultimately prevail, and that you will in due course reconsider your decision, so that we can at least contain the simmering anger and bitterness. Had it not been

―――――――

i   Sir Quett Ketumile Joni Masire (1925–2017), second president of Botswana 1980–98.

ii   Dr. Gaositwe Chiepe (1922–), former Botswana cabinet minister.

iii   Mandela's brother-in-law Sefton Vutela, who was working for the Botswana Book Centre in Gaborone.

iv   Dan Tloome (1919-92), leader of the ANC and the South African Communist Party who was working for the ANC in Botswana, and who spent many decades in exile in Zambia.

v   Ishmael and Martha Matlhaku, political activists and friends. They went into exile in Botswana.

vi   ANC activists Euphenia and Solly Hlapane, who were refugees in Botswana.

vii   K. D. Mantanzima (1915–2003) – see the glossary.

viii   A reference to him being a descendant of King Ngubengcuka who was also Mandela's great-great-grandfather.

ix   Mandela could be referring to K. D. Matanzima's actions regarding King Sabata Jongunhlanga Dalindyebo (1928–86), paramount chief of the Transkei homeland and leader of the Democratic Progressive Party, who fled to Zambia after he was convicted of violating Matanzima's dignity in 1980 and died there in 1986.

for my current circumstances I would long have come down, as I did in 1955, to discuss these problems with you. When conditions change for the better I will certainly arrange to see you, and I only hope that an attempt to resolve the matter will then still be timely and fruitful.

I need hardly remind you that our political beliefs differ most radically, and it is my duty to remind you of this fact whenever you tend to ignore it. But I still regard you as an important member of the family whose friendship and co-operation is essential for the preservation of family unity and peace. I will not consciously insult or belittle you, or any other person for that matter. But I must stress with all the emphasis at my command that a public figure, whether – as you would put it – he is a "dangerous revolutionary", or a mere Bantustan leader, who allows his image to be so severely dented by recrimination, touchiness and intemperate language is no model for my own approach to people and problems.

Fondest regards and best wishes to you, Bambilanga,[i] Mzimvubu,[ii] Ngangomhlaba,[iii] Zwelidumile and Wonga. I miss you all. Ngubengcuka!

Very sincerely,
Dalibunga

◇◇◇◇◇◇◇◇◇◇◇

Nelson Mandela's health became the subject of widespread public discussion and concern when it became known that he had been admitted to a Cape Town hospital for prostate surgery on 3 November 1985. He was sixty-seven years old and the idea that he could die in prison was as alarming to the regime as to his family and supporters. While he was recuperating, he had 'a surprising and unexpected visitor,[46] *the then minister of justice, Kobie Coetsee. Although Mandela had written to Coetsee asking for a meeting to discuss potential talks between the government and the ANC, he had not expected to see him in the hospital. Coetsee became a crucial connection in talks Mandela began with a government team the following year. These exploratory talks were planned to investigate whether*

---

i   Nxeko (also known as Bambilanga) is the brother of King Sabata Jonguhlanga Dalindyebo, paramount chief of the Transkei homeland.

ii   George Matanzima (1918–2000), K. D. Matanzima's brother, Transkei leader and chief. While Mandela was at University College of Fort Hare with KD, George studied at nearby Lovedale College.

iii   Chief Ngangomhlaba Matanzima, a relative.

the government could enter into formal negotiations with the ANC about the end of white minority rule.

It is suspected that the dampness of Mandela's single cell away from the sunshine of the roof of Pollsmoor Prison also contributed to the illness that permanently removed him from that prison. Almost a year before he fell ill with tuberculosis, he petitioned the authorities about what he saw as a threat to his health.

═══════════

To the head of prison, Pollsmoor Maximum Security Prison

D220/82: NELSON MANDELA

6.10.86

Head of Prison
Pollsmoor Maximum Security Prison

Attention: Major Van Sittert

I would like to be transferred, at the earliest possible convenience, from my present cell to the opposite and empty cell across the passage primarily on health grounds.

My present cell has proved to be quite unhealthy and, if I continue staying in it, my health will eventually be impaired. At no time of day does the cell get the natural light, and I am accordingly compelled to keep the electric lights burning throughout the day.

The interior window panes are opaque and thick and the exterior fittings are made of louvre boards, all of which make the cell dark and depressing. Six panes have been removed and the cell becomes unbearable on cold and windy days.

Part of the wall and floor are perpetually damp and, during the ten months of my stay here, I have had to endure this inconvenience. You will readily appreciate, I trust, that it is not desirable that I should be compelled to live under such unwholesome conditions when there is a far better cell right in the same unit in which I could stay with relative comfort.

I must add that the dampness, as well as the metal fittings on the walls, also affect the reception in both the wireless and television set, resulting in uncontrollable flickering on the screen.[i] I believe that I would get a better performance in a dry and properly ventilated cell which is not cluttered with metal material. I accordingly suggest that you allow me to move to the opposite cell.

You will recall that on 26 September 1986 I requested an urgent interview with the Commanding Officer, and I would urge you to remind him again about the request. In conclusion, I would like to point out that no explanation has been made to me as to the conditions under which the television set has been made available to

P.T.O. [The letter ends abruptly. We are unsure if the second page was not copied or if it is not held by the National Archives and Records Service of South Africa.]

To Frieda Matthews,[ii] friend & wife of his university professor Z. K. Matthews

D220/82: NELSON MANDELA   25.2.87

Our dear Rakgadi,[iii]

You have no idea just what your visit to Pollsmoor has meant to all of us here. A visit to a prisoner always has significance difficult to put into words. Routine is the supreme law of a prison in almost every country in the world, and every day is for all practical purposes like the day before: the same surroundings, same faces, same dialogue, same odour, walls rising to the skies, and the ever-present feeling that outside the prison gates there is an exciting world to which you have no access. A visit from your beloved ones, from friends and even from strangers is always an unforgettable occasion, when that frustrating monotony is broken & the entire world is literally ushered into the cell.

---

i   The Rivonia prisoners at Pollsmoor were allowed to have television sets in 1986. Mandela received one in his cell at Pollsmoor Prison on 1 October 1986.
ii   Frieda Matthews (1905–98) – see the glossary.
iii 'Sister' in Setswana.

Your visit was typical and it made one feel that, after all, he is still part of the world to which we were born and grew up. It lighted a corner in me and a whole panorama of pleasant memories going as far back as 1939, flashed across the mind. Under different conditions we would have urged you to visit Robben Island, Pretoria, Diepkloof and Kroonstad[i] to take to them directly the same sentiments you expressed to me. But of course that is not possible. . . .

It pleased us to learn that Kgosie, together with J.J. and company, visited you. That is the field to which a Matthews should be active, and we were happy indeed to know that he is keeping the family tradition alive. I hope he has inherited Bakwe's[ii] excellent gift of wide and disciplined reading. During the Treason Trial[iii] Bakwe had a set pattern from which he rarely deviated. On returning from the case he would chat with the family for some time, have his supper, retire to the bedroom and get stuck to his reading for hours on end. Equally important was the fact that he knew how to absorb what he read and to apply it to his political work. I have missed him and Fiki over the years.

As far as the other grandchildren are concerned, you are mistaken to think that talking about them may bore me. On the contrary, the progress made by children can be very fascinating, even when they are your grandchildren. Admittedly, and having regard to your family background, there is nothing particularly astonishing in your grandchildren reaching out for the stars. The very achievements of their parents and grandparents are in themselves a challenge and an inspiration. But even when making allowance for that, what they have achieved gives a person in prison a fairly clear picture of the far-reaching changes which are taking place in Southern Africa today, and put the social turmoil in this region in perspective.

It would seem that some kind of diaspora is in full swing and children from urban townships and simple country villages alike are scattered all over the world and, in the process, horizons are widened beyond recognition, and new ideas acquired; with this background

---

i   Prisons where other political activists were incarcerated.
ii   Bakwe (Joe) Matthews (1929–2010), political activist and son of Frieda and Z. K. Matthews – see the glossary for these three individuals.
iii   The Treason Trial (1956–61) was a result of the apartheid government's attempt to quell the power of the Congress Alliance, a coalition of anti-apartheid organisations. In early-morning raids on 5 December 1956, 156 individuals were arrested and charged with high treason. By the end of the trial in March 1961 all the accused either had the charges withdrawn or, in the case of the last twenty-eight accused (including Mandela), were acquitted.

they return home to an environment not yet ready to accommodate them. This phenomenon is evident in many of the letters we receive and I am happy to note that your grandchildren are right in the centre of this process. I congratulate all of them and send them my fondest regards and best wishes.

I see Walter and others[i] now and again and we had a pleasant get together on Boxing Day. We are like a family and share almost everything we have. Naturally, we miss you all and literally crave for the open veld, some fresh air and plenty of sunshine.

Much love, Rakgadi,

Very sincerely,
Nelson

To Helen Joseph,[ii] a friend

1.4.87

Our dear Helen,

Please do not tell me that last yr I forgot to send you birthday greetings. I invariably keep copies of my outgoing correspondence, whether in the form of letters, birthday cards or telegrams. I have just gone through my letter book &, despite my firm belief that I sent you the message, I found no record to that effect. But I want to assure you that this time last yr you were constantly in my thoughts, especially because it was your 80th birthday.

After all, a card is of secondary importance; it is no more than a mere expression of how a person feels towards a friend. That love & loyalty to you will always be there whether the card reaches you or not. It was all there in April last yr & it is in this spirit that I send you my warmest congratulations on your 81st birthday. I hope the girls will all

---

i   Walter Sisulu and the other Rivonia trialists imprisoned at Pollsmoor (for Walter Sisulu, see the glossary).

ii   Helen Joseph (1905–92), teacher, social worker, and anti-apartheid and women's rights activist – see the glossary.

be there to rejoice with you. In my last letter to Amina[i] I suggested that she should arrange a tea party & invite Muriel,[ii] Virginia, Catherine, Rahima,[iii] Bertha,[iv] Greta, Onica[v] & co. to commemorate praiseworthy efforts & precious contributions – the deathless yrs. Perhaps you can take up the matter with her & Ntsiki? The response may far exceed your expectations.

How about it, Helen? By the way, do you still remember my reply when you told me that the late Dr Moroka[vi] had celebrated his 92nd birthday? You abhorred the prospect of living till that age. It would seem that the gods want you to drink that cup. Now it is my turn to say that I hope I will not live as long as Helen. How do you like that?

Caroline Mashaba[vii] disappointed me very much. When I sent her a letter of sympathy on the death of Andrew, I asked her to give me certain information on him which I needed urgently. Andrew did far more than we expected both outside & especially on the Island, & we had a duty to acknowledge that contribution. That was not possible without that information. I cannot understand why she chose to be so flat-footed in a matter of this nature. In May last yr, I also wrote to Esther Maleka;[viii] until then she was as good a correspondent as you, but I never heard from her again. There was also no response from Onica to my letter of sympathy on the occasion of her mother's death. I would not want you to actually travel in order to ascertain what happened. But if & when you bump against them do find out if they received the letters. How is Ruth,[ix] Sheila[x] and others? I trust that they still look after you. Ruth & Sheila are very good children & I am always happy to hear about them. It is, however, not so easy to

---

i   Amina Cachalia (1930–2013), friend and anti-apartheid and women's rights activist – see the glossary.

ii   Muriel Sodinda, anti-apartheid activist and singer.

iii   Rahima Moosa (1922–93), anti-apartheid activist and one of the leaders of the Women's March in Pretoria in 1956 to protest the extension of pass laws to women.

iv   Bertha Mashaba (1934–2010), anti-apartheid activist, feminist, and trade unionist. Alternatively he could be referring to Bertha Mkhize (1889–1981), an ANC Women's Leaguer and a vice-president of the Federation of South African Women.

v   Onica Mashohlane Mashigo from Alexandra township was an ANC activist who participated in many of its important campaigns and boycotts.

vi   James Moroka (1892–1985), medical doctor, politician and anti-apartheid activist, president of the ANC, 1949–52.

vii   The wife of former Robben Island prisoner, Andrew Mashaba.

viii   Sister of ANC activist Tito Maleka, who played a role in taking letters from him to his family during his Africa trip.

ix   Ruth Fischer (1941–) is the eldest of Advocate Bram Fischer's two daughters.

x   Sheila Weinberg (1945–2004) was the daughter of activists Violet and Eli Weinberg. An activist in her own right, she was detained as a teenager. At the time of her death she was a member of the Gauteng Provincial Legislature.

reconcile myself with the fact that I will never see their parents again – Braam, Molly, Violet & Eli.[i] When you see Nadine[ii] do give her my fondest regards & best wishes. She has turned out to be a forthright & formidable communicator whose message reaches far beyond the visible horizons. How such girls have become so precious today!

By now you probably know that Aunt Freda Matthews[iii] from Botswana paid me a special visit last November & brought along a whole library. Except that she has become shorter, she is in many respects like you. She carries her 81 yrs with much grace & charm & is very strong & alert. I enjoyed the visit very much. I have, however, no hope of seeing you, Amina & Fatima.[iv] All my efforts from this side to make such a visit possible have been unsuccessful. But we will always be in touch through correspondence & you will constantly be in my thoughts.

Lastly, I must tell you that I saved a piece of fruit cake which I hope to enjoy as you celebrate in a few days time. Although I have tea leaves & condensed milk I don't think I will be able to prepare it as well as you make yours. Nevertheless, it will be a very enjoyable moment for me. Have a wonderful time! Love & best wishes.

Very sincerely,
Nelson

◇◇◇◇◇◇◇◇◇◇◇◇

When Nelson Mandela was first sent to serve a prison sentence he was the father of five children aged from nearly two years old to seventeen. By the late 1980s he was a grandfather of twelve, with some of his grandchildren living abroad. His relationships with them were stitched together by birthday cards, simple notes, and in the cases of the older ones, extraordinary efforts to help them in their own endeavours at school and university. In this letter to his oldest grandson Mandla, he speaks of assisting his mother and his stepfather. Throughout, Mandela continued his long-distance parenting of his children and their spouses, cajoling and encouraging and in some cases admonishing them, even though they were grown and had children of their own.

---

i   Violet and Eli Weinberg. Violet Weinberg was a member of the Communist Party and the ANC. She left South Africa in 1977 to join her husband in exile.

ii   Nadine Gordimer (1923–2014), the South African author.

iii   Frieda Matthews (1905–98), friend and wife of his university professor Z. K. Matthews (Mandela has misspelled her name as 'Freda') – see the glossary for both individuals.

iv   Fatima (1928–2010) and Ismail Meer (1918–2000), friends. Fatima was a professor, author, and anti-apartheid activist. Imail was a lawyer and anti-apartheid activist – see the glossary for both these individuals.

To Mandla Mandela,[i] his grandson and the son of his son Mak-gatho[ii]

D220/82: NELSON MANDELA

9.7.87

My dear Mzukulu,[iii]

Why do you not write to me? Did you get the birthday card I sent you?

How are you getting on with your studies? We are trying to get you a scholarship to go to Waterford,[iv] and I sincerely hope that you will pass the test for admission.

I am keen to see you and I have told Grandma[v] to bring you down so that we can talk about your school work.

Our friends in London have met Mum Rennie[vi] and they are help-ing her to get glasses for her eyes. Uncle Adrian[vii] has already got work with a building firm in London.

[I] am sending you R50,00 for pocket money.[viii] Please look after it.

Love and fondest regards. Affectionately,
Tatomkhulu[ix]

[Envelope]
Mandla Mandela,
c/o Prince Kuzulwandle Dlamini,
Ministry of Education,
MBABANE, Swaziland

---

i   Mandla Zwelivelile Mandela (1974–) – see the glossary.
ii   Makgatho Mandela (1950–2005), Mandela's second-born son – see the glossary.
iii   'Grandchild' in isiXhosa.
iv   Waterford Kamhlaba school in neighbouring Swaziland.
v   Winnie Mandela.
vi   Rose Rayne Mandela-Perry, known as Rennie, Mandla's mother. After her marriage to Makgatho
      Mandela ended, she married Adrian Perry.
vii   Mandla's stepfather, Adrian Perry.
viii Mandela received money from family, friends, and supporters.
ix   'Grandad' in isiXhosa.

To Nandi Mandela,[i] granddaughter & eldest daughter of his late son Thembi[ii]

D220/82: NELSON MANDELA

17.8.87

My darling Mzukulu,[iii]

I enjoyed the last visit very much and it is a great pity that one visit is no more than a mere 40 minutes. Even more regrettable is the fact that we may not be able to see each other until early next year, because of the limited number of the remaining visits. But it is just possible that there may be one spare visit towards the end of the year which we could use. I would accordingly suggest that you telephone again, say, during the last week in October to find out whether you and Thumeka[iv] could come round. Remember that I love you and it is always a great day when you walk into the visiting room.

As I pointed out during the last visit, 43% and 44% in Economics and Accounting respectively, and bearing in mind the whole background, and that this is your first year, is by no means a bad performance. I am confident that, if you work harder during the next two months, you may be able to overcome, at least, some of your difficulties and improve your over-all performance.

Zindzi[v] ought to have been here on 5 August but she never turned up. I sincerely hope that she will be here one of these days. Have you written to Mandla?[vi] Tell Mamphela[vii] that I fully reciprocate the sentiments she expressed and keenly look forward to seeing her one day. Meantime, I send her my fondest regards and best wishes.

You must tell me a little more about your boyfriend. I never knew

---

i   Nandi Mandela (1968–) – see the glossary.
ii   Madiba Thembekile (Thembi) Mandela (1945–69), Mandela's eldest son – see the glossary.
iii   'Granddaughter' in isiXhosa.
iv   K.D. Matanzima's daughter Tumeka Matanzima.
v   Zinziswa Mandela (1960–), his middle daughter.
vi   Mandla Mandela (1974–), son of Mandela's youngest son Makgatho Mandela and Rose Rayne
        Mandela, known as Rennie.
vii   Mamphela Ramphele (1947–), anti-apartheid activist and a founding member of the Black
        Consciousness Movement, medical doctor, academic, and businesswoman – see the glossary.

until the last visit that he was also at UCT.[i] All you told me a year or two ago was that he was working at Umtata[ii] and studying through Unisa.[iii]

Fondest regards to Herbert[iv] & Nono[v] and to your room-mate Pearl Ralei.

Tons and tons of love and a million kisses, darling!

Affectionately,
Khulu[vi]
Miss Nandi Mandela, 718 Tugwell Hall, UCT, Rondebosch, 7700

<><><><><><><><><>

Mandela learned of Professor Mzobanzi Mboya when he was based at the University of Cape Town, where Mandela's daughter, Zindzi, and his granddaughter Nandi were studying. A PhD graduate of the University of Washington in Seattle, Mboya was a special advisor on transformation to Principal and Vice-Chancellor Dr. Stuart Saunders, focused on assisting black students by raising funds and providing academic guidance. Mandela initially contacted Professor Mboya via Professor Herbert Vilakazi to ask him to assist Zindzi and Nandi.

Later Mandela also asked Professor Mboya to obtain certain books to be sent to him in prison and requested that he collect some of his family members from the airport when they arrived in Cape Town to visit him. Professor Mboya also unsuccessfully lobbied the University of Cape Town to name one of its buildings after Mandela and initiated an international chain letter amongst academics calling for his release.

---

i   University of Cape Town.
ii   Umtata (now called Mthatha) was the capital of the Transkei homeland.
iii   University of South Africa.
iv   Herbert Vilakazi (1943–2016), professor of sociology.
v   Noni Vilakazi. It seems that Mandela may have spelt her name incorrectly.
vi   'Granddad' in isiXhosa.

To Professor Mzobanzi Mboya,[i] an acquaintance

D220/82: NELSON MANDELA   Pollsmoor Maximum Prison
P/B X4, Tokai, 7966
1.3.88

[Prison censor stamp dated 88/3/2]

Dear Mzobz,

It was a source of comfort for me to know that Herbert had requested you to help Nandi[ii] in her studies. If he had not done so, I would independently have approached you to undertake the task. There is a big gap between her matric performance and the first year academic standard at a university, a gap which she must close. This may be quite difficult without some professional help. I am confident that she will benefit immensely from your guidance. Meantime, I have advised her to do no more than two university courses this year and to take advantage of the orientation course offered by the university.

Your residential address reminds me of the memorable days I spent in Langa,[iii] first, the three months' stay there in 1948 during which I met prominent men like Johnson Ngwevela,[iv] Lwana, Ntshinga[v] and others. In 1955 I toured the whole country spending a fortnight with Rev Jeka[vi] of the Methodist Church of that township. I returned for the third time in 1961 and, this time I stayed with Rev Thethiwe[vii] and family of the Presbyterian Church. I also spent a lot of time with Dr A.C. Jordan, as he then was, who lectured at the UCT department of African Studies.

I miss Langa very badly and sometimes wish I could stand on Table Mountain, just as I did in 1948, and see even if merely its distant outline.

---

i   Professor Mzobanzi Matthewson Mboya (1949–), an academic in the education department of the University of Cape Town and special advisor on transformation to Principal and Vice-Chancellor Dr. Stuart Saunders.

ii   Nandi Mandela (1968–), Mandela's second grandchild and youngest daughter of Thembekile Mandela, his eldest son to his first wife, Evelyn – see the glossary.

iii Langa is a suburb in Cape Town.

iv   Johnson Ngwevela (d. 27 July 1987), ANC member and the South African Communist Party.

v   ANC members.

vi   In a conversation with Richard Stengel in 1993 Mandela recalled that Ngwevela and Rev Jeka were 'members of the Communist Party' and 'devout churchmen'.

vii Rev. Velaphi Elliot Thethiwe (1921–86), Albertina Sisulu's brother (for Albertina Sisulu, see the glossary).

My cousin, Mrs Grace Matsha, stays in 5 Sandile St. We used to correspond regularly, but she suddenly stopped responding, possibly as a result of pressure from some well-known quarters. Do give her and children my regards.

In conclusion I want to thank you for all that you have done for me. I would otherwise not have managed. I look forward to the day when I may have the opportunity of shaking your hand very warmly. Meantime, love and best wishes to you and your family.

Very sincerely,
Tata[i]

---

i   'Father' in isiXhosa.

TYGERBERG HOSPITAL & CONSTANTIABERG MEDICLINIC

||||||||||

AUGUST–DECEMBER 1988

n 1988, at the age of seventy, Mandela was taken to Tygerberg Hospital, where he was diagnosed with tuberculosis. While he was being treated in hospital he remained a prisoner of Pollsmoor Prison in Cape Town, which remained his address and point of contact for official requests and correspondence. He arrived at night on Friday 12 August 1988 at the government hospital in Bellville, known as Tygerberg Hospital, which serves as a teaching institution for Stellenbosch University. He had last been there fifteen months previously for surgey to repair a 'torn retina' of his right eye. That admission was not public knowledge and only became known through his personal calendar after his release.

The first doctor he saw in August 1988 announced that there was 'nothing wrong' with him.[47] The next morning he was examined by a Professor de Kock, head of internal medicine, who sent him straight to theatre where 2 litres of fluid were drained from his lung. Tuberculosis was found.[48] This time, news of his hospitalisation went global. The world's most famous prisoner was being treated for a serious illness while South Africa staggered through constant protests and continued repression. It was as if the universe held its breath.

Almost three weeks later, on 31 August 1988, after nineteen nights in hospital, he was transferred to the comfortable private hospital Constantiaberg MediClinic, close to Pollsmoor Prison, where he continued to be treated for tuberculosis. While there he received a string of visitors, including his wife and other family members as well as the minister of justice Kobie Coetsee, Reverend Anthony Simons, his lawyer, and the anti-apartheid activist and MP Helen Suzman.

Coetsee arrived on Mandela's first morning at the clinic just as Mandela was about to tuck into bacon and eggs instead of his prescribed cholesterol-free diet. 'They brought two eggs and a lot of bacon and then cereal, and then the Major . . . said, "No, Mandela, you can't eat this food – it's against the instruction of the doctor." I say, "Today I am prepared to die; I am going to eat it." Yes, I hadn't had eggs and bacon for a long time,' he laughed.[49]

He also befriended several of his nurses, delighting in their tales of life outside prison and hospital walls.

At the clinic, Mandela continued to meet with Coetsee and the 'secret committee' of government officials. It was during those talks that Coetsee told him that he would like to see him 'in a situation halfway between freedom and confinement' without explaining what he meant.[50]

He discovered what Coetsee was referring to on 7 December 1988 when unusual movement and tense conversations began between prison officials in his ward. 'I could see something was afoot but I didn't know what it was. Eventually in the evening, then the Major came in and said, "Mandela, prepare yourself, we are taking you to Paarl."[i] And I said, "What for?" He says, "Well, that is where you are going to be now." And at nine o'clock we left with a big escort.'[51]

---

i   A city in the Cape province (now the Western Cape province).

Throughout his illness and hospitalisation, Mandela continued to study for his law degree and spent some considerable effort in the last months of his imprisonment pressuring the University of South Africa to recognise some of the credits he had already obtained. He wanted not to have to complete the courses in practical Afrikaans and practical isiXhosa, his home language, but to be credited with a course he had already passed in another South African language, Sesotho, in order that he may complete the degree.

To Professor W. J. Hosten

Student no: 240-094-4

25.11.88

[Stamped] censored 88.11.26

Prof WJ Hosten,
Dean of the Faculty of Law,
Unisa,
P.O. Box 392,
Pretoria.
0001

Dear Sir,

I hope it will be possible for me to get an exemption from Practical Afrikaans (PAF100-A) and Xhosa I (XHA100-F), both of which I am expected to write in January 1989.

I had intended to write the four remaining subjects for the LL.B Degree during the October/November 1988 examinations, but I became indisposed at a crucial stage in the preparation for the examinations.

I fell ill on 28 July 1988, was admitted into Tygerberg Hospital on 12 August, and I was compelled to suspend studying until 15 September when I was able to resume preparations. However, I had by then already completed all the assignments set for the four subjects, and obtained passing marks in all of them.

I am presently being treated with a combination of drugs which will probably be maintained until early in February 1989. Dr. Stoch, the

District Surgeon of Wynberg,[i] whose letter is attached here, has since 1 September visited me daily for the various examinations indicated in the management of my illness. I also receive regular visits from three consultants from Tygerberg who are the heads of their respective departments at the hospital.

Although I am now feeling far better compared with the beginning of the treatment, the possibility that drugs may induce side-effects which may affect stamina and concentration, as well as the standard of performance in the examinations, continues to worry me.

I must point out with regard to Practical Afrikaans that, if I complete the degree I do not intend to practice either as an attorney or advocate. I must further point out that in 1963, I passed the London University examination on the history of English Law, and I hope you will be able to take this fact into account when considering the application for exemption from Xhosa I. The University of London will readily send me written confirmation in this regard, should you require such confirmation,

It would have been proper for me to make this application after the publication of the examination results in December. But as it is more than likely that you may be away on vacation by then, I thought it advisable to submit it now.

Yours faithfully,
[Signed NRMandela]
NELSON MANDELA

---

i   Wynberg is a suburb of Cape Town.

VICTOR VERSTER
PRISON

IIIIIIIIII

DECEMBER 1988–FEBRUARY 1990

On the evening of 7 December 1988 Nelson Mandela was taken from his hospital ward at Constantiaberg MediClinic and driven to Victor Verster Prison, about an hour away. The destination was the bungalow of a former prison warder and it had modern furnishings, a large garden, and a swimming pool. Warrant Officer Jack Swart, who had first encountered Mandela in the early days on Robben Island, was instructed to cook for him and run the house.

Swart recalls that Mandela was not restricted in the number of letters he could write while he was at Victor Verster Prison but he remembers three boxes containing 'hundreds of letters' that were not given to him.[52]

The next morning Mandela was visited by the minister of justice, Kobie Coetsee, armed with a housewarming gift – a case of wine. He told Mandela that it had been decided that he would be held in the house so that he could continue the discussions he had begun with government officials in 1986.

The talks with the 'working group' continued apace. The schedule depended on a request to meet from either the government team or from Mandela, who would communicate through the commanding officer of the prison.[53] The meetings were not negotiations, but rather an attempt by Mandela to get to a point where the ANC and the government could eventually negotiate about the end of apartheid. They were later described technically, as 'talks about talks'. He used these discussions with the officials to arrange the release of the remaining six Rivonia Trial colleagues still in prison. The oldest, Govan Mbeki, had been freed in November 1987 and Denis Goldberg was released in 1985.

While prospective visitors still had to apply to see him, and their applications were still sometimes rejected by the authorities, Mandela had many visits from his wife, Winnie Mandela, their children, and grandchildren and other family members as well as friends and comrades. His letters were similarly less controlled and they assumed the role of an instrument for him to reach back into the world he seemed increasingly likely to inhabit again.

In 1988 Mac Maharaj, his comrade from Robben Island, had been infiltrated back into South Africa as part of an underground strategy, called Operation Vula, to smuggle MK operatives into South Africa in case the government did not negotiate in good faith. Maharaj devised a method for Mandela to communicate from the prison to Oliver Tambo and other ANC leaders in exile. He informed Mandela's attorney Ismail Ayob of a nickname they had arranged before Maharaj's release from prison and told him to refer to it on one of his visits. This signalled to Mandela that Ayob was conveying a message from Maharaj. The first one was a tiny rolled-up note the size of a matchstick. It asked him to participate in a secret exchange of messages that would be hidden inside a book cover. Mandela agreed. In this way, Mandela and the organisation were able to share information on the discussions he was having with the government team.[54]

A mark of Nelson Mandela's character was his determination to stick at his
law studies; throughout his imprisonment he persevered with the law stud-
ies toward his LLB that he had begun as a young man in 1943. Although
he was permitted to practise as an attorney with only a diploma in law, he
had set his heart on achieving this goal when he was an activist studying at
the University of the Witwatersrand in Johannesburg and started his three
years of legal articles at the firm Witkin, Sidelsky and Eidelman within
weeks of enrolling as a student.

While imprisoned at Pretoria Local Prison in 1962 he signed up to Lon-
don University to continue his studies, and faced challenges at every turn.
Studying at night after almost eight hours toiling in the quarry, digging out
lime from 1965 to 1978, was not his biggest obstacle. His correspondence
reveals that he often did not receive the correct study materials or not on
time. The scenario he would sketch for university officials from the Univer-
sity of London, and during his subsequent studies through the University of
South Africa, went on for many years. Finally, at the age of seventy, knowing
that it was highly unlikely that he would ever practise as a lawyer again,
Mandela learned that he would indeed graduate with a law degree.

To Professor W. J. Hosten, University of South Africa

Student no: 240-094-4

23 December 1988

Prof W.J. Hosten,
Dean of the Law Faculty,
Unisa,
P.O. Box 392.
Pretoria
0001

Dear Prof Hosten,

I thank you for your letter of 5 December 1988 in which you advise
that I have completed the LL.B degree.

It was fitting that you should be the first to congratulate me on this achievement. I firmly believe that, without your support, my request for exemption from the languages would probably not have succeeded. The accomplishment will certainly strengthen my ties with Unisa,[i] and will enable me to join the scores of men and women, inside and outside South Africa, whose ability to serve their respective communities has been considerably enhanced by obtaining this degree.

Kindly convey my thanks to the Faculty Board and to the Registrar (Academic and Student Affairs), to Prof Wiechers for his complimentary press comments, to Prof P.A.K le Roux, who provided me with prescribed literature, and all the lecturers who guided me so well in my studies.

Yours sincerely,
[Signed NRMandela]

To Dumani Mandela, his grandson and his eldest daughter Makaziwe's[ii] son

1335/88: NELSON MANDELA   28.2.89

My dear Mzukulu,[iii]

I am told that you are doing well at school, and that you are particularly good in Mathematics. This subject is very difficult but very important. If you always get the best marks and pass well in the end, you will always have a good job wherever you may be.

I believe that you are also doing well with the trumpet. Perhaps in your letter you will tell me who teaches you music, and whether you have any music book to guide you. Exercise is also very good. Taking part in sport like running, swimming and tennis will keep you healthy, strong and bright. But swimming is also a very dangerous sport. You must have a good coach and never swim in the absence of the coach until you have mastered the hobby.

---

i   University of South Africa.
ii   Makaziwe Mandela (1954–)– see the glossary.
iii   'Grandchild' in isiXhosa.

Please tell your Mum that I got her letter and that I spent years trying to persuade Uncle Kgatho[i] to go back to school. There is absolutely nothing more I can now do. Books, clothing and videos will not be allowed. Buying and sending them will be a waste of money, as they will not be given to me.

I have recovered from illness and I now feel well and strong. The other matters mentioned in Mum's letter will be discussed when she visits the country next June.[ii] I miss you, Tukwini and Kweku[iii] very much and look forward to seeing you one day.

My love and best wishes to you all.

Affectionately,
Khulu[iv]

[Envelope]
Mr Dumani Mandela,
108 University Apartments,
Amherst,
Massachusetts,
01002
U.S.A.

To Candie Lawless, a nurse who took care of him at Constatiaberg MediClinic

<u>1335/88: NELSON MANDELA</u>

4.4.89

Dear Candie,

I have been expecting your letter ever since my discharge from the Constantiaberg MediClinic.[v] I am indeed very happy that it has come at last.

I am even more pleased to hear that you and Trevor are engaged.

---

i   Makgatho (Kgatho) Mandela (1950–2005), Mandela's second-born son – see the glossary.
ii   Makaziwe Mandela was living in Boston, United States.
iii Dumani Mandela's sister and brother.
iv   'Grandfather' in isiXhosa.
v   He was admitted to Constantiaberg MediClinic while he was recovering from tuberculosis in late August 1988.

My warmest congratulations! I am sure he will make a fine husband; a source of lasting happiness and security to you. If he had not proposed by now, I would have urged you to seize the bull by its horns and propose to him. After all, the acceptance of the principle of the equality of the sexes gives you that right when the young man drags his feet.

From your sketch it would seem that the engagement ring will be very special, and Trevor's salary increase should be able to cover the price without difficulty. Again, my warmest congratulations!

I am very sorry to hear about Kitty's death. But that is the way of life, and it is far better to be realistic and to accept what has happened. My deepest sympathy to you and Trevor.

The clinic will miss you very much, as they regarded you as one of their best sisters. But I will rejoice with you if you find your new job rewarding. I will be holding thumbs for you.

Meantime, I send my fondest regards and best wishes to you, Trevor, Dara, Tami (whose success in the exams delighted me), Kim and your parents.

Sincerely,
[Signed NRMandela]

To Mike Tyson,[i] American heavyweight boxing champion

1335/88: NELSON MANDELA

10.5.89

Dear Champ,

It pleased me and my family very much to learn that the Central State University[ii] has awarded you an honorary doctorate, an honour which is rightly deserved. Please accept our warmest congratulations.

We must also thank you for the pair of boxing gloves which you sent to mark my 70th birthday.

---

i   Mandela met Mike Tyson and other American boxers in the United States on 22 June 1990.
ii   University in Wilberforce, Ohio, United States.

It is such messages of solidarity which has enabled me and scores of others to remain so strong and full of hope throughout these trying times.

Fondest regards and best wishes,

Sincerely,
[Signed NRMandela]

[Envelope]
Dr Mike Tyson
Heavyweight Boxing Champion of [the] World
c/o President Arthur E Thomas
Central State University
WILBERFORCE, OHIO 45384
USA

To Tim Wilson, director of the Alexanda Health Centre[i]

1335/88: NELSON MANDELA

Victor Verster Prison,
P/B X6005,
Paarl South,
7620.

23.7.89

Dear Tim,

The significance of an institution lies not merely in the size of its buildings, staff or budget, but mainly in the quality of its service to the community. On this standard the Alexandra Health Centre[ii] is a unique project in more senses than one.

---

i   Tim Wilson was director of the Alexandra Health Centre in Alexandra township in Johannesburg during the turbulent, and often violent, period of the 1980s, and the son-in-law of lawyer and political and anti-apartheid activist Bram Fischer (1908–75). For Bram Fischer – see the glossary.

ii   The Alexandra Health Centre and University Clinic in Alexandra, Johannesburg, was initially established in 1929 as a maternal and child health centre before evolving into a primary health care centre.

For one thing, it brings hope where there was despair, and even life where death would have triumphed. Its independence from government control, the diversity of its benefactors, its goals and range of activities all make it an effort of far-reaching potential; an example of what would happen in the new South Africa we are all striving to build.

Sixty years of community service is an appropriate occasion for celebration, and I send the Centre my congratulations and best wishes.

***

I spent some exciting years in Alex in the early forties,[i] and the mere mention of that famous township makes me more than nostalgic. I intend visiting the place at the earliest opportunity when better times return.

Meantime, I think of you, Ilse[ii] and Ruth[iii] with warm regards,

Sincerely,
Uncle Nelson

To the commissioner of prisons

1335/88: NELSON MANDELA

11.9.89

Commissioner of Prisons
Pretoria

The release of the following prisoners, all of whom are serving sentences of life imprisonment, will be widely appreciated:[iv]
1. Kathrada, Ahmed,
2. Mhlaba, Raymond,

---

i   Soon after Mandela arrived in Johannesburg in 1941 he moved into the township of Alexandra, where he boarded with the Reverend J. Mabutho of the Anglican Church at his home in Eighth Avenue. He later moved into a room in the yard of the Xhoma family in 46 Seventh Avenue.
ii   Ilse Wilson, Tim Wilson's wife and daughter of Bram Fischer.
iii Ruth Fischer, Tim Wilson's sister-in-law and daughter of Bram Fischer.
iv   This was part of Mandela's secret negotiations with the government. He later wrote: 'I pressed the government to display evidence of its good intentions, urging the state to show its bona fides by releasing my fellow political prisoners at Pollsmoor and Robben Island.' (NM, *Long Walk to Freedom*, p. 661.)

3.   Mlangeni, Andrew,
4.   Motsoaledi, Elias,
5.   Sisulu, Walter.[i]

All of them were sentenced in June 1964, and all of them are now more than 60 years of age, Mr Sisulu having turned 77 last May and Mr Mhlaba 70 last February.

6.   Mr Wilton Mkwayi[ii] was sentenced in December 1964. Although he was arrested after the above persons had already been convicted, he is for all practical purposes a co-accused, the only difference being that he escaped the police net when the others were arrested in July 1963.

7.   *Messrs Meyiwa and Mdlalose, both of whom are held in Robben Island, were released in the Seventies after each had served eight years. They were again arrested and this time sentenced to life imprisonment together with Mr Harry Gwala,[iii] who was released last year on medical grounds.

8.   Mr Jeff Masemola,[iv] presently held in Diepkloof,[v] was sentenced to life imprisonment in 1963. All his co-accused have been released, some of them as far back as four years ago. But the Department of Prisons continues to hold him in spite of his poor state of health and age.

I should add that the release of one or a couple of these men only will no longer have any significance.

---

i   For more on these Rivonia Trialists, see the glossary.
ii   Mkwayi was serving a life sentence for his role in the Little Rivonia Trial. The Little Rivonia Trial took place in November 1964, five months after the Rivonia Trial (see the glossary) ended, after Laloo Chiba, Mac Maharaj, Wilton Mkwayi, Dave Kitson and John Matthews were charged with sabotage for their activities on behalf of MK. The former three were sent to Robben Island and the other two, being white, were held in Pretoria.
iii   Harry Gwala (1920–95), ANC activist who was charged with sabotage for recruiting members to MK and sentenced to eight years in prison on Robben Island. Continued his activism on his release in 1972 and in 1977 he was sentenced to life imprisonment and returned to Robben Island – see the glossary.
iv   Jafta Kgalabi 'Jeff' Masemola (1929–90), teacher, member of the ANC Youth League, member of the Pan Africanist Congress, and political prisoner – see the glossary. After being arrested in 1962 and charged with sabotage for blowing up power lines and smuggling freedom fighters out of South Africa he was sentenced to life imprisonment in July 1963. He was released from prison on 15 October 1989, and on 17 April 1990 he was killed in a mysterious car accident.
v   A prison in Johannesburg.

If you grant this request, as I hope you will, then I would like to see them before they are released. I can see Mr Masemola immediately after he is released.

[Signed NRMandela]

*The full names are

Matthews Meyiwa
Zakhele Mdlalose

[In another hand]: Oscar Mpetha – added on request of Mr Mandela[i]

To Fatima Meer,[ii] friend and comrade

1335/88: NELSON MANDELA

28.9.89

Dear Fathu,[iii]

Your letters of 7 and 14 September were delivered to me only yesterday, and the nature of the issues you raise in the correspondence demands a prompt reply.

I fully agree with Iqbal's[iv] suggestion that the services of Mr Geoffrey Bindman[v] should be retained.

With regard to the publication of the local edition, I enclose for your attention authority empowering you to choose the publisher. Unfortunately, my information on the Madiba Trust is very scanty, but I will respect your decision if you nonetheless consider it wise to publish under it. Would IBR[vi] not be better able to undertake it? In my opinion distribution by the CNA[vii] would be a good arrangement.

---

i   All except Meyiwa and Mdlalose were released on 15 October 1989.
ii   Fatima Meer (1928–2010), writer, academic, and anti-apartheid and women's rights activist – see the glossary.
iii   A nickname for Fatima Meer.
iv   Fatima's nephew, Iqbal Meer.
v   A London attorney who was assisting with the publication of Fatima Meer's book about Mandela, *Higher Than Hope: The Authorized Biography* (New York: Harper & Row, 1988).
vi   The Institute for Black Research.
vii   A book retailer called Central News Agency.

I suspect, ben,[i] that you easily forget that you are still fairly young and wide awake. You have no reason whatsoever to behave like a sexagenarian. We discussed Anant's[ii] offer to make the film and I expressly assured you that I accept the offer.[iii] Iqbal can draw up a formal acceptance document if one is required.

Sidney Potier[iv] is a super-star and it would be a shot in the arm for him to act in the film. But he is probably very rich now to accept our offer. I am making an application to the Department of Prisons for you and Iqbal to visit me. But, as you know, it may take quite some time before we get a reply.

The new cover for the South African edition looks impressive and I am happy with it. I would have preferred that we renew the contract with Skotaville.[v] But bearing in mind your views on the matter I would suggest that either the Institute for Black Research or the Madiba Trust or any other agency of your choice should handle publication.

As far as legal representation is concerned, Krish[vi] has already done a lot of good work and I suggest that he should represent us in this matter.

Unfortunately, I have no information on the significance of the words "authorised version". But if this will contribute to the success of the project then I sanction the suggestion both for the overseas and local editions.

Love and best wishes.

Sincerely,
Nelson

◇◇◇◇◇◇◇◇◇◇◇◇

During his talks with government in prison, which he hoped would lead to eventual negotiations with the ANC, Mandela had repeatedly called for the release of other prisoners. De Klerk made an announcement on television on

---

i   'Sister' in Gujarati.

ii   Anant Singh, South African filmmaker.

iii   Anant Singh and Fatima Meer had discussed making a film version of *Higher than Hope*, which Mandela agreed to. Singh met him at Meer's house two weeks after he was released and Mandela indicated that he had written his autobiography and was going to publish it. 'We both then agreed that we should wait until that is published to get the movie made.' (Anant Singh, email to Sahm Venter, 7 September 2017.) Singh eventually produced the feature film based on Mandela's autobiography, *Long Walk to Freedom*, and it was released in 2013.

iv   Sidney Poitier (1927–), Bahamian-American actor, film director, author, and diplomat. *Higher Than Hope* was never adapted into a film but Poitier later played Mandela in the 1997 television film *Mandela and De Klerk*.

v   The first South African publisher of *Higher Than Hope*.

vi   Krish Naidoo, a lawyer.

10 October 1989 the remaining five of his Rivonia Trial colleagues would be released. Five days later his imprisoned comrades Walter Sisulu, Ahmed Kathrada, Andrew Mlangeni, and Raymond Mhlaba[i] were free. They were joined by ANC prisoners Oscar Mpetha, Wilton Mkwayi and Jafta Masemola of the Pan Africanist Congress.

As 1989 rolled to an end, rumours of Mandela's own release from prison began to grow daily. They had already reached a new height on 5 July 1989 when he was taken from prison before dawn to meet with President F.W. de Klerk who had assumed leadership of the National Party and the country after P.W. Botha suffered a stroke. On Friday 2 February 1990 protests demanding the release of Nelson Mandela dissolved into street celebrations when De Klerk announced that he would at long last be freed. He also immediately legalised the ANC, the PAC and all other banned political organisations – other steps Mandela had called for to level the playing fields.

The following letter was written on the day of De Klerk's announcement. It concerns a report of a meeting of the ANC in exile, which Mandela wanted to be sent to Minister Gerrit Viljoen, who at the time was part of the government team talking with Mandela. The letter reveals that he had had a telephone conversation with a leading figure of the exiled ANC, Thabo Mbeki, eleven days before De Klerk's historic speech.

———

To the commissioner of prisons

1335/88: NELSON MANDELA

2.2.90

General WH Willemse
Commissioner of Prisons
Cape Town

Dear Gen Willemse,

Please ensure that the attached statement reaches Dr Gerrit Viljoen[ii] at the earliest possible convenience.

———

i   They were held at Pollsmoor Prison. The other remaining Rivonia trialist, Elias Motsoaledi, was still on Robben Island (see the glossary for notes on these individuals).

ii   Gerrit Viljoen (1926–2009), minister of constitutional development.

With kind regards,
[Signed NRMandela]

[This whole resolution is in Mandela's hand.]

Resolution adopted at a meeting of the National Executive Committee of the African National Congress attended by the internal leaders
released from prison.[i]

The meeting reaffirmed the significance of the Harare and United
Nations declarations,[ii] the latter unanimously adopted by the General
Assembly for the political settlement in our country. It emphasised
the importance of the fact that these documents are supported by
the overwhelming majority of the people of South Africa, the rest of
Africa and the international community.

It reiterated that in keeping with the provisions of these declarations, no negotiations can take place until the necessary climate for
such negotiations has been created. The refusal of the Pretoria regime[iii]
to take the appropriate action in this regard is yet another element
confirming its unwillingness to see the apartheid system ended with as
little bloodshed and destructions as possible.

In this regard the meeting reaffirmed the importance of the immediate and unconditional release of Nelson Mandela and other political
prisoners. It paid tribute to our dear comrade and fellow leader, Nelson Mandela, and expresses its full support for his continuing action
even from within prison, which are fully in keeping with the policies
and objectives of our movement, to take [forward] the struggle to end
apartheid.

The meeting further reaffirmed the preference of the A.N.C. for
a settlement arrived at by political means. The A.N.C. has held this
position from its very foundation. Throughout the 78 years of its existence it has done everything it could to prevail on successive white

---

i   The meeting was held in Lusaka, Zambia.
ii   At a meeting in Harare, Zimbabwe, on 21 August 1989, the Organisation of African Unity endorsed
     a statement by the ANC which outlined five preconditions in order for negotiations with the South
     African government to begin. These included the release of all political prisoners, the unbanning of
     political parties, removing troops from townships, an end to political executions, and the end of the
     State of Emergency. This became known as the Harare Commonwealth Declaration. On 14 December
     1989 the United Nations General Assembly adopted the 'Declaration on Apartheid and its Destructive
     Consequences in South Africa', which called for an end to apartheid and the establishment of a non-
     racial democracy.
iii A reference to the government-led apartheid regime. Pretoria is the South African government's
     administrative capital.

minority regimes to adopt the same position to no avail. The meeting reaffirmed that our commitment to these positions is not in doubt. It is fundamental to the nature of the A.N.C. as a movement which seeks democracy, peace and justice for all. At the same time the process of ending apartheid through negotiations requires that the Pretoria regime should itself demonstrate its commitment to a political solution by taking the necessary action which would make such a solution possible.

The meeting warned that no solution can be arrived at while the apartheid regime seeks to impose its will on the majority of our people and their representatives. A negotiated settlement must address the fundamental aspirations of all the people of our country, with those aspirations having been expressed by the people themselves in open political activity and debate.

The National party and its Government, therefore, needs to take a decisive step forward by meeting the conditions for the creation of a climate conducive to negotiation, and recognise the central importance of the genuine representatives of the people of our country.

The above statement was read over to me by Mr Thabo Mbeki[i] on 22 January 1990,[ii] and contains no reference whatsoever to violence.

[Signed NRMandela]
2.2.90

[A note in Afrikaans by General Willemse]
Min. G Viljoen
Here is the requested information following yesterday's conversation.

[Signed]
WH WILLEMSE
90/02/02

---

i   Thabo Mbeki (1942–), head of the ANC's department of internal affairs who was living in exile at the time. He was deputy president of South Africa, with former president F. W. de Klerk, from 1994 to 1999, then succeeded Mandela as the second president of a democratic South Africa, serving from 1999 until 2008.

ii   Mandela didn't have a phone in the house at Victor Verster, and would have had to have gone to a next-door office to take any calls (Jack Swart in conversation with Sahm Venter, 28 June 2017).

◇◇◇◇◇◇◇◇◇◇◇◇

At a press conference on 10 February 1990, De Klerk advised the media that Mandela would walk free from Victor Verster Prison the next day at 3 p.m. He actually walked through the gates some ninety minutes later, when he was released the following day, bringing to an end his 10,052 days in prison. He had entered custody a forty-four-year-old father of five children and left it as a seventy-one-year-old grandfather.

It is likely that this is Nelson Mandela's last letter from prison. On Sunday, 11 February 1990, before he walked through the gates of the prison, the future president wrote to the commissioner of prisons referring to a photograph taken with officials the night before. He is either confusing that occasion with photographs taken with De Klerk two nights before or else there remains a photograph of which the world is so far unaware.

To the commissioner of prisons

1335/88: NELSON MANDELA   11 February 1990

General W.H. Willemse
Commissioner of Prisons
Cape Town

Dear General,

I acknowledge receipt of your letter of 10 February 1990, contents of which have been noted and for which I thank you.

Last night a series of photographs of me[i] and some officials was taken. The identity of some of these officials was disclosed to me by Brigadier Gillingham only after the photo session. I then requested him to

---

i   Jack Swart (1947–), Mandela's prison guard and his chef at Victor Verster Prison cannot recall any
     meeting with officials on the night before Mandela's release or any pictures being taken. Mandela only
     met with his lawyer, Dullah Omar, and his colleagues. Pictures taken with President F. W. de Klerk
     on the night of 9 February were published. Swart and Mandela had a good relationship and Mandela
     invited him and his wife, Marietha, to his inauguration on 10 May 1994 and his first State of the Nation
     address at the opening of Parliament on 24 May 1994. He also invited him and his wife to tea on more
     than one occasion after his retirement.

inform Dr Roux[i] that I would prefer that these photos should under no circumstances be published without first consulting me. I hope steps will be taken to ensure that this request is respected. I must add that I had hoped that I would by now have got some of the photos we took in July and this year's[ii] [meeting].

Yours sincerely,
[Signed NRMandela][iii]

i   Possibly General Jannie Roux, a prison official and psychiatrist who was involved in the media's visits to Robben Island in 1975. Later he served as director-general in the presidency under Mandela.
ii   Mandela may have been referring to the meetings he had with P. W. Botha in July 1989 and FW de Klerk on 9 February 1990.
iii On the same day the Commissioner of Prisons, W.H. Willemse replied and said: "Thank you for your letter dated 1990/02/11. The photos that you are concerned about have not yet been processed and are in good hands. They will be dealt with in such a fashion as to accommodate your request. Some of the other photos that you refer to will first have to be cleared with the parties involved. Thereafter I will contact you again."

GLOSSARY

ANC

Established as the South African Native National Congress (SANNC) in 1912. Renamed African National Congress (ANC) in 1923. Following the Sharpeville Massacre in March 1960, the ANC was banned by the South African government and went underground until the ban was lifted in 1990. Its military wing, Umkhonto weSizwe (MK), was established in 1961, with Mandela as commander-in-chief. The ANC became South Africa's governing party after the nation's first democratic elections on 27 April 1994.

Aucamp, Brigadier

Based in Pretoria, he was in charge of security in all prisons that had political inmates. He would visit Robben Island Maximum Security Prison several times a year. He was also a member of the Prison Board which had the task of monitoring prisoners and to recommend them for a higher grade. In Mandela's autobiography written in prison, he wrote: 'Brig. Aucamp: (a) Did well as officer commanding (b) position of Security Officer difficult – changes man's personality (c) had direct access to Minister (d) became quite unpopular (e) allowed correspondence between self and Zami [Winnie Mandela]'.

Ayob, Ismail

(1942–). Qualified as a barrister in London and returned to South Africa where he practised law from 1969, acting mainly for opponents of the apartheid regime. He served as an attorney for Mandela while he was in prison and for some years after his release. The pair split acrimoniously in 2004.

Benson, Mary

(1919–2000). A friend of Mandela's, Benson was a journalist, author, and anti-apartheid activist. After serving as an aide to various generals in World War II she settled in England. She returned to South Africa in 1957 and worked to raise funds for the defence of Mandela and 155 other accused in the Treason Trial. Mandela visited her in London on his clandestine trip out of South Africa in 1962. Among her books is *Mandela: The Man and the Movement* (New York: W. W. Norton, 1986).

Bernstein, Lionel (Rusty)

(1920–2002). Architect and anti-apartheid activist. Leading member of the Communist Party of South Africa. Founding member and leader of the Congress of Democrats, one of the participating organisations in the 1955 Congress of the People at which the Freedom Charter was adopted. Defendant in the 1956 Treason Trial. After being acquitted in the Rivonia Trial, he and his wife, Hilda, went into exile (they crossed into neighbouring Botswana on foot). He remained a leading member of the ANC, whilst practising as an architect.

Bizos, George
(1927–). Greek-born human rights lawyer. Member and co-founder of the National Council of Lawyers for Human Rights. Committee member of the ANC's Legal and Constitutional Committee. Legal advisor for the Convention for a Democratic South Africa. Defence lawyer in the Rivonia Trial. Also acted for high-profile anti-apartheid activists, including the families of Steve Biko, Chris Hani, and the Cradock Four during the trials of the Truth and Reconciliation Commission. Appointed by Mandela to South Africa's Judicial Services Commission.

Botha, P. W.
(1916–2006). Prime minister of South Africa, 1978–84. First executive state president, 1984–89. Advocate of the apartheid system. In 1985 Mandela rejected Botha's offer to release him on the condition that he rejected violence. Botha refused to testify at the Truth and Reconciliation Commission in 1998 about apartheid crimes.

Brandfort
A small town in the Free State province that was established in the mid-1800s in honour of President Brand of the then Orange Free State (now Free State) after he visited a church on a farm. It housed a British concentration camp for Boer women and children during the Second Boer War (1899–1902). Prime Minister H. F. Verwoerd completed his high school education in the town. Winnie Mandela was banished there by the apartheid regime in 1977 and lived there until 1985.

Buthelezi (née Mzila), Irene
A family friend and also the wife of Chief Mangosuthu Buthelezi. Mandela also refers to her as Mndhlunkulu and Umdlunkulu, a royal term. When Mandela worked in the mines in 1942 and 1943 he stayed at the Witwatersrand Native Labour Association Compound. It was here that he met Irene Mzila, the daughter of the compound manager.

Buthelezi, Mangosuthu Gatsha (also called by his clan name Shenge; Mandela sometimes spelled his surname Butelezi and sometimes spelled his first name as Mangosutu)
(1928–). South African politician and Zulu prince. Founder and president of the Inkatha Freedom Party in 1975. Chief minister of the KwaZulu Bantustan. Appointed South African minister of home affairs 1994–2004, and acted as president several times during Mandela's presidency.

Cachalia (née Asvat), Amina (also referred to as Aminabehn or Aminaben – *ben* is the Gujarati word for 'sister')
(1930–2013). Anti-apartheid and women's rights activist. Member of the ANC and Transvaal Indian Congress. Co-founder and treasurer of the Federation of South African Women. Founder of the Women's Progressive Union. Married Yusuf Cachalia. Banning orders from 1963 to 1978 prevented her from attending social gatherings or political meetings, entering any place of education or publishing house, and leaving the magisterial district of Johannesburg.

Cachalia, Ismail Ahmad (Maulvi)
(1908–2003). Anti-apartheid activist. Leading member of the South African Indian Congress, Transvaal Indian Congress and ANC. Key participant in the 1946 Passive Resistance Campaign. Deputy volunteer-in-chief to Mandela in the

1952 Defiance Campaign, and amongst the twenty accused in the Defiance Campaign Trial. With Moses Kotane, he attended the Bandung Conference, a meeting of African-Asian states focused on peace, decolonisation, and African-Asian economic development, in Bandung, Indonesia, in 1955. Fled to Botswana in 1964 and set up ANC offices in New Delhi. His father, Ahmad Mohamed Cachalia, was a close associate of Gandhi's and was chairperson of the Transvaal British Indian Association, 1908–18.

Cachalia, Yusuf

(1915–95). Political activist. Secretary of the South African Indian Congress. Brother of Maulvi Cachalia. Husband of Amina Cachalia. Co-accused with Mandela and eighteen others in the 1952 Defiance Campaign Trial. They were convicted and sentenced to nine months imprisonment, suspended for two years. Banned continuously from 1953.

Carlson, Joel

(1926–2001). One of Mandela's attorneys who began representing opponents of apartheid after his 1957 exposé of the brutal working conditions of farmworkers. He presented nearly 100 cases of torture to the courts. Several attempts were made on his life and he left South Africa in 1971 and lived in the United States of America.

Chiba, Isu (Laloo)

(1930–2017). Anti-apartheid activist. Member of the South African Communist Party and Transvaal Indian Congress. Platoon commander of MK. Tortured by the South African security police causing him to lose the hearing in one of his ears. Member of MK's Second National High Command, for which he was sentenced to eighteen years' imprisonment, which he served on Robben Island. Assisted in transcribing Mandela's autobiographical manuscript in prison. Released in 1982. Member of the United Democratic Front. MP, 1994–2004. Received the Order of Luthuli in Silver in 2004 for his lifetime contribution to the struggle for a non-racial, non-sexist, just, and democratic South Africa.

Coetsee, Hendrik (Kobie)

(1931–2000). South African politician, lawyer, administrator, and negotiator. Deputy minister for defence and national intelligence, 1978. Minister of justice, 1980. Held meetings with Mandela from 1985 about creating the conditions for talks between the National Party and the ANC. Elected president of the Senate following South Africa's first democratic elections in 1994.

Communist Party South Africa (Communist Party of South Africa)

(*See* South African Communist Party.)

Congress Alliance

Established in the 1950s and made up of the ANC, South African Indian Congress, Congress of Democrats and the South African Coloured People's Organisation. When the South African Congress of Trade Unions was established in 1955, it became the fifth member of the Alliance. It was instrumental in organising the Congress of the People and mobilising clauses for inclusion in the Freedom Charter.

Congress of the People
The Congress of the People was the culmination of a year-long campaign where members of the Congress Alliance visited homes across the length and breadth of South Africa recording people's demands for a free South Africa, which were included in the Freedom Charter. Held 25–26 June 1955 in Kliptown, Johannesburg, it was attended by 3,000 delegates. The Freedom Charter was adopted on the second day of the Congress.

Cyprian, King Bhekuzulu Nyangayezizwe kaSolomon
(1924–68). King of the Zulu nation from 1948 until his death in 1968. He succeeded his father, King Solomon kaDinizulu. He was the father of the current king of the Zulus, Goodwill Zwelithini.

Dadoo, Dr. Yusuf
(1909–83). Medical doctor, anti-apartheid activist and orator. President of South African Indian Congress. Deputy to Oliver Tambo on the Revolutionary Council of MK. Chairman of the South African Communist Party, 1972–83. Leading member of the ANC. First jailed in 1940 for anti-war activities, and then for six months during the 1946 Passive Resistance Campaign. Was among the twenty accused with Mandela in the 1952 Defiance Campaign Trial. He went underground during the 1960 State of Emergency, and into exile to escape arrest. Awarded the ANC's highest honour, Isitwalandwe Seaparankoe, in 1955 at the Congress of the People.

Dalindyebo, Buyelekhaya Zwelibanzi a Sabata
(1964–). The son of Sabata Jonguhlanga Dalindyebo, he reigned as Thembu king from 1989 until December 2015 when he was imprisoned for offences including culpable homicide, kidnapping, arson, and assault. He was customarily dethroned as a result.

Dalindyebo, Chief Jongintaba
(d. 1942). Chief and regent of the Thembu people. Became Mandela's guardian following his father's death. Mandela went to live with him at the Great Place at Mqhekezweni when he was twelve years old.

Dalindyebo, King Sabata Jonguhlanga
(1928–86). Paramount chief of the Transkei, 1954–80. Leader of the Democratic Progressive Party. Nephew of Chief Jongintaba Dalindyebo. Fled to Zambia in 1980 after being convicted of violating the dignity of President Matanzima of the Transkei. Sabata was the great-grandson of King Ngangelizwe.

Daniels, Edward (Eddie; Mandela sometimes refers to him as Danie)
(1928–2017). Political activist. Member of the Liberal Party of South Africa. Member of the African Resistance Movement which sabotaged non-human targets as a statement against the government. Served a fifteen-year sentence in Robben Island Prison where he was held in B Section with Mandela. He was banned immediately after his release in 1979. Received the Order of Luthuli in Silver from the South African government in 2005.

de Klerk, Frederik Willem (F. W.)
(1936–). Lawyer. President of South Africa, 1989–94. Leader of the National Party,

1989–97. In February 1990 he unbanned the ANC and other organisations and released Mandela from prison. Deputy president with Thabo Mbeki under Mandela from 1994 to 1996. Leader of New National Party, 1997. Awarded the Prince of Asturias Award in 1992 and the Nobel Peace Prize in 1993 with Nelson Mandela, for his role in the peaceful end to apartheid.

Defiance Campaign Against Unjust Laws (Mandela also refers to it as the Defiance Campaign)

Initiated by the ANC in December 1951, and launched with the South African Indian Congress on 26 June 1952, against six apartheid laws. The campaign involved individuals breaking racist laws such as entering premises reserved for 'whites only', breaking curfews, and courting arrest. Mandela was appointed national volunteer-in-chief and Maulvi Cachalia as his deputy. Over 8,500 volunteers were imprisoned for their participation in the Defiance Campaign.

Dingake, Michael Kitso

(1928–). Joined the African National Congress in 1952 and went into hiding after the Rivonia arrests in 1963. He left South Africa to work underground. As he was born in the British protectorate of Bechuanaland (Botswana) he had the protection of the British government. Nevertheless, in 1965 he was taken off a train in Southern Rhodesia and unlawfully handed over to South African police. He was driven to South Africa where he was tortured, charged, and convicted for sabotage. He was sentenced to fifteen years' imprisonment which he served in the same section on Robben Island as Mandela. In late 1967 he was transferred from the island to Pretoria where he was again tortured for information. A few weeks later he was returned to Robben Island. On his release in 1981 he was repatriated to Botswana.

Fischer, Abram (Bram)

(1908–75). Lawyer and political and anti-apartheid activist. Leader of the Communist Party of South Africa. Member of the Congress of Democrats. Charged with incitement for his involvement in the African Mine Workers' Strike for better wages in 1946. Successfully defended Mandela and other leading ANC members in the Treason Trial. Led the defence in the Rivonia Trial, 1963–64. Continually subjected to banning orders, and in 1966 he was sentenced to life imprisonment for violating the Suppression of Communism Act and conspiring to commit sabotage. Awarded the Lenin Peace Prize in 1967.

Freedom Charter

A statement of the principles of the Congress Alliance, adopted at the Congress of the People in Kliptown, Soweto, on 26 June 1955. The Congress Alliance rallied thousands of volunteers across South Africa to record the demands of the people. The Freedom Charter espoused equal rights for all South Africans regardless of race, as well as land reform, improved working and living conditions, the fair distribution of wealth, compulsory education, and fairer laws. The Freedom Charter was a powerful tool used in the fight against apartheid.

Goldberg, Denis

(1933–). Anti-apartheid and political activist. Member of the South African Communist Party. Co-founder and leader of the Congress of Democrats. Technical officer in

MK. Arrested at Rivonia in 1963 and subsequently served a life sentence in Pretoria Local Prison. On his release in 1985 he went into exile in the UK and represented the ANC at the Anti-Apartheid Committee of the United Nations. Founded Community HEART in 1995 to help poor black South Africans. Returned to South Africa in 2002 and was appointed special advisor to Minister of Water Affairs and Forestry Ronnie Kasrils, who was named as a co-conspriator in the Rivonia Trial.

Gumede, Archibald Jacob
(1914–98). The son of Josiah Tshangana Gumede a founder of the South African Native National Conference (SANNC), a precursor to the ANC, Gumede, an anti-apartheid activist and lawyer, joined the ANC in 1949. He was an accused with Nelson Mandela and 154 others in the infamous 1956 Treason Trial which went on for four and a half years and resulted in all the accused being acquitted. In 1983 he was elected as a joint president with Albertina Sisulu and Oscar Mpetha of the United Democratic Front. He and a group of activists famously sought refuge in the British consulate in Durban in 1984 when the security police threatened to detain them, which they did when they left the building after ninety days. They were charged with high treason. Charges against Gumede and eleven others were withdrawn in December 1985 and also for the four remaining accused in June 1986.

Guzana, Knowledge (Mandela refers to him as Dambisa)
(1916–unknown). A fellow student at University College of Fort Hare with Mandela, he went on to a political career in the Transkei after qualifying as an attorney. He was the leader of the New Democratic Party in the Transkei which rejected 'independence' of black homelands or Bantustans. He led the party until 1976 when he was replaced by Hector Ncokazi.

Gwala, Harry (also called by his clan name Mphephethe) Themba
(1920–95). Known as 'The Lion of the Midlands', he was a school teacher and activist in the South African Communist Party and the ANC Youth League. In 1964 he was arrested and charged with sabotage for recruiting people to MK. He was sentenced to eight years in prison and served his sentence on Robben Island until 1972. He was arrested again in 1975 and sentenced to life imprisonment and sent again to Robben Island. He contracted motor neuron disease, which led to the loss of the use of his arms. As a consequence of his illness he was released in 1988. In 1992 he was awarded the ANC's highest honour, Isitwalandwe Seaparankoe.

Healdtown
Healdtown was a boarding school in Fort Beaufort, run by the Methodist Church. Nelson Mandela enrolled there in 1937 and completed his matric there in 1938. He took up long-distance running there and in his second year became a prefect.

Joseph (née Fennell), Helen
(1905–92). Teacher, social worker, and anti-apartheid and women's rights activist. Founding member of the Congress of Democrats. National secretary of Federation of South African Women. Leading organiser of the 1956 Women's March of 20,000 women to Pretoria's Union Buildings. An accused in the 1956 Treason Trial. Placed under house arrest in 1962. Helped care for Zindziswa and Zenani Mandela

when their parents were both imprisoned. Awarded the ANC's highest honour, Isitwalandwe Seaparankoe, in 1992.

Jozana, Xoliswa
(1952–). A daughter of K. D. Matanzima's by Princess Nosango. In 2017 she retired from the Department of Rural Development and Land Reform in South Africa where she was the chief director responsible for co-operation and development.

Kantor, James
(1927–75). Lawyer. Despite not being a member of the ANC or MK, he was put on trial at Rivonia, possibly due to the fact that his brother-in-law and business partner was Harold Wolpe who had been arrested at Liliesleaf Farm and named as a co-conspirator in the Rivonia Trial. Was later acquitted and fled South Africa.

Kathrada, Ahmed
(1929–2017). Anti-apartheid activist, politician, political prisoner, and MP. Leading member of the ANC and of the South African Communist Party. Founding member of the Transvaal Indian Volunteer Corps and its successor, the Transvaal Indian Youth Congress. Co-accused with Mandela in the Defiance Campaign Trial of 1952, and one of the last twenty-eight accused in the Treason Trial who were acquitted in 1961. Placed under house arrest in 1962. Arrested at Liliesleaf Farm in July 1963 and charged with sabotage in the Rivonia Trial. Imprisoned on Robben Island, 1964–82, then Pollsmoor Prison until his release on 15 October 1989. MP from 1994, after South Africa's first democratic elections, and served as political advisor to President Mandela. Chairperson of the Robben Island Council, 1994–2006. Awarded Isitwalandwe Seaparankoe, the ANC's highest honour, in 1992; the Pravasi Bharatiya Samman Award from the President of India; and several honorary doctorates.

Kente, Gibson
(1932–2004). Considered by many to be the father of black theatre in South Africa, between 1960 and 1990 he produced more than twenty plays in the genre of what became known as the 'township musical'. He wrote music for Miriam Makeba in the 1950s. Mandela refers to him as 'nephew' in his letter to him as they were both from the Madiba clan.

Kruger, James (Jimmy)
(1917–87). Politician. Minister of justice and police, 1974–79. President of the Senate, 1979–80. Member of the National Party. Infamously remarked that Steve Biko's death in detention in 1977 left him 'cold'.

Le Grange, Louis L.
(1928–91). Joined the cabinet of the ruling National Party in 1975. In 1979 to 1980 he served as minister of prisons and from 1979 to 1982 as minister of police. From 1982 to 1986 he was minister of law and order.

Lukhele, Douglas (Duggie)
Former legal colleague. Moved to Swaziland and became the attorney-general there. He did his articles at the firm Mandela and Tambo in the 1950s.

/

Luthuli, Chief Albert John Mvumbi
(1898–1967). Teacher, anti-apartheid activist, and minister of religion. Chief of Groutville Reserve. President-general of the ANC, 1952–67. From 1953 he was confined to his home by government bans. Defendant in the 1956 Treason Trial. Sentenced to six months (suspended) in 1960 after publicly burning his passbook and calling for a national day of mourning following the Sharpeville Massacre. Awarded the Nobel Peace Prize in 1960 for his non-violent role in the struggle against apartheid. Awarded the ANC's highest honour, Isitwalandwe Seaparankoe, in 1955 at the Congress of the People.

Luthuli, Nokhukhanya
The wife of Chief Albert Luthuli. When Mandela writes Nkosikazi Luthuli, it means Mrs. Luthuli.

Madikizela, Columbus Kokani
Also known as C. K., he was Winnie Mandela's father. In letters to his wife, Mandela referred respectfully to him as Bawo. A history teacher, he later became the minister of forestry and agriculture in the Transkei government under K. D. Matanzima.

Madikizela-Mandela, Nomzamo Winifred (Winnie, Nobandla, Nomzamo, Mhlope, Zami and Ngutyana)
(1936–2018). Social worker and anti-apartheid and women's rights activist. Member of the ANC. Married to Nelson Mandela, 1958–96 (separated 1992). Mother of Zenani and Zindziswa Mandela. First qualified black medical social worker at the Baragwanath Hospital in Johannesburg. Held in solitary confinement for seventeen months in 1969. Placed under house arrest from 1970 and subjected to a series of banning orders from 1962 to 1987. Established the Black Women's Federation, 1975, and the Black Parents' Association, 1976, in response to the Soweto Uprising. President of the ANC Women's League, 1993–2003. ANC MP.

Maharaj, Sathyandranath (Mac)
(1935–). Academic, politician, political and anti-apartheid activist, political prisoner, and MP. Leading member of the ANC, South African Communist Party, and MK. Convicted of sabotage in 1964 and sentenced to twelve years' imprisonment which he served on Robben Island. Helped to secretly transcribe Mandela's autobiography, *Long Walk to Freedom,* and smuggled it out of prison when he was released in 1976. Commanded Operation Vulindlela (Vula), an ANC underground operation to establish an internal underground leadership. Maharaj served on the secretariat of the Convention for a Democratic South Africa. Minister of transport, 1994–99. Former envoy to former president Jacob Zuma.

Maki
(*See* Mandela, Makaziwe.)

Mandela (née Mase), Evelyn Ntoko (also referred to as Mqwati or Ntoko)
(1922–2004). Nurse. Married to Nelson Mandela, 1944–57. Mother to Madiba Thembekile (1945–69), Makaziwe (1947) who died at nine months old, Makgatho (1950–2005) and Makaziwe (1954–). Cousin of Walter Sisulu who first introduced her to Mandela. Married a retired Sowetan businessman, Simon Rakeepile, in 1998.

Mandela, Madiba Thembekile (Thembi; Mandela also spells it Tembi sometimes)
(1945–69). Mandela's eldest son to his first wife, Evelyn. Died in a car accident.

Mandela, Makaziwe
(1947). Mandela's first-born daughter to his first wife, Evelyn. Died at nine months old.

Mandela, Makaziwe (Maki)
(1954–). Mandela's eldest daughter to his first wife, Evelyn.

Mandela, Makgatho (Kgatho)
(1950–2005). Mandela's second-born son to his first wife, Evelyn. Lawyer. Died of AIDS complications on 6 January 2005 in Johannesburg following the death of his second wife, Zondi Mandela, who died from pneumonia as a complication of AIDS in July 2003.

Mandela, Mandla Zwelivelile
(1974–). Mandela's oldest grandson and first-born child of Makgatho Mandela. He is now Chief of the Mvezo Traditional Council.

Mandela, Nandi
(1968–). Mandela's second grandchild and youngest daughter of Thembekile and Thoko Mandela. She was a year old when her father was killed in a car accident.

Mandela, Ndileka
(1965–). Mandela's first grandchild and eldest daughter of Thembekile and Thoko Mandela. She was four years old when her father was killed in a car accident.

Mandela, Nkosi Mphakanyiswa Gadla
(d. 1930). Chief, counsellor, and advisor. Descendant of the Ixhiba house. Mandela's father. Deprived of his chieftainship following a dispute with a local white magistrate.

Mandela, Nolusapho Rose Rayne (referred to as 'Rennie')
The mother of Mandela's grandson Mandla Mandela. She was married to Mandela's second son Makgatho.

Mandela, Nosekeni Fanny
(d. 1968). Mandela's mother. Third wife of Nkosi Mphakanyiswa Gadla Mandela.

Mandela, Thoko (aka Molly de Jager)
The wife of Thembekile Mandela and the mother of their two daughters. She was in the car accident which killed her husband and her sister Irene Simelane. Her brother was injured in the same accident. Newspaper articles on the accident refer to her as Molly de Jager which is a name she adopted from a relative which meant she could be classified under apartheid laws as coloured and live in a better area. Mandela also refers to her as *molokazana* which means daughter-in-law. After her husband's death she went back to her maiden surname of Mhlanga.

Mandela, Winnie
(*See* Madikizela-Mandela, Nomzamo Winifred.)

Mandela, Zenani (Zeni) Nomadabi Nosizwe
(1959–). Mandela's first-born daughter to his second wife, Winnie. Her names mean 'What have you brought?' and Battle of the Nation. She is South Africa's high commisioner to Mauritius.

Mandela, Zindziswa (Zindzi)
(1960–). Mandela's second-born daughter to his second wife, Winnie. Her first name means 'well-established'; she is named after the daughter of the Xhosa poet, Mqhayi. She is South Africa's ambassador to Denmark.

Mandela, Zoleka (1980–)
Mandela's granddaughter and only daughter of Zindziswa Mandela.

Masemola, Jafta Kgalabi ('Jeff')
(1929–90). Known as the 'Tiger of Azania', he was a member of the ANC Youth League and a founder of the armed wing of the Pan Africanist Congress. After being arrested in 1962 and charged with sabotage for blowing up power lines and smuggling freedom fighters out of South Africa, he was sentenced to life imprisonment on July 1963. On 13 October 1989, while still in prison, he met with Nelson Mandela at Victor Verster Prison. It was rumoured that they discussed unity between the ANC and the PAC. He was released from prison on 15 October 1989, and on 17 April 1990 he was killed in a mysterious car accident.

Matanzima, Kaiser Daliwonga (K. D.) (also referred to as Wonga)
(1915–2003). Thembu chief and politician. Mandela's nephew. Member of the United Transkei Territorial Council, 1955, and an executive member of the Transkei Territorial Authority, 1956. Chief minister of the Transkei, 1963. Established and led the Transkeian National Independence Party with his brother George Matanzima. First prime minister of the Transkei Bantustan when it gained nominal independence in 1976. State president of the Transkei, 1979–86. He was the great-grandson of King Matanzima.

Matanzima, Mthetho
(d. 1972). A son of K. D. Matanzima's by Princess Dade. He was educated at University College of Fort Hare, passing his law examination in 1968. Chief of the Noqayti region. He died in 1972.

Matthews, Frieda Deborah Bokwe
(1905–98). The daughter of Reverend John Knox Bokwe, a leading Xhosa intellectual and hymn writer of the 1880s. She was one of the first black women to earn a university degree in South Africa. A teacher herself, she married educationalist Z. K. Matthews. She published *Remembrances* in 1984.

Matthews, Vincent Joseph Gaobakwe (Bakwe)
(1929–2010). Matthews was the son of Professor Z. K. Matthews and Frieda Matthews. Both he and his father were charged with treason in 1956 along with 154 other anti-apartheid activists. He qualified as an attorney and while in exile became assis-

tant attorney-general of Botswana. He returned to South Africa in 1992 and that year left the ANC. He was a member of Parliament for the Inkatha Freedom Party from 1994 and deputy minister of safety and security from 1994 to 1999.

Matthews, Professor Zachariah Keodirelang (Z. K.)
(1901–68). Academic, politician, and anti-apartheid activist. Member of the ANC. First black South African to obtain a BA degree at a South African institution, 1923. First black South African to obtain an LLB degree in South Africa, 1930. Conceptualised the Congress of the People and the Freedom Charter. Following the Sharpeville Massacre, with Chief Albert Luthuli he organised a 'stay-away', a national day of mourning, which took place on 28 March 1960. In 1965 he retired to Botswana, and became its ambassador to the USA.

Mbeki, Archibald Mvuyelwa Govan (clan name, Zizi)
(1910–2001). Historian and anti-apartheid activist. Leading member of the ANC and the South African Communist Party. Served on the High Command of MK. Father of Thabo Mbeki (president of South Africa, 1999–2008). Convicted in the Rivonia Trial and sentenced to life imprisonment. Released from Robben Island Prison, 1987. Served in South Africa's post-apartheid Senate, 1994–1997, as deputy president of the Senate, and its successor, the National Council of Provinces, 1997–99. Awarded the ANC's highest honour, Isitwalandwe Seaparankoe, in 1980.

Meer, Professor Fatima (also referred to as Fatimabehn and Fatimaben – *ben* means sister in Gujarati)
(1928–2010). Writer, academic, and anti-apartheid and women's rights activist. Married Ismail Meer, 1950. Established Student Passive Resistance Committee in support of the 1946 Passive Resistance Campaign against apartheid. Founding member of Federation of South African Women. First black woman to be appointed as a lecturer at a white South African university (University of Natal), 1956. Banned from 1953 and escaped an assassination attempt. She embraced the Black Consciousness ideology. Founded the Institute of Black Research, 1975. First president of the Black Women's Federation, established in 1975. Author of *Higher Than Hope* (published 1988), the first authorised biography of Mandela.

Meer, Ismail Chota I. C.
(1918–2000). Lawyer and anti-apartheid activist. He met and befriended Nelson Mandela in 1946 when they were studying law at the University of the Witwatersrand in Johannesburg. He joined the Communist Party of South Africa while at university and played pivotal roles in the 1946 Passive Resistance Campaign and the 1952 Defiance Campaign as well as participated in the drawing up of the Freedom Charter. He was married to Professor Fatima Meer.

Mhlaba, Raymond (clan name, Ndobe)
(1920–2005). Anti-apartheid activist, politician, diplomat, and political prisoner. Leading member of ANC and South African Communist Party. Commander-in-chief of MK. Arrested in 1963 at Rivonia and sentenced to life imprisonment at the Rivonia Trial. Imprisoned on Robben Island until he was transferred to Pollsmoor Prison in 1982. Released in 1989. He was involved in the negotiations with the National Party government leading to the democratisation of South Africa. Member of the ANC National Executive Committee, 1991. Premier of the Eastern Cape, 1994.

South African high commissioner to Uganda, 1997. Awarded the ANC's highest honour, Isitwalandwe Seaparankoe, in 1992.

MK
(*See* Umkhonto weSizwe.)

Mkwayi, Wilton Zimasile (clan name, Mbona; nickname, Bri Bri)
(1923–2004). Trade unionist, political activist, and political prisoner. Member of the ANC and South African Congress of Trade Unions. Union organiser for African Textile Workers in Port Elizabeth. Volunteer in the 1952 Defiance Campaign, and later active in the campaign for the Congress of the People. Escaped during the 1956 Treason Trial and went to Lesotho. Joined MK and had military training in the People's Republic of China. Became MK's commander-in-chief after the arrests at Liliesleaf Farm. Convicted and sentenced to life in what became known as the Little Rivonia Trial. He served his sentence on Robben Island. Released October 1989. Elected to the Senate in the National Assembly in 1994, then deployed to the Eastern Cape Provincial Legislature, where he served until his retirement from public life in 1999. Awarded the ANC's highest honour, Isitwalandwe Seaparankoe, in 1992.

Mlangeni, Andrew Mokete (clan name, Motlokwa; nickname, Mpandla)
(1926–). Anti-apartheid activist, political prisoner, and MP. Member of the ANC Youth League, ANC and MK. Convicted at the Rivonia Trial in 1963 and sentenced to life imprisonment. Served eighteen years on Robben Island and was transferred to Pollsmoor Prison in 1982. Awarded the ANC's highest honour, Isitwalandwe Seaparankoe, in 1992.

Motlana, Ntatho Harrison
(1925–2008). Dr. Ntatho Motlana, a medical doctor, community leader, political campaigner, businessman, and close friend of Nelson and Winnie Mandela. He entered extra-parliamentary politics in the 1940s and was appointed secretary of the ANC Youth League in 1949. Charged with Mandela and eighteen others in the Defiance Campaign Trial of 1952. He served two banning orders and one period of detention. In the 1970s he helped to establish the Black Parents' Association to help those affected by the 1976 student uprising. He also founded the Committee of Ten, an influential organisation of Soweto residents. In the 1980s he led the Soweto Civic Association, a body affiliated to the broad-based United Democratic Front.

Motsoaledi, Elias (clan name, Mokoni)
(1924–94). Trade unionist, anti-apartheid activist, and political prisoner. Member of the ANC, South African Communist Party, and Council of Non-European Trade Unions. Banned after the 1952 Defiance Campaign. Helped to establish the South African Congress of Trade Unions in 1955. Imprisoned for four months during the 1960 State of Emergency and detained again under the ninety-day detention laws of 1963. Sentenced to life imprisonment at the Rivonia Trial and imprisoned on Robben Island from 1964 to 1989. Elected to the ANC's National Executive Committee following his release. Awarded the ANC's highest honour, Isitwalandwe Seaparankoe, in 1992.

Mpetha, Oscar
(1909–94). A trade unionist and political activist from the Transkei, he joined the ANC in 1951 and in 1958 became president of the Cape ANC. In 1983 he was sen-

tenced to five years in prison for inciting a riot in which two white people were killed. In the same year, he was elected as one of three co-presidents of the newly formed United Democratic Front. He served most of his prison sentence wheelchair-bound in hospital after both legs had been amputated due to diabetes. He was released on 15 October 1989 with a group of prisoners including the last remaining Rivonia trialists.

Naicker, Dr. Gangathura Mohambry (Monty)

(1910–78). Medical doctor, politician, and anti-apartheid activist. Co-founder and first chairperson of the Anti-Segregation Council. President of the Natal Indian Congress, 1945–63. Signatory of the 'Doctor's Pact' of March 1947, a statement of cooperation between the ANC, Transvaal Indian Congress, and Natal Indian Congress, which was also signed by Dr. Albert Xuma (president of the ANC) and Dr. Yusuf Dadoo (president of the TIC).

Naidoo, Indres Elatchininatha

(1936–2016). A member of the South African Communist Party and the Transvaal Indian Congress, he spent ten years on Robben Island for his activities on behalf of MK. On his release he published the book *Island in Chains: Prisoner 885/63*. A son of Ama and Thambi 'Naran' Naidoo and brother to Shanti Naidoo.

Naidoo, 'Shanti' Shanthivathie

(1935–). The eldest of five children of Ama and Thambi 'Naran' Naidoo, she became a political activist while still at school. She was a member of the Transvaal Indian Congress and the Federation of South African Women. Banned from the 1960s, she was detained in 1969. When she refused to testify against Winnie Mandela she was convicted and sentenced to two months in prison. Her banning orders meant that she could not visit her brother Indres Naidoo who was imprisoned on Robben Island from 1963 for ten years. She was refused permission to leave the country until 1972 and visited him in prison for the first time before she left South Africa. She lived in England and at the ANC's school in Tanzania. She returned to South Africa with her husband Dominic Tweedie in 1991.

Nair, Billy

(1929–2008). Politician, anti-apartheid activist, political prisoner, and MP. Member of the ANC, Natal Indian Congress, South African Communist Party, South African Congress of Trade Unions, and MK. Named as co-conspirator in the Rivonia Trial, he was charged with sabotage in 1963 and imprisoned on Robben Island for twenty years. Joined the United Democratic Front on his release. Arrested in 1990 and accused of being part of Operation Vula, an underground operation to smuggle freedom fighters into South Africa and keep the lines of communication open with ANC leaders in prison, at home, or in exile. MP in the new democratic South Africa.

National Party

Conservative South African political party established in Bloemfontein in 1914 by Afrikaner nationalists. Governing party of South Africa, June 1948 to May 1994. Enforced apartheid, a system of legal racial segregation that favoured minority rule by the white population. Disbanded in 2004.

Ngoyi, Lilian Masediba

(1911–80). Politician, anti-apartheid and women's rights activist, and orator. Leading member of the ANC. First woman elected to the ANC Executive Committee, 1956.

President of the ANC Women's League. President of Federation of South African Women, 1956. Led the Women's March against pass laws, 1956. Charged and acquitted in the Treason Trial. Detained in the 1960 State of Emergency. Detained and held in solitary confinement for seventy-one days in 1963 under the ninety-day detention law. Continuously subjected to banning orders. Awarded the ANC's highest honour, Isitwalandwe Seaparankoe, in 1982.

Njongwe, James 'Jimmy' Lowell Zwelinzima

(1919–76). One of the first two black male graduates of the University of the Witwatersrand medical school in 1946, he was the first black medical doctor to open a practice in Port Elizabeth in the Eastern Cape. He was on the executive of the ANC Youth League and later president of the ANC in the Cape. He was banned and forced to resign from his position. He left Port Elizabeth and established his practice in Matatiele in the Transkei. He was detained in the 1960 State of Emergency.

Nokwe, Philemon Pearce Dumasile Nokwe (Duma)

(1927–78). Political activist and advocate. Taught by O.R. Tambo at St. Peter's High School, Johannesburg and was elected to the executive of the ANC Youth League while a student. He was, with Mandela, in the last group of accused in the 1956 Treason Trial. He attended Mandela's marriage to Winnie Madikizela. Nokwe served as the secretary-general of the ANC from 1958 to 1969. Named as co-conspirator in the Rivonia Trial. He went into exile in 1963 and died in Zambia.

OR

(See Tambo, Oliver.)

Pan Africanist Congress

Breakaway organisation of the ANC founded in 1959 by Robert Sobukwe, who championed the philosophy of 'Africa for Africans'. The PAC's campaigns included a nationwide protest against pass laws, ten days before the ANC was to start its own campaign. It culminated in the Sharpeville Massacre on 21 March 1960, in which police shot dead sixty-nine unarmed protesters. Banned, along with the ANC, in April 1960. Unbanned on 2 February 1990.

Paton, Alan

(1903–88). Teacher and author of the famous South African novel *Cry, the Beloved Country* (published 1948). Principal of the Diepkloof Reformatory, 1935–49. In 1953 he founded the Liberal Party of South Africa which fought against the apartheid legislation of the ruling National Party. He gave evidence in mitigation of sentence at the Rivonia Trial for Nelson Mandela and his colleagues.

Pogrund, Benjamin

(1933–). A journalist and friend of Mandela's, he worked for the *Rand Daily Mail* from 1958 and covered the Sharpeville Massacre on 21 March 1960. Mandela soon told him of his belief that the days of non-violent protest were over. Pogrund moved to London in 1986.

Pollsmoor Maximum Security Prison

Prison in the suburb of Tokai, Cape Town. Mandela was moved there along with Walter Sisulu, Raymond Mhlaba, Andrew Mlangeni, and, later, Ahmed Kathrada in 1982.

Qunu

Rural village in South Africa's Eastern Cape province where Mandela lived after his family moved from his birthplace of Mvezo.

Ramphele, Mamphela Aletta

(1947–). Anti-apartheid activist and a founding member of the Black Consciousness Movement, medical doctor, academic, and businesswoman. When she was the partner of Steve Biko she was banished in 1977 by the apartheid regime to Tzaneen in the then Northern Transvaal (now Limpopo province) where she remained until 1984. She joined the University of Cape Town as a research fellow in 1986 and one of its vice-chancellors in 1991. In 2000 she was appointed one of the four managing directors of the World Bank.

Rivonia Trial

Trial between 1963 and 1964 in which eleven leading members of the Congress Alliance were initially charged with sabotage and faced the death penalty. Named after the suburb of Rivonia, Johannesburg, where six members of the MK High Command were arrested at their hideout, Liliesleaf Farm, on 11 July 1963. Incriminating documents, including a proposal for a guerrilla insurgency named Operation Mayibuye, were seized. Mandela, who was already serving a sentence for incitement and leaving South Africa illegally, was implicated, and his notes on guerrilla warfare and his diary from his trip through Africa in 1962 were also seized. Rather than being cross-examined as a witness, Mandela made a statement from the dock on 20 April 1964. This became his famous 'I am prepared to die' speech. On 11 June 1964, eight of the accused were convicted by Justice Qartus de Wet at the Palace of Justice in Pretoria, and the next day were sentenced to life imprisonment.

Robben Island

Island situated in Table Bay, 7 kilometres off the coast of Cape Town, measuring approximately 3.3 kilometres long and 1.9 kilometres wide. Has predominantly been used as a place of banishment and imprisonment, particularly for political prisoners, since Dutch settlement in the seventeenth century. Three men who later became South African presidents have been imprisoned there: Nelson Mandela (1964–82), Kgalema Motlanthe (1977–87) and Jacob Zuma (1963–73). It is now a World Heritage Site and museum.

Sikhakhane, Joyce Nomafa

(1943–). Journalist and anti-apartheid activist. Wrote about the families of political prisoners, including Albertina Sisulu and Winnie Mandela, which resulted in her being arrested under the Protection Against Communism Act, then re-detained under the Terrorism Act and forced to spend eighteen months in solitary confinement. Banned on her release. She fled South Africa in 1973. Employed by the Department of Intelligence in the democratic South Africa. In his letter to her, Mandela calls her Nomvula as she was engaged to a relative of his, John Fadana. They never married, as after they registered the marriage at the Magistrates Court the security police accused her of having broken her banning and restriction orders by going to the court without permission and that therefore the marriage was invalid. John Fadana was banished to the Ciskei where he married another woman and later died.

Sisulu (née Thethiwe), Nontsikelelo (Ntsiki) Albertina

(1918–2011). Nurse, midwife, anti-apartheid and women's rights activist, and MP. Leading ANC member. Married Walter Sisulu, whom she met through her nursing friend, Evelyn Mase (Mandela's first wife), 1944. Member of the ANC Women's League and Federation of South African Women. Played a leading role in the 1956 women's anti-pass protest. The first woman to be arrested under the General Law Amendment Act, 1963, during which time she was held in solitary confinement for ninety days. Continually subjected to banning orders and police harassment from 1963. She was elected as one of the three presidents of the United Democratic Front at its formation in August 1983. In 1985 she was charged with fifteen other United Democratic Front and trade union leaders for treason in what became known as the Pietermaritzburg Treason Trial. MP from 1994 until she retired in 1999. President of the World Peace Council, 1993–96. Recipient of the South African Women for Women Woman of Distinction Award 2003, in recognition of her courageous lifelong struggle for human rights and dignity.

Sisulu, Walter Ulyate Max (clan names, Xhamela – sometimes spelt by Mandela as Xamela – and Tyhopho)

(1912–2003). Anti-apartheid activist and political prisoner. Husband of Albertina Sisulu. Met Mandela in 1941 and introduced him to Lazer Sidelsky who employed him as an articled clerk. Leader of the ANC, and generally considered to be the 'father of the struggle'. Co-founder of the ANC Youth League in 1944. Charged with Mandela and eighteen others under the Suppression of Communism Act for playing a leading role in the 1952 Defiance Campaign. Arrested and later acquitted in the 1956 Treason Trial. Continually served with banning orders and placed under house arrest following the banning of the ANC and Pan Africanist Congress. Helped establish MK, and served on its High Command. Went underground in 1963 and hid at Liliesleaf Farm, in Rivonia, where he was arrested on 11 July 1963. Found guilty of sabotage at the Rivonia Trial, and sentenced to life imprisonment on 12 June 1964. He served his sentence on Robben Island and at Pollsmoor Prison. Released on 15 October 1989. One of the ANC negotiating team with the apartheid government to end white rule. Awarded the ANC's highest honour, Isitwalandwe Seaparankoe, in 1992.

South African Communist Party (also referred to as the Communist Party of South Africa)

Established in 1921 as the Communist Party of South Africa, to oppose imperialism and racist domination. Changed its name to the South African Communist Party in 1953 following its banning in 1950. The South African Communist Party was only legalised in 1990. The South African Communist Party forms one-third of the Tripartite Alliance with the ANC and Congress of South African Trade Unions.

South African Indian Congress

Founded in 1923 to oppose discriminatory laws. It comprised the Cape, Natal, and Transvaal Indian Congresses. Initially a conservative organisation whose actions were limited to petitions and deputations to authorities, a more radical leadership that favoured militant non-violent resistance came to power in the 1940s under the leadership of Yusuf Dadoo and Monty Naicker.

State of Emergency, 1960

Declared on 30 March 1960 as a response to the Sharpeville Massacre. Characterised by mass arrests and the imprisonment of most African leaders. On 8 April 1960 the ANC and PAC were banned under the Unlawful Organisations Act.

Suppression of Communism Act, No. 44, 1950

Act passed 26 June 1950, in which the state banned the South African Communist Party and any activities it deemed communist, defining 'communism' in such broad terms that anyone protesting against apartheid would be in breach of the Act.

Suzman, Helen

(1917–2009). Academic, anti-apartheid activist and politician. Lecturer in economic history, University of Witwatersrand, early anti-apartheid campaigner and later opposition MP for thirty-six years (1953–89). Entered Parliament as a representative of opposition party the United Party, before breaking away with eleven others to form the Progressive Party in 1959. The only Progressive MP to retain their seat in the 1961 election, she remained its sole representative in Parliament for thirteen years. The first (and only) opposition political leader permitted to visit Robben Island, Suzman continuously raised the issue of political prisoners in Parliament. She first met Mandela on Robben Island in 1967 and despite applying to the authorities every year to visit him in prison, was only granted permission to do so on a further seven occasions.

Tambo (née Tshukudu), Matlala Adelaide Frances (also referred to as Matlala and sometimes spelt Matlale)

(1929–2007). Nurse, community worker, and anti-apartheid and women's rights activist. Married Oliver Tambo, 1956. Member of the ANC Youth League. Participated in the Women's March, 1956. Lived in exile in London, UK, until 1990. Recipient of numerous awards including the Order of Simon of Cyrene, July 1997, the highest order given by the Anglican Church for distinguished service by lay people; and the Order of the Baobab in Gold, 2002.

Tambo, Oliver Reginald (OR) (Also referred to as Reggie, Reginald)

(1917–93). Lawyer, politician, and anti-apartheid activist. Leading member of the ANC and founder member of the ANC Youth League. Co-founder, with Mandela, one of South Africa's first African legal practices. Became secretary-general of the ANC after Walter Sisulu was banned, and deputy president of the ANC, 1958. Served with a five-year banning order, 1959. Named as a co-conspirator in the Rivonia Trial. Left South Africa in 1960 to manage the external activities of the ANC and to mobilise opposition against apartheid. Established military training camps outside South Africa. Initiated the Free Mandela Campaign in the 1980s. Lived in exile in London, UK, until 1990. Acting president of the ANC, 1967, after the death of Chief Albert Luthuli. Was elected president in 1969 at the Morogoro Conference in Tanzania, a post he held until 1991 when he became the ANC's national chairperson. Awarded the ANC's highest honour, Isitwalandwe Seaparankoe, in 1992.

Thembu royal house

Nelson Mandela was a member of the Thembu royal house, descended from King Ngubengcuka (c.1790–1830) who united the Thembu nation before it was subjected to British colonial rule.

Transkei

Transkei is a region of South Africa in what is now the Eastern Cape province. During the apartheid era, under Mandela's nephew K. D. Matanzima it accepted nominal independence with the neighbouring Ciskei as a homeland or Bantustan set aside for people of Xhosa origin.

Treason Trial

(1956–61). The Treason Trial was the apartheid government's attempt to quell the power of the Congress Alliance. From 5 December 1956, 156 individuals were arrested and charged with high treason. By the end of the trial in March 1961 all the accused either had the charges withdrawn or, in the case of the last twenty-eight accused including Mandela, were acquitted.

Umkhonto weSizwe (MK)

Umkhonto weSizwe, meaning 'spear of the nation', was founded in 1961 and is commonly known by the abbreviation MK. Nelson Mandela was its first commander-in-chief. It became the military wing of the ANC. After the 1994 elections, MK was disbanded and its soldiers incorporated into the newly formed South African National Defence Force with soldiers from the apartheid South African Defence Force, Bantustan defence forces, Inkatha Freedom Party's self-protection units, and Azanian People's Liberation Army, the military wing of the Pan Africanist Congress.

University College of Fort Hare (UFH)

Originally the South African Native College, the University College of Fort Hare was founded on the site of an old fort through the initiative of the United Free Church of Scotland. Until 1960 it was the only university for blacks in the country. It offered training to students from all over Southern Africa and from as far afield as Kenya and Uganda. The National Party government took over control of the university from 1959 and turned it into an ethnic college for Xhosa speakers. Leaders such as Nelson Mandela, Robert Mugabe, Robert Sobukwe, Mangosuthu Buthelezi, and Oliver Tambo studied there.

University of South Africa (UNISA)

UNISA is one of the largest distance education institutions in the world, and the university through which Nelson Mandela achieved his LLB degree. After he was forced to end his studies through the University of London, he continued through UNISA and graduated, in absentia, in 1989. He was able to practise as a lawyer before he was imprisoned as, in those days, only a diploma in law was necessary.

Victor Verster Prison

Low-security prison located between Paarl and Franschhoek in the Western Cape. Mandela was transferred there in 1988, and lived in a private house inside the prison compound. There is a statue of Mandela just outside the prison gates. Now named Drakenstein Correctional Centre.

Wolsey Hall

Situated in Oxford, United Kingdom, and established in 1894, Wolsey Hall is a distance education provider which caters for students at various levels and through the University of London. Mandela began his correspondence LLB studies through the University of London.

Xaba, Niki Iris Jane Nondyebo
(1932–85). Winnie Mandela's eldest sister who was detained at the same time as her in 1969. Then unmarried and called Iris Madikizela, she brought a case against the government to stop her and her fellow accused being assaulted.

Zami
(*See* Madikizela-Mandela, Nomzamo Winifred.)

Zeni
(*See* Mandela, Zenani.)

Zindzi
(*See* Mandela, Zindziswa.)

8115 Orlando West
In 1944 when Mandela married his first wife, Evelyn Mase, they were allocated a two-roomed house in Orlando East, Soweto, and early in 1947 they moved to a red-brick three-roomed matchbox house at number 8115 Orlando West. He later lived there with his second wife, Winnie Mandela. The South African government declared it a national heritage site in 1999 and it is now a museum.

PRISON TIMELINE

5 August 1962:	Nelson Mandela, wearing a coat, cap, and dark glasses, is arrested along with his friend, Cecil Williams, at a road-block at Cedara, a town outside Howick in KwaZulu-Natal. His twenty-seven and a half years in custody begins.
6 August 1962:	Appears in court in the nearby town of Pietermaritzburg and is remanded to Johannesburg.
8 August 1962:	Appears in the Johannesburg Magistrates Court in handcuffs. He is defended by attorney James Kantor. No evidence is led. He only admits his identity and is remanded until 16 August.
16 August 1962:	Appears in the Johannesburg Magistrates Court wearing a jackal-skin kaross and is remanded for trial in the Johannesburg Regional Court.
15 October 1962:	Transferred to Pretoria Local Prison. He appears in the Old Synagogue, Pretoria, which has been transformed into a 'Special Regional Court' for his trial. Mandela wears a jackal-skin kaross, shirt, khaki trousers, sandals, and a necklace in the yellow and green colours of the ANC. He complained that the last minute change of venue from Johannesburg to Pretoria was a deliberate attempt by the government to deprive him of his attorney Joe Slovo, who was restricted to Johannesburg.
22 October 1962:	Makes an hour-long speech from the dock for the recusal of the magistrate, saying that as a 'black man in a white man's court' he would not get a fair trial. He pleads not guilty to incitement in connection with calling a national strike on 29, 30 and 31 May 1961, and leaving the country without a passport. Mandela conducted his own defence, and was assisted by advocate Bob Hepple.
7 November 1962:	He is convicted of inciting workers to stay at home and on leaving the country without a passport, and is sentenced to five years in prison. He begins serving his sentence in Pretoria Local Prison.
27 May 1963:	After being transferred without reason or warning, he arrives at Robben Island Maximum Security Prison.

12 June 1963:	Transferred back to Pretoria Local Prison.
11 July 1963:	Police raid his former hideout at Liliesleaf in the Johannesburg suburb of Rivonia. Many of his comrades are arrested and held in solitary-confinement detention.
9 October 1963:	Mandela appears in the Palace of Justice in Pretoria for the first time with ten other accused in connection with 222 charges of sabotage committed between 1961 and 1965, in what becomes known as the Rivonia Trial. The case is remanded to 29 October.
29 October 1963:	He and ten others are charged with 199 acts of sabotage in the Rivonia Trial. The defence applies for the indictment to be quashed.
30 October 1963:	It is announced that one of the accused, Bob Hepple, will be called as a state witness. Charges against him are withdrawn and he is released. He did not testify and fled the country. The indictment against the remaining ten is quashed, but they are immediately rearrested in court and charged with 199 acts of sabotage.
12 November 1963:	A new indictment splitting the sabotage charges into two parts is presented in the Rivonia Trial by prosecutor Percy Yutar to Mr. Justice Galgut. The case is remanded to 25 November.
26 November 1963:	The 199 acts of sabotage are reduced to 193 and the defence applies to have the new indictment quashed. Justice de Wet dismisses the application.
3 December 1963:	Mandela and nine fellow accused plead not guilty to sabotage and the first evidence is heard. The indictment lists 24 co-conspirators, 23 of which left the country, and one of whom died in police detention.
2 March 1964:	The State's case comes to an end.
4 March 1964:	Fellow accused James Kantor is acquitted.
20 April 1964:	The defence case begins. Wearing a blue suit, Mandela makes a speech that lasts almost four hours, and famously ends it by saying that he is prepared to die for a non-racial, democratic South Africa.
11 June 1964:	In a brief judgment, Judge Quartus de Wet convicts Nelson Mandela, Walter Sisulu, Govan Mbeki, Ahmed Kathrada, Denis Goldberg, Raymond Mhlaba, Elias Motsoaledi, and Andrew Mlangeni of sabotage. Rusty Bernstein is acquitted but is immediately rearrested on another charge.

12 June 1964:	Alan Paton, president of the Liberal Party, gives evidence in mitigation of sentence for the accused. Judge Quartus de Wet sentences Mandela and seven others to life imprisonment. He says the offences were essentially 'treasonous' but that they were not charged with treason.
13 June 1964:	Nelson Mandela, Walter Sisulu, Govan Mbeki, Ahmed Kathrada, Raymond Mhlaba, Elias Motsoaledi, and Andrew Mlangeni arrive on Robben Island. (Denis Goldberg, because he is white, is sent to Pretoria Central Prison.)
24 September 1968:	His mother dies. His request to attend her funeral is refused.
13 July 1969:	His eldest son, Madiba Thembekile, is killed in a car accident. Mandela's letter to the prison authorities requesting permission to attend his funeral is ignored.
31 March 1982:	After almost eighteen years at Robben Island Maximum Security Prison, Mandela is transferred with Walter Sisulu, Raymond Mhlaba, and Andrew Mlangeni to Pollsmoor Maximum Security Prison at the foot of the mountains outside Cape Town. They held together in one large cell. On 21 October, Ahmed Kathrada joins them.
10 February 1985:	After rejecting an offer from President P. W. Botha to release him if he renounces violence as a political strategy, his statement of rejection is read out to a rally in Soweto by his daughter, Zindziswa.
3 November 1985:	Mandela is admitted to the Volks Hospital in Cape Town for prostate surgery.
17 November 1985:	Visited in hospital by South Africa's minister of justice, Kobie Coetsee, and the commissioner of prisons.
23 November 1985:	Discharged from the Volks Hospital and returned to Pollsmoor Prison, but held separately from his comrades. During this period he begins exploratory talks with members of the government over the creation of conditions for negotiations with the ANC.
11 June 1988:	A twelve-hour pop concert to celebrate Mandela's seventieth birthday, held at Wembley Stadium, London, UK, is broadcast to sixty-seven countries.
12 August 1988:	Admitted to Tygerberg Hospital in Bellville, Cape Town.
13 August 1988:	Diagnosed with tuberculosis and pleural effusion.

31 August 1988: Transferred from Tygerberg Hospital to Constantiaberg MediClinic, Cape Town, where his tuberculosis treatment continues.

7 December 1988: Discharged from Constantiaberg MediClinic and transferred to Victor Verster Prison near Paarl where he is housed in a bungalow once occupied by a former prison warder.

8 December 1988: He is visited by Minister of Justice Kobie Coetsee who tells Mandela that it has been decided that he will be held in the house so that he can continue the discussions he began with government officials in 1986.

17 May 1989: Graduates with an LLB degree in absentia at the University of South Africa.

5 July 1989: Meets President P. W. Botha in his office in Cape Town.

15 October 1989: The remaining Rivonia Trialists, apart from Mandela, are released from prison.

13 December 1989: He is driven before dawn from prison to meet President F. W. de Klerk at his office in Cape Town.

9 February 1990: He is taken to Tuynhuys in Cape Town to meet President F. W. de Klerk.

11 February 1990: He is released from Victor Verster Prison at 4:22 p.m. He addresses a crowd from the balcony of the City Hall in Cape Town and spends the night at Archbishop Desmond Tutu's official residence in Bishopscourt.

MAP OF SOUTH AFRICA, c.1996

East Rand
Benoni
Germiston
Kempton Park

Pretoria
Monument Hill

Johannesburg
Bantu Men's Social
Centre
Braamfontein
Coronation Hospital
Ferreirastown
Killarney
Milner Park
Mzila
Nasrec

Soweto
Baragwanathan Hospital
Donaldson Orlando
Community Centre
Jabavu
Moroka

Gazankulu

LIMPOPO

Lebowa

Nylstroom

White River

Nelspruit

Zeerust

Mmabatho

Mafikeng

NORTH WEST

Potchefstroom

Klerksdorp

Kuruman

Vryburg

Kroonstad

Wallmansthal

PRETORIA

GAUTENG

Witbank

MPUMALANGA

Ogies

Evaton

Bethal

Sharpeville

Boipatong Standerton

MBABANE

Manzini

SWAZILAND

Hluti

Bethlehem

Vryheid

Upington

Griekwastad

Kimberley

Welkom

FREE STATE

Brandfort

Phatakahle

**SOUTH
AFRICA**

Bloemfontein

Botshabelo

MASERU

LESOTHO

Trust Feeds

Groutville Reserve

Howick

Ohlanga

Pietermaritzburg

Kwazulu-Natal
Nongoma
Mahlabatini
Groutville
KwaDukuza
(formerly Stranger)
Umfolozi River
Mahlabatini
Inanda
uMgungundlovu
Imbali

NORTHERN CAPE

De Aar

Calvinia

Victoria West

Middelburg

Engcobo

Port Shepstone

Mqhekezweni Qunu

Mvezo

Tsolo

Mthatha
Bityi
Baziya

Vanrhynsdorp

Queenstown

Beaufort West

Cradock

Fort Beaufort

EASTERN CAPE

Alice

Bisho

Qumbu
Shawbury College

Durban
Claremont
Cato Manor
Hammarsdale
Hillcrest
Sydenham
Umgeni Rd
Westville

Robben Island

Table Bay

Cape Town
Bellville
Constantiaberg
MediClinic
Mowbray Retreat
Rondebosch
Tokai
Tygerberg Hospital

Worcester

Paarl

Simonstown

Oudtshoorn

Swellendam

Grahamstown

East London

Port Elizabeth

Eastern Cape
Mbongweni
Ezibeleni
Bizana
Great Kei River
Butterworth
Matatiele
Sterkspruit
Qumanco
Mqanduli
Peddie

Cofimvaba
Deckert's Hill
Qamata

PROVINCE	CITY/TOWN/VILLAGE	DESCRIPTION
Eastern Cape	Mvezo	Mandela's birthplace.
	Qunu	Village where Mandela lived as a child and built a home after his release from prison.
	Mqhekezweni	The Great Place where Mandela moved to when he was around the age of twelve.
	Engcobo	Clarkebury Boarding Institute where Mandela obtained his junior certificate.
	Fort Beaufort	Attended college at Healdtown.
	Alice	Attended University College of Fort Hare.
Gauteng	Johannesburg	Moved to Johannesburg in April 1941.
		Lived in Alexandra and Soweto before his imprisonment.
		Lived in Soweto and Houghton upon his release.
	Pretoria	Pretoria Central Prison, 1962–63, 1963–64.
		Location of his trial in 1962 and the Rivonia Trial.
	Sharpeville	Sharpeville Massacre, 21 March 1960.
	Rivonia	Liliesleaf Farm, the underground safe house.
KwaZulu-Natal	Pietermaritzburg	All-In African Conference, 22 March 1961.
	Howick	Arrested, 5 August 1962.
Western Cape	Robben Island	Imprisoned on Robben Island for two weeks from May 1963, and for eighteen years from 13 June 1964 to 30 March 1982.
	Cape Town	Imprisoned at Pollsmoor Prison, March 1982 to August 1988.
		Treated at Tygerberg Hospital, 1988.
		Treated at Constantiaberg MediClinic, 1988.
	Paarl	Held at Victor Verster Prison, 7 December 1988 to 11 February 1990.

When South Africa's first democratically elected government came to power in 1994, the government reorganised the ten existing Bantustans, or homelands, and the four existing provinces into nine smaller fully integrated provinces as shown on this map. The four provinces that existed from 1910–94 were reorganised into the new provinces as follows:

OLD PROVINCES	NEW PROVINCES
Cape Province	Eastern Cape
	Northern Cape
	Western Cape
Natal	KwaZulu-Natal
Orange Free State	Free State
Transvaal	North West
	Limpopo
	Mpumalanga
	Gauteng

ENDNOTES

1   Mac Maharaj (ed.), *Reflections in Prison*, (Cape Town: Robben Island Museum and Zebra Press, 2001), p. xi.

2   Nelson Mandela, summarised statement minuted at Robben Island Prison, Robben Island, 11 December 1978.

3   Robert Vassen, 'Life as a Political Prisoner', South Africa: Overcoming Apartheid, Building Democracy, a project of MATRIX: The Center for Humane Arts, Letters, and Social Sciences; the African Studies Center; and the Department of History, Michigan State University, http://overcomingapartheid.msu.edu/sidebar.php?id=65-258-8&page=3.

4   Walter Sisulu, introduction to *Letters from Robben Island*, Ahmed Kathrada (ed. Robert D. Vassen) (Cape Town: Mayibuye Books and East Lansing: Michigan State University Press, 1999), p. xvi.

5   Eddie Daniels, *There and Back: Robben Island 1964-1979* (Cape Town: CTP Book Printers, third edition, 2002), p. 160.

6   NM in conversation with Richard Stengel, Johannesburg, 14 December 1992, CD 6, Nelson Mandela Foundation, Johannesburg.

7   Eddie Daniels, *There and Back: Robben Island 1964-1979*, p. 160.

8   Elinor Sisulu, *In Our Lifetime: Walter & Albertina Sisulu* (Cape Town: David Philip Publishers, 2002), p. 200.

9   NM, summarised statement minuted at Robben Island Prison, Robben Island, 11 December 1978.

10 NM, letter to the commissioner of prisons dated 12 July 1976, *The Prison Letters of Nelson Mandela* (New York: Liveright Publishing Corporation, 2018), pp. 293–315, reference p. 308.

11 Michael Dingake, 'Comrade Madiba' in *Nelson Mandela: The Struggle is My Life*, (London: Idaf, 1986), p. 224.

12 Ibid.

13 Ibid.

14 Ibid., pp. 224–5.

15 Ibid., p. 225.

16 Ibid.

17 NM, speech at the 46664 Concert, Cape Town, 29 November 2003, http://db.nelsonmandela.org/speeches/pub_view.asp?pg=item&ItemID=NMS950&txtstr=46664.

18 NM in conversation with Richard Stengel, Johannesburg, 16 April 1993, CD 51, Nelson Mandela Foundation, Johannesburg.

19 'Mandela Wins Week's Adjournment', *Cape Times*, 16 October 1962.

20 NM, speech to the court, Old Synagogue, Pretoria, 22 October 1962, http://db.nelsonmandela.org/speeches/pub_view.asp?pg=item&ItemID=NMS011&txtstr=recusal.

21 NM in conversation with Richard Stengel, 16 and 17 April 1993, CD 52, Nelson Mandela Foundation, Johannesburg.

22 Bob Hepple, *Young Man With a Red Tie: A Memoir of Mandela and the Failed Revolution, 1960–1963* (Johannesburg: Jacana, 2013), p. 48.

23 'Mandela Gets 5 Years: Described as Master-mind', *The Argus*, 7 November 1962.

24 'Shouts, Clenched Fists, Songs, as Mandela is Gaoled, *Cape Times*, 8 November 1962.

25 Ibid.

26 'Mandela is Asked Not to Become "Difficult"', *Rand Daily Mail*, 25 October 1962.

27 NM in conversation with Richard Stengel, Johannesburg, 16 April 1993, CD 51, Nelson Mandela Foundation, Johannesburg.

28 NM in conversation with Richard Stengel, Johannesburg, 3 December 1992, CD 2, Nelson Mandela Foundation, Johannesburg.

29 NM in conversation with Richard Stengel, Johannesburg, 16 and 17 April 1993, CD 52, Nelson Mandela Foundation, Johannesburg.

30 NM, *Long Walk to Freedom* (London: Abacus, 2013), p. 414.

31 Ibid.

32 Joel Joffe, *The State vs. Nelson Mandela: The Trial that Changed South Africa* (London: One World Publications, 2007) p. 41.

33 Ibid., p. 42.

34 Ibid.

35 'Sir Bob Hepple Obituary', *The Guardian*, 26 August 2015, https://www.theguardian.com/law/2015/aug/26/sir-bob-hepple.

36 NM, *Long Walk to Freedom*, p. 444.

37 Ibid., p. 447.

38 NM in conversation with Richard Stengel, Johannesburg, 3 December 1992, CD 2, Nelson Mandela Foundation, Johannesburg.

39 Christo Brand, *Doing Life with Mandela* (Johannesburg: Jonathan Ball, 2014), p. 46.

40 Indres Naidoo, as told to Albie Sachs, *Island in Chains: Ten Years on Robben Island by Prisoner 885/63* (Harmondsworth: Penguin Books, 1982), p. 87.

41 Mac Maharaj, 'Interview with Mac Maharaj', 1978, in *The Struggle is My Life*, p. 208.

42 Ibid.

43 NM, *Long Walk to Freedom*, p. 458.

44 Joel Carlson, *No Neutral Ground* (London: Davis-Poynter Ltd, 1973), p. 291.

45 Ahmed Kathrada and Sahm Venter, *Conversations with a Gentle Soul* (Johannesburg: Picador Africa, 2017), p. 87.

46 NM, *Long Walk to Freedom*, p. 608.

47 Ibid., p. 646.

48 NM in conversation with Richard Stengel, Johannesburg, 8 February 1993, CD 19, Nelson Mandela Foundation, Johannesburg.

49 NM, *Long Walk to Freedom*, p. 647.

50 NM in conversation with Richard Stengel, c. 2 and 3 February 1993, CD 17, Nelson Mandela Foundation, Johannesburg.

51 Ibid.

52 Jack Swart, telephone conversation with Sahm Venter, 7 September 2017.

53 Padraig O'Malley, *Shades of Difference: Mac Maharaj and the Struggle for South Africa* (New York: Viking, 2007), p. 312.

54 Ibid., p. 313.

LETTERS AND COLLECTIONS

Nelson Mandela Prison Archive, National Archives and Records Service of South Africa: commanding officer, Pretoria Local Prison – 25 October 1963; Bram Fischer – 2 August 1964; Major Visser – 25 August 1965; Adelaide Tambo – 5 March 1968; Knowledge Guzana – 14 October 1968; Mangosuthu Buthelezi – 4 November 1968; minister of justice – 22 April 1969; Nkosikazi Nokukhanya Luthuli – 8 June 1970; Winnie Mandela – 20 June 1970; commanding officer, Robben Island – 4 April 1971; commanding officer, Robben Island – 14 June 1971; Winnie Mandela – 1 June 1972; Helen Suzman – 1 March 1974; minister of justice – 13 May 1974; Winnie Mandela – 1 February 1975; Yusuf Dadoo – 1 November 1975; commanding officer, Robben Island – 12 July 1976; commissioner of prisons – 23 January 1976; commissioner of prisons – 12 July 1976; Winnie Mandela – 19 August 1976; Thorobetsane Tshukudu (Adelaide Tambo) – 1 January 1977; Duma Nokwe (Gcwanini Miya) – 1 January 1977; head of prison, Robben Island – 19 May 1977; head of prison, Robben Island – 18 September 1977; Ndileka Mandela – 21 January 1979; Winnie Mandela – 21 January 1979; Makaziwe Mandela – 13 May 1979; Alan Paton – 29 July 1979; Zindzi Mandela – 9 December 1979; Winnie Mandela – 30 July 1980; Zindzi Mandela – 1 March 1981; Winnie Mandela – 26 April 1981; Petronella Ferus – 3 May 1981; Dr. Ayesha Arnold – 15 November 1981; Ismail Meer – 29 January 1985; P. W. Botha – 13 February 1985; Sheena Duncan – 1 April 1985; Archie Gumede – 1 July 1985 (from 1975); Archie Gumede – 8 July 1975; Victoria Mxenge – 8 July 1985; Joy Motsieloa – 17 February 1986; K. D. Matanzima – 19 May 1986; head of prison, Pollsmoor – 6 October 1986; Frieda Matthews – 25 February 1987; Helen Joseph – 1 April 1987; Mandla Mandela – 9 July 1987; Nandi Mandela – 17 August 1987; Prof. W. J. Hosten – 25 November 1988; Prof. W. J. Hosten – 23 December 1988; Dumani Mandela – 28 February 1989; Candie Lawless – 4 April 1989; Mike Tyson – 10 May 1989; Tim Wilson – 23 July 1989; commissioner of prisons, Pretoria – 11 September 1989; Fatima Meer – 28 September 1989; commissioner of prisons – 2 February 1990; commissioner of prisons – 11 February 1990.

The books into which Mandela transcribed his letters (the Donald Card Collection housed at the Nelson Mandela Foundation): Zenani and Zindzi Mandela – 4 February 1969; Makaziwe Mandela – 16 February 1969; Lilian Ngoyi – 3 March 1969; Gibson Kente – 3 March 1969; Winnie Mandela – 2 April 1969; Zenani and Zindzi Mandela – 23 June 1969; Niki Xaba – 15 July 1969; Winnie Mandela – 16 July 1969; Evelyn Mandela – 16 July 1969; Makgatho Mandela – 28 July 1969; Sefton Vutela – 28 July 1969; Zenani and Zindzi Mandela – 3 August 1969; Irene Buthelezi – 3 August 1969; Nolusapho Irene Mkwayi – 29 September 1969; Winnie Mandela – 16 November 1969; Thoko Mandela – 29 November 1969; Winnie Mandela – 1 August 1970; Senator Douglas Lukhele – 1 August 1970; minister of justice – 14 September 1970; Winnie Mandela – 1 October 1970; Joyce Sikhakhane – 1 January 1971; commanding officer, Robben Island – 2 January 1971; Zenani Mandela – 1 March 1971; Thoko Mandela – 1 April 1971.

The Himan Bernadt Collection housed at the Nelson Mandela Foundation: Frank, Bernadt & Joffe – 20 May 1969.

The private collections of: Amnesty International: The Secretary Amnesty – 6 November 1962; Amina Cachalia: Amina Cachalia – 12 December 1977; Nick Carter: Ray Carter –

4 March 1985; Meyer de Waal: Adele de Waal – 29 August 1983; Michael Dingake: Michael Dingake – 24 April 1986; Adelaide and Paul Joseph Collection: Adelaide Joseph – 1 March 1975 and 25 February 1985; Helen Joseph Collection at Historical Papers, University of the Witwatersrand: Helen Joseph – 19 October 1978 and 28 March 1983; Fatima Meer: Fatima Meer – 1 March 1971; Mzobanzi Mboya: Professor Mzobanzi Mboya – 1 March 1988; Morabo Morojele: Lionel Ngakane – 1 April 1985; Sylvia Neame Collection at Historical Papers, University of the Witwatersrand: Sylvia Neame – date unknown; Coen Stork: Coen Stork – 11 June 1964; Emily Wellman: Peter Wellman – 27 May 1979.

ACKNOWLEDGEMENTS

We are grateful to Zamaswazi Dlamini-Mandela for her invaluable assistance on this book and for her beautiful foreword. As she says, *The Prison Letters of Nelson Mandela* helps us understand how people like her grandfather who were 'caught opposing the apartheid government's system to oppress an entire race of people, endured terrible punishments'.

This is so much more than the collected words of an imprisoned freedom fighter and world icon, and greater than the work of an editor and an associate editor. It is the result of a sustained collective effort over many years.

The long journey to publication began in 2006 when Verne Harris, Nelson Mandela Foundation director of archive and dialogue, approached Nelson Mandela for permission to access the letters written during his twenty-seven years in prison with a view to publishing them some day. He assigned Anthea Josias the task of cataloguing everything in the scores of boxes that comprise Mandela's prison record at the National Archives and Records Service of South Africa. In the next stage, I went through the correspondence to identify all his letters to family and friends. During this research, I discovered a range of compelling official letters to and from prison officials and various institutions, many of which appear in this collection. Gerrit Wagener, Natalie Skomolo, and Zahira Adam worked tirelessly to assist in the copying of the letters.

The task of collating and transcribing the letters took years, and in the process other letters were unearthed, both in the archive of Mandela's personal papers at the Nelson Mandela Foundation, the Historical Papers research archive at the University of the Witwatersrand, and in private collections. Our thanks go particularly to Nicholas Carter, Meyer de Waal, Michael and Sithembile Dingake, Emily Wellman, Morabo Morojele, Sylvia Neame, Adelaide Joseph, Nadia Joseph, Gabriele Mohale, Professor Mzobanzi Mboya, and Hlubi Mboya for offering us letters we had previously not seen. Our gratitude also goes to Ruth Muller and Zofia Sulej. Amnesty International gave us a copy of a letter we were unaware of, which Mandela wrote in 1962 and which is housed in its London archive. The late Coen Stork gave us the letter Mandela wrote to him in 1964. The late Himan Bernadt, who was one of Mandela's lawyers while he was in prison, donated his papers to the Nelson Mandela Foundation. In 2004, a former security policeman, Donald Card, handed back to Mandela the two hardcover books containing copies of his letters which he had kept for decades after they had been confiscated from his prison cell. They are now housed at the Nelson Mandela Foundation.

We also deeply appreciate the assistance from Vanessa van Copenhagen and the executors of Madiba's estate, Archbishop Emeritus Desmond Tutu, Chief Mangosuthu Buthelezi, the Rev. Frank Chikane, Dr. Richard Maponya, Tumeka Matanzima, Xoliswa Matanzima Jozana, Nqaba Ngoyi, Vicky Kente, Duma and Thandeka Gqubule, Trevor Tutu, Anant Singh, Shamim Meer, Her Excellency Nomvuyo Nokwe, Joyce Sikhakhane Rankin, Ilse Wilson, Tim Wilson, Nosizwe Macamo, Nina Jones, Sanja Gohre, and Albie Sachs.

Mandela did not write only in English, some of the letters included in this collection were written in his mother tongue of isiXhosa and some in Afrikaans. We are grateful to the following people for their translation skills: Pumeza Gwija, Luzuko Koti, Diketso Mufamadi, Vukile Pokwana, Benjamin Harris, Nosisa Tiso, and Jeannie Adams. Thanks also to those who translated various terms in other languages as well as identifying individuals and explaining cultural practices and historical events: Zanele Riba, Florence Garishe, Razia Saleh, Ramni Dinath, Fred Khumalo, Zubeida Jaffer, Siraj Desai, Jimi Matthews, and Zohra Kathrada Areington.

It was a mammoth task to identify individuals and other details in the letters, and without the assistance of many people the supplementary information would not have been as rich as it is. Mac Maharaj never refused one request for information and spent considerable time providing much detail of prison life and of individuals.

Others who did not hesitate to pitch in when we requested their help were John Allen, Edwin Arrison, Christo Brand, Belinda Bozzoli, Laloo Chiba, Tony Eprile, Dali Tambo, Andile Xaba and Sino Xaba, the family of Dr. Gordon Handelsman, Sharon Gelman, Bobby Heaney, Carmen Heydenreich, Willie Hofmeyr, Stanley Kawalsky, Libby Lloyd, Sam Mabale, Mosie Moolla, Saleem Mowzer, Nthabiseng Msomi, Bruce Murray, Prema Naidoo, Shirona Patel, Greta Soggot, Faiza Sujee, Jack Swart, Luli Callinicos, and Lyndith Waller. We are also indebted to Zodwa Zwane, Lucia Raadschelders, Claude

Colart, Zandile Myeka, Lerato Tshabalala, Khalil Goga, Joe Ditabo, Mongezi Njaju, Sophia Molelekoa, Kerileng Marumo, Tshwarelo Mphatudi, Mark Seftel, Ntsiki Sisulu, Beryl Simelane, and Effie Seftel.

Robert Weil of W. W. Norton & Company waited patiently for years after he first expressed a desire to publish the letters and provided wonderful support. Ruth Hobday and Geoff Blackwell of Blackwell & Ruth joined the partnership to publish this book and gave it wings. We are indebted to Rachel Clare's exceptional and thorough editing and dedication to this book, Cameron Gibb for his handsome design and Elizabeth Blackwell for her assistance.

Sello Hatang, the chief executive of the Nelson Mandela Foundation, encouraged this book from the beginning and continues to use every opportunity to promote it. We would be remiss in not thanking the rest of the Nelson Mandela Foundation team who have all contributed in different ways to this publication. They are Ethel Arends, Victoria Collis-Buthelezi, Lee Davies, Maeline Engelbrecht, Fikile Gama, Yase Godlo, Sylvia Graham, Heather Henriques, Sumaya Hendricks, Lungelo Khanyile, Gregory Katsoras, Lesego Maforah, Ann-Young Maharaj, Aletta Makgaleng, Clive Maluleke, Palesa Manare, Namile Mchunu, Koketso Mdawo, Limpho Monyamane, Kholofelo Monyela, Kealeboga Morembe, Lunga Nene, Eric Nhlengetwa, Patronella Nqaba, Buyi Sishuba, Lindiwe Skhosana, Morongoa Thobakgale, Given Tuck, Noreen Wahome, and Louisa Zondo.

Members of the Mandela family generously helped with identifying people mentioned in the letters. Winnie Madikizela-Mandela was exceptional and spent many hours assisting us. HRH Princess Zenani Dlamini-Mandela, Her Excellency Ms. Zindziswa Mandela, and Ndileka Mandela also gave us essential information. We would also like to thank other members of the Mandela family, Nandi Mandela, Makaziwe Mandela, Tukwini Mandela, Kweku Mandela, Dumani Mandela, Zinhle Dlamini, Zaziwe Manaway, Zoleka Mandela, Chief Zwelivelile Mandela, and Nolusapho Rayne Rose Mandela.

Nelson Mandela's pain at being separated from his family runs prominently through this valuable chronicle, as does his recognition of their own suffering during those twenty-seven years. We owe them all our deep gratitude.

Sahm Venter
Editor

PERMISSIONS
ACKNOWLEDGEMENTS

We are grateful for permission to reproduce the following items.

Extracts from recordings of Nelson Mandela in conversation with Richard Stengel (Johannesburg: Nelson Mandela Foundation, 1992–3), copyright © Nelson R. Mandela, used by permission of Nelson Mandela Foundation. Extracts from 'Comrade Madiba', *Nelson Mandela: The Struggle is My Life* (London: International Defence and Aid Fund for Southern Africa, 1978), used by permission of Michael Dingake. Extract from *Young Man With a Red Tie: A Memoir of Mandela and the Failed Revolution, 1960–1963* by Bob Hepple (Johannesburg: Jacana Media, 2013), used with permission. Extracts from 'Shouts, Clenched Fists, Songs, as Mandela is Gaoled', *Cape Times*, 8 November 1962, used with permission. Extracts from *Long Walk to Freedom* by Nelson Mandela (London: Abacus, 2013), copyright © Nelson R. Mandela, used by permission of Nelson Mandela Foundation, Johannesburg. Extracts from *The State Vs. Nelson Mandela: The Trial that Changed South Africa* by Joel Joffe (London: One World Publications, 2007), used with permission. Extract from 'Interview with Mac Maharaj', *Nelson Mandela: The Struggle is My Life* (London: International Defence and Aid Fund for Southern Africa, 1978), used by permission of Mac Maharaj. Extract from *Island in Chains: Ten Years on Robben Island by Prisoner 885/63* by Indres Naidoo (Joahnnesburg: Penguin Books, 2012), used with permission. Extracts from *Saving Nelson Mandela: The Rivonia Trial and the Fate of South Africa* by Kenneth S. Braun (New York: Oxford University Press, 2012), used with permission. Extract from *491 Days: Prisoner Number 1323/69* by Winnie Madikizela-Mandela (eds. Sahm Venter and Zamawazi Dlamini Mandela) (Johannesburg: Picador Africa, 2013), used by permission of Winnie Madikizela-Mandela.

Photographs: pages ii–iii, 49, 65, 75, 92 and 117 Donald Card Collection housed at the Nelson Mandela Foundation, photographs by Ardon Bar-Hama; page 7 Amnesty International, courtesy Nelson Mandela Foundation; pages 9 and 21 Matthew Willman; page 20 Coen Stork, courtesy Nelson Mandela Foundation; page 63 Himan Bernadt Collection housed at the Nelson Mandela Foundation, photograph by Ardon Bar-Hama; pages 149, 192, 195, 203, 233, 263 and 281 Nelson Mandela Prison Archive, National Archives and Records Service of South Africa; pages 161, 164 and 259 from the personal collection of Adelaide and Paul Joseph, used with permission; page 249 Mikhael Subotzky, Installation view: 'Die Vier Hoeke' exhibition, in the Nelson Mandela Cell, Pollsmoor Prison, South Africa, 2005, courtesy of the artist and Goodman Gallery; page 301 Getty Images/TSJ MERLYN LICENSING BV/Gallo Images; and page 307 Getty Images/Matthew Willman.

INDEX

Page numbers beginning with 325 refer to glossary.